EVANGELICAL-UNIFICATION
DIALOGUE

Edited by
Richard Quebedeaux
Rodney Sawatsky

Distributed by
The Rose of Sharon Press, Inc.
New York

Conference series no. 3
First edition
© 1979
by
The Unification Theological Seminary
Barrytown, New York 12507

Distributed by
The Rose of Sharon Press, Inc.
G.P.O. Box 2432
New York, N.Y. 10001

Grateful acknowledgement is made to the following:
   Christianity Today for permission to quote from "Meeting the
Moonies on their territory," by Joseph Hopkins, August 18, 1978
   Concordia Publishing House for permission to quote from *The
Possible Years*, by Donald L. Deffner, ©1973
   Theology Today for permission to quote from "Dialogue with
the Moonies," by Rodney Sawatsky, April 1978

Printed in the United States of America
Library of Congress Cataloging number 79-89421
ISBN 0-932894-02-X

CONTENTS

PREFACE

At the invitation of the president of Unification Theological Seminary, Barrytown, New York, a formal theological dialogue was convened in June, 1978, between a group of Unificationist seminarians and a group of Evangelicals (or "born again" Christians) at Barrytown, followed in October of that year by a second and concluding gathering with most of the same participants and several others. The tapes of these two sessions were transcribed, then integrated and edited into book form by the conference convenor (Richard Quebedeaux) and moderator (Rodney Sawatsky), and *Evangelical-Unification Dialogue* is the finished product we present here.

Each participant has had the opportunity to read his or her transcribed remarks and make appropriate corrections in the text. The editors have attempted to maintain as much of the original dialogue as possible, despite the problems of repetition and organization. The transcript has been punctuated to present the dialogue as it was actually spoken. Because of the controversial nature of the gatherings, two participants have found it necessary to take on pseudonyms.

True "dialogue" is risky business because "conversion" is always an inherent possibility in the process. At least dialogue may force the participants to change their minds about each other. To our knowledge, none of the Evangelicals here have become "Moonies," and none of the Moonies have become Evangelicals. But a large number of persons on both sides did change their minds. Stereotypes were broken, and all participants, we feel, gained a better understanding of what it really means to be a Unificationist or an Evangelical in contemporary American society.

The significance of this experiment in dialogue for Evangelicals and Unificationists alike—and for those who don't identify themselves by either label as well—will become apparent, we hope, to each reader of *Evangelical-Unification Dialogue.* Furthermore, it should be noted at this point that most of the evangelical participants in these events were grounded in the Reformed tradition (subsequent Unification/Evangelical dialogues were attended by Arminian Wesleyan Evangelicals and by Pentecostal Charismatic Evangelicals—with different results). Readers should be aware that this work is not a finished systematic theology. Rather, it is the transcribed result of eight days of spontaneous theologizing. Thanks are in order to all of the following men and women who, by their hard work, helped to make this book a reality: Jeanne Bannister, Patricia Gleason, Sylvia Grahn, Barbara Mallory, Michael Mickler, Lynn Musgrave, Lorna Skaaran, Helen Subrenat, Valarie Weber, Andy Wilson, Sarah Witt, and to Anthony Guerra and Patricia Zulkosky who helped to organize the conferences. Special thanks, in addition, is due M. Darrol Bryant who supervised the final copy editing, and John Maniatis, librarian of Unification Theological Seminary, who supervised the technical aspects of the production of *Evangelical-Unification Dialogue* in their entirety.

September 20, 1979

Richard Quebedeaux
Rodney Sawatsky
Editors

PARTICIPANTS

Charles Barfoot, author, Berkeley, Ca.

Thomas Bower, Director of Development, University of Dubuque, Dubuque, Ia.

Mark Branson, Secretary, Theological Students' Fellowship, Los Angeles, Ca.

Roy Carlisle, Chairman of the Board, New College, Berkeley, Ca.

Tom Carter, student, Unification Theological Seminary (UTS), Barrytown, N.Y.

Virgil Cruz, Professor of New Testament Studies, University of Dubuque Theological Seminary, Dubuque, Ia.

Daniel Davies, graduate of UTS and student, Perkins School of Theology, Dallas, Tx.

Donald Deffner, Professor of Christian Education and Homiletics, Pacific Lutheran Theological Seminary, Berkeley, Ca.

Paul Eshleman, Assistant to the President, Campus Crusade for Christ, San Bernardino, Ca.

Evangelical X.

Evangelical Y.

Franz Feige, graduate of UTS and student, Drew University, Madison, N.J.

Sharon Gallagher, editor of *Radix,* Berkeley, Ca.

Beatriz Gonzales, graduate of UTS and Unification Church campus minister.

Anthony Guerra, graduate of UTS and student, Harvard Divinity School, Cambridge, Ma.

Jack Harford, graduate of UTS and Unification Church campus minister.

Irving Hexham, Assistant Professor of Philosophy and Religion, Regent College, Vancouver, B.C., Canada.

Joseph Hopkins, Professor, Westminster College, New Wilmington, Pa.

Lloyd Howell, graduate of UTS and Unification Church campus minister.

Frank Kaufmann, graduate of UTS and student, Vanderbilt University, Nashville, Tn.

Warren Lewis, Associate Professor of Church History, UTS, Barrytown, N.Y.

Patrick Means, Campus Crusade for Christ, Monterey, Ca.

Richard Quebedeaux, author, Berkeley, Ca., convenor of dialogue.

Rod Sawatsky, Director of Academic Affairs, Conrad Grebel College, University of Waterloo, Waterloo, Ontario, Canada; moderator of dialogue.

John Scanzoni, Professor of Sociology, North Carolina State University, Greensboro, N.C.

Letha Scanzoni, author, Greensboro, N.C.

Tirza Shilgi, graduate of UTS and Unification Church campus minister.

Whitney Shiner, graduate of UTS and student, The Divinity School, University of Chicago, Chicago, Ill.

Pete Sommer, San Francisco Bay Area Director, Inter-Varsity Christian Fellowship, Redwood City, Ca.

Johnny Sonneborn, member of Unification Church and student, New York Theological Seminary, New York, N.Y.

Rachel Spang, member of Unification Church and student, University of Pennsylvania, Philadelphia, Pa.

Nora Spurgin, member of Unification Church and counselor (M.S.W.), UTS, Barrytown, N.Y.

Helen Subrenat, member of Unification Church and Registrar, UTS, Barrytown, N.Y.

Ulrich Tuente, graduate of UTS and Unification Church campus minister.

Jan Weido, graduate of UTS.

Jonathan Wells, graduate of UTS and student, Yale University, New Haven, Ct.

John Wiemann, graduate of UTS and Unification church campus minister.

Mark Wilenchik, student, UTS, Barrytown, N.Y.

Patricia Zulkosky, graduate of UTS and student, School of Theology at Claremont, Claremont, Ca.

A cross section of participants at the June 1978 conference. From left to right: Patricia Zulkosky, Mark Branson, Roy Carlisle, Rachel Spang, Paul Eshleman, Beatriz Gonzales, Anthony Guerra, Rodney Sawatsky and Warren Lewis.

A cross section of participants at the October 1978 conference. From left to right: Johnny Sonneborn, Rodney Sawatsky (conference moderator), Tom Carter, Dan Davies and Richard Quebedeaux (conference convener).

TESTIMONIES

Rod Sawatsky: Let me just state one assumption before we get into our discussion, and then I want to go into a more detailed introduction. In contrast to most of the theological conferences conducted here, this is to be a dialogue. Prior to this conference, they have been fairly much monologues in terms of supplying information from the Unification church to the guests that have come. Our assumption here is that we're speaking in both directions, in that Unification people will speak to the Evangelicals and vice versa. The agenda will be set in both directions, because the questions that we want to work at will come just as much from the Unification side as from the Evangelical side. Accordingly, when we pick up a certain topic such as christology, after the Unificationists tell us what they understand to be the nature and meaning of the mission of Christ, then we'll ask the Evangelicals to do the same. And if differences emerge among Unification people about their definitions, which will probably happen, I would also assume that there will be differences on the other side, because there are no monolithic positions on any of these subjects. At least, that's my impression.

Now, I think that we should begin our conversation by talking about ourselves in a confessional, testimonial way. What I'm interested in having us tell each other is who we are, where we come from, and when and how we entered the faith, that is, the Evangelical faith or the Unification faith. Evangelicals know all about testimonials and so do the Unificationists, so we have a commonality here. And I think we'll begin to know each other more closely, more deeply, and in fact, our initial agenda for the morning may well grow out of these testimonials. I would also like you to say something about your expectations for this dialogue, particularly in terms of one or two questions uppermost in your mind about the other group—those questions which have been particularly disturbing, perplexing, and so on. Is this a good way for us to start?

I'm wondering where we'd best start? I'm going to suggest that we begin with Richard, since he was here on an earlier occasion, and since the conference was his idea, so I think we're going to let him set the pace for the rest of us in our introductions. Then we'll move on to Anthony and around clockwise.

Richard Quebedeaux: I'm Richard Quebedeaux. I was born in Los Angeles as was my father, which is a rarity. I think Los Angeles was very important in my development because it has produced an amazing number of religious movements. The whole Southern California ethos is conducive to that, I think.

My father was a "culture Presbyterian," which means that my father's whole family way back was in the church for business, social and traditional reasons. My mother was a Roman Catholic, but when my parents got married, my father wouldn't be married by a priest, so that was the end of her Catholicism. My father was really always looking for something. He started reading Plato and Aldous Huxley and a whole bunch of things. Finally both he and my mother went to a Presbyterian church in Los Angeles where I was baptized the *first* time.

Then my parents were "saved"—they became Baptist because of the persistence of a family down the street who "worked on" my parents relentlessly for a whole year. Finally, on Easter Sunday, my father gave in and cussed all the way to the nearby Baptist church—and then boom! I was in the fourth grade and I also walked down the aisle. That was the tradition. But I don't consider that any kind of a conversion experience for me because I didn't know what was coming off really. I was a smart kid—but I just don't think I understood what was happening.

I was raised in that church and was president of this, that, and everything. Then I also went to what is called a Christian day school for high school. It's very evangelical, so of course, I got the full fundamental, evangelical background in formal studies and in my church. I was cultivated to go to Wheaton College in Illinois, what I call the Harvard of evangelicalism. If you were a good student and from my background, there was just one place to go. I had to give a testimony in front of the church, you know—isn't it wonderful Richard is going to Wheaton—I lasted one week there. Everything came to a head, in that I really felt it was time for me to go into the secular world. I got there and met all kinds of other freshmen. The first thing they would talk about is how they could do things incognito that they couldn't do "legally" at Wheaton. It turned me off because I had been leading a double life myself all the way through, and felt that the time had come for me to find out who I was and to be myself, so luckily I had applied to UCLA, which didn't start until later. I called my folks up and said, "Well, I'm going to UCLA and if you won't send any money I'll hitchhike home." So I came home and my parents saw that as the beginning of my decline—secularism and liberalism and all that stuff.

I went to UCLA and I maintained my church involvement. I was also a member of a Christian fraternity, which may be a contradiction in terms, but it was a fraternity that was trying to be in the inter-fraternity council and then also be Christian, to do things and not do other things—it was very difficult, but that was another good experience. At the end of my sophomore year I really reacted to all this evangelical stuff. I had discovered at UCLA that there were Christians who were not Baptist, and I really didn't know that before, quite frankly, and it became very confusing for me. I also discovered *Christianity Today,* which is an evangelical magazine. I started reading it, and that was really enlightening for me at that time. It's called a conservative magazine by a lot of people now, but it was very radical to me at that time. In my junior year in college I left the fraternity and started associating mainly with secular Jews who I thought were better people. They were more honest, more real, and more interesting. I really got into the academic thing, and from UCLA I went to the Harvard Divinity School. I went there through a quirk. I didn't even know Harvard had a divinity school—I thought the only seminaries were Fuller and Dallas and my own church's school, Bethel Theological Seminary, in St. Paul, Minnesota. But I discovered the Harvard catalog, and one of my professors had been at a conference there and thought that I should go. I wanted to go into church history as a Ph.D. eventually. So I went to Harvard and of course that extended my liberal training. All my doubts then became systematized. (laughter) I wasn't really shocked because I had done enough reading to know what was coming and was glad I went there because it was so extreme that I could see the weaknesses. I had hoped to go there to find an alternative to my bigoted fundamentalist background and I discovered a new kind of fundamentalism, but it was fundamentalism on the left. I was still looking for the open liberalism which I always heard about. And that experience was very interesting to me because it really turned me off to both conservatism and liberalism in Christianity. I got to the point where I had to decide if I was going to really be a Christian. I was so disillusioned by everything —so disillusioned by the hypocrisy of what I saw on both the right and the left—that I suppose during this time I really became a Christian in the sense of really affirming my evangelical roots and my relationship with Jesus Christ. Yet I was very vague and uncertain as to where this was going to go.

My church virtually put me out by making me a "non-person" because I was against the Vietnam war. I was invited to come back and teach the college class the summer after my first or second year in seminary—this was the beginning of the Vietnam thing—and we were talking about attitudes toward war and peace in the New Testament. I didn't do much talking but all the students were really getting into it. The director of Christian Education sat in on the class and didn't like it, and indicated to me subtly that if he had anything to do with it, I would have nothing more to do with that church's leadership. Well, that was the end, and that's what happened. So I was without a church and in seminary. I joined the United Church of Christ, which was affiliated with Harvard. It's a very liberal denomination and I'm really much more conservative than most of the people, but at least I found the freedom to be a token conservative in a liberal denomination and got along better than as a token liberal in a conservative denomination. At least I could live the way I wanted and people wouldn't criticize me. So I became UCC and became involved quite by accident in a lot of ecumenical ministries.

I went back to UCLA after I graduated from HDS to do a Ph.D. in medieval church history. This is what I had originally wanted to do out of college, but seminary got me into the present. I decided I didn't want to spend the rest of my life going over Latin manuscripts. I was really into the late '60s concerns and into social justice and all these kinds of issues. So I got tired of medieval history and decided I really didn't want to stay at UCLA, so I finished a Master's degree there in history. Then I got an unexpected scholarship from the World Council of Churches to go to Oxford for one year. I got that probably because I came across as an evangelical and the WCC would occasionally pick up a token evangelical.

I went off to Oxford for one year. I took a leave of absence. I didn't want to go back to UCLA. I didn't have anything to do at Oxford, because if you weren't going for a degree at Oxford there was really very little to do. So the principal of my college said, "Find somebody to supervise some reading for you." So I found this guy who was an authority on Pentecostalism and it just so happened that while I was in seminary my parents had gone from Baptist to Pentecostal in the extreme form—the Church of God (Cleveland, Tennessee). They were literally "rolling in the aisles" and dancing and screaming in ecstasy. And that sort of shocked me. Even my father, who is a rational person and very much an intellectual, got into that and I couldn't believe it. My mother I can understand because she's very emotional and likes that sort of thing very much. But anyway, in the course of their involvement and the involvement of some of my friends, I learned a lot about Pentecostalism and was interested in it. I impressed a professor at Oxford and he said, "Well, why don't you do a doctorate here and do something on the Charismatic movement?" which he'd just found out about and wanted somebody to do something on. So I said, "Well, if you can get me in for a degree program I'll do it." And he did. That's how I wound up there.

I spent two years at Oxford and then came back to the States where it took me four more years to finish my dissertation. During that time I didn't have any money, so I had to do some work. Through a number of contacts and interests I got into this kind of "bridge building" business. I guess I reacted so much to my fundamentalist past and the "pure church" idea that I decided there was no such thing as a pure church and really, we Christians needed to find each other and get together.

I became very ecumenical during that time—I met a man named John Coleman Bennett at Pacific School of Religion who used to be president of Union Seminary. He had graduated from my college at Oxford, so I went and talked to him. I told him that the evangelical movement was finally developing a sense of social concern. I was looking at Urbana '70, the big Inter-Varsity campaign of which I had seen a favorable review in *The Christian Century* that shocked me. So I told him about this and he too was shocked. He asked me to write an article for his magazine *Christianity and Crisis* and I wrote an article on that. Harper and Row was looking for someone to do a book on that topic, so they invited me to do it, and that is how I got into writing.

I did the book, and then I spent almost a year in campus ministry at the University of California at Santa Barbara because the campus minister there who had become a friend of mine was going on a sabbatical. He wanted somebody to go there and try to build some bridges between the evangelical campus ministry and the liberal mainline campus ministries, and this was a really good opportunity for me to put into practice what I had just finished writing in *The Young Evangelicals** which hadn't come out yet. So I went over there and at that point was forced to deal with the conservative groups which I didn't want to touch after my own personal experience. In the process of doing that I found out they were a lot different from what I thought — they had changed. And so that project went very well. Then my book came out, I got a name and I was hired by the Southern California Conference of the United Church of Christ for a year to do the same kind of bridge-building for them. They were sitting right next to Fuller Seminary and really they had never met each other because they thought Fuller Seminary was a real Bible-thumping fundamentalist institution. I spent a year putting together various kinds of meetings, getting liberal and conservative ministers together, and I enjoyed doing that.

I was also finishing my dissertation on the Charismatic movement at that time — I flew back to England, was examined, got my degree, and came back. Then I got a job for the United Church Board for Homeland Ministries, which is the home missions board for the United Church of Christ, and did essentially the same thing for them for a year and a half: that is, organizing ministers' conferences all over the country to introduce UCC clergy to leading Evangelicals. The UCC, a very liberal denomination, was getting to the point of being interested in what was going on with all these Evangelicals and the fact that the Evangelicals were finally getting into social action. I really became involved in this whole ecumenical quest, which I had really believed in for years. Then my dissertation was published and I really got into writing. I was very free in my writing, I suspect,

---

*Richard Quebedeaux, *The Young Evangelicals*, New York: Harper & Row, 1974.

because I didn't have anything to lose. Unlike most evangelical types, I didn't have to worry about losing a job or being fired, so I could say some things that I wanted to say and then I really didn't care what people thought. In so doing, I discovered that a lot of people identified with what I said because they were thinking the same, but were either afraid to say it or really couldn't articulate it. So, that sort of brought me into the present.

My experience in working with liberal Protestants has been somewhat mixed, in the sense that it's good that we all get together and talk, but I came to the conclusion that there was not an awful lot to gain there. I was tired of pursuing that because it was always Evangelicals saying what *they believe,* so the issue was about seeing how much the liberals could tolerate, rather than what they believe. I got rather bored with this because we weren't really having dialogue. It was a monologue—just our trying to get them to come around to accept us—which had mixed amounts of success. But basically I got into the situation—I still feel this way—where I really felt that I had a knack for bringing people together to talk on various things, and I enjoyed doing that. Now I no longer look for Christian unity in the institutional sense, and I've begun to appreciate our diversity and feel that many of us are doing different parts of the gospel better than other parts and that probably by talking together and occasionally working together we can probably get nearer to what the whole gospel is all about. That's basically where I am today. Now I'm constantly in the process of re-evaluating. My latest book—if you read between the lines—will tell you a lot about where I am, because it's something of a spiritual autobiography, and a lot of the questions that I raise are still the questions that I have.

Rod Sawatsky: Anthony, your life hasn't been as long. (laughter)

Anthony Guerra: I was born in Boston into a Roman Catholic family, and attended a Catholic grammar school, high school, and university. When as a child I was first learning about Catholicism I was very pious. Every day I would say several thousand ejaculations—short phrases like "Lord Jesus, have mercy on me....Forgive my sins" and I was very avid. When I turned twelve I began reading philosophy in particular, and I began to doubt my religion. Further, I felt then that the Catholic nuns and priests that I knew were not a model for the life that I wanted to adopt. And so, at a very early age I proclaimed myself an agnostic, and for the next five or six years, throughout high school, I became a philosophical skeptic in the tradition of Bertrand Russell. I agreed with Russell that religion, as the dragon standing before the threshold of the door of progress, had to be slain in order to solve the problems of the world. And I pursued my agnosticism vehemently.

When I was in high school I ran for president of the student body. This was a Catholic high school and there was compulsory mass attendance once a month. I actually ran a campaign on a platform opposing compulsory mass attendance. I had a friend take from the yearbook an image of a lamb and draw it on a huge banner, and when I gave my nomination speech, I held it over my head and said, "Here, this is what the administration of this school thinks about you. They interpret the parable of the sheep and shepherd a bit too literally, and you are the sheep." Needless to say, the administration, the faculty and the students all disagreed about the merits of that speech. The administration refused to print any of my subsequent statements in the school newspaper, and I lost the election by about twenty votes. Two days later I was called out of my homeroom over the loudspeaker by the Prefect of Studies to come into his office and speak to him. I had been a very good student, already accepted to Georgetown University with a full scholarship, and I was a senior, so I didn't have too much fear of being expelled before I entered his office. But as I sat down the first thing he said was, "Well, I guess you know that you're in a lot of trouble. The community has met, the brothers and priests, and they're thinking about expelling you." I didn't say anything. He said, "Do you know why? It is for blasphemy." I said, "Blasphemy? What do you mean?" And he explained that, in my ignorance, the image which I had blown up was actually the *Agnus Dei,* the Lamb of God. Where I was ideologically, I could have shirked that off and said, "So what? Why is that blasphemy?" But somehow my feeling was to keep silent, and although I didn't in any way apologize before the Prefect, when I left, I felt regret in my heart. I had a profound religious experience. It was my private reformation you might say, where I realized that you could separate your love for Jesus Christ from the Catholic church as an institution. And that was a profound experience. I do not want to belabor that because it didn't change my life in any way, and I didn't even think about it until several years later.

I was undaunted by my failure in politics. I began with a friend from Harvard University an organization called "Youth for Massachusetts" which involved about 500 students in Massachusetts; this group was responsible for getting the voting age lowered to eighteen. I traveled to various high schools giving my political testimony to people. The organization was very successful in an immediate sense. But as we were working, I would talk to my friend and I'd have all these deep doubts about what the value of all this was. I questioned, "Is this really going to solve people's problems? Is this going to solve the suffering in the world?" And I knew the answer was no. So, even as I was engaged in this, I felt a sense of purposelessness, and the more I thought about it, the less and less enthusiastic I became about my involvement in politics.

When I went away to college, to Georgetown in Washington, D.C., I became apolitical. I was still mostly irreligious. During my first year in college I encountered Marxism. I had one internal commitment, which was that if I found something which I thought was reasonable, which I thought was true, and which would solve the problems of mankind, then I would follow it, I would dedicate my life to it. Marxism promised that it was all of those things. It was scientific, it was reasonable, and it was going to solve the world's problems. So I had to confront this very seriously. However, there was one problem: even though, as I said, I wasn't very spiritual, all the people I met who were Marxists repelled me spiritually. I felt a spirit of hatred. I would feel almost sickened, especially by the more vehement, violence-oriented Marxists. But I couldn't in any way admit the validity of that objection, given my own hermeneutics at that point. So what I did was to study Marxism very intensely and to take the equivalent of six credits in writing a paper on it in which I concluded that it was irrational. Therefore, I didn't become a Marxist.

The following year I had a spiritual awakening and I shed my religious biases and became open spiritually once again. This happened in a two-fold way: First, it was through the writings of Sören Kierkegaard, who of course would appeal to me because of his attack on cultural Christianity. I realized that one could be against cultural Christianity and still find some essence, reality and meaningfulness in it. I actually had a profound conversion experience to something (not God or Jesus). I decided to totally change my life after reading Kierkegaard, and I went on a long fast that lasted over thirty days. I also gave the keys to my car away, trying to shed all of my material belongings. During this period when I was fasting, I had what I might term a personal revelation. This was in 1970 in Washington, D.C., when, as you know, there were riots against the Vietnam war and many of my friends were involved in them and believed that the seeds of a new civilization were going to be formed from this revolutionary movement. During this time, I received word that these riots were rather the ashes of a burnt-out civilization. I felt from that experience that we were living in the last days, that we were living in an apocalyptic, eschatological time.

Well, I didn't know what to do about that personal revelation, so I let it lie and decided that all of this spirituality was not getting me anywhere and that I might as well just get my life together. So I compromised my idealism and decided to become a lawyer. As a matter of fact, I planned to study Japanese and pursue a law degree so I could hook up with a firm that did business between Japan and America, so that I could study karate in Japan. I was into karate at that time.

In December, 1970, I met two members of the Unification church—they were called Unified Family at that time—who came to me and said they wanted to talk to me. I said, "O.K., come into my room and I'll talk with you." They said they were members of a religious community and I said, "Well, that's nice. I'm not interested in religion; I'm not interested in communities. What do you want to talk about?" But I was profoundly appreciative of the sincerity that I noticed in these people. One of the sisters visited me for a period of several months, coming to me, befriending me, bringing me cookies, and expressing her desire that I go to one of their workshops to hear the teaching of this community. I didn't want to go. I was busy on the weekends. I used to go to karate tournaments about every weekend. I thought I had more important things to do. Finally, however, I felt a kind of personal obligation to go to hear the lectures because she seemed to be putting herself out so much and was so sincere and so dedicated that I thought I owed it to her to go. I went to hear the teaching of the church and I must admit I was profoundly appreciative of what I thought was a rational explanation of the faith, something I had never encountered before. I left after two days, saying to myself, actually saying to someone else who had attended the workshop with me, "This is a dirty trick. I thought I was just coming to some nice weekend, but if this is true, I'm going to have to change my entire lifestyle, and I wasn't prepared for that." The first thing I did at home was to read the *Divine Principle* book to see if all the things they had said had been written down somewhere, and they had. After that time I actually didn't have much communication with the movement. I went back to the campus. However, based on the testimonies that I heard from people after the workshop about their prayer life, I decided to begin praying seriously for the first time in my life. And in prayer I realized that God was a real being and that He was concerned for me. Finally, I had encountered the ground of my life, and in the relationship with God I found what I had been looking for.

A few months later, I called up the Unification church center in Washington, D.C. and I said, "I read the book, and I've had a number of experiences, and I think it's true. I'd like to join the community. What should I do?" They were completely flabbergasted, because when I went to the workshop I had asked many abstruse and seemingly objecting questions, and they never expected to see me again. They were really surprised. However, I did not move into the community for several more months. I finally moved in at the end of my junior year, and throughout my senior year I lived in the community and commuted to school. After finishing my undergraduate degree, I then traveled with the One World Crusade team, which was comprised of members from Europe, Asia, and America. We traveled extensively throughout the east coast of America from Florida to Maine. I worked for some time doing research on the Unification theology book that Miss Kim wrote;* I went to Louisiana to do missionary work; and I came to New England and was state director for the Unification church in New Hampshire and in Massachusetts. Later, I worked in various campaigns in which Rev. Moon spoke throughout America, and I was the state director in Tennessee before coming to the Seminary. That was two years ago.

For me, the Unification church and its teaching have helped me overcome my bias and resentment toward religion—actually toward God—and have opened up a tremendous relationship

---

*Young Oon Kim, *Unification Theology and Christian Thought*, New York, N.Y.: Golden Gate, 1975.

with God which I feel is the most essential thing in my life. After I leave here, I'm going to be attending Harvard Divinity School where I hope to systematize my convictions. (laughter)

Rod Sawatsky: Do you want to ask any questions for this particular discussion?

Anthony Guerra: One of the questions I have after reading Richard's book is how Evangelicalism deals with maintaining its spiritual standard, its dedication, its Christlikeness, while enjoying social success—the tremendous acceptance that you have in society. How, in fact, do you maintain your spirituality and deal with the obvious temptations that arise from such success?

Rod Sawatsky: Well, we've had equal time for two of you. I think our introductions will really have to try to stick to five minutes. You're running closer to fifteen. You probably weren't aware of it, but you were.

These are fascinating stories, of course. But if everybody's going to tell their fascinating story, we'll be here forever. (laughter) I think I saw people beginning to listen closely, Anthony, when you started to say how you joined the Unification church itself, and what you've done with it. I think a greater emphasis on those things would be more valuable. Let's see if we can try for five minutes each.

Roy Carlisle: I think I'll start a year before I entered into the evangelical world. I was a senior in a small high school, won a large scholarship to go to college, was voted most likely to succeed, and just a whole pile of things. I went off to a very good college. In the course of that first year I went from a 4.0 to about a 2.3 and got my mind blown, because I'd never seen a C on a report card in my life. It shattered me emotionally. In the process I had met Christians who were a part of my fraternity. Those Christians, who were very evangelical, cared about me in a way that nobody I'd ever known cared about me. They loved me, and brought me into their community at the end of my freshman year in college. I made a kind of a C. S. Lewis attempt at trusting God, although I didn't really understand who Jesus Christ was at that time. But I was in a very academic community and that community was working those questions through.

Over the course of the next three years I became very stable in that faith. It was basically enlightened fundamentalism. In the course of that time I decided that I wanted to go on to seminary. I was a philosophy major. It was incredibly boring, and I decided that theological studies would be much more exciting. So I went to Fuller Theological Seminary. After the first quarter, I had a crisis of faith because it was not just enlightened fundamentalism at Fuller. It was a radical change for me. I dropped out, went to do a counter-culture thing, by editing a Jesus-people newspaper for a year. Finally I started to put my act together. In those years, my life of faith really came together.

The Jesus people movement was a charismatic movement, which I'd never heard of before that time. But I was confronted with a dimension of spiritual vitality that I'd never seen before. It profoundly influenced me. So I went back to Fuller to finish my seminary training and in the course of that did become charismatic. My charismatic experience began to integrate faith and life for me. In this process I felt led to get more involved ecumenically. I was freed by that experience not to be tied by fundamentalism or fundamental Evangelicalism, and I felt that I would walk into any circle and be who I was, share my faith and not be uncomfortable with it.

In the course of that I felt quite strongly moved to go into publishing and prepared myself for that direction. Also, I met Richard Quebedeaux while I was the bookstore manager at Fuller Seminary. He doesn't know it, but he was a real influence in my life then, because he was always blasting my evangelical notions to the pit (laughter) and I had to go back to my Saturday night charismatic group and get put back together. I found it a healing experience to get crushed and built up every week. (laughter) Actually, the way Richard did it was so gracious, I couldn't blame him. It was just a matter of him talking frankly about things that I had struggles with, but it really helped me in many, many ways. I went on to join a major publishing house. My responsibility for evangelical publishing forced me to deal with the great questions I have as an Evangelical.

Now I know they are questions about process. The spiritual process that goes on among people who are moving from non-faith to faith and the in-between places. And that is one of the reasons I was very intrigued about the conference. Living at Berkeley, of course, you see examples of faith and non-faith from every spectrum under heaven. You have to become aware of what that means, I think, in the world. I'm also involved in a seminary. It's a new theological training center, and we're having to speak as Evangelicals in a process way in a situation where things are changing. My questions of the conference are questions of how you come along the path and how the paths go. Also it's important because I've received several manuscripts on Unification and the only thing I've ever seen in a manuscript is negative. I've never seen one that was pro. As an editor, to maintain my own integrity, I believe that I need to see the other side of the story. So that was part of my reason for attending as well.

Rod Sawatsky: That was ten minutes. We're doing better.

Paul Eshleman: I was raised in South Florida, the son of a Baptist minister. I was part of a group of high school students that went to church because it was family tradition. We brought things to amuse ourselves during the sermon. We'd bring watches with sweep-second hands so we could practice holding our breath to build up our lung capacity for skin-diving on Sunday afternoon, and other important things. I went to Michigan State and quit most of my religious activities. As a child I had asked Jesus Christ to come into my life. I'm sure that He did, but I had very little personal commitment to the Lord. I basically forgot about it until my junior year. I was in the Student Union at Michigan State one day when a student from a Jewish background came up to me and said, "Have you ever thought about a personal relationship just between you and Jesus Christ?"

My ordinary reaction would have been, "Look, talk to somebody who needs it. I've had that for eighteen years." But, because he was Jewish, I said, "I thought Jews didn't believe in Christ. Why are you talking to me about it?" He shared with me that he had read the Old Testament, that he had become convinced that Jesus of Nazareth was that promised Messiah. And, on that basis, he had committed his life to Him, and his whole life had changed.

This came at a point in my life when there were kicks and good Saturday night parties, but there was an empty feeling that somehow wasn't being met in my life. I didn't do anything about it at that time. I was interviewed for a number of jobs, but about a year and a half later I was asked to counsel at a church camp. I was in no condition spiritually to counsel at the camp, but I didn't want my friends who were committed Christians to think I was a bad person, so I said I'd lifeguard. On the third day of the camp a girl that I'd been dating came up to me while I was lifeguarding and said, "Paul, what are you going to do with your life?" And I said, "Well, I'll probably go into the reserves for six months, and then go to work for Standard Oil and make some

money." And she said, "What are you going to do with your life?"
I said, "O.K., I know what you're getting at. What am I going to
do for Jesus?" And she said, "You know, Paul, most of your
friends who are here don't really respect you because you're just
fooling around with Christ and Christianity. Get off the fence."
And I thought, I don't need this. I've been nice enough to give
my time, and all I get is a sermon.

I went home and tried to watch television, tried to read, but
all I could think about was what she had said. By 2 o'clock in the
morning I was having an incredible battle. I said, "Lord, I've
gone to camp and made new vows that I'll be a better Christian
and it never worked. I'm 23. I know what I'm doing. I'm not
making any more new vows or new starts." But that night a verse
of scripture started to go through my mind and it was this:
"Pharaoh's heart was hardened, and he would not listen to them;
as the Lord had said." And I knew in my own experience that it
had been years since my heart had been soft enough for God to
really talk to me. And I was desperately afraid that if I said "no"
there wouldn't be another opportunity. I obviously believe that
God always gives people more opportunities, but I knew in my
own mind how long it had been since I'd been soft enough for
Him to talk to me. And so that night, at 2 o'clock in the morning,
I got down by my bed and I said, "Jesus Christ, You might
already be in my life, I'm not sure, but not only do I want You to
come in if You're not there, but I want to give You my whole life.
I'm willing to do whatever You want me to do."

Having been raised the son of a minister, I thought the worst
thing that could possibly happen to anybody was to have to be a
minister, or if not that, to be a missionary in Africa. That's what
all the committed people did. That night I said, "I'm willing to do
whatever You want me to do. I'll even be a missionary in Africa
or a minister." There was such a tremendous freedom that came
into my life after that. I had an assurance that I had an eternal
relationship with God.

I saw changes in my life. Instead of trying to use people for
my own ends, I began to develop a love and a compassion that
wasn't me, but was supernatural. I began to find a purpose for
living far beyond making money. I saw that I could invest my life
to see other people's lives change, and through that I could see
the world change. If enough individual lives were changed, the
world could be changed. I gave my life to that.

I came into contact with Campus Crusade for Christ; they taught me how to share my faith. In 1966 I joined the staff of Campus Crusade for Christ as a new trainee and learned all the things that you have to learn as a trainee. I took out the garbage at the director's house and all those kinds of things. I was then made the campus director at the University of Wisconsin. I started the ministries of the Campus Crusade all over the state of Wisconsin and in Northern Michigan. I then moved to Dallas in 1970 and spent two years in preparation for a conference called Explo '72, in which we had 85,000 high school and college students for a week of training in how to share their faith. On the final day almost a quarter of a million attended the Jesus Music Festival.

I went from there and took over the directorship of 600 campus ministries for Campus Crusade nationally, and then finally 2,500 full-time field staff in the United States working on the campus, in high schools, among laymen, military, athletes, prisoners, and in several other areas. Then, in 1975-6, I directed the "I Found It" campaign nationally, working with 17,000 churches. For the last year I have been in New York City on a special assignment—the Genesis project—serving as vice president of a firm that's producing the Bible on film for distribution throughout the country and throughout the world.

Rod Sawatsky: Any more specific questions?

Paul Eshleman: As I've read the materials that have been sent out, I obviously disagree in strong measure with much of the doctrinal content that I have read in the statements and in the book that I have been sent. I am not vindictive, nor am I judgmental because I know there were people who thought that I would never amount to anything. I think everybody is on a pilgrimage of discovery, the pilgrimage to find a relationship with God, so I don't write off the Unification church. I believe there are people here who are genuinely searching for God. Every time I have an opportunity to share my faith, I do that. I don't understand how the Unification church would hope to succeed without the primacy of a living vital faith in Jesus as king and Lord and master and ruler of the universe. I think without that primacy in the central part of the doctrine that it can't possibly succeed.

Mark Branson: My early life was within the liberal tradition and it included everything from liberal Methodism to process theology to Campus Crusade to Inter-Varsity and quite a few things in between. Now as long as I can remember, I have wanted to be a preacher. That's from when I was five or six. There has always been a basic desire to serve God. I haven't had any traumatic experiences or any big emotional conversions or even second blessings or whatever. It's been a slow growth. I got started early and it's taken every bit of that time! (laughter) The continuous and constantly growing ingredient for me has just been more and more coming to love Jesus. His life and what He taught were an attraction to me very early. My understanding was that He was head of the church, so I was a part of the church. It was during high school that I met Chuck Melcher, an older high school friend, who shared with me the idea that Jesus was more than the head of the church, that Jesus could forgive personal sins, and I found this true in life. That began an incredible new change in my life. Although it wasn't dramatic, it began my commitment.

Over the college years as a religious-studies major and at seminary, education has always played a part, though minor, in my life. During the early '70s, I moved from Kansas to California to become involved in some street ministry in Hollywood. While there I also helped TA at Claremont Men's College and completed a degree at the School of Theology in Claremont. More and more the focus for me was Jesus. Even though I'd read the gospels and the whole New Testament, the focus came down very much to the study of the gospels with the quest of knowing and imitating Jesus Christ. This concern went deeper and deeper in my life. This involved several different chains of events at that point in which a contemplative life became more significant to me. I became involved in what was called Evangelicals for Social Action at that time, finding some camaraderie with some other individuals who felt the gospel was not something spiritual but the good news that included all areas of one's life and therefore had political, economic, and social ramifications, not only for the believers, but also for the believers' behavior in the world. How do we imitate Jesus and serve the world in the way that He did as an agent of the good news? Issues of traditional evangelicalism have not been attractive to me. I generally have been very much annoyed with institutionalism, yet I see that it can be an agent of grace as many things can.

I now work at a Presbyterian church in Los Angeles. I'm not

ordained. My main thrust still is ministry with college and seminary
students. I like conducting Bible studies. I work with a Theological
Students' Fellowship (that's a ministry basically to Evangelicals
who are in "liberal seminaries"). Many evangelical students studying
at mainline seminaries are working with faculties who don't have
the background to understand evangelical theology and to offer
those resources. We work in providing those resources, and
we're very close to some of the faculty in those schools. Our
membership grew from 200 to 1,000 over the last couple of years.
I've spent a lot of time traveling, speaking and working with
fellowships at the seminaries. So my job's about half and half—it's
college ministry half the time, and travel for the TSF half the
time.

The focus for me still really comes down to what it means
for God to be incarnate in Jesus. What did Jesus do? Because if
He is the main way I understand God, as He is, I know God
because I know Jesus Christ. Then, how do I proclaim the gospel
in my actions, my words and the words of forgiveness, the words
of new life, the words of the kingdom, and the words of what it
means for the King to be alive?

The main questions I bring to the conference are twofold:
one has to do with integrity. I have been tricked by comments of
friends who have been formally involved with the Unification
church. One friend was involved for eight years. My questions
have to do with them explaining certain Unification beliefs to me
and saying, "You may bring these up but they will be denied."
Also, there are different issues about the conversion process
which sometimes I find are very similar to evangelical conversion
processes, so I'm led to question my own tradition at the same
point. But the whole issue of honesty, the issue of methods, the
issue of integrity are very key questions in my own thinking. If I
get answers to my questions, are they honest answers? I'm not
interested in dialogue that doesn't have a presupposition of honesty. The other question I bring is the one that Paul mentioned,
and that is of christology, of messiahship. I obviously don't like
the understanding that Jesus did not complete the job, did not do
what He was supposed to do, did not do what was intended for
Him. And then, there is the understanding of how Rev. Moon has
instead done that and takes care of God's needs.

Pete Sommer: Pete Sommer is my name and I work with
Inter-Varsity. My parents were converted the year I was born,

out of a background on the one hand of Christian Science, and on the other of post-Jewish Gnosticism. I was born in 1949 and raised perforce in a Christian home. My earliest encounter with God, I guess, would be when I was seven. We went down to the Cow Palace in San Francisco when Billy Graham was conducting his crusade and at the end of the meeting that night, he asked people to come forward, and I saw all these adults getting out of their seats and it looked like the thing to do. And my parents turned to me and said, "Now, do you know what you're doing?" and I said, "I don't know. Don't you think I should?" So I went down to the front, and I was surrounded by adults who were weeping over the issue of sin and having their guilt forgiven and experiencing cleansing, and I had no idea really of what was going on. And I think my counselor at the crusade understood that and he just kind of patted me on the back and brought me back to my mom and dad. But the one thing that I did come away with from that meeting was an indelible impression that this was really the question—the spiritual question.

Then I forgot about that and got into some deep emotional trouble in my junior high years a few years later. I was on an ulcer diet and a few other things at the age of thirteen, went off to a camp in California known as Mount Hermon, which is a prominent evangelical conference site. That week I had a counselor at the camp who just showed me a love and a toleration for my antics which somehow penetrated the screen, and I was really convinced that somebody could know who I was and still love me. And at the end of that week I finally realized that I could have a deeply personal experience with the living Jesus Christ, and I asked Him to come into my life and to forgive my sins. And in that instant, I felt a deep cleansing of myself, and I felt utterly free and loved and known and forgiven. I was in a state of euphoria for two weeks, after which I promptly forgot all about it and lived my life my way for two or three years.

I started to receive some help in high school through a movement known as Young Life, which is touched on briefly in Richard's book, and also in my Presbyterian church. Our church was very involved in social action throughout the San Francisco Bay Area as well as in very active evangelism. I went to the Urbana Missionary Convention which Inter-Varsity does every three years. I'd never heard of Inter-Varsity at that time, my freshman year of college in 1967. And there for the first time I

was confronted with people from seemingly every country and
cultural background and I was confronted with the question of
what I would do with my life and that again was a deep watershed
experience for me. I saw Jesus Christ as the one who was really
the answer to the needs of man. It had an interracial and
international, supernatural thrust; it hit me deeply and I committed
myself to it at that time. The conversion experience that was
really exciting for me is my wife's, and I'm sorry that she can't be
here to tell her story. It's really a miraculous story, if any of you
want to ask about it, you can. It's short. I now work in the Bay
Area. We both work together supervising a team of sixteen staff.
Every time I count them off it comes out a little different. We're
having some turnover right now. But I'm based near Stanford
University, and it's exciting to see students responding to the
gospel. That's what I do.

Rod Sawatsky: Do you want to say anything, Pete, regarding
this particular discussion? Questions?

Pete Sommer: The few things that have provoked me as
I've read all the material sent to me and some other material as
well and as I've talked with former members of the Unification
church who are in our Presbyterian church on the peninsula, are,
first of all, the christological issue again, the failure, or whatever
you want to say, of the mission of Jesus, and therefore the
necessity of Moon to improve upon or, say, to fulfill, the mission
of Jesus in a way that Jesus Himself did not succeed in doing. Yet,
I would just say I radically disagree with that, but I hope we will
unpack that and get at it. And secondly, again, is the honesty
question that I am very interested in. The stories that I get from
the former members and then from you is that of real variance,
and I would hope that we can talk absolutely frankly about that.
I've done a little bit of research but not much. So those are the
two things.

Lloyd Howell: My name is Lloyd Howell and I'm a second-
year student here. I'll begin my story when I was in college. In
college I took engineering, which was enough for my mind
because it stimulated my thinking, but there was something missing
in my heart. There was always an emptiness that I filled up with
poetry. I really found poetry to be a vehicle to help me along
during that period with "heartistic" expression and creative explor-
ation. When it came time for job interviews, I just couldn't go to
them. In my heart I said, "I don't feel a call, a pull, an urge or

anything in that kind of direction. I'm just not going to the job interviews."

I graduated from college and I thought I would just go on writing poetry. I got a job at a supermarket for a little while, and finally I thought I would check out this engineering. I had to at least see if it was worth something, if it wasn't just some concept I had about big business, or being swallowed up by some organization to which I didn't feel I could be loyal. I went to a couple of engineering jobs. Then there were layoffs and I hitch-hiked around the country, which had always been one of my dreams. It was during one of these layoff periods that, on one trip around the country, I met Rev. Moon. He had just finished a campaign in New York. His picture was plastered on all the billboards. I had seen enough of his picture, and a friend said to me, "This guy thinks he's the second coming of Christ." And I said, "Well, another one, that's good." It didn't mean much to me.

I went to an Episcopal church—and I never found anything there. I got tired of the word "church" and I got tired of their inability to answer my questions. I have to admit, it wasn't a very lively church; some churches are alive and some people in the church are alive. I didn't think much of the word "church." When I met someone in Oregon from the Unification church, I liked the person and I liked the word Unification. The person, I could feel, was concerned more about me than about himself. He said to me, "Do you want to come to this meeting? We're concerned about a world brotherhood and God," and I said, "Well, I'm going to a movie; I think I can find God at the movie."

At that time I was into the I-Ching, and I figured there were cosmic principles and true laws. But I didn't know the heart of God; I didn't have anything personal going on. So I tested this person. I said, "Why don't you come to the movies with me, God is there I know." And the person said, "Yes, I'll walk with you." And I felt something really sincere; there was no thought in my mind that this was wishy-washy. I realized that that person just wanted to know me for an "I" reason, for a purpose of love. I then said, "I don't want to go to the movies. What is this lecture?" So I went to the lecture. I wasn't impressed. They wanted me to go to the weekend workshop. I had plans to go to the Oregon coast. But I went to the workshop. I wrote a letter back to my girlfriend and said, "You know, these people are different from how I imagined them in New York." When you meet people in New York everybody's just a hassle. (laughter) You go to Port Authority and you meet the Black Panthers and the Black Muslims, and maybe you meet a Moonie and everyone else, and you just want to make it home. (laughter) So I said to her, "These are good people, you know." And that's it; I wrote the letter.

I went back to New York. To me, love was important, but the kind of love as I understood it came between a man and a woman. Then about a month later, my girlfriend met this church and she was invited up to Barrytown, at the time when they had workshops here. She disappeared for a couple of days and she came back and she wasn't happy about her experience. So the relationship really just fell apart, and to me love was all I cared about. I didn't care about money; I didn't care about jobs. Those things were all at the bottom of the list, and so without my love I didn't know what to do. It was about four or five months later she got an inspiration to go back and check out whatever she ran away from the first time. So she came back up here. I supported her. I knew she needed to change some and I needed to change some. Something had to get better. So she came to the three-day and the seven-day workshops and I was angry. She said that they were detaining her. I wanted to go up, put her in the car, go on a picnic and just take her back. These kinds of feelings came over me but I fought through them and I said to myself, "If there's trouble going on inside her and she really wants to change, then I'm just going to support her 100% even if she's not going to be orbiting around my life; something good is happening to her—I can feel that from my perspective. And as I did that I received many revelations, things that I was later to find out coincided with the Divine Principle. I came to realize I had to live my life for God; I had to give it to God 100%. There was no doubt that the love between her and me wasn't anything that could sustain me, or carry things on. I, from the middle of my I-Ching and whatnot said, "I'm going to give my life to God and I'm just going to get on a boat and go." I guess spiritually I understood it, as I wanted to leave this world and just find God and that was it.

I was going to go into the merchant marine—I had everything prepared—but I went around to visit this church a bit—I thought I should go. In fact, my girlfriend was beginning to change her life. And I went around and she said, "Why don't you come to a weekend workshop?" And I said, "Fine, but I can't get in the way of what I have to do which is to find God."

As I came here I felt that there was no fooling around. I felt some kind of commitment to something, and I had a fear inside me that this was the time when I had to make my decision. And I heard these lectures and I had deep experiences of repentance during the lectures on creation, on the fall of man, and on Jesus. I went into the chapel there and said, "I'm giving up my old way of life, and I'm just going to give everything to this direction." I'm always glad to tell you more, to share more, but that's enough.

Rod Sawatsky: Do you want to say anything about our discussion here?

Lloyd Howell: Well, I have a number of questions, such as, I meet people who say, "Are you born again?" What must you do to be born again? I'm always wondering what they want to do once they're born again. What do you do after you're born again? What is discipleship? I went to the Jesus '78 and I saw a lot of healing. They wanted to heal the body of Christ. But I didn't see any tears of repentance around me. I didn't see people weep; I didn't feel they would be willing to pay a price. I thought that somehow they thought the spirit would come down to heal the body and I understand that a man has a responsibility and role in this and I want to know how my evangelical brothers and sisters feel towards healing the body of Christ. How is God working in this world? Socially? And on different levels? As I have my ways of comprehending His work, I want to comprehend your understanding.

Ulrich Tuente: My name is Ulrich Tuente. I'll try to make this short because my conversion is not so dramatic. I feel that I've not much to say. I'm from Germany, and my parents are farmers. My father's from a Reformed background. My mother is from a Lutheran background. I met the Unification church in 1973 at the University of Mainz. I actually was not very impressed by the members when I encountered them standing there in front of the campus witnessing and approaching students. There were two women who were then in the center, and I really was not very much impressed with them. But I was interested when they spoke about the idea of the unification of religion, and I was especially interested because their ideas encompassed all the practical aspects of life, even the political and economic realms. This attracted me very much and this was the reason I came to the lectures. I didn't particularly feel any love, but I felt that I definitely had the responsibility to do this if it was right, if it really was going to

establish God's kingdom, and if it would accomplish the will of
Jesus Christ for today. After I was convinced of this, I decided to
join.

   Patricia Zulkosky: My name is Patricia Zulkosky. I'm originally from Seattle, Washington. I got my bachelor's degree in
occupational therapy from the University of Washington. From
the time I was very young, I was very greatly distressed by man's
suffering and by the whole question of good and evil and how it all
fit into the world. I couldn't accept sin. I felt that I always made
the most conscientious decision possible in any given circumstance.
I might make mistakes, but I didn't feel that I sinned. Eventually,
I left the Catholic church because no one could explain sin to me
in a way that I could understand. And when I was a junior, one of
my nuns had told me to stop asking questions because I was
destroying the life of faith of the people in my class. It was at a
time when I was thinking about entering the convent, so it was a
rude awakening to me that people didn't have the answers to the
questions that I was searching for.

   Eventually I went into occupational therapy and my whole
life was dedicated to serving others. My apartment was a drop-in
center. At some point in my little apartment I had as many as
nine people living, all dependent on me, including a 13-year-old
foster daughter and a 30-year-old man who'd been in prison for
fifteen years and anyone else I knew who needed help. I took
phone calls at any hour of the day or night from people who were
in distress. So I was really into helping people. Halfway through
college I came into contact with eastern philosophy to the
extent that for the first time I got the idea that perfection was
not only possible but also the goal of man. And so when someone
witnessed to me on campus, he happened to say the word
"perfection" and that caught my attention because I knew the
drive to reach perfection. It was like an innate feeling to me. But
also I was the first person he ever witnessed to in his life. He was
obviously trying too hard to share something which was precious
to him and he was scared to death to try to witness to me. Since I
was into giving success to people (laughter), I told him that I'd
come over and hear his group.

   At that time there were twenty people in the Unification
center from many different countries living in a two-bedroom,
one-bathroom house, but it was a temporary situation—they
were passing through on a traveling team. It was clean and the

atmosphere was so pure that you would never believe such a thing. As a matter of fact, most of them didn't even speak English, but it didn't interrupt the harmony at all; as a matter of fact, the harmony was that much greater. It was clear to me that somehow these people had something that I didn't have, or they were closer to perfection in a way that I wanted to be. So I listened to the people, and I could understand how uniting around an ideology could bring people together. And I think in the past five years I've come to a much deeper relationship with God, especially with Jesus, through the Unification church. I guess we all have numerous spiritual experiences that we can share, but this particular conference is very important to me because I'm very interested in evangelical Christianity.

I want to raise the question of perfection and the direction we must go to become perfect. I'm one of those people who studies the lives of the saints thoroughly, upside down and inside out, to understand mystical relationships with Jesus, how people became who they became, and what kind of life of sacrifice they led to become a channel through whom God could do something great. So I greatly admire many of the saints and reformers of the past, but I'm really seeking to learn how to apply those things of the past, those examples of a life of faith, today, and how we can become this kind of really powerful vehicle to reach so many people, and to bring them back to God and to really revolutionize this world in a deep way.

Joseph Hopkins: I'm Joe Hopkins. I was here in March and enjoyed myself so much that I came back again. I have a rather unconventional background, I guess. My father was Quaker; my mother, a Presbyterian. I graduated from high school in Laurel, Maryland, when I was barely sixteen, so I was sent to Westtown school, a Quaker school, for a year before going on to college. Then I went to Westminster College, my mother's alma mater, and struggled to find myself spiritually. I remember going to the minister of the United Presbyterian church in Wilmington and telling him that I'd come to the point where I didn't know whether there was a God. He advised, "Don't cut loose from your moorings. Keep praying, reading the Bible, and attending church. Continue to pursue your search for God with the assurance that He will reward your search." A verse that has come to mean a great deal to me is Jeremiah 29:13, "You will seek me and find me; when you seek me with all your heart." In the course of time my quest was rewarded, though I can't point to a specific experience when I committed my life to Christ. But in time, God came to be real to me and I answered God's call to the ministry.

After graduation from Pittsburgh-Xenia (now Pittsburgh Seminary), I served a church for a year, then served for two years as a navy chaplain, and after that returned to Westminster to teach—and I've been there ever since. Over the years I have grown into a more mature faith—not a *mature* faith, because there is always room for improvement. During the '50s and '60s I guess I was a radical, because I was a militant crusader for racial equality and later against the Vietnam war. I resigned from my national fraternity over the racial issue. During the late '60s I preached a sermon denouncing the Vietnam war in a large suburban church. During the course of the sermon, a number of people got up and walked out. It was a very traumatic experience for me. I feel I'm in Richard's category of the evangelical left. I very strongly believe in the born-again Christian experience, and feel I have come to know God through the surrender of my life to Christ as my Saviour and Lord. My first concern in the conference is the question of authority. The biblical authority versus the concept of continuing revelation. I think that's very basic. Another thing that concerns me—in addition to christology, which has already been mentioned—is the doctrine of salvation by grace alone versus grace plus works.

Rod Sawatsky: Next man up.

Virgil Cruz: If you don't give me at least half an hour I should probably plead racial prejudice or something! (laughter) My work is now in Iowa, but my home is in upstate New York. I was brought up in Cambridge, which was the home of my mother. We like to say that we've been in that tiny town forever. Our family dates back from about 1790 there, so when other Blacks had to engage in a search for roots, I always was able to say that I know who I am because I know my predecessors. We have an interesting racial mingling in my family, including a component from a native American background.

I was brought up in the old United Presbyterian church which Joe knows; I can't point to a specific time of a conversion experience. I can point to a general period in my life at the time of graduation from high school, after which, I can say, a relationship with God became a vital thing for me. So that's the native United Presbyterian way of looking at a kind of conversion experience.

After having had two years between high school and college, I did go off to Houghton College; some of you know that college—a poorer sister of Wheaton College. There as a Presbyterian I had a difficult experience encountering for the first time the second blessing phenomenon, sanctification, and so forth. I attempted to receive that blessing, because I, of all people, knew I was not perfect and could really benefit from that kind of thing. I remember the counsel of an upper classman after I had gone to an altar call a number of times seeking the second blessing. He said, "Cruz, why don't you just forget it and remain Presbyterian?" (laughter) "Don't you think that it is completed at the end of your time here? Why don't you just remain Presbyterian?"

While I was in college I had planned to major in history and teach history ultimately. During college I received a call to the gospel ministry, and turned to a pre-seminary program. Also I discovered Greek at that time and became a Greek major at Houghton. My seminary was Pittsburgh-Xenia, an institution of the old United Presbyterian church of North America. Having graduated from seminary, I had a pastorate in New York for four years. It was just a marvelous experience for me. It was the first time in the old denomination when a Caucasian congregation called a person from a minority race its pastor. And while maybe we didn't accomplish a lot of responsible ministry together, we had an awfully good time. I sometimes feel guilty about the enjoyment I experienced in that pastorate. It was a marvelous time for me. While there I received a fellowship from the Hazen Foundation of Chicago to study wherever I might choose, and I finally decided upon the Free University in Amsterdam. That was just a marvelous experience for me. I was coming out of a very conservative background, and it was great for me to be at a place that was really a crossroads of theological ferment. We experienced radicalism out of Germany and were influenced by the sanity of England many times.

I really had a fine experience in educational formation at the Free University; it moved me out of my theological provincialisms. When I went to Europe I was also provincial with respect to political-social stances. I remember once—you mentioned the business of working with students and organizations—I organized a protest in Amsterdam, a counterdemonstration against those leftist students who were saying bad things about my nation, my country. We had a permit and were all set to go, but it rained, so that major event didn't take place. I had known when I went to Holland that socialism is of the devil; when I got there and found out that so many of my Christian friends were involved in one or another expression of socialism, that was a great enlightening change.

A major event in my life happened in the Netherlands. I married. I met my wife who was a student. Her field was Spanish. I was married later in life, so God planned it that way in bringing me and this one individual into contact. My marriage is extremely important in my life.

I've been at the University of Dubuque Theological Seminary, a Presbyterian school, since 1966. My professional interests are the apocalyptic writings, in general, and especially the book of Revelation. My dissertation, published in Amsterdam by Academic Press, deals with the interpretive problems in Revelation. I enjoy very much my work at Dubuque, and maybe the Unification church would be interested in looking at what we're doing there. We have really far-reaching, ongoing ecumenical cooperation there. In addition to the Presbyterian and Methodist schools in that city, there is a vital Lutheran seminary, Wartburg (ALC Lutheran), and there is an active Roman Catholic school of theology which is ecumenical in its own right, both Dominican and Franciscan. And we're totally integrated in our academic program. It's fun to look out and see nuns in habits and nuns also in shorts, Dominican brothers, Lutheran men and women, Presbyterian men and women. It's a marvelous attempt to work through to some sort of cooperative position, all the while keeping in mind the fact that we have differences. And we enjoy and respect each other enough that we can face those differences.

In the city of Dubuque, I've become involved in social action and have had some real good run-ins, fights with the establishment there, which have resulted in, I think, improvement. Governor Ray of Iowa has appointed me to the State Crime Commission, which has given me another means whereby I think I can do ministry in the state. I've had fun the last few years doing things for the larger church, for the denomination. Perhaps the most significant responsibility has been the ordination exams which each of the Presbyterian candidates for the ministry must take and pass. I had particular responsibility for the open Bible exegesis exam and Bible content exams. This has been a good involvement on my part and a worthwhile expenditure of time.

For four summers I've also been on the staff of the Young Life Theological Institute in Colorado Springs, and have had just a great time getting to know that group. I learned one summer that Jeb Magruder was going to be in my class, so I decided even before class started that I would flunk him and the whole class at once, but as a result of our engagement, we became rather good friends. I have appreciated him and know that his testimony is legitimate.

I, too, am interested in the question of christology, and a whole cluster of issues surrounding that; I'm sure they will begin to emerge as we begin to discuss. The other point that I'd like to mention has been alluded to also: the phenomenon of new scripture. There's no place for that in my theology, so I think it will be very helpful for me to understand how this phenomenon can indeed be advanced by the Unification church. Particularly, I have problems with new revelations, with new scriptures, when I think they are at variance with biblical writings. So, frankly speaking, this would be a real issue I'd like to engage in.

Rod Sawatsky: There's some iced tea in the corner there, and some ginseng fizz! (laughter)

(BREAK)

How are we doing, folks? Is everyone keeping their interest up? Very much so? I'm finding it fascinating. I think it's worthwhile. Maybe we can speed up just a little bit more so that we can get done by noon. Can we do that? Just a little faster pace? Let's see if we can. If we can't, it's O.K.

Jan Weido: My name is Jan Weido. I was born in Nemacolen, Pennsylvania, which is a small coal-mining town named after Nemacolen, an American Indian. I was raised a pagan Catholic pantheist, and at the age of thirteen, my parents just got sick of the hypocrisy they saw in the Catholic church (at least where I was raised), so they just gave it up. That pleased me, because I didn't have to go to catechism; I didn't have to go to church. My religion became athletics. I became a superjock—played football, basketball, track, whatever. That was my religion and my discipline. At the end of my senior year, I started to question and search and get out of the provincial little coal-mining town. I began to become radicalized. I had a deep sense of the "haves" and the "have nots," being a coal-miner's son and seeing the oppression,

the exploitation, that goes on with the workers. I think Malcolm
X, his autobiography, moved and changed me during that period
in my life more than anything else I've ever read or heard.
Basically, that area is pretty racist, and I'd had a pretty racist
upbringing. I think there was one Black at our school. All that
changed for me. I took a scholarship to play basketball at a small
school in Maryland. I lasted about a year. I started smoking pot,
got involved with campus radicals, and became one of the leaders
on campus. That was my first conversion, into the counter-
culture, into the radical culture. I accepted that as my "lord and
saviour" first. I wanted to continue on in school, so I decided to
look for another school. Rutgers University was developing an
experimental program so I decided to go there.

Later, I did some traveling; I really got into art, into that
Bohemian artist kind of trip. At that point, I had totally rejected
Christianity. I didn't want to be bugged by Jesus freaks. I thought
they and Christianity were a justification of the death machine in
America. They blessed the bombs, lived in suburbia, and did
their thing with America. That turned me off. What turned me
on was the eastern spirituality, the kind of internal search for self
and God. So I went that route. Where I really started to relate to
Christianity and Christ was at the end of my senior year in
college. I had a professor who was pushing me towards getting
into art more, going to graduate school, and getting into the New
York art scene. But I was turned off by civilization, so I decided
the thing to do was to get a little piece of land off in the country
somewhere.

I had a very good relationship with a woman. I was very
spiritual. We meditated together. We were very open and honest
with one another. We were very loyal to one another, and we
were searching together. We understood that our relationship
was part of a spiritual search. So we worked and we bought some
land in West Virginia with a few other people back in the hills,
figuring that if there was a nuclear war, we were far enough away
from Pittsburgh that the fallout wouldn't get us, and when it all
came to a grinding halt, that we could last it out eating roots and
berries and things like that. Who knows, maybe somewhere
along in there we would reach enlightenment; we were basically
neo-Buddhist Hindus. (laughter) After we had decided to do that,
things started happening. I met my patron saint, Thomas Merton.
He's not a "saint" yet, but I look to him as a saint. I've taken him

on as my patron saint. As with Jacob, God or the Archangel or someone came in and threw my body out of place, so that I had to continue to struggle; but I had also to stop. I twisted my knee and tore the cartilage, so I had to stay in bed for about a month. It was at that point, I think, that the Holy Spirit began to work in my life. I was really into reading all of Thomas Merton's books, and it just happened that one friend brought me one of them, so I told my girlfriend to go to the library and get his other ones. I read through all of them, and as I lay there and watched life revolve around me, my friends into their trips, into their spirituality, I was at the mercy of God, at the mercy of other people (because I couldn't get up too much). I had a lot of time to think. A voice came to me one night and said, "O.K., you want to go out into the woods and do your thing out there. How about the suffering people in the world?" I think I was convinced in that moment by the Holy Spirit, or by God or Christ or whatever, that life wasn't to be escaped from, but is to be lived for other people. At that point, I read in one of Merton's books about a Catholic apostolate up in Ontario, Canada. Something moved me to inquire about it. I played with the idea of either becoming a Trappist monk, following his course in modeling God, or going to this Christian Catholic apostolate and checking it out. Their vows of chastity, obedience and poverty I could accept. My leg got better. I had another experience with the Holy Spirit. I had a choice of whether I should get an operation or let it go. I made the decision that I believed God could heal, that there was a healing force in the universe, so I said rather than put my faith in the hands of a surgeon, I would put my knee in the hands of God and let Him take care of it. And it happened. Many times I would experience a warm current flowing through my leg. I haven't had to have an operation. I can predict the weather sometimes with my knee. (laughter) It's O.K.!

Then, one night I met some Christians. I was outside the Rutgers Student Center. I had just come back from New York City and was waiting to be picked up. I was sitting there very tired. I noticed that God works in my life a lot when I'm pushed to the physical extremes, when I'm very tired or injured. He has to cut my feet down underneath me, because I'm a very active person. I was very tired and wiped out, when these people, these Christians, were witnessing and they came up to me and surrounded me; basically, they were pretty arrogant. This one girl kept calling me "dirty old man" and laying the hell and damn-fire thing on me. "What if you die tonight in a car accident, where will you be?" That really turned me off very much. It just turned me off. But there was one person there who was very loving. He didn't come on like that. He just spoke to me as a person. It was Halloween night, October 31, 1974, that I accepted Christ. At that point, I knew my life was, as you said last night, "O.K., what do you want me to do?" That's the kind of attitude I've taken since. Now, I said, "O.K., I'll put Christ or God—I didn't make too much of a difference there—on the throne of my life."

Things started happening. I started talking to my friends about Christianity, and they were turned off by it. They were I-Ching'ers, and Taoists, and T'ai Chi'ers; some of my friends were Guru Mahara-ji people. They didn't want to hear about Christ. Not one person could help integrate things for me in my life, show me how Christianity and how Christ related to the world's religions, to Buddhists, to Hindus, and all these other people. What turned me off about this little group of Christians that I met was that they were very judgmental. They condemned Buddhists. They said, "Hindus are satanic and they're doomed to hell; they might have good intentions, but the road to hell is paved by good intentions." I couldn't buy that. I couldn't buy that there was a loving Father, God, who was going to throw people into this cosmic burning junk-heap forever and ever because they didn't buy a western Christian trip. It didn't sit right with me. Thomas Merton spoke to that, and Paramahansa Yogananda spoke to that. I had a week of vacation coming. I decided to go visit the place in Ontario. But I couldn't get in touch with the people. A lot of things happened. It was Easter week and I felt something symbolic was happening. Merton gets into the liturgy and the meaning of the Christian year. I was re-connecting with that, with my Catholic past, in a way. But Ontario didn't work out, so I had this week to space out. I was disappointed. But I accepted it. I thought maybe there was something else God had in mind for me.

I went to the dentist one day. I got an overdose of sweet air. If you've never had that experience, it's kind of nice. I OD'd on it, and got sick. I went home and went to sleep and I woke up with this craving for strawberry Continental yogurt. Strange how God works. (laughter) I went into a health food store and sat down to my first Continental strawberry yogurt. I wanted another one; so I ate another one. Then, this friend of mine, whom I hadn't seen in a while, came in and started talking about this Christian group in Barrytown, New York, but I wasn't paying any attention to him. He was talking to these Guru Mahara-ji people, and they were kind of negative on it. They would say, "Oh, Rev. Moon, the Bible, that's a bunch of baloney." They were against his whole enthusiasm. But he was looking for someone to talk to; so he came over to me, and he started talking to me and I said, "O.K., I'll listen to you." He wasn't a convert or anything; he'd just attended a workshop, and he said, "There's a spiritual community. They're into integrating eastern religions and Christianity." My ears perked up, and he said, "I'm going to go back up there. What do you think?" I said, "Yeah, I'll go with you. Let's go. I'll go check it out." I thought—I'd be open to this. I'll see what they have to say. We hopped into his junker and made it as far as the turnpike and then it broke down, so we had to go back. We stayed at his house. We took a bus into the city but I still ended up here in Barrytown for a three-day workshop. I was freaked out by all the short hair and that everybody seemed so happy. I said what's going on here! But I was open to it. I had realized in my life that my plans had to be put aside, that I had to let things happen, let God work in my life. So I listened to the lectures. I got into it. I prayed deeply and for the first time really could understand God's heart, and the personal God. And also repentance. I was brought to a very deep sense of repentance at Barrytown, not just through the lectures, but through the attitude of the people, the prayer, the fellowship that we had. So I decided to stay for another week to hear more and to see what was going on.

I called my girlfriend up and I said, "Why don't you come and check this out?" She said O.K., and she came; but I didn't want to influence her. If this is my path, then I'll follow it, but maybe this isn't her path. So I wouldn't tell her she should do this if she loved me. Actually, I avoided her. I wasn't cold to her, but I didn't speak too much about how I felt about it. After a week, I decided, O.K., I'll join. She stayed around another week, and decided separately that she would also join. So we went back and got all our possessions together, put them in our truck, gave a lot of things away to our friends, because Jesus said, "Sell all that you have, and distribute to the poor...and come, follow me." I moved into the community, and went through some training workshops here, became a pioneer, which is kind of a missionary. I went to Minnesota, where I encountered Christianity on another negative note. It also brought me to an understanding of Christ, because those who persecuted me the most were the evangelical Christians, the Lutherans, and all these so-called followers of Jesus, who had nothing but hate and venomous words and judgment for me as a Moonie and as a person. I didn't see any love manifested there, so I became resentful and turned off to their whole thing. That's what happened to Jesus, too, you know. I worked that out here, but I think in our movement there are still a lot of people with resentment which we have to work out towards Christians who have persecuted us. It's very strong persecution. I was once in a group of people who were all calling me Satan and pointing their finger at me and shouting Bible verses at me. They thought they were going to exorcise me when, in fact, one of their own people got possessed and freaked out. It was a very negative experience. Then I became a state leader in Nevada for a couple of months, until I came to the Seminary.

Here, it's been a very challenging experience. This isn't a place where your faith is just reconfirmed. Your faith is challenged here. I think I changed a lot of my ideas about our faith and other world religions and the Christian faith. I have grown a stronger sense of mission and calling toward working with world religions. And that's one of the questions I have for you people here. How do Evangelicals relate to the world's religions—to Africans, to the Confucians? I don't think they're going to end up in hell. There might be some Christians in hell, and I don't think these other people are necessarily going to go to hell or stay there. I also see this as a question for my Moonie brothers and sisters. How do we relate to the world's religions? When we become too sectarian, get turned off? We're really supposed to be the Unification church or the Holy Spirit Association for the Unification of World Christianity. Some of the things that are important in my faith are the idea that God is personal, that God works through history, through governments; I relate to Jesus more as an elder brother. God is my Father and Jesus is my elder brother. He's also my Messiah, and I know it's through Him that I learned to repent, to find God's forgiveness. I also believe that God is speaking today and I'm open to other scriptures, other revelations, not just the *Divine Principle,* but other people. I think that God is speaking through the world's religions, to the Moonies, to those traditions that aren't Christian. What are the Evangelicals going to do in response to that, other than write books that denounce them? What *positive* things are the Evangelicals going to do? Also, what's your response to Marxism? It has become very important for me to bring my faith into social action. I think the Unification church has to move in that direction a lot more. Other than that, I'm glad you folks came. (laughter)

Rod Sawatsky: Let's keep running. Jonathan.

Jonathan Wells: O.K. I'll just hit a few points here. I was raised a nominal Presbyterian, but I promptly abandoned it when I left high school. I found myself attending the University of California at Berkeley in the mid-60s, and was caught up in the feeling that our generation was going to be a force to change the world and bring about a new society. And in the course of that I got very righteous about civil rights and the anti-war business. So one thing led to another, and I wrote letters of rebellion and refusal to the army. One day I was walking down the street next to the Pacific School of Religion when a black limousine drove up and three plainclothesmen jumped out and packed me in the back seat and took me off to jail where I spent the next year for protesting the war. During this time I wasn't religious, except in a very general sense, but my models were Jesus and Gandhi and King. And every chance I got, I read about these three men. I read things by them and was very idealistic while I was in prison. When I got out in '69 and came back to Berkeley, I felt that things had changed somewhat. There was a lot of violence, bitterness, destruction, and window-breaking. People had died. When I went back to my old friends and associates, I found a strong Marxist influence which I noticed particularly because I had been away during a critical time. And I still can't say that I was religious, that I believed in God, but I was really turned off by the Marxists and I was really turned off by the violence.

So, lacking anything else to turn to, I left the Bay Area and headed for the hills, up in Mendocino County, which some of you may know. I lived in various cabins, bought a farm eventually, and read a lot of the same things that Jan just described, and I had a lot of friends who were neo-Buddhist-Hindu, American Indian, this and that. At that time I underwent a conversion experience, centered on the Old Testament, and I realized that God was real. Then, through the Old and New Testaments, I realized that God was personal. I was in the mountains, partly to avoid the holocaust that I felt was coming, because I knew the impetus that our movement had built up and I felt that this country was headed for very serious trouble. I just didn't want to have any part of it at that point. But at the same time my conscience bothered me because I knew that a lot of people were unhappy, that the world needed something. So I was looking for a movement that could combine the dynamism of the one I had left with the spirituality that I had found in Mendocino County.

About the same time, I encountered the Unification church by visiting an old friend of mine who had joined the Oakland church, and just about the same time I read the *Time* articles about Rev. Moon, accusing him of being this and that. I heard various things from all kinds of people against Rev. Moon and against the church, but because of my experiences in the '60s, I know better than to believe anything the first time I hear it from anybody, anywhere. So I did a lot of checking and spent about a year and a half actually looking into not just the Unification church but also these other Christian and non-Christian groups, and I gradually became more and more impressed with the Unification church. So, through my prayer life, which was deepening quite a bit at that time, I decided that this might be the group that God was leading me to. So I decided to join, but I decided to join on a very conditional basis. The church membership form is just, you know, one piece of paper that lists name, address, educational background, job experience, and one spiritual question: "When did you accept the Divine Principle?" I never did answer that, because I didn't know whether to accept the Divine Principle or not. I wanted to test it and felt the best way to test it was to become involved in the church activities. But I didn't know whether Rev. Moon was a preacher, a guru, a businessman, a fascist, or the antichrist. I just had to see for myself.

So I found myself in 1974 in New York City at a rally in Manhattan to fire people up for the Madison Square Garden campaign. Rev. Moon spoke to a group of maybe 2,000 church members and got them all excited, and by the end of the speech they were standing up and throwing their fists in the air saying, "Monsei!" which is Korean for "Victory!" With all this power and excitement, they were going to go hand out leaflets and invitations for the MSG rally which was a week away. I was standing at the very back of the church when this was going on, fresh from the hills of Mendocino County, and I was horrified because here was all this power and energy, and I didn't know whether to trust this group or not. When Rev. Moon finished and the shouting died down he stepped off to the side of the stage and the head of the German Unification church got up and started speaking in a very heavy German accent (laughter) and I thought, "Wow! This is it! If this isn't a neo-fascist group I don't know what is!" (laughter) The look on my face must have been terrible. Nobody could see me, except Rev. Moon, who I noticed was looking at me. He pointed his finger directly at me, until he realized that I was fully conscious of his awareness of me. Then he lowered his finger. Nobody else, apparently, saw what he had done. Just after that, the meeting broke up and I went to stay at my mother's house in New Jersey to begin writing an article that I was going to submit to the New York newspapers exposing this fascist group. It was a pretty fair article, not too unlike the ones that you've seen. But as I wrote the article I remembered Rev. Moon looking at me, and I prayed very seriously because I wanted it to be honest. Finally I realized that what I was doing was projecting my own fears and suspicions—and my own sin actually—on what I had seen in New York. When I looked at it really objectively, I realized that all I'd noticed was a lot of energy. There hadn't been any talk of nationalism. In fact, it had been the most international group I'd ever seen. There hadn't been any talk of hatred, or racism. All they were going to do was stage a rally for God in New York City, which I knew was probably the most sinful place in America. Well, in a way, this was my idea. I wanted to find the group that had the courage to go into the worst place in America and have a rally for God. That's what I wanted. And so, I tore up the article I was writing, threw it away, and went back to attend the rally and stay in the church. But ever since then I've tried very hard to maintain that kind of skeptical distance at the same time that I'm involved, to make sure that what I'm doing is for God.

In response to some of the things I've heard from our visitors, I have to say that some of the criticisms of us are undoubtedly true. Some of them I've looked into myself and found that they're false. As for what I expect to get out of this conference, I don't know how much we're going to agree on by the time the weekend's over. I don't have too many illusions about strong-willed people changing their minds in three days, either way. But I do have to say, especially after reading Richard's book last week, that I feel a strong tie of brotherhood and sisterhood with the Evangelicals. I admire them more than many other religious groups in America. So I'm looking forward to a lot of good fellowship and clarification and I hope this all serves God's providence somehow.

Rachel Spang: My name is Rachel Spang. I'm from Massachusetts. My father is Roman Catholic, my mother was Protestant and I was brought up in a little town outside Boston in a Congregational church. I was really very active in politics, sports and social life in high school, and it was very easy for me to cruise along and have a good time or really get into whatever I was doing without really even thinking about God or a spiritual life. When I got to college, the University of Pennsylvania, because of certain experiences I had—some tragedy in my family and just certain personal experiences—I was really open to searching, so I made a whole new start in my life. Early in the year I was met by Campus Crusade for Christ, which I talked to Paul about last night. That was a very big turning point in my life, because I attended their meetings and their fellowship. It was just a whole new experience to put my trust in Christ and really feel and experience that God really has a personal relationship with me. You just feel spiritually that that's where real truth and love start. I was just so disturbed by the dichotomy among all of these supposedly intelligent and very capable, brilliant people at Penn, knowing how different their emotional and personal lives were. That was very disturbing to me. So I just got more and more involved with Campus Crusade, which I honestly felt was a little bit superficial in answering certain spiritual questions I had. Nevertheless, it was my introduction to my spiritual life, and by the end of the year I became very intense about furthering what that really meant in my life. I went to Geneva, Switzerland, for a year to get out of the American environment, my own culture, and experience what that could mean.

My interest in the experiential aspects of my faith was very conducive to my living in the woods for quite a long time to feel what it was like to live in the creation and, since this was God's world, feel what that meant. So I did that. I was also very influenced by eastern philosophy, and I integrated that into the

Gospel of John and the life of Jesus particularly, especially what He said our life was meant to be like in the world. And if this is God's world, then how are we to experience that reality as children of God in this world? Beyond the fact that we're saved, what does it mean once we're reborn, with reference to our relationships and in every aspect of our life?

So I came back to the United States and I still was dissatisfied with a particular direction. I really was directionless spiritually; I wasn't going to associate with a group, but nevertheless I was very intense about my spiritual life. Then I got into my Volkswagen van, made a little home, got my Bible and decided that the next step was to see further what God had in mind for me. I would travel around the country and really get a feel for America and the spiritual times that we were living in and what that meant for me in terms of what God wanted me to do in this life. I just didn't know because, living in Europe, I heard so much criticism about America. I really wasn't too concerned about politics at that time but just wanted to feel my way around. So I traveled around the country. When you spend so much time alone things become very internal for you and you react very sensitively to every little thing you see. Every part of the country had such a different spirit, and in every different part of the country I listened to Christian radio stations. Sometimes I'd stop in different churches in different parts of the country and sheepishly walk in and participate to get a feeling of where other spiritual people are at, or what their faith means to them.

And so I was cruising around the country. I went out to California. I had an interview. I thought maybe I should transfer to a Christian college and I had an interview at a Christian college out in California—I don't remember the name of it—but I felt like it was too set on such a uniform way of acting, thinking and approaching the gospel; it was just so western. I felt narrowed down by that so I kept going. I traveled to Illinois and had an interview at Wheaton; that was a pretty deep experience for me also. It was not that I wasn't impressed, but I also felt a little bit narrowed down. I felt that the person who interviewed me there couldn't cope with the experience that I was having, he couldn't relate to it. I was pretty intense at the time so maybe... because I'd just come off from being alone, just searching and being so serious about what I was experiencing that it was difficult for somebody really plugged into a set way of doing things to just be totally open and embrace that experience. So I decided I really didn't want to go to one of these Christian colleges. I went back to Penn and decided to major in religious studies, although all the time I was still searching, because one thing I really discovered while I was doing this is that even though I'd spent so much time on my own—being alone or living in the woods with either one or two other people—very simply, I absolutely felt responsible to God to do something in the world. I really wasn't led to associating with a group at that point. Sometimes you become a little aimless in that position, but you just don't know what to do about it.

At that point I did meet the Unification church through a friend in New York. When I was over at the center I was very moved by the experience of the community way of life. I believe the Christian life is a way of life, not only a faith, but a way of life. I think the whole confrontation with the oriental way of life is very important for Christians today to learn how to live in a smaller and smaller world. Since I've been in the movement, I've been involved in its ecumenical wing. I've been working interdenominationally for about four years, setting up theological conferences, and also being involved with minority and social action projects. I'm working in Harlem; I have been for about three years. Since I've been in that wing of the movement, I've also gone back to Penn and am getting my Master's in Religious Studies there.

Through the conference here, I'm not really expecting anything. I really respect everybody's point of view, where they're at in their life of faith. And I just hope that we can fully realize how seriously each one of us is dealing theologically with the questions of the Christian gospel, the purpose of creation, the fall of man, the nature of evil (and how it works in the world), the nature of Satan, and how we can overcome sin within ourselves. I think that we can share many things in common at that level, even though on specific theological points we're obviously different. But there is an internal aspect where I think we can learn to respect and love one another.

Rod Sawatsky: I think we're going to have to break here. It's lunch time. We have only covered about half of the participants. But I think we are accomplishing, at least in part, what we're hoping to accomplish with this conference. I think we'll simply continue the same approach after lunch.

(LUNCH BREAK)

Rod Sawatsky: The basic value of the testimonials has been achieved. We have been getting various Unification stories and various Evangelical stories, and I think that from here on in we can just shorten them a bit, so that we can get on to the other issues.

Irving Hexham: I've noticed a lot of people have been talking about their religious backgrounds—how they were brought up in Christian homes and so forth. Well, I'm going to start off by saying that I wasn't brought up in an evangelical home. My experience is different, in that when I was eleven, I took an exam which English children took at that time called the *Eleven Plus*. It decided whether you went to a grammar school or a secondary modern school. I failed it and went to a secondary modern, along with 90% of the school population. That meant I left school at fifteen, and I became an apprentice in the gas industry as a gas fitter. I worked there for nine years. That was a very interesting experience because the main aim of most of the people I worked with was getting to bed with the woman of the house we were working in and similar things. On hot days in summer we would go swimming in the afternoons and fiddle our time sheets pretending to be working. When I was eighteen, I met some Christians who asked me if I'd read the Bible. I started to read the Bible and after a few months became a Christian. I was converted after having a very vivid dream in which I realized Christ had risen from the dead. That made a big change in my life, because I could no longer go along with fiddling time sheets and so on. The change made me a very unpopular apprentice, and I very soon found I was on my own. No one would work with me, so I was given jobs I could do on my own without having to be with anyone else.

When this conversion happened, a change in my social class occurred as well because people in British churches are very middle class and I was in the working class. The people I worked with never went to church or expected to go to university. All the young people I met at church were expecting to go to the university. Three people I knew went up to university to do theology. Over the next couple of years they all lost their faith. I couldn't see how one could really lose one's faith through study. So I became interested in reasons for faith and theology. As a result I became a Calvinist through reading Calvin's *Institutes.* I then met Clark Pinock, who was at Manchester University. He suggested I visit L'Abri in Switzerland. There I met Francis Schaeffer and was strongly influenced by him. He suggested that I ought to go to university, so I started to study for matriculation. I entered Lancaster University in 1967 to read philosophy. As it happened, the year I went, a Ninian Smart came there—some of you know his work—and started a new course. It was the first course in Britain in religious studies. So I enrolled for religious studies.

The courses I took raised many questions relevant to this discussion. There I learned that you do not understand Buddhist or Islamic traditions if you make the kind of statements folks are making here, because religions are fundamentally different. I'd like to hear your replies to this view of religion. The other big influence in my life is my marriage to a South African who had been brought up an agnostic and converted in England. I say this because her mother was very active in politics in South Africa in opposition to the government. So when we were married in '69 in South Africa, my mother-in-law's cry was, "How on earth can you be a Christian? Even worse, how can you be a Calvinist, when you see what has happened in South Africa?" This led to my doing my Master's degree in course work on African religions and my writing a thesis on a new religious movement in England. I then did my doctorate on the relationship between Calvinism and apartheid, taught for a few years in England, and then came to Regent College in Vancouver. Regent is particularly designed for laymen. I've been there since September. One of my main research interests is new religious movements; I teach a course in that area. The other interest, of course, is African studies.

Helen Subrenat: My name is Helen Subrenat. I was raised in a rather liberal Christian home. We moved around a lot and so tended to go to the local church, whatever it was, whether it was Methodist, Presbyterian, or Congregationalist. My mother is a Quaker, so I spent about ten years going to Friends Meetings as well. Thus, I was raised believing in Jesus but not believing in any particular way of following Him.

My parents didn't feel that any one denomination was necessarily right, but I didn't really have a personal relationship with Jesus until my senior year in high school, when I was living away from my family, missing them a great deal and facing a lot of personal crises. A friend of mine had had a born-again experience over the summer and he had really changed so much that I knew something definitely had happened to him. He shared his experience with me, and through that, I became a born-again Christian. Then I began to frequent mostly Baptist churches, went away to college, and really began to break away from the fundamentalist Christianity which I'd found in the Baptist church. I sought the way I wanted to commit myself to serving God through Christ. I had many friends who weren't Christian at all and sometimes I'd try to convert them, but through those experiences I came to the realization that I had to love them as human beings and respect them and their own beliefs. Many of them were Islamic and Buddhist, and so I had to realize I couldn't force my Christianity upon them. I could be a witness through my life, but not necessarily through my words, and I again made a conscious commitment to serving Christ.

I had some experiences before college in which my credo became I Corinthians 13—that is, to live a Christian life I had to be able to love unconditionally. I really had to be able to do that to be His representative. So then I began shopping around different churches—this was in New York City in 1965, '66, '67. Nora (Mrs. Spurgin) and I were both going to an Inter-Varsity Christian Fellowship at NYU and were pretty active in that. It was a pretty small chapter, but I was really turned off by the narrowmindedness of most of the people who were in Inter-Varsity at that time.

The next year I lived in a Christian dormitory, the ideal of which was really beautiful—that of having a Christian community, building on that community, and going out into New York City to serve it in some volunteer way. Through that I encountered Paul Tillich's *Dynamics of Faith*, and the one phrase that always kept striking me during this time was, "Faith is the act of being ultimately concerned." I knew I wasn't ultimately concerned. I wasn't really centering my life on God and couldn't find anywhere an example of Christ in a church. I went to Episcopalian, Baptist, and Methodist churches, etc. I couldn't really find any specific way, so I just prayed a lot and searched a lot. My other concerns were world religions and uniting the different religious groups. How can we work together for a family of man? All these things were influencing me, and in my sophomore year of college I was witnessed to by a member of the Unification church. Many questions I had had about the Bible, specifically, which came up about six months previous to my being witnessed to, all began to be answered through the lectures. The thing that really struck me, however, was that this was a true community centered on God which I hadn't been able to find anywhere else, one which was really manifesting Christ's love. I had been struggling with the question of who Jesus really was and what He wants us to do in this twentieth century. I felt very clearly that Jesus had guided me to the Unification church, to a deepening relationship with God, and also to a deeper relationship with Him. Of course, we'll discuss our christology, which is a little bit different, but I've had many experiences through prayer and some inspirations or whatever you want to call them. I've really come to a much deeper relationship with Jesus, a personal relationship, than I had before, or was able to find in other churches. Since I joined the Unification church I've done missionary work in Berkeley. I was in Berkeley for three years. I also worked in Los Angeles, directing a nursery school that was owned by the church. Then at one time I was part of a tour with Rev. Moon. Most recently I've been a missionary in Gabon, West Africa, for two years. I've just come back from that. That's it in a nutshell.

Rod Sawatsky: Actually, my story is really very uninteresting compared to most of yours, because I was raised Mennonite, my parents were Mennonites. I am a fourth generation North American Mennonite, my ancestors having come from Russia in the 1870s. My undergraduate years were spent in Mennonite colleges in Winnipeg and in Kansas. I find myself quite comfortable in Anabaptist-Mennonite theology and feel myself very much to be a Christian within that context. Therefore I see myself as neither Evangelical nor Liberal. In fact, Mennonites usually insist that they are somewhere in between, and—I think—rightly so.

One of my biggest concerns theologically is our view of the Church. My own position is that the Christian faith calls for a very high view of the Church. My belief is that evangelicalism by and large, and liberalism as well, have a relatively low view of the Church, in the sense that for them the two primary agencies for building God's kingdom are the individual in his search for personal salvation and the nation or state as a redemptive community. By contrast, I see the Church as the primary agency of God's reconciliation in the world. In this I feel somewhat at one with Unification in some of its emphases.

I am, at the same time, somewhat of a heretical Mennonite,

in that Mennonites, like Unificationists, have a very strong commitment to faith made active in works, usually defined as discipleship. And there is always a latent perfectionism in the Anabaptist-Mennonite tradition, while I'm not a perfectionist at all. In fact, on this point I find myself very much with Luther and pretty much with Evangelicals, in that I feel that which I would, I do not; and that which I do, I would not. And so constantly I have to return to God for His grace for what I'm not. In fact, I find when people make statements about how intensely they're committed to following Jesus I have to constantly say, "Isn't that nice? I wish I was." I have a deep commitment to the Christian faith but I think my profession is very weak. In comparison to many others, that commitment is probably very thin. And I have to live with that and struggle with my faith accordingly. So I guess, given my background, the way I was raised, my own faith and commitment, I'm a mixture of many things—in part Evangelical, in part more Liberal, and maybe that brings me to this role here as moderator.

I first became fascinated with evangelicalism during the Vietnam war. I was doing a Master's program in history at the University of Minnesota. Timothy Smith was there at the time—some of you know him—the Church of the Nazarene historian. I was working with him, and I did my thesis on "The Influence of Fundamentalism on Mennonite Nonresistance." I was rather concerned at that point to hear people like Billy Graham serving basically as military recruiters. And so I did a little bit of research back into the 1920s and '30s and found that this has a long history among Fundamentalists. I learned that the reticence of the Mennonites to speak out in the twentieth century on what they traditionally claimed they believed was largely due to the growth of fundamentalism among them. And I've been trying to undo some of that in my own work since then. So I have from that time on continued my fascination with fundamentalism and evangelicalism, and I now teach a course on evangelical Christianity.

There are very few courses in religious studies departments across North America on evangelical Christianity. I use some of Richard's books as texts. The reason is that Evangelicals have not written their own history, by and large. There's hardly anything available other than what Richard has done. But it's a movement which I take very seriously, which I respect very deeply, in part, because I have at least one foot in it. Besides, students in universities need to be taught another angle on the history of Protestantism besides the basic history that goes through the rise of liberalism, neo-orthodoxy, on to the theology of hope and so on. We need other angles to tell the whole story of modern Christianity. So that has convinced me to work on this area. The students are fascinated by it, which is rewarding.

I have also been working in the field of newer religions. I know a little about the problems of minority traditions given my own heritage. My first experience here with Unification was an exciting one. Since being here a year ago and then working with some other religious movements, we formed a society in Canada known as Canadians for the Protection of Religious Liberty. Religious liberty problems are becoming more intense in Canada. I think they will also become more intense in the United States, not around deprogramming issues only, but primarily because the psychologists are defining legitimate religion under the rubric of healthy religion. Evangelicals have as much to fear here as Scientologists, Moonies, and others. So I have involvements either through my own faith or scholarly interests on both sides of our discussion here, and find my role and participation here very fascinating.

Johnny Sonneborn: My last name is Sonneborn, spelled with two n's in the middle. My given name is John Andrew; people call me Johnny. I'm a Jew. I was born in 1930 in New York City in a middle-class home. My grandfather had been borough president in Manhattan and held other kinds of political offices. My family had absolutely no connection with any religious institution of any kind, my mother being a militant atheist. I myself have been interested in mythology and supernatural types of things all my life, the present life being so unsatisfactory. At the age of twelve I decided I was going to be a musician, and I became a musician, a classical musician. One of the first times I was ever in church was when I went with a family friend to hear a music program at her church, and she was probably the only Christian, probably the only religious person who was one of my family friends. She had been an employee, and she was a member of the church in Harlem. And later on I went to take organ lessons from the organist there at St. Mark's Methodist Church in Harlem.

After high school I went to Bucknell University in Pennsylvania where I sang in the chapel choir because I loved the music so much. I'd been told many things about the Christian church by my mother. I guess they described the Christian church in Germany around the time of Marx, Freud, and others like that, which was that it always favored the bourgeoise, the capitalists, with emphasis especially on conformism. If there was one thing I was against it was conformism. I was 100% non-conformist. I didn't care what somebody else thought. I was going to be exactly as I liked to be. I was singing in the chapel during Religious Emphasis Week, and minister McCracken from Riverside Church, the number-one Protestant church in the country—any New Yorker knows that— came out. His topic was *The Perils of Conformity*. This was mind-blowing; he preached that Jesus was the original nonconformist—you know the scriptural texts as well as I do. So this began to reduce some of my prejudices against Jesus and Christianity, and through attending chapel services in order to sing, I began to listen to what Jesus had to say, and it made a lot of sense. Some of it I had figured out myself, and other parts of it I saw were sharp thinking. I saw that He was really a great teacher, and was smarter than I. And that was about as far as I went for a year.

There were many IVCF people on the Bucknell campus, and they walked around with the light of Jesus in their eyes. I was attracted to that, but I didn't have any way of relating to them personally—because they didn't offer me anything directly. But I always remembered that. Instead, the Methodist Youth Fellowship was a really embracing fellowship; they could take a nonconformist in and make him comfortable, and they were socially active. I was becoming a World Federalist and becoming active in social concerns. I transferred the next year to the University of the Redlands in California, which is a very accepting place, a wonderful school. There I quickly became a pacifist, and from then on my interests in Christianity and pacifism were just inextricably linked; this was the way of peace and the way of love. I began to take very, very seriously the teachings of Jesus, and I became a religion minor and a music major. At this time I was really into church music as well.

After one year of helping in the liturgy in the Methodist church there (the community I was in was the Methodist Youth Fellowship and the Methodists Student Movement, all of whose leaders were in jail during the Korean War for draft evasion), I became a conscientious objector and worshipped with the Quakers. For most of my life after that I worshipped with the Quakers, finding this was the way to God most open to an intuitive person.

By the time I graduated, I had begun to realize that prayer was not just self-hypnosis but that there really was a God and also that my respect for Jesus had been not just for one more great teacher but for somebody who was at least such a super doctor that if I couldn't understand Him I knew He was right anyway. He was the one who really knew it all. The only question was how I was going to appropriate it.

I came back to New York and entered the field of music. My sister had been converted very dramatically in her first year at college. She had been a stronger atheist than I and had never been interested in supernatural things at all, although she had always believed in fate. She became a Southern Baptist. I was very pleased with her conversion. When I was back in New York she began saying simple Baptist formulas to me which actually began to sink in.

A number of years later I looked back and I realized that Jesus wasn't just a teacher but there was, through Jesus, an experience of God and that Jesus had changed me. There was the "Rock experience." I could really stand on this. I could never really disbelieve again. I had been saved. I knew that God and Jesus are really with me, and it's only a matter that I sometimes recognize it and sometimes I don't, but they're never going to leave me, so why should I want to turn away from them?

I was a musician for many years, working as organist in church and in synagogue and as a pianist. And I also associated very much with Catholic Worker people. So I really began studying theology and talking to many different people, and my theology concerning Jesus became much more conservative, in terms of the incarnation of the second person and so forth, although I was still very liberal on certain world-views and lifestyles. I had a very low opinion of eastern religions, and I had a strong argument with a very important Catholic who said he could be a Christian and a Buddhist at the same time. I said, "You can't be; you have to be one or the other." I was always turned off by people who were into eastern religions and self-help and so forth. Also, I was influenced strongly by Tillich, and Leslie Dewart, the Canadian who showed that to have faith you have to be completely open; that you can't just have faith that you know what God's going to tell you to do. Rather, you don't know what God is going to ask you to do, but you have to have open faith and be ready to do it anyway.

I came to the end of my career as a musician and I thought

of going into the Christian ministry, but I had become so degraded
personally the last years of my musical life that I felt I wasn't
qualified to do this, so I became Regional Executive for the
Fellowship of Reconciliation, the Christian pacifist organization,
for three years. This was '68, '69, and '70, during the height of the
Vietnamese protest. I was organizing protests, and vigils and
doing draft counseling. I was very strongly into faith and love but
I understood love only in relation to individual people.

With the Fellowship of Reconciliation I could never speak
openly about Jesus, and I always could argue any point on both
sides equally unless I put Jesus on one side. I always came to that
conclusion. So I felt frustrated with the Fellowship. I just had to
go into the Christian ministry, so I chose the Presbyterian church.
I enrolled in Union Theological Seminary to become a Presbyterian
minister.

Three weeks before my first class I heard the principle of
creation in the Unified Family. As it came about, it was given by
a young woman I had known in the musical field when she was in
high school, who had had a very strong relationship with God the
Father and Jesus the Son since she was fourteen. I had known her
to be a very pure and quiet person. I spoke to her on the phone
one day and said that I was going to go to Union and she said,
"Oh, I'm into religion now, too." I said, "Susan, you've always
been in a deep relationship with God and Jesus," and she said
that this was something new. I realized in the conversation that she
had changed, so I wanted her to tell me more about it. She had
joined the Unification church in a period of ten days, earlier that
spring. So in September we met and she told me a few things
about the church, that it was really dedicated towards changing
the whole world and had a strong emphasis upon the family. She
knew that I'd always valued the family emphasis in Catholicism. I
went to a lecture, and later on that fall I wanted to hear the rest
of the Divine Principle. They didn't have any workshops at that
time. The Unified Family was living with fifteen people in New
York City in a slum on the edge of Spanish Harlem. I liked the
people and I went back to hear the ideas, arguing all the way. But
the person who taught me had all the answers, so I was really
convinced by the teachings. At the same time I was very much
into Union Seminary. So first I thought of Union Seminary,
"Well, since I'm learning this much and here's an extra free class
from the Unified Family—I'm learning a great deal." But by the

time we got into Moses and the Old Testament and all that material about the Completed Testament age, the three ages, I realized I was viewing everything at Union as extra courses and the Divine Principle as the main course by which I was interpreting everything. So, therefore, I believed the Divine Principle and Rev. Moon as the truth-teller who had given this.

But the question was, could I trust him as a leader? He was in Korea and very few people here had met him. So it took me the better part of a year before I was finally able to read things that he had written about God's heart and God's grief, and I came to the conclusion I could trust him, so I joined the church. Since I've been in the Unification church I've completed my Master of Divinity at Union Seminary. I've been doing theological studies and research, especially studying the Divine Principle itself, analyzing what it says on a point, comprehensively, although there's always a problem to really *understand* what it says, not just to *know* what it says. I've lectured on the Divine Principle to members of the church and done Interfaith lecturing on it. Currently I'm doing advanced studies at Union Seminary. I've taken four semesters, each with six credits in systematic theology and the history of Christian thought.

I have been sharing ideas with professors of religion and philosophy whom I encounter in New York, learning, and sharing our ideas, and also trying to work out ideas within the movement. I've written a number of essays based on the Divine Principle for the movement.

In the dialogue here at this conference there are two issues that I find very central—they are related. The first is that I think many Christians believe we are sinners who have been justified by Jesus. But we aren't happy being sinners. How will this ultimately be changed so that we won't always be such miserable people? And the second is that it's obvious that Jesus established the kingdom and that He has active spiritual lordship; the question is about political governments of the earth, which in light of what I've just said are made up of sinful people. Does Jesus want to change them and if so, how would He go about doing this? The Unification church has certain answers. What are the evangelical answers to these questions?

Dan Davies: My name is Daniel Davies. I was born May 27, 1948, in Winlock, Washington, a small town of five hundred people. My childhood was a happy one; my parents were good and my brothers and sister were very close. My father and mother often took us into nature. My father was very kind, wise, and a leader in the town. My mother served us night and day; but we five children were too much for her and her health broke trying to take good care of us. My family went downhill until my parents were divorced in 1963. We moved from Winlock to Seattle when the divorce finally took place. We all suffered a great deal from this.

I sought a profession in the first year of college, 1967-68. I wanted to be a doctor. I thought this was the way that I would make a name for myself and find my place in society. But when my brother, Marc, returned from Vietnam, he brought with him the Buddhist religion and philosophy. We talked for hours about this religion and about truth. I had several experiences with love I had never experienced before while we talked. The love was not coming from any person; it completely surrounded me and gave me the greatest comfort and joy. I experienced the love of truth and I changed my direction from the medical profession to be a seeker of truth, a philosopher. Marc and I found Ramakrishna Vedanta especially attractive. Basically, Vedanta respects all the leaders of the world religions and believes that all religions are paths to God.

America was involved in Vietnam and I had to struggle with whether to participate or not. I was threatened by the draft in the 1969-70 school year. I had been persuaded by the communists on the University of Washington campus that America was fighting Vietnam for imperialistic reasons. I decided not to fight in Vietnam, but rather, join the National Guard. I joined a missile unit near Seattle and did not learn until later the missiles carried atomic warheads. My job included installing the arms plug into the missiles prior to firing. The arms plug is the final step before the missle can be fired. My action made it possible to explode the atomic warhead. The men on the base were convinced we were going to blow up the world.

My education at the University of Washington was bringing me to the conclusion that the world lives in a crisis. The population explosion would be out of hand by the year 2,000. There would not be enough food or space for all the people of the world; that meant the world was on the verge of war, famine, pestilence, and genocide. A hungry man has no choice but to fight for his food if he is starving.

I had an opportunity to receive many scholarships for graduate study in 1970-71. I had thoughts of raising a family. But I realized, "How can I bring up children in a world headed for destruction?" I decided to give up thoughts of graduate school, a family, and look for some way to change the direction the world was headed for instead. I would have been foolish to live my life as if everything was O.K.

I left Seattle in the summer of 1971, owning nothing but what I was carrying on my back. I flew to London, England, with a one-way ticket and a determination to find a better way of life or die. I had faith God would lead me to a better way if one existed. If a better way didn't exist, I'd rather not live anyway.

I traveled for two years throughout Europe, the Mediterranean and finally Israel. My journey was a day-by-day journey. I prayed that God would lead me His way. I worked in Germany when my little money ran out. I spent most of the time on the move, except when I arrived in Israel; I lived on Kibbutz Sasa in Galilee for about one year.

I was given an invitation to join the kibbutz community and I seriously considered it. I felt they had a better way of life than any people I had ever seen before. But, I felt they didn't quite have the answer. Their ideology, essentially Freud and Marx, was not holding up to the tests of reality.

Their children were leaving the community and never returning. I could predict that in about twenty or thirty years their decline would be complete. They would be without an ideology they could believe in within one or two generations. They would then be like a suburban community in the United States: upper middle class with all the upper-middle-class problems. They would have all the material comforts they wanted, no dream to live for, and no God. I realized the need for God to be central in community life for the community to be successful.

I left the kibbutz in spring 1972 and began to travel around Israel. I rededicated myself to find God. I took part in the movie "Jesus Christ Superstar" for several months. I played a stand-in for Ciaphas, a wine-merchant in the temple, a friend of Jesus, a leper in the Valley of the Lepers, in a dance scene with Simon Peter, and a friend of Jesus at the crucifixion.

I had my first encounter with Jesus Christ during the filming. Three days after the crucifixion scene, Jesus appeared to me in a dream and said, "I am the divine Son of God." I was shocked; I hadn't believed Jesus Christ was real at the time. I told others about the experience and I was made to think seriously about Jesus Christ through this experience.

I developed the dream to establish a God-centered community in New Zealand while working on the film. I thought the kibbutz was the right idea, but God had to be at the center of the community. I went to work in Elat, Israel, after the film, to earn the money I would need to leave the country and travel to New Zealand. But I came to the traumatic realization that I could not find a place in the world where we could live out our lives in peace and freedom. I realized there was a conflict going on within myself and between myself and others that I could find no place on earth to escape from. I realistically viewed the world situation and realized it was only a matter of time before communism took over the world. New Zealand would be easy pickings after the communists had defeated the United States and the rest of the Free World. I was not looking for an escape from the real problems of life. I was looking for a place to live in a God-centered community, raising my family in peace and freedom. I realized that the peaceful way of life I was looking for was not possible on any continent on earth. I lost my last ideal. I reached the bottom-point of despair. I had absolutely no direction and no will to go on.

I met a kindly Jewish woman on December 19, 1972, the day I reached the bottom-point of despair. She asked me if I knew Jesus Christ. I thought, "Ah, you're kidding me! Here you are, a Jewish lady in Israel asking me if I know Jesus Christ!" My first reaction was to laugh, but I was told intuitively that I was in no position to laugh and that I had better listen. She said something that clicked, and I experienced a rebirth at the time, but over the next few days my heart gradually changed. I began to feel love in my heart that I had never experienced before. I completely lost the thought for drugs and the thought of immoral sex became completely contrary to the love in my heart. My mind and life changed. I experienced the baptism of the Holy Spirit several days later in Bethlehem on Christmas Eve.

I spent the next four months from Christmas until Easter living in Jerusalem waiting for the return of Jesus Christ to Israel. I was baptized in a fresh-water spring on the Dead Sea below the Qumran Cave where the Dead Sea Scrolls were found. I began to read the Bible seriously. I spent a lot of time in the Sinai desert reading the Bible, praying, and asking for direction from God. I did not join any one Christian group exclusively. I believed we are all members of the body of Christ. I had fellowship with all Christians with gratitude for the love we had to share with one another.

I noticed Christians were arguing over the day to worship, how to baptize, how the Lord was going to return, etc., and separating from one another when they disagreed. I did not want to argue. If one group wanted to worship on Saturday and another group wanted to worship on a Sunday, I would worship on both days! I believed that when Christ returned it didn't matter where I was; it didn't matter which group I belonged to or the denomination of the congregation. If I was living the will of Jesus Christ then I'd be with Him when He returned. I reached the point where I was trying to live by the Bible.

I lost many friends trying to live by the Bible. Most of them would fight with me on certain points, such as that I had to work eight hours a day. But I could never find that in the Bible. I found that you were supposed to work long enough to provide for yourself, your family, to provide help for the needy, and the rest of the time was to be used to spread the word of God. I didn't see anything about working eight hours a day. I lost several friends on that one. The time I wasn't spending in prayer, reading the Bible, and working for a meager living, I spent evangelizing. I wanted to help all people to experience the love of God I was experiencing.

I received direction from God during prayer in Jerusalem and in visions in the Sinai desert to return to America in March, 1973. I struggled to confirm this direction. America was the last place on earth I wanted to go to. But the direction was confirmed by many signs. I flew from Israel on Easter morning and landed in Nice, France, to visit my brother, Marc, who was studying there, for three weeks. I was very narrow in my beliefs then; I believed the Bible was the only truth and Christianity was the only true religion. He helped me to understand that other people's religions have value too. My brother was the only one close enough to me to help me out of my religious bigotry, but he did it with patience, love, and understanding.

I traveled to Holland to visit a friend after leaving my brother in Nice and then flew from Belgium to New York City. I arrived in New York City late at night, so it was necessary for me to wait until morning before I could leave the airport. I made the decision to take the bus into New York City and find a way out as quickly as I could; New York was the last place on earth I wanted to go.

I got off the bus in front of Grand Central Station and immediately began walking up 42nd Street toward the Public Library. The buildings were so enormous; I had never seen anything like them before. I didn't know where God wanted me to go or what He wanted me to do, so I decided to head toward the West Coast where my family lives unless God showed me something else He wanted me to do. I was thinking two things as I walked up 42nd: first, I wanted to study history so I could avoid making mistakes Christians have already made; and second, I'd like to find a quiet place in the country to spend the Sabbath, seeing that it was Friday afternoon already.

I noticed several people on the sidewalk wearing banners and talking with people as I walked toward Fifth Avenue. I thought, "Brother, there are all kinds in New York! Those people are communist." I was stopped by a girl who was talking a mile a minute saying, "We're changing the world and helping everyone," and so on and so forth. Well, I was willing to listen to what anyone had to say and then afterwards I'd tell them about Jesus Christ. I asked her if she knew Jesus Christ when she gave me the break. She answered, "Oh, yes. We're Christian!" I was so happy to find a Christian in New York City. I had thought that no Christians existed in New York. She invited me to their center for fellowship, and I gladly accepted. They had a van nearby and people in the van were from all over the world. We drove a long way and finally came to a beautiful white marble building on 71st Street. I entered the building, and the people I saw seemed to be radiating. I was impressed; these people really had it together. They were serious about their witnessing and went about their calling with a very high standard. I thought, "If these people are true, I'd like to work with them. If they're not, I'll stay until I save them all."

I listened to two lectures. I had the deepest religious experience of my life during the first lecture. The lecture dealt with history and answered many questions I had about the right way to live as a Christian, one of the two questions on my mind before I met these people. The religious experience I had was as if a fountain of living water gushed out from my soul and showered everywhere.

I was overwhelmed by the internal testimony I had had to the truth of what I had heard.

I was invited to go to a workshop in the country starting that evening. This seemed an answer to my second prayer. I wanted a place in the country to spend the Sabbath, so I accepted. The workshop was held in Tarrytown, New York, on a beautiful estate called Belvedere. I was impressed; these people do what they do very well. The workshop lasted the entire weekend. By the end I had been presented an entirely new view of the Bible, history, science, and common-sense truth that was harmonized into one consistent and beautiful truth. The Divine Principle was deep beyond my ability to fathom.

The experience is properly called a workshop. The Divine Principle without the example of people living it out would not have been as moving. I decided to spend forty days living in their center in New York without leaving. I still had a big question or two that needed answering. I knew that this was the best place for me to witness to my faith in Jesus Christ. I received answers to my questions at the end of the forty days, from the Bible, and I decided to throw my lot in with the Unification movement completely.

I joined when no negativity existed about the church in America. I worked in New York City from May '73 to October '73, witnessing, fundraising, and campaigning for Rev. Moon's Carnegie Hall speech. I set up pioneer witnessing centers with a team of missionaries across upstate New York from October '73 to March '75. I worked in the training programs at Barrytown from March '75 until March '76. I finished my B.A. degree at the University of Washington and spent a lot of time with my family from March '76 until September '76 in Seattle. I am now attending the Unification Theological Seminary and will graduate in June, to go on to Perkins School of Theology in Dallas, where I plan to enroll in the Master of Theology program.

Tirza Shilgi: My name is Tirza Shilgi and I was born and raised in Israel in a kibbutz. When I finished high school I went to the army, like everybody else in Israel. After the one month of combat training that they give everybody, I was sent to train as a nurse, and served in a military hospital for two years. When I finished the army I came back to the kibbutz to work as a gesture of gratitude before leaving the kibbutz (because I already knew that I would like to go on studying in college). I was in charge of the sickrooms in the kibbutz. While I was there, I realized that one of the things that I'm most interested in is finding some real values—truth. I didn't exactly know what it would be, but somehow, in the kibbutz, in the life I saw around me, I felt that something was missing, although externally and socially it was almost the ideal. People have social security from the day they're born to the day they die. They have friends, leisure to pursue interests, and many other things, but I had the feeling that something really fundamental was missing somewhere in their relationships to each other and in some spiritual goals and development.

When I went out to study, I decided to go into art. I liked art, and I had some ability in that area, but also, I chose art because I couldn't picture myself enjoying a routine 8-to-5 type job. Art, I felt, was so open, offered a large variety of occupations, and was constantly in development. At that time, I felt there was some kind of search still ahead of me, and I had to find answers to all my questions about life and about relationships with people, but I really didn't think much about religion. When I graduated from college I came to America to live with some friends, and I had in mind to look for some philosophy groups or study some meditation. I had the feeling that something was going on in that direction, and maybe there were some answers somewhere. In the first month I was here, I met a person from the Unification church who invited me to come to their center. But a year before, I visited their community in Jerusalem and I really did not like it much. We talked some more, and finally I felt that if I was really interested in finding the truth and in finding answers, then I should be able to look anywhere, even if it came from a most unlikely place. I felt I should at least listen to what they had to say before I could mindfully reject them and say no.

One thing that bothered me in the past was that I heard a lot of people saying things that were good and important, people who spoke of high ideals, and morals, but who did not have a sufficient explanation of why these ideals were good and were to be pursued. For example, why is it good to refrain from sexual relationships before marriage, and why is it good to sacrifice for others? There was never a rational explanation for that. Even though intuitively I felt that yes, much of it is right, for some reason I didn't know exactly why and therefore felt that I was not willing to follow anything unless it could be explained very clearly and rationally.

When I was in Jerusalem, just before I was finishing school, I was in a period of great distress personally and also with respect to school. One day as I was thinking of it all, the pressure felt unbearable with no way out. One verse from the Bible came to my mind, one from Psalms which says, "From the very deep I called your name, O God." I don't know why I said it because I was not into the Bible at all. As I said it, all of a sudden, this very warm and embracing feeling came down and there was a definite presence in the room. A presence that communicated in some kind of a voice, "Don't worry, everything will be all right." I was shocked, because it was undeniable—the experience was totally undeniable. It lasted, I'm not sure how long, and it was overwhelming. In the following months, things indeed turned out all right. I could not deny that experience, and in my spiritual search, I had to take things from that point on. I realized that there is something more than just what I thought there was. I think that that experience had a lot to do with my decision to listen to Unification teachings.

While I was listening to Unification lectures, I was already enrolled in a philosophy course in a school in Boston. Ideologically and socially, the philosophy was very appealing to me. However, because of this experience, I knew that now for a philosophy to be satisfactory to me it had to explain God very clearly. Unification church teachings did, and so this was one of the main experiences that led up to my being in the church. Still, even then, it was a long struggle. I didn't want to be a part of a movement or a community. I was too individualistic in my ways. Gradually, a feeling started growing in me, and there were a lot of spiritual experiences and dreams that came along with it—some very strong feelings of responsibility. For example, I had a feeling that God was revealing to me His heart and suffering in the past through the teachings of the Divine Principle, and here I was sitting and not willing to do anything about it, just because of some personal inconveniences. My joining the church eventually was more of a surrender than a heroic commitment. I just gave up to that internal feeling of responsibility. I felt like someone who just witnessed the discovery of a cure for cancer, and for one reason or another, was not willing to do anything about it.

After a period of four months of wrestling with these thoughts, I decided to join. Still, most of my understanding was highly intellectual. I could understand the intellectual aspect of the teachings pretty well, but it came to the point that my center director, who was also from a Jewish background, said to me that I would not be able to advance in my understanding much more unless I understood the New Testament and Jesus' message, upon which Divine Principle is based. I was surprised to find that one had to go through that in order to understand the heart-aspect of the Divine Principle. I was generally not very interested in the New Testament. I thought it was a collection of stories about Jesus' life, and I was not sure it had much relevance for our lives today. He bought me the New Testament in Hebrew, for one of my excuses for not reading the New Testament was that I could not read English well enough. From that point on, in a period of three months or so, I went through an experience of what Christians, as I later found out, call rebirth. I decided to get up in the morning early and to go out into an open field nearby to read a chapter of the New Testament and pray. One morning, while praying after reading a chapter, I saw Jesus standing on a hillside of Nazareth, a place I knew very well. He looked very uncared-for; His feet were all dusty and the dust went up to His knees. His disciples were scattered around, each doing something else, and it seemed like nobody was taking care of Him. This feeling of agony He felt came through to me so strongly I couldn't stop crying for a long time. I think this was the main starting point of my relation with Jesus. I felt a great feeling of agony for whatever responsibility the Jewish people had for the pain and misery that He had to go through. And then I was wondering what I could do now; I wished I had been alive then when I could have done something. When He stood there and looked at me, I had the feeling that He was communicating: "By giving yourself to God and to me now, you can help me just as much." I realized, at that point, that it's true: you can understand the Divine Principle intellectually very well, but in order to understand and experience the "heartistic" message, the internal aspect of it, Christ is definitely first. It is indispensable, I think, to a comprehensive understanding of the Divine Principle message, and even more, to the complete realization of the Divine Principle way of life. Since then, I have been two years in the United States, one year in Japan and Korea, and I am now finishing my second year in the Seminary.

John Wiemann: I can in a way pick up where Tirza left off. In my life my search hasn't been for truth—it's been for love.

I'm just going to talk about my experience in the Unification church, I think, and not about experiences before then. I always believed in Christ, but that wasn't enough, because I didn't know how I could follow Him. Everybody else seems to have analyzed what they were thinking or what they were doing in their own past, whereas I haven't thought about the past enough to be able to explain it so vividly in a conceptual way. But I do know that my search has been for love and acceptance, a very unconditional acceptance. I can bluntly say that I've never found it anywhere else. I'm not saying that it wasn't around; I just didn't find it. But I found it in the Unification church, and that was probably why I joined.

I came to believe in the Divine Principle, which enlightened me to a much deeper extent than the Bible alone. For three years I went on that initial experience which I had when I first joined the Unification church. But I'd say, within the last six months, I realized that that experience wasn't enough. I prayed before, but it was never really deep, because something was blocking me from God. And I found out what that thing was in very real terms last night. It started when I listened to the lecture by Paul. Actually, I knew intellectually what it was, but I just didn't really know fully what it was. So I listened to the second spiritual law, which is sin. I realized the reality of sin very deeply last night. I decided that if I'm really going to become a religious person, a person who wants to live a life with God (which I had in three years said I wanted to do but was not so sure I actually wanted to do), then I'd better just pray. I'd better just go off to God and leave my past behind. I went down near a trail by the lagoon, and I knew that it was going to get dark soon and I wouldn't know how to get back (it's just a trail and it's not easy to find your way in the dark) but it didn't matter. As I was going there I felt something in my back where I had recently pulled a muscle. It seemed to be a sensation of perhaps healing. At any rate, I ended up down there for four hours and at one point I repented very deeply; I guess that was the essence of it, and I never did that before. I experienced God's love and also experienced the first spiritual law, namely that God has a plan for my life and that God loves me. I never experienced that before. I had always wanted to have a relationship with Jesus. I have felt Jesus very closely with me previously, but I never really felt this sense of repentance for sin. I always thought, "Oh, I'm O.K., I'm not a bad guy," and actually I'm not, I'm very easy-going. (laughter) Well, I found out last night that I'm not so great, at least I recognized it and I spoke about it to God frankly. There was one point at which I said, "God, I'm just leaving, I'm just getting up and I'm not staying here any more." I repented but I didn't know if God wanted me to stick around any more, so I tested God. I never did that before either. I said, "If you want me to stay here longer, then I want a sign." You know, I felt like Job. "I just want a sign," and I waited. I really was kind of indignant at God. It felt good in a way but anyway, I said, "In three minutes I'm leaving, if you don't show me a sign," so a minute passed and I said, "I'm warning you, I'm really going." Right after that I heard what sounded like footsteps in back of me and I looked around. I didn't see anyone there but it sounded like they were coming closer so I said, "O.K., God, I'm staying—I'm staying right where I am!" He must have said O.K. because they stopped. I don't know what the sound was but it was real for me. I stayed there two more hours.

I'm on a new journey now, on a new track, and I feel good about that. I feel that this conference is really important in my life. A lot of things are coming together that I've been struggling with a long time and this has really been a good experience so far. And I know there is going to be a lot more.

Warren Lewis: As I get ready to go through my list of spiritual arrogances, it is interesting that practically everyone in this room seems to be some kind of mystical Calvinist. These experiences, of the kind you must testify to to get voted into the Baptist Church, certainly tie us all together. Analogous to the world religions problem, the experiences are absolutely different and totally alike. This proves two things: it proves that religious experience is not the arbiter of true religion, and, I think, it proves that it is.

When I was three years old, my grandmother used to stand me up on her footstool and have me preach, pray, lead singing and administer the Eucharist to her (laughter) under the signs of Premium Saltines and tapwater! By the time I was ten, I was drawn by the preaching of the gospel to the obedience of my Lord, Jesus Christ, in baptism and was therefore as a penitent sinner totally immersed in the cold waters of baptism in the Fierman Avenue Church of Christ in Corpus Christi, Texas, where I was born—twice. (laughter) I've drunk deeply at the saline wellsprings of Texas fundamentalism. I went to church because I wanted to, because God wanted me to, because we communed every Sunday and because I believed the angels were there. Whenever I found the sermon boring, as I occasionally did, I would take quick peeks at the clear glass windows—we don't have stained-glass windows in our church house, so God's light could get through to us—to see if I could see any angels' wings disappear around the corner. I was convinced that I saw them once or twice. I grew up totally surrounded by God—God was the atmosphere that I breathed; I've never seriously questioned God's existence, though I do not believe any arguments for God's existence.

There was a stage of natural religion; the spirits of the air found me and inspired me to establish my own pagan religion. It had to do with animal sacrifice and prepubescent sexuality on the banks of the creek on our ranch near Austin, Texas. Pity the poor garter snakes and turtles who went up in holocaust to those gods! One good thing came of it: the spirits of the air communicated to me how long I would live. They told me this by ordering me to walk from the center of the sorghum field, where I was standing, to one end of the row and then to the other end of the row, and to count the steps in both directions. It was one hundred five steps to the end in one direction and thirty-five steps to the end in the other direction. Then they told me: "You will live then to be either thirty-five or one hundred five." I'm now thirty-eight and feeling good about the revelation.

During the time I was studying at Abilene Christian College, I was a minister for the Churches of Christ. Our congregations are distinguished from the Disciples of Christ and Christian Church, in that we do not play instrumental music in our worship and consider that anybody who does is going to hell. (laughter) I was a missionary to Mexico where I preached to the Indians in the mountains, and from there I went to Harvard Divinity School. There, I regained my faith in the Bible, especially in the Old Testament, after the stupidity of the biblical-infallibility notions which were communicated to me at Abilene, which made me disbelieve more than believe. While at Harvard, I wrote a book about the Lord's Supper which was published by a Church of Christ press. After the first edition sold out in one year and we were well into the second edition, 4,000 copies of it were burned as heretical in Austin, Texas. I'm singularly proud of that. (laughter)

My third born-again experience happened at my Harvard commencement: I was converted from a Texas Republican to a liberal Democrat by the commencement speech of Adlai Stevenson.

Also while at Harvard, I worked in the field-work program. As part of the trial and the test there, I became involved in a struggle against witchcraft, and subsequently stood trial for sodomy and rape of two Black children as a result of the attacks from the spirit world. There was insufficient evidence to decide guilt or innocence, one way or the other; only God, those children, and I know whether or not I was guilty or innocent. But it was a religious experience in that I had to process the possibility of life imprisonment, and I got a lot out of that.

From Harvard, I went to Toronto to study Roman Catholic theology at the Pontifical Institute for three years and while there became a charismatic. I received the baptism of the Holy Spirit two days after Christmas, 1967. Subsequent to that experience, I received many charismas of the Holy Spirit. Following Toronto, I went to Tübingen, where I wrote my doctorate in Franciscan spirituality of the late thirteenth century and the Franciscan "spirituals'" understanding that St. Francis was the second coming of Christ, the Lord of the Second Advent. Before, during, and after those times, I was involved in establishing a ghetto project in a slum in East New York, where I got involved in race riots. During one of these riots, the Blessed Virgin appeared to me and protected me from certain death in a harrowing situation.

After returning from Tübingen, I was a minister on Long Island for two years and I found it a delightful activity except for the hardship it worked on my marriage. Those of you who are ministers know whereof I speak. Our marriage was not too secure even as we came back from Germany. It ended in divorce. But, because one is not allowed, if one is a minister, to have a divorce in the Churches of Christ, I was disfellowshipped by my congregation. During this time, I was teaching pastoral theology and church history at New York Theological Seminary. Around about this time, I had my (is it a fourth or fifth?) rebirth in a vision of the Lord Jesus in apocalyptic glory seated upon the atom. My eschatology changed. I was convinced that rather than He coming to meet us, we are going to meet Him.

Shortly afterwards, I got a new job through *The New York Times*. I answered an ad to become Church History Professor at Unification Theological Seminary. I took the job because, as I told the Rev. Moon when he asked me, "Why do you want to teach here?"..."As a church historian, I specialize in the history of heretical sectarians, and you represent to me the outstanding example in our time of a sectarian heretic. I want to study you as closely as I can to see what makes you and your movement tick." He loved that, and came forth with an uproarious guffaw, walked over and embraced me, and said, "Dr. Lewis, everyone else around here calls me 'Father,' but you may call me 'brother.'" And I thought to myself, we have a good initial understanding of one another. I started teaching here because it was the best job I could get at the time, was intellectually stimulating, and paid well. I continue to teach here because I consider Sun Myung Moon to be the outstanding religious mind of the century. To cast it in church historical terms, he is the Tertullian of the orient. He is the first person in the history of Christianity to wed successfully the Christian Gospel with the categories of the thought-world of the orient. No one has done that before. As I work here, with and for him and on his projects, I'm deeply involved in plans for a global congress of world religions.

When Herb Richardson* and I were discussing this conference this weekend, he said, "Now, let's see, Warren, you'll be there for the Unification side—no, let's see, you'd better be there for the Evangelical side—no, let's see, you'd better be there for the Unification side—which side do you want to be on?" In terms of what I hope for this weekend, I'm prepared to preach it both round and flat, depending on who's talking at the moment. I believe in the virgin birth of Jesus and bodily assumption of the Virgin Mary; I believe that Jesus is Lord, and so is Krishna; I believe that God inspired the whole Bible, including the contradictions. And I believe that Rev. Moon is the Lord of the Second Advent and that after he has accomplished his providential purpose Jesus will descend on the clouds with the archangelic shout and blast of the trumpet, walk over to Rev. Moon and say: "Sun Myung Moon, you've done a good job. I'll take over now." (laughter) I see my role this weekend as keeping both sides honest. Just as quick as you Evangelicals lay a subjectivist, bibliolatrous trip on these Moonies, I'm going to shoot you down in flames, if I can. And just as soon as any of you Moonies practice "heavenly deception" or anything like it on any of these unsuspecting Evangelicals, I'm going to air the family's dirty laundry. (laughter)

Nora Spurgin: My name is Nora Spurgin. I grew up in a

*Herbert Richardson is a theological consultant to the Unification Church and is the author of *Toward an American Theology* and *Nun, Witch and Playmate* and other works.

Mennonite community in Lancaster, Pennsylvania, in a very conservative Mennonite home. I quit school when I was a freshman in high school—this is what other friends and relatives did in the Mennonite community in which I lived—and helped my parents on the farm. There were nine children. I'm the oldest and only after I was twenty-one did I finish high school by studying on my own. I spent two years working in Mennonite Voluntary Service with migrant workers, and then went on to Eastern Mennonite College. I always felt that I was close to God and close to Christ, but there was never a specific experience, a specific point at which I felt that I had a conversion experience, although I suppose seventeen, when I made the decision to join the Church, was a very crucial point. While I was in college, however, I had some friends who became charismatics. For about six months I studied the Bible and I felt that they had something I wanted. I didn't want to just seek after some gift from God. It had to be a meaningful experience for me. So I prayed, "God, if you want me to have this charismatic experience, I know you'll give it to me." The "Baptism of the Holy Spirit" opened up a whole new relationship with Christ, and a whole new experience of Christianity to me. I probably wouldn't be here if I hadn't had that experience, because it took me out of a very narrow way of thinking and opened up a whole new level of really feeling something, not just intellectualizing Christianity and the Bible and praying, but really feeling the spirit.

After I graduated from Eastern Mennonite College I went on to graduate school at New York University and there, for the first time, I was confronted with the so-called "outside world," the secular world. I approached it with a great deal of interest, excitement, and vigor, and I felt like Christ wanted us to be able to be tested by everything, including my atheistic psychology professors. I *had* to be able to deal with "worldly knowledge;" if I couldn't, then I'd better take another look at my Christianity. It had to somehow meet the test, and it did. I had always felt that with intellectual pursuit, Christianity should be able to grow and blossom and become even more exciting. I was doing my Master's thesis on the extent to which religion changed value systems, for I believed that it was possible for people's value systems to change with a powerful experience of Christ. However, there was also the possibility that one had a certain set of values that always remained with that person.

I was quite active in Inter-Varsity Christian Fellowship and the night that someone from the Unification church witnessed to me, I was speaking on a panel at Columbia University. "Heart and Mind" was the name of the discussion. After the session was over, I was so aware of two girls who were in the audience, and they happened to both be Unification church members. They were not sitting together, but I had singled out these two girls to talk to them afterwards, to witness to them. But I felt some kind of kinship, some real feeling of spiritual attraction. I talked to them and it turned out that another person they were with, a third person, an older lady, walked up to me and she said, "I saw you last night." I looked at her—you never say that to anyone in New York City, you just never remember who you saw the night before, and I looked at her and I said, "How come you remember?" And she said, "Oh, you have the kind of face," or something like that. It turned out that she was going to witness to me the night before. It was just so incredible in New York City that this would happen.

I went to the center to hear the Divine Principle; actually, because I was doing research for my paper. Although I was always open to something that would give me a better spiritual life, at the same time I was very happy with what I had and was not seeking. When I went to the center, (there were just two girls in New York City), and listened to the lectures that they gave, immediately I began to think, "Wow, this is incredible!" and I started taking many notes. I didn't realize at that time that what they told me was based on the teachings of Sun Myung Moon; somehow for some reason, I just didn't hear that introduction. It didn't click. Of course, I didn't know anything of Sun Myung Moon at that point. Nobody knew him in America, except for a few people. There were probably about fifty members in the church at that time. So I heard the lectures and I took copious notes on them and thought, "These girls have really got it together. How in the world did they ever come up with such lectures? I could use this for teaching my Sunday School class. I could use this for all kinds of things." I was just fascinated with the basic principles. When I heard the part on original sin, the fall of man, I felt this was a real key, because I'd been studying and trying to find out where Christianity fits in with all the different psychological personality theories. Then, when I heard the lecture on the mission of Jesus I was so moved. There was no way that I could deny the feelings I had. I remembered that just a couple of weeks before I had written a little note on my dresser that said, "Isn't it something, how we all could possibly walk by Jesus on our way to worship in the church? Where is Jesus? In the church? Or could I walk by Him on my way to church?" When I realized what the lectures were leading up to, I thought, "I'm going to have to make a decision at the end of this if I hear the whole thing! Do I want to make the decision? If I don't I'd better stop right now." But I couldn't do that. I had to hear the whole thing. I had to face the responsibility of making a decision.

I didn't really like the communal style of life. I'd come from a Mennonite background and I guess I was becoming more individualistic. I wasn't attracted by the lifestyle in the church, but the philosophy itself was so powerful that I couldn't stay away from it. So I struggled with it for about four months. Actually at one point I thought, "Who can I go to? If I go to my pastor, I know what he'll say. Who can I go to? I have to work this out between myself and God." I went to the library one time and I got eight commentaries on the Book of Revelation, and started reading them. Often, for a break, while writing my thesis, I'd read the *Divine Principle* and the commentaries on the Book of Revelation. At one point I just got so frustrated that I took the whole eight volumes and dumped them on the floor! Each was some person's interpretation. How could I find the answer? It boils down to this: "I have to make the decision myself." I prayed and prayed about it and said, "Come on, God! Where are You? You've been leading me—all along You've led me, and now, suddenly, where am I going?"

I had felt that I was at a point where God was going to lead me to some great mission because I was graduating from school and was ready to go out in the world and become a missionary or something, and I was just saying, "God, the world is the limit and You are the Master. Where shall I go?" That was my prayer. And I never thought that He was leading me into the Unification church. At first I looked at it as just something to listen to in connection with my thesis. Suddenly it occurred to me, "God, do You mean that You've been leading me here? Was there a more personal reason that I needed to hear this?" And I kept praying about it until finally I realized that I knew it was true, but was resisting making a decision. When I said, "God, wherever You need me, even if it's a place I don't want to go, even if it is the

Unification church, I'll go." I felt such a flood of joy and knew that I had made the right decision. My head had been saying, "Come on, now. You've got to be careful what you espouse." But in my heart I knew that it was the truth and I couldn't get away from it; therefore I would be hounded the rest of my life if I didn't conscientiously respond to this. This was my sincere feeling, that I couldn't live with myself if I didn't make this kind of response.

At that point I committed myself to this church as I knew it then—that was eleven years ago—and it's been an incredible experience, a walk of faith in the church. I believe that this is the way God is working at this time in history, and that my Christian life in the past was definitely a preparation for this; the charismatic experience was definitely a preparation for this, and now I'm here. I consider myself a charismatic, post-Mennonite Unification-ist. I'm married and have three children. We live just down the hill and my husband is now doing graduate work at Union Theological Seminary in New York.

Whitney Shiner: My name is Whitney Shiner. I'm from Indiana. I came from a very irreligious family. My father sent me to Sunday School when I was in second grade so that I could understand what was going on in this society. Because American culture is based on Christianity, he thought I should have at least some understanding of the church. So they sent me to Sunday School. But actually, in church I suppose I would have become a Christian, but even when I was little, I was very intellectual, and after a few years I gave it up on intellectual grounds. I think one thing that decided me against Christianity when I was in the fourth grade was that they taught that Christians would go to heaven and other people were going to hell. I looked at the world and I realized that that meant that people in America were going to heaven and everybody else in Africa or non-Christian places was going to hell without having heard about Jesus. If that were true I thought that God was totally immoral and I knew from my own experience of the love of God that that couldn't be true. I think that ever since then I have never taken established Christianity seriously. I was very socially conscious even when very young because of some feeling of the spiritual kinship of all people. For this reason I couldn't believe in the idea of a personal God because I just couldn't understand how a personal God could love each person and still allow so much suffering. The explanations

I heard of this weren't very good. But then I was left with the experience of God and no explanation. So I was always very interested in religion, because I was always seeking an explanation.

When I was in junior high school I went to confirmation classes with one of my friends although I thought at this point that I was an atheist. I was the only one who was interested in the class; everybody else was throwing spitballs at the girls. Everybody else joined the church and I didn't. (laughter) When I was in high school I developed my own mystical pantheistic theology—and I was even more interested in politics at that point. Religion and politics were always separated in my life—I was a Marxist in high school, but then I went to college and I met the Marxists, and that cured me of my Marxism. I just couldn't deal with where they were spiritually. I kept going back and forth between trying to understand God and trying to accomplish something politically and socially, getting more and more disillusioned each time I switched from one to the other. I just couldn't find anybody I could follow—I couldn't make any sense out of any religions or theologies. I decided very early that there weren't any good guys to follow.

I was going to the University of Chicago where I became interested in eastern religions—not enough that I ever got involved in them in a serious way. At one point I thought I would become a Vedanta monk. I was very interested in Vedanta because it seemed more like the experience of God that I had had. But at that time I was engaged to be married in a month,...so I decided not to become a monk. My religion was very mystical and unconcerned with this world, but the rest of my interest was in various social concerns, so it seemed that I had to choose one or the other.

After I graduated I studied architecture for two years and was trying to make my peace with society. I was pretty disillusioned at this point. I finally decided I just couldn't live that way, and I dropped out of architecture school. I also left my wife. I was still searching but I had absolutely no theological construct. I was feeling more and more that this search for God was the most important thing because I had realized that social problems are really spiritual problems. I can remember one day my girlfriend told me that I was looking for God in the wrong place, that the greatest reality of God was in relationships between people. Then I experienced a blinding flash of light. I took this as a sign that I should be more serious about my search for God. At that point I decided to leave home, hoping that I would find some people with some answers. I headed out to California because I had several friends from college in California who were interested in spiritual things. So I went out to California and that's where I met the Unification church, in Berkeley. I was quite fascinated by the girl whom I met, by her spirit, because I saw in her a sincere kind of love, a depth, and spiritual solidity that I'd seen in very few people, probably in fewer than half a dozen people in my life. I didn't want to join anything organized, but I was fascinated by all the people in the church in spite of what they were doing. In a way witnessers seemed very strange animals—they have an almost stylized sort of friendliness, especially younger members. But I thought in spite of that I could see that they knew something very deep and important.

I left Berkeley, but I decided that I had to come back and figure out what it was that they knew. And finally I decided to join. There were two things that made me join. One was that I felt the presence of God in a way that I had very seldom felt it since the middle of my college career when I lost the feeling of the love of God because my heart was becoming hardened. And the other thing that made me join was the idea that God was suffering. This changed my whole understanding of what is possible because, for the first time I could conceive of a personal God. There were an awful lot of intellectual struggles because the Divine Principle was so far away from my own way of thinking. But I figured I had at least to some extent to be able to see the world in that perspective before I could reject it. I tried to be able to see God in a personal way through prayer. After a few weeks God became personal to me. I can remember that after a lecture on the fall of man, I finally realized what it meant in a real personal way, my sin towards God. I remember crying and crying all afternoon.

Maybe I should mention something about my relationship to Jesus, because I think at certain points in the church it's helped me through some problems in my spiritual growth when I prayed to Jesus instead of to God. I think because I feel His spirit is more supportive or more personal, or something like that.

Don Deffner: I grew up in Wichita, Kansas. At the age of thirteen I left for prep school, and spent nine years of my life in dormitories. So this is like coming "home" again to be in the buildings here. I studied in St. Louis, was at Concordia Seminary, and then interned at Kalamazoo, Michigan, where I had a broadening, relaxed, slow kind of "conversion" as I really grew in knowing Christ more personally than just reading the Bible for classes in prep school. I went to the University of California as campus pastor in 1947, where I stayed for twelve years. I left in 1959, just in time. I was in St. Louis for ten years as a professor at Concordia Seminary, and left there in '69, again just in time, because several years later came the ousting of the Seminex group which I had been with (Dr. John Tietjen and company). Now I have been at Berkeley for nine years and I don't know what's going to happen next.

But really, my becoming a Christian, I believe, was by God's grace through Jesus Christ in my baptism when I was three weeks old. I would like to extol the grace and mercy of God and I think we'd do well to talk about God's grace here, as one of the cardinal doctrines to discuss. It was God working in me and not my choosing God. I believe my salvation is God's workmanship. It is God working in me. Our life lived in this world is actually His life lived in us. Ephesians 2:8 and 9 is a crucial passage here too. "For by grace you have been saved through faith, and this is not your own doing, it is a gift of God—not because of works, lest any man should boast." And what we need is a whole rediscovery of the righteousness of God, which is God's imputed gift to us—not what *we* do. So I think the concept of "my responsibility" or "what *I* do"—as I hear the phrases used in Unification theology— is something I'd like to see discussed a lot more. I find a lot of disillusionment and disenchantment in the backgrounds shared here. I think much of the problem often is between our failing to distinguish between the church, as an organization, and our Lord Jesus Christ Himself. I think we need to look at Christ Himself again as the only way of salvation, the only way to the Father for anyone...the Holy Spirit being the one who does that work in us. It's not believing in Christ *plus* something else. For me as a Lutheran Christian, the means of grace is all important. I don't believe that God comes in with a great big zap. I believe He works through Scripture, through the study of it, through baptism and the Lord's Supper.

Let me tell you the story of a boy on a bicycle in the slums. One day he was hit by a car. He came from a very impoverished home where even a glass of milk was often shared with a brother and sister. After the accident he was taken to a hospital and bathed and put between clean sheets and the nurse brought a great big tall glass of milk for him. And he, looking at the glass of milk, remembering the times he had to share it, said, "How deep shall I drink?" and the nurse said, "Drink all of it. It's yours."

My point is, we should "drink" from our Lord Himself—and drink deeply—and not from any other sources. We should know Him as "the Christ cradled in the Scriptures" (as Luther put it).

There were some questions particularly that I'd like to see addressed here if we can get at them some time. First, a clear definition of words that both groups use, like "gospel; Christian; liberal; conservative." Secondly, I'd like to discuss what is absolutely normative to *being* a member of the Unification church. I found in reading through an earlier dialogue's transcript a wide diversity of opinions. What would you say is the *sine qua non* to be a member of the church? Thirdly, I would like to hear you air what your hermeneutical principle is. How do you determine what is figurative and what is literal in Scripture? For example, I would question the exegesis of Dr. Moon on the Jude passage in *Divine Principle** (p. 71) where he speaks of the original sin being sexual rather than the eating of the fruit; or page 183, that the dead were resurrected on the day that Christ died and these were actually Old Testament spirits. The Greek New Testament says nothing more than that "the dead people were raised" and Moon adds a great deal to that. Again, I would like to ask if you see the *Divine Principle* as authoritative, as Scripture, or as secondary *to* Scripture. Again, in terms of the Seminary here, what are the criteria for being admitted as a seminary student? And what are the criteria for being graduated as a seminary student? Again, to come back to my original question about our salvation being 100% the work of God in men, does man (woman) in effect get some credit for salvation, or is it *sola gratia,* totally by God's grace? Then, another question, and I know Ulrich will speak to this—did Christ "fail," or not? Or was He a "success" and so on? And then another question: Is your theology essentially universalistic? There's also the question of how your polarity relates to your theology. These are some of the questions.

Beatriz Gonzales: My name is Beatriz Gonzales and I'm from Texas. I was raised in a Roman Catholic family but we were also shamanistic. From time to time our parents took us to

*All references are to the *Divine Principle,* 2nd edition, New York, N.Y.: Holy Spirit Association for the Unification of World Christianity, 1973.

church. Sometimes they would take us during the Mass, but most of the time it was just to go and light candles and pray. I really learned from the church about my relationship with God and how to live. I think that I'm going to talk a bit about this relationship with Jesus. This was very crucial in my life and in coming into the Unification church.

When I was five years old my parents used to take me to this shrine. On the altar up on the side there was a life-size statue of Jesus on the cross and it was carved of wood. It looked very real, especially because it was life-size and because it came down low enough for me to be able to see it really clearly when we went up to the altar to light the candles. I was struck. I remember asking my mother, "Who is that?" And she told me it was Jesus and God, and I said, "Who did that to Him?" And my mother said, "He died on the cross." And I said, "But *why* is He up there? Who put Him up there?" And my mother said, "He died for our sins. He came to die for us." I couldn't reconcile it in my heart, and it wasn't until later that I realized why I couldn't reconcile what my mother had said. I had seen my sister die just about a year before and I knew what it meant to die. My sister and I were playing outside and my sister went in the house and died. I knew that to die meant that you just died. And I knew that Jesus was put up with nails on wood, and I knew that somebody had put the nails there, so for me He had been killed. We lived on a farm and my uncles used to hunt rabbits. They would bring the rabbits, pin them up and strip the skin off and then they would hang the skin up against the wall, with some nails. And to me that was killing. When I saw Jesus up on the cross like that, there was a difference between dying and being killed. To me Jesus was killed. So I told my mother I couldn't accept that Jesus had died. I asked her if my sister died or if she had been killed, and my mother said she died; I asked her if the rabbits died or if they were killed, and she said, they were killed. So to me this was something that I could not accept. I saw Jesus up there and I saw that He was killed, and so when we went to the church to light candles and pray I couldn't take my eyes off Him because I felt He was so sad and that He was bleeding; the blood looked very real. So after everyone started to walk out, I would walk up where He was. There was a little stool for people to pray and I would step on the stool and I would kiss His feet and I would walk out. My family would all walk out but I always stayed behind to kiss His feet.

The reason that I did it was because I wanted to recognize Him. I wanted Him to know that I knew that He was suffering and I knew that He was there. I was embarrassed for my family to see me, but I did this all the time. As I grew up I had a continuous conversation with Jesus. I remember that when the kids in school were asking questions about whether the earth was round or flat, I was really concerned about whether Jesus had been killed, the cause of His killing, and why everyone justified His killing without question.

I was raised with the medicine people. The life that they lived was totally selfless. There was one medicine woman in my community who had a really pure heart. She sacrificed everything for others; she was always healing people, and she had a beautiful clean room with an altar, statues, and a baby Jesus. One thing that humbled me about her was that when it didn't rain, she would go out in the corn fields and walk through them praying. She would fall on her knees and cry and pray that rain would come. I remember one day it rained. It came pouring down. It hadn't rained for a long time and I ran out to look at the field because I wanted so much for it to rain too. I saw her running out to the field. It was pouring and there was lightning and thunder. Once in the field she just bowed to God; she was just totally humble before God. She bowed before God over and over again. I was very moved. I saw someone praying and asking for something from God and God responding and man humbling himself before God. And I saw the power of prayer and the power of the love of God for us. And to me this woman was like Jesus. I studied Jesus when I was going to make my first communion and learned that He had healed people, He was very common, very simple, and He never had anything. This medicine woman was like Jesus. She just gave her life totally for others. She was very simple.

In church, I asked the nuns at catechism why Jesus was up on the cross, and they told me the same thing that my mother did. I knew that they didn't know everything, and besides, they didn't have that spirit about them that the medicine woman had. So anyway, I grew up with these experiences. As I grew older I promised Jesus, pledged to Him that someday I would help Him. I would give my life to do the same things He tried to accomplish. I knew He was trying to do something good but He had been killed.

I left home when I was about eighteen and I went to work in

Houston where I later started college. Actually, I completely gave myself to people. I worked in a halfway house for girls out of a penitentiary, and I worked in a veterans' hospital. I did every kind of volunteer work that I could do. I just completely gave of myself, except to have a job to send money home to my family. Later on, I became involved in the civil rights movement and became a community organizer in west side Chicago with the Industrial Areas Foundation. I wanted to change the world as Jesus had done. I wanted to do something for Him. At that point I became very bitter and somewhat distant from God. I didn't have much of a religious experience. I worked in the civil rights movement about seven years and I came to the realization that as much as I was trying to do to change politics, standards, rules and regulations that were discriminatory, I was only changing external things, but not the hearts of people. This is where the root of the problem was. At that point I was looking into communism and considering going to Cuba. But I realized that there were some things about communism that were just not right, and that I didn't agree with. It denied the existence of God and yet I had a commitment to God and I had a relationship with God. So I didn't go to Cuba.

I was at the University of Texas where I was very involved politically on the campus. I was the president of the Mexican-American organization. I was trying to find a direction in my life and I began to talk to Jesus again. I began to talk to God and to try to find direction again in my life, and I read many books. At this time I met people from Campus Crusade. During a period of maybe five or six years I studied the Four Spiritual Laws about four times. I really loved the Campus Crusade people very much. They were good, very sincere people, but one thing that I couldn't relate to was that they also told me the same thing—that Jesus had come to die for my sins—and I didn't accept that. By now I knew why Jesus had been killed, because I had tried to do many things also, and I had seen that always the people who put their lives on the line for what they believed were the people who were the most misunderstood and persecuted. I saw this in Martin Luther King and in Gandhi. People who were really living the life of Christ—not so much preaching but really living it day to day—these were the people who were "crucified." So I understood clearly that Jesus had been killed, and I knew in my heart that that was not meant to be. I couldn't reconcile in my heart that

God sent His son to be killed. I just couldn't. I could see how sincere and wonderful the people from Campus Crusade and other Christian groups were, and I loved to be with them, but I couldn't agree with their theology or doctrine. One day I met the Unification church. I came by myself to the center because I found a leaflet about it on the campus. I heard the whole Principle. Here were the first Christians that preached that Jesus had not come to die on the cross. So I stayed. That's why I'm here. I've been in the Unification church for five years.

Rod Sawatsky: O.K. We've made it all the way around. This has been very interesting to hear this fantastic variety of experiences.*

---

*Participants who joined the conference in the second session did not give personal introductions.

"HEAVENLY DECEPTION"

Mark Branson: The question of "heavenly deception" has come up as a result of conversations with some people who were formerly involved with the Unification church. But I might also say that ex-Christians who are no longer part of the church would suspect the same thing of our testimonies. Out of our spiritual pride we have a sense of needing to defend what we say or believe, whether that's rationalizing for ourselves or supposedly protecting the beliefs or integrities of other people around us. Cathy, who was with the Unification church for eight years, filled me in on many beliefs and activities. She often said, "They will deny this. They will deny this. They will deny this!" That just automatically raised the concern for me. Can I ask questions and know that the answers I'm getting here will be true, both concerning doctrine and concerning history? Obviously a lot of us are going to be in situations where we can say we don't know and where we must be free not to know. But, when it comes down to an issue and I receive an answer from a Unification church member, can I count on that being a true answer?

Rod Sawatsky: Does anybody want to speak to that?

Irving Hexham: A point that's worth making is that many groups have a policy of teaching simple things first, which in many ways is sensible. Then they gradually move to more complicated things. The Mormons, for instance, do this. With new converts they use the *Book of Mormon,* which is fairly close to the Bible; then they move on to the *Pearl of Great Price* and more difficult works which take them away from the established Christian tradition. Very often this is taken as deception, although

I don't know if it really is intended as such. In discussion with people generally, it may not always be wise to say exactly what you believe because they may reinterpret what you've said and misunderstand it. Therefore, you've got to build a pattern so they can begin to understand what's really being said. So I wonder if we could perhaps get to the point and you could ask one or two explicit things which you've been told that members of the Unification church will deny, and then they could explain how they understand them. Can we accept that we're all here under a certain obligation to communicate, and that, if we hear things that could be embarrassing, we could agree not to pass them on, because we may not have fully worked through what's involved, and it's easy to take things out of context. And that must not be done.

Rod Sawatsky: O.K. Let's try one or two.

Mark Branson: I'm not sure that simply throwing out the question will serve our purpose. I could ask some of the more common questions and see the contradiction between evangelical responses, such as Yamamoto*, and some of the things I read. These mainly concern conversion experiences. What I could ask, simply, is whether people are detained against their will in the three-day weekend, because I've read about that and I've talked to at least three people who've said that they were fully detained during the training experience, were not allowed to leave even though they had transportation, etc.

Jonathan Wells: May I respond to that?

Rod Sawatsky: Yes, please.

Jonathan Wells: Of course, it's not enough for me to say that I wasn't detained or restricted because that wouldn't prove anything one way or the other. But, as someone who has been accused many times of being involved in a nefarious group, I've done a lot of checking. The facts of the matter are that this whole issue has come to trial several times, in several different courts of law, and also in various legislative investigations, several of which I was involved in. And, of course, we all know that things can happen that cannot be proven in a court of law; but, every time the issue has come to some kind of adjudication, the church has

---

*Reference is to J. Isamu Yamamoto, *The Puppet Master, An Inquiry Into Sun Myung Moon and the Unification Church,* Downers Grove, Ill.: Inter Varsity Press, 1977.

been found innocent. Not only that, but a certain other class of people, namely the deprogrammers, has been found guilty numerous times. This, incidentally, is the class of people which most commonly makes the accusations against us. So, their accusations have not held up in court, but the church's accusations against them have.

Now, it seems to me that conversion is one thing, but coercion is another. Evangelicals wouldn't survive without conversion experiences and neither would we. But coercion is no good. It's not fair, it's not legal, it's not God's way, and I certainly don't condone it. And I don't know anyone in the church who does. In fact, we've been so thoroughly investigated already that, if we did do something like that, several of us would be in jail. Now, one other point in my experience is that many of these stories about being detained, in fact, come from people who have gone out through deprogramming. Now you'll have to check yourself in your own experience to see statistically how that works out—I'm not saying in every case—but, in my own experience, something like 90 or 95% of those stories come from people who confess to having left the church through a deprogramming experience, where coercion was applied in some form or another. Now, if you, as an evangelical Christian, were to give up your faith under coercion, then either you would have to repent of that failure, or you would be likely to turn on your faith and say that the faith was counterfeit all along, and that's why you gave it up. You certainly wouldn't like to admit that you gave in under pressure. And I find that that's common among people who go through deprogramming.

Pete Sommer: A point of clarification. What I've found is that with one exception, I think, they're all people who did not leave the church through deprogramming. We personally are against deprogramming. Our position is outlined in Yamamoto's book, *The Puppet Master,* which Andy Wilson said he didn't read because of the offensive cover. I would encourage you not to be put off by that and to read what we have to say about the unethical nature of deprogramming especially. But I will bear witness with Mark that I've talked with kids who've tried to leave but were prevented from leaving, who've had the phones cut off, and things like that. These stories are not from deprogrammed people.

Patricia Zulkosky: I've been one of the major lecturers of the Unification church in three-day, seven-day, and twenty-one day workshops, and my personal experience is that it is not at all advantageous to keep a negative person at a workshop if he wants to leave. There's the contamination factor among others. So, in my own experience, as one who taught the Divine Principle extensively, if someone has this kind of strong feeling, then it's one of my primary objectives to see that he gets back to his destination with all possible speed; otherwise, it is not conducive to the spiritual atmosphere of the workshop.

Pete Sommer: During the workshop I would grant that. But I've heard people who have said, "Once I had decided to join the church, for six months I was not permitted to have contact with my parents." And I know of two cases where people tried to leave: one was a girl who decided after pressure to stay in (and did for a couple of weeks), and another was a fellow who did leave in Berkeley; actually an Inter-Varsity guy helped him break out.

Patricia Zulkosky: I can well imagine that through counseling or something like that, someone may be convinced not to go out; but, when I went fundraising, I was dropped off somewhere and I had tons of time when no one checked up on me. When I was witnessing, I'd go out on the street, and I'd do anything I wanted anywhere I wanted. I could even call anyone I wanted. I could disappear if I wanted. I was not being watched to the extent that I'd be forced to break out if I wanted to go.

Pete Sommer: But you know that you would be reminded of the doom you might face if you left, that people would certainly call and pursue you if you did. What I'm interested in is what these two people have talked about, a kind of six-month quarantine and indoctrination before one is sent out fundraising and witnessing. Now I don't know that that's a Unification general procedure, but it was in this case.

Anthony Guerra: Well, I think one has to make some distinctions. It's possible, although I don't know of any cases, that one or two individuals in the church have done something like you're indicating. But, in terms of church policy, in terms of all of the experiences in all of the states and all the people that I know who are leaders of the church, this has not been done. As a matter of fact, the policy is that we oppose coercion because we're a religious movement, and we believe that truth and spirit are what convert a person. Now, I think that it is important to define what you mean by coercion, because that word may be used by some people who want to discredit not only our movement but any religious movement. The legal definition, also the definition that most people can agree upon, is that coercion is the use of force to prevent someone from pursuing his will. Could we agree upon that as a definition? That is legally what physical coercion is. Now, I don't think there's ever been that. That's what the courts have adjudicated. But, acting as a spiritual leader of the Unification church, I certainly wouldn't say, if someone wanted to leave the church, "Well, you want to leave? Well, go right ahead. I was thinking of leaving yesterday too. That's the thing to do." But, I would take it very seriously and try to counsel that person, speak confessionally, and do as much as possible on a spiritual level to see that that person would remain and come to a deeper understanding. I think that's exactly what any good Evangelical would do, if I'm not wrong. And that's very serious. When people experience that and still leave anyway, they later interpret that intense pleading as being coercion. I don't believe that's coercion. It's just a bare fact which is an inherent factor of any religious movement, that there's that kind of conviction and there's that kind of spiritual embracing that you have. But the assertions, as Jon pointed out, are that we have been detaining people physically, and that's absolutely false; yet the deprogrammers, who are the source of that accusation to a great extent, have detained people that way, and we, on religious principles, absolutely object to it. On religious principles, we would never conduct any type of forcible detainment.

Pete Sommer: I know of at least one situation where that was the case. I could relate the story.

Jonathan Wells: Physical detainment?

Pete Sommer: Yes. The guy was in the Hearst Street house in Berkeley. He went to the San Francisco airport. He was interested in going back to his family in San Diego. He was on the telephone to his mother at the airport and said, "I'm on my way home." Two gentlemen from the church hung up the phone for him, and she, that is, his mother, didn't know what was coming off; so she phoned our area director in San Diego, who called my predecessor in the Bay Area. My predecessor went to the house and, through conversation, helped the guy get out and onto a bus. So, it was a matter where two people followed him to the airport, hung up the phone for him in the middle of the conversation, and took him back to Berkeley. So, I mean, at that point, I guess it's a matter of my word against anybody else's.

Jonathan Wells: No, no, I don't think anybody's doubting your word.

Pete Sommer: And I'm sure that it was under the excuse of a we-know-best-what's-good-for-you kind of thing and that they may have done it with the best of intentions.

Jonathan Wells: I wouldn't necessarily defend the action that they took. I mean, as Anthony said, all of us know that there are cases when our members don't act up to the best standards.

Pete Sommer: So you need to know that it has been done. Let me just register that point.

Lloyd Howell: Yes, sure, I know there have been examples like that. It's no secret, but I think the issue here is whether you can bring a person to God through your own love and example; and if your love and connection with God isn't strong enough, you might resort to another method, especially if you're young in the faith. If you're just a spiritual baby yourself and you try to bring someone in, you hardly understand what love is and how to reach into a person's heart and touch him. I had a guest at a workshop once; I was very new in the church, and I tried very hard to convince him. He was a very troubled person. I saw slashes on his wrist. I'd met him in the street, and I cared for this person, about where his life was going. He was ready to commit suicide. He'd tried it before. I brought him to a workshop. I wanted him to experience God, but before the workshop even began, he got all these negative feelings. He said, "I want to go back." It was very difficult for me to want to let him go. I didn't really know how to love him enough. And a thought came to my mind—he said he had a plane ticket to go to Florida—and the thought came into my mind, throw the plane ticket in the fire, you know. What the heck does he need to go to Florida for, when we want to give him God here? But I didn't understand. I tried to talk to him, and then we let him go. We drove him down to the road where he wanted to go and that was it. But that temptation came into me. I think you learn how to love, and you grow, and, if you don't know the difference, if you don't know what love is, you might try to grab people because you really care for them. This may be confused with "compel them to come in." You have to compel them through your life and your example. I just want to make that distinction.

Rod Sawatsky: The other issue is that coercion can also be nonphysical.

Tirza Shilgi: There may be such cases, but I don't think that there are many. I want to refer to the theological side of it. What Anthony just touched is very basic to our beliefs. Anything meaningful in our life with God, or anything meaningful at all in terms of our spiritual growth, has to be done out of total freedom. Freedom is one of the most fundamental things that God gave to man. It is important that we believe that one of the reasons the fall was not prevented by God or stopped by God was in order to preserve this very fundamental freedom which God saw as indispensable for man. In other words, for man to become a son of God and resemble Him, he needs to have freedom, creativity, and responsibility. God even let man fall away in order not to take that freedom away from him; this is very fundamental to our beliefs. Freedom is fundamental for man's growth as a son of God. So, when you have organizations with thousands and thousands of people who are doing all kinds of things under all kinds of circumstances, I would not stand up and say, "No, I do not believe there are such cases." I believe there were, and I believe that they are very unfortunate, and I would say they are completely against what we believe.

Mark Branson: Yes, there are questions here of motivation. I know there can be different motivations, and they may be wrong. I also know there's freedom, but it could be argued that the concern for the individual is such that if that person returns to his parents he won't have the freedom to decide. The only place he has freedom to decide is in this seminar with us, and that can still provide a motivation for detention.

Rod Sawatsky: Irving, would you add something?

Irving Hexham: I was just thinking that these things cut both ways. I could, but don't want to, wash some other dirty linen in public. I'm sure Evangelicals can be accused of many similar things, certainly psychological pressure. All new religions get accused of this sort of thing. I wondered if there are more specific claims.

Mark Branson: Irving, I'm interested in comparing the conduct of one of their initial weekends with, say, an Inter-Varsity weekend with generous room for free time to let people talk at length with other young Christians who are there. And those are the points at which my friends say they didn't have much time for private conversations at all. They got long lectures, with little sleep. And I'm sure we understand what that is.

Irving Hexham: I've seen things like that, as well, to get the message across.

Warren Lewis: Is the question here what they do or what we think of the method? Or is not the original question: Will these people operate with you truthfully? Will they answer your questions honestly? How are they doing?

Anthony Guerra: I want to make our position clear. If it is done, it's against our teaching, it's against our stance, and I would be the first one to see that corrected, legally and in any other way. I want to make that clear, so that you can make it clear to your friends.

Pete Sommer: But we don't find that in the training manual. We don't find any written policy. Instead, we find talk of "heavenly deception," and I think this is what concerns Evangelicals as they survey your literature. I'm willing to believe you have integrity in telling that to me, and I find it interesting that there is an admission on your part that this, at least, does happen once in a while, even though you might disassociate yourself from it and say it's not part of your policy. It interests me to see it as a written policy.

Rod Sawatsky: Would somebody like to speak about what "heavenly deception" is? What is "heavenly deception?"

Paul Eshleman: I'll give you an example of it. When I was at Arizona State University, the members of CARP* were raising money in the name of Campus Crusade for the Unification church. I would say that would be a good example of "heavenly deception." How is that disciplined in your movement? Or do they just count the bucks when they bring them back?

Johnny Sonneborn: We have a written statement from the president of our church to all fundraisers, saying what is not permissible to do. It is sent out every year. I don't have it handy, maybe someone does.

Pete Sommer: Inter-Varsity would love to have a copy.

Johnny Sonneborn: It says that fundraisers are to wear badges saying that they are Unification church members.

---

*CARP (Collegiate Association for the Research of Principles) is an international student organization which studies the relationship between various academic disciplines and the Divine Principle.

Irving Hexham: But what is "heavenly deception?" Is it like the Buddhist doctrine of Skill in Means?

Nora Spurgin: I would like to make a few comments about the concept of "heavenly deception." I'd never heard of it until it came from our opposition. We traced the history back in the church and discovered that someone did coin the term somewhere along the line. I'd like just to make a couple of comments in terms of its historical developments.

For one thing, a very strong American value is honesty, but our movement is not just American. Honesty is one of those values we're taught in the very beginning: honesty, equality, freedom, etc. In dealing with orientals—I'm not talking about Rev. Moon here, I'm talking about all the orientals in our church who come and work side by side with us—I've discovered that honesty does not have a high priority in their value system. Honesty is a very Christian concept, while, in the East, loyalty is a much higher value. You're dealing with two groups of people who were raised with two different value systems, and you're putting them together. Out of that, I believe, will eventually emerge a heavenly value system. That's why it's hard for us to say, "Oh, there's a policy." We never felt we needed to make a policy about it until all of a sudden we were faced with these accusations. Those of us who never in any way deceived anyone when we were fundraising suddenly discovered that somebody else had been doing it. Historically, I think, it began developing when we began to get a lot of persecution. You get young members who were scared to admit that they were Unification church members because they were facing possible physical danger. They experienced violence, and you'd see them backing down and saying, "Well, I'm a member of a Christian group," trying not to mention the fact that they were from the Unification church. We don't want this to happen. And, as we discover it, we make the kinds of policies that Johnny is talking about. That comes after we discover that these things are happening. It was never Rev. Moon's intention at all for this to happen. Never.

Irving Hexham: You're saying there's no doctrine of "heavenly deception?"

Nora Spurgin: There's no doctrine!! (laughter) I'm not denying that some leaders in our church at some point coined that phrase and encouraged members to use it. However, again, it matters what is meant by "heavenly deception." There are times when one, out of wisdom, reserves a little bit in order to protect the young—even as Jesus advised...

Irving Hexham: In the Buddhist doctrine of Skill in Means, the Bodhisattva, in his compassion for all sentient beings, realizes that compassion alone is not sufficient. You need wisdom. And, in his wisdom, he realizes that certain people will not come to enlightenment of their own volition. Therefore, he must make the path to enlightenment sufficiently attractive to them so that they will attain enlightenment. This seems similar to "heavenly deception" and makes sense in an eastern context.

Anthony Guerra: Yes, Paul talks about the same thing, about feeding milk to babes. I think that that's true, but the term "heavenly deception," if it means you deliberately lie or falsify statements, is something distinct from that doctrine. In other words, to reserve something because a person is not ready to hear it is one thing. But, to falsify a statement, or to deny a fact, is something else. And I would say certainly we have a doctrine that truth is taught in stages, but I don't believe that we have the doctrine of "heavenly deception."

Irving Hexham: You're saying truth has got to be presented in stages. I think that raises an important question concerning concepts of truth. Are you working with an oriental or a western concept? In Buddhism, there isn't this problem because of the inherently contradictory nature of reality, whereas with western Aristotelian logic, you've got problems. Skill in Means doesn't present the same problems in an eastern context that it does in the West. Now, which concept of truth do you work with?

Anthony Guerra: I'm a westerner, and I work with the western concept of truth. I think that what Nora was alluding to is precisely your point: that there are Asians in the church who have the view that to make a person feel good is more important than giving him truth which is related to the capacity of reason. And, therefore, Asians might not say things, or might say things which seem inaccurate to someone from a western point of view, because they're basically trying to uplift him or make him feel good. But, as far as "heavenly deception" is concerned now, I would say we can't go with that. I would not call it a doctrine of the church. I think it's a false opinion.

Patricia Zulkosky: Lloyd and I just remembered where the term may have come from. It actually dates back to the Old Testament and the story of Jacob and of how Rebecca learned that Jacob was to receive the blessing and the inheritance, even though Esau was the eldest son. Because of the revelation which she received, she inspired or encouraged Jacob to take Esau's place at the time of the blessing by pretending that he was Esau. This is what is called "heavenly deception." That term, then, was picked up. Some might have said that fundraising in the name of another group is "heavenly deception." I don't think this direction comes from God in any way. I think this is downright deceit, and, if it is reported, then it can be dealt with. But if it's never reported, we may never be able to track down the people to correct their ways. By reporting these situations to church officials in the area, you can do something.

Jan Weido: I agree with what you are saying. I was a new Moonie when I met the director of fundraising who was here. He was a western person, but he was very much united with an eastern person. Sometimes, when we would go fundraising, we'd get a little pep talk like the kind maybe the Campus Crusaders get when they rev up their spirit a little before they're going to go out and meet the people. And this is the theological rap that comes down about Jacob and Esau, and also Tamar seducing her father-in-law: "Look what happened! That was the Messiah's lineage; therefore, cosmically, that little deception was nothing compared to the ultimate event of Jesus being born." But there was more: the examples given were more things like ways of sneaking into businesses past the guards and how to "become invisible." I think what happened is that these people, Japanese people in particular, do not understand the American covenant of openness. We've broken that covenant and I think we need to be rebuked when we do those kinds of things, and we need to change those things. I also want to say I can affirm that, whenever Rev. Moon and the church hierarchy heard about this, there was a very strong statement made against it all.

Paul Eshleman: Can you recall specific instances when you were told to use another name?

Jan Weido: Not use another name; but, because of the publicity, instead of saying "Unification church, Rev. Moon," you might say, "a Christian youth group."

Paul Eshleman: We got calls one day from people selling flowers saying they were with the Crusade.

Patricia Zulkosky: It could be One World Crusade.*

---

*A mobile evangelical unit of the church. It is composed of people of many different races and nationalities who travel throughout the world.

Jan Weido: Yeah, that's a name. The Moonies have been accused of using a lot of "front organizations," which were not devised as an attempt to deceive the American people; it's just that we have different organizations that do different things. "New Hope Singers" might be fundraising, and they're going to say that they're "New Hope Singers." If I'm fundraising, I tell people that I'm a seminary student at the Unification Theological Seminary. And if they ask me if that's Rev. Moon, I say, "Yes, he founded the seminary, and I'm a member of the church."

Pete Sommer: Part of evangelical sensitivity to this kind of thing has come in connection with Transcendental Meditation, which has tried to deny its religious nature from the word go, though we have now partly established that they are religious in a court of law. We became tired of their rap when we clearly saw that they were committed to a Hindu agenda. I'm perfectly happy to deal with a Hindu any old time, but to pass off the religion as a relaxation technique is something that Inter-Varsity has just waded through, and we're sensitive to these issues.

The other thing I'd like to know is what status Ken Sudo has in the movement? In reading the training manual by him, what am I reading? Am I reading something that is now passé? Is his word law? I noticed talking with Johnny last night that you called him a "very important person" with "very daring interpretations." This made me wonder if he is in the experimental end of the theology. Why was he director of your training? This would seem to be a fairly central role? I'm not accusing anybody, but I'd just like to know — what's he all about?

Patricia Zulkosky: Having been his assistant for a year and a half, I can say he was one of the very early members in Japan who came in with a good education and began lecturing from the early days in Japan and became one of the major lecturers there. When the American church was developing and had very little theological foundation, he came to America, studied English and tried as best he could to teach us things on internal guidance and the like. Each lecturer has a different way of expressing the Divine Principle. I know that through Ken Sudo's lectures, the American family came much closer to Jesus because Ken Sudo himself has a very deep relationship with Jesus. Where the very early American family didn't understand enough about Jesus, Ken Sudo really brought a whole level of undertanding of Jesus into the American Unification church. It was an understanding far beyond what we had had until that time. There are things he has said that not everyone would agree with; but, then, I'm sure you'll find in this room, on any given topic, not all of us will agree on anything, other than basic principles. Our interpretations of the Principle are influenced by our personal life experiences, as is the case with Mr. Sudo. He also had the opportunity to discuss many aspects of the Principle with Rev. Moon directly.

Irving Hexham: Could I ask a question about Ken Sudo?

Rod Sawatsky: Go ahead.

Irving Hexham: You said Ken Sudo had a great experience with Christianity and Christ before he came; was he ever connected with the "No-Church" movement in Japan?

Patricia Zulkosky: No. It was because of a healing experience. He was a traditional Christian.

Irving Hexham: Traditional Christian?

Patricia Zulkosky: Baptist.

Irving Hexham: Baptist!

Richard Quebedeaux: I want to go back to the fact that I think that evangelical Christianity in its various movements in my experience has been guilty of this very same thing. Example: I did my undergraduate work at UCLA in the early '60s, and Campus Crusade really was very unpopular with the administration because, at that time, some of their functions were not labeled and they were constantly being accused of deception. I think, on some campuses, even Inter-Varsity was occasionally accused of that. In the last five or six years, though, I've noticed that there is much more boldness about "saying who we are." I've definitely seen a transition here. It may be because of the maturity of the movement. It seems very logical to me that young converts —and I get this from Paul at a meeting we both attended— who may just be off drugs or whatever, sometimes will appear to be in positions of authority but are doing things which are very contrary to the teachings of the movement. Another problem has been with some of the messianic Jewish groups, not Jews for Jesus, but some of the others who have held meetings saying they are Jewish and they want all Jews to come, without identifying themselves further. And this has caused a great deal of concern, especially on campuses where the administrations have been concerned that people be very honest about who they are. Another thing about Campus Crusade: in one of the early drafts of the book I'm writing, I had a statement saying, "In Campus

Crusade, the ends justify the means."* O.K. that is a long-standing criticism of Campus Crusade which I've heard for years and years, and I thought was probably true. In other words, I thought that Campus Crusade felt that the issue was to get people converted to Christ, and it was really rather secondary how this happened. I crossed that out of my text, not just because I happened to be writing a book on Campus Crusade which is basically sympathetic, but because I really felt that that was a wrong accusation. Yet I see how people could look at Campus Crusade in this way. It's a result of its aggressiveness.

Now, again, I would say that probably those in the Unification church in Berkeley are a lot more honest this year than they were a year or two ago. I mean, about ten times more so. Now, I don't know if this has to do with the initial enthusiasm versus maturity, or what. I would say that this is not something that is peculiar to the Unification church; it is common to many other religious movements, including Evangelical movements. But I do think that now there seems to be much more willingness on the part of the people to be honest and to become very clean. I think it's good.

Rod Sawatsky: I think we need to wrap up. Just one or two further comments and we can conclude this discussion.

Anthony Guerra: I just want to emphasize that we are not concerned about constructing a theological apologetic for "heavenly deception." We don't believe in it. I just want to make that clear.

Pete Sommer: No, but it still has to assume some importance, since it's in the training manual.

Anthony Guerra: But they're not the standard lectures that are given in workshops anymore.

Pete Sommer: Is there a new manual, and is that available to our eyes?

Patricia Zulkosky: There are two-hour, four-hour, and six-hour lecture cassette tapes and also a video tape that's all set up ready to play. (laughter) Mr. Kim** loves to show people the lecture tape. We don't have training manuals *per se,* but now

---

*Richard Quebedeaux, *I Found It!,* San Francisco: Harper & Row, 1979.

**David Sang Chul Kim is President of the Unification Theological Seminary and a founding member of the Unification Church.

there's a standard little two-hour lecture booklet you may have seen. It's a brief formal presentation of the Divine Principle; and then there is a more lengthy one and a still more lengthy one. So, it's not for the purpose of training the members the way Ken Sudo's was. It's more for a unified way of presenting our theology to the public.

Pete Sommer: You mean, this thing was secret at one time?

Jonathan Wells: No, it wasn't secret. It just wasn't distributed publicly. There's a difference.

Warren Lewis: There's a difference between "private" and "secret." Much of the literature and a little of the gnosis of the movement is private, but it's not "secret." If you want to know, you may know. All you have to do is ask.

Pete Sommer: I'm aware of that. I'm thinking of the woman who directed the San Francisco State work and said that was really secret.

Warren Lewis: It was probably important to her to be involved in a movement that has some secrets. (laughter)

Johnny Sonneborn: Mr. Sudo was director of training during a certain period of time. It was an experiment to see if we could find a new and more successful way of evangelizing. Pioneers were sent out, after quite a long period of training, by themselves, in small groups; and these methods were used. Later on, we stopped having the long training programs and used other methods. Mr. Sudo is now the director of evangelical work in New York City, where it is very important to have a successful leader.

Warren Lewis: When I was at Harvard I heard Joe Fletcher's lectures on situation ethics. Although situation ethics when used by the fraternity brother as an excuse for getting in bed with his girl friend are not something that any of us approve of; on the other hand, when Pastor Wurmbrandt sneaks Bibles past the Soviet border guard, we think of him as a saint.

Pete Sommer: Oh no, we don't!

Warren Lewis: All right, you don't. I do. The point I'm making is this: everybody in this room, at one time or another in his life, has used "doctor's lies" to moderate the truth that would have been too harsh in that situation. We would probably defend the action now as being the ethical thing to do in that situation, the ethic that transcended the moral norm without breaking it. Why is this such a difficult concept?

Jonathan Wells: That was Jesus' problem too, wasn't it? I

mean, among other things, He told people not to spread the word that He was the Messiah, after they discovered the secret. But that's still different from deliberate lying. Now, you haven't quoted from Mr. Sudo's lectures, so I don't know quite what you're finding fault with, but the church does not advocate lying.

Lloyd Howell: Just one biblical point. There's a verse where St. Paul says to the Jews, "I am a Jew," and to the people under the law, "I'm one under the law," and so on. If I wanted to attack somebody, I could certainly work on this passage and build up something, and say, is Paul going around practicing "heavenly deception?" I don't think so. We could examine the verse, but that's another angle on the situation.

Nora Spurgin: I just want to say one thing: I feel that we Americans have to take responsibility. I don't want to blame the orientals. I know that some Americans have done wrong. I know that, in a growing movement that has many undefined characteristics, each person is called to define on the spot, and the definitions come out very differently. But I think that there have also been Americans who have deliberately lied; we all bear that sin and, I think, ask forgiveness for it.

(The following continues the discussion of the same topic but is based on additional questions which were posed to the seminarians at the second conference in October 1978.)

Patrick Means: You may already have discussed this in your last get-together, but I haven't had the opportunity to read the transcripts. If that's so, I'll pick it up from one of you during the breaks. Now, I'm not intending to be provocative in bringing this up here, but this is something fundamental. I'd like us to give some time to the whole concept of "heavenly deception." I'd like someone either to set me straight on that, or have some light shed on that, because it affects the credibility of all the other issues.

Patricia Zulkosky: I think I can get you the transcripts of the last conference, because we opened with a lengthy discussion of that topic. It might be good to make a couple of transcripts available for people who didn't attend that session.

Joseph Hopkins: I really think we ought to discuss that at this conference as well, because an ex-Moonie wrote a letter in rebuttal to my article in *Christianity Today*,* a letter in which he said I had been a victim of "heavenly deception." And he stated that deception is a consistent pattern in the operation of the Unification church. So I really think this ought to be aired at the outset.

Warren Lewis: That touches me more directly than anything else we've talked about. I'm glad you've said that, because I see myself on both sides of this issue as a kind of score-keeper to keep the Evangelicals honest with the Unificationists, and the Unificationists honest with the Evangelicals. I know both sides; so if you feel you've been hoodwinked in any way, heavenly or otherwise, then that says to me that I too am deceived, or duped, or that I participated in the deception.

Joseph Hopkins: I'm not saying I feel I've been deceived. I'm saying that a former Moonie made that accusation, so I do think we ought to talk about it.

Warren Lewis: As somebody down in the New York City Unification headquarters told me the other day in a moment of heavenly honesty, "heavenly deception" is fine until you start using it on one another. (laughter)

Roy Carlisle: I had an encounter about a week ago with two former Moonies in Berkeley, and I specifically talked to both of them about "heavenly deception." They both said that where the rubber meets the road with that doctrine for them is with the whole understanding of the Lord of the Second Advent. The critical statement, I understand, was that to be a Unificationist, you must honestly be committed to the Lord of the Second Advent. That to me is the critical thing here, too. If we're damning "heavenly deception" at that very critical and most important point, then that needs to be aired for me to feel comfortable again. When we get into it, I would like some Unificationists to tell us about the Lord of the Second Advent, what they really believe, and push that whole doctrine out into the center aisle and really examine it.

For one ex-Moonie, the most critical thing was the Unification belief about the Lord of the Second Advent. He said they could be pushed anywhere else on any other issue, but *that* one they could not be pushed on. They would lie to cover that issue,

*Dan Glissman, "Heavenly Deceit," *Christianity Today,* 22:2:9-10, October 20, 1978.

and those are strong words. If we look in the transcript, there is tremendous divergence at that point among Unificationists.

Paul Eshleman: One wondered if it was a hold-over from good field technique that was flowing in our meeting, and that what was coming out in regard to the Lord of the Second Advent was the line you would give the uninitiated who had not had time yet to have hundreds of hours of background or whether it was from personal conviction. There weren't people who said, "I believe that the Lord of the Second Advent is sinless, he's perfect." There were not those kinds of clear statements being made about Moon at the last conference.

Dan Davies: I would like to raise the question: What do you think a disciple of Jesus would say about who he thought Jesus was after he had been told not to tell anyone Jesus was the Messiah?

Patrick Means: He'd probably say Jesus told him not to tell.

Dan Davies: Do you think so? It's easy to say now, but if you were in that situation . . .

Patrick Means: He wouldn't lie about it.

Dan Davies: But what would he say? Put yourself in the disciple's situation and reflect upon it.

Patrick Means: I'm picking up a parellel here. Are you admitting to lying about Moon's identity because he told you not to tell people?

Jonathan Wells: Wait a minute. Wait a minute. I haven't heard any actual lie. Haven't we jumped the gun here? Where's the lie we're talking about?

Patrick Means: I'm not bringing anything up. I'm trying to understand what this brother said.

Dan Davies: I just asked a simple question.

Evangelical Y: I think you're asking a contradictory question, because, if truth is anything, it is central to the Scriptures. Therefore, for Jesus to command His followers to lie is like saying here's a four-sided triangle. It doesn't work, so your question is an unanswerable question, which means that nobody can possibly respond to it.

Dan Davies: But when you apply it to this situation that we're in...

Evangelical Y: Well, Jesus made a very strong statement about truth, whereas Rev. Moon apparently has not made an equally strong statement about truth, which means I enter into calumny when I talk about Jesus commanding some people to lie. But I don't get into that same position when I talk about Rev. Moon commanding that. To me, it's not logically possible to think of Rev. Moon commanding that. To me, it's not logically possible to understand what in the world you'd be talking about to have Jesus do that same thing.

Jonathan Wells: How did this word, "lie," come into this conversation?

Rod Sawatsky: Daniel introduced it. (laughter)

Dan Davies: No, I didn't mention the word, "lie." I said, "What would you do if Jesus had told you..."

Jonathan Wells: I wouldn't answer the question. But somehow the word, "lie," got in there, and Rev. Moon has never told *me* to lie. I never heard him tell anybody to lie. The first thing we have to resolve is what do we mean when we talk about deception—is it deception, or is it, as Paul mentioned, strategy from the field? Is it a pedagogical approach? Or is it something kind of unethical in the way we are talking to people?

Warren Lewis: Or, to stick with Daniel's question, is it the messianic secret?

Jonathan Wells: Or is it the messianic secret?

Paul Eshleman: I guess what we're saying right here is that we don't want any more things of this from the field. We want to know...

Jonathan Wells: ...about the messianic secret?

Rod Sawatsky: I think messianic secret is a fair answer. To say simply, "We have been told not to tell," is a legitimate answer. But is that the way you would want to answer the question here?

Johnny Sonneborn: There's a further problem, because Jesus told us in the Scriptures: "If anybody says to you, 'Lo, He is here,' or 'Lo, He is there,' don't believe it." (I forget the quotation exactly.) Therefore, I think it's not really right to ask somebody if you know where the messiah is. If you are a Christian, you shouldn't believe them if they do claim to know. It really puts us in a bind. In other words, why would Jesus say that? I think, as I understand it, and I think I've heard this in Unification church, it's because each person must find out for himself. Each eye must see.

Patrick Means: Do you see why that causes us some problems when we're here to try to understand what we see as a central issue in this whole area of how Christian, how biblical the

Unification church movement is? Christ's identity and role is so central, and Moon's identify and role is so central, that when we sense there is a common understanding of who he is, when we ask anyone directly, they say, "Well, we're told in the Scriptures not to really say." To me that seems superspiritual and not speaking to the issue, not being totally transparent.

Johnny Sonneborn: I think there are two things about that. First, it is very clear what Unification teaching is concerning the nature of the Lord of the Second Advent: that it's going to be a person of a different name, who will be born on earth, and so forth. Whether it's Sun Myung Moon or someone else is open to debate. The theology stands the same. That is one aspect.

The other aspect is that it's widely reported in journals and analyses that most Unification church members believe that Sun Myung Moon *will be* the Lord of the Second Advent—at least, no one has denied that statement. It's easier to say that than to talk about personal situations. But, still, the basic issue is, can the Lord be someone with a different name, or does it have to be someone with the same name coming on the clouds, and so forth? Will He be coming back in a resurrected body, or in another body?

Anthony Guerra: I think that the question of "heavenly deception" is quite separate from the notion of a messianic secret. I would say directly, concerning this so-called doctrine of "heavenly deception," that it is not a teaching of the Unification church, Rev. Moon, or any other responsible church leader! There is no such teaching that deception is necessary to build the kingdom of heaven. Precisely the opposite is held.

It is also interesting to note, from a sociological perspective, that the few people quoted as accusing the Unification church of "heavenly deception" are mostly ex-members. I think you must all be cognizant of the fact that the ex-member of any organization can be a highly questionable source of information concerning the organization from which he has disengaged, possibly very painfully. Certainly, Joe, I would be skeptical about accepting the evaluation of anyone who writes me admitting that he was brainwashed!

In any case, I want to make absolutely clear that it is in no way a doctrine of the Unification church that its members should go around deceiving anyone for some greater good.

Patrick Means: I don't believe it's just ex-Moonies who make the charge of "heavenly deception." There have probably been a number of us in here who have had personal experiences with that. My wife on the streets of her home town was approached by a Unificationist, collecting funds. My wife asked her whom she was representing, and the Unificationist said, "Campus Crusade for Christ." She pursued the conversation with this young lady and said, "Well, I don't believe you are with Campus Crusade for Christ. Isn't it true that you are working for Rev. Moon?" The girl denied it for a while, finally admitted it, got very vehement, and went on. You could say that she was a gal who was green. We've had green people in Campus Crusade that have done bad things out there too, and I'm willing to accept that. But, it seems like there are numerous instances of this being reported. So, perhaps it's not just green ones. I'm really open to being turned around in the impression I've gathered, but I really need an understanding of this as a foundation for discussion.

Anthony Guerra: I was not saying that there is no one in the Unification church that at some time has deceived another person. I was addressing the theological question whether or not we hold to a doctrine of deception as a requirement of religious life, and we simply do not. I could quote you several examples of Campus Crusaders who have come up to me and said a lot of nasty things, even using foul language. Now, I don't suppose for a moment that such behavior is doctrinally demanded by the Campus Crusade organization.

Warren Lewis: Isn't the question, "Are *you* guys going to deceive *you* guys?" That's the question. How do you know they're telling the truth? Isn't that the question?

Paul Eshleman: You remember, I raised the question last year of "heavenly deception" on the very issue of fundraising? We then got out the one-hundred-day training manual and we worked through those passages that very clearly pointed out how to deceive somebody, and what needed to be done in the fund-raising context. We read through those, and you very eloquently said, "Some guy out to lunch wrote these training manuals, and he's not around any more in a leadership position. We don't use them anymore."

Anthony Guerra: I think that there were never any passages that I saw that were telling anyone to deceive anyone. You were reading a different script than I was.

Paul Eshleman: Then let's get out the manuals again.

Anthony Guerra: I think it's instructive to understand, as Harvey Cox has pointed out in an article that we can perhaps make available,* that it has been common practice in the history of religion, when a new religious movement dawns, to accuse it of deception, and then to proceed to disbelieve anything that is said by anyone of that movement. Furthermore, when you do find specific individuals in that movement who do lie—and you'll find such individuals in any religious movement—you then take these instances as proof of the theory. And that is something that has been done to Mormons and Catholics and every new religion that has arisen in America.

Paul Eshleman: Yes, but who coined the phrase?

Anthony Guerra: The phrase was coined in reference to a specific understanding of the role of Jacob in gaining the birthright, in Scriptures. Now, that may have been coined by Unification theology,but it is in no way intended to refer to the kind of ethical activity prescribed for humanity at the present time. We do believe that Jacob deceived his father and got the birthright, as it says in the Scriptures, and that, in those circumstances, he actually accomplished something which was in God's providence in spite of the ethical violation. Now, we're not saying that an ethical violation is something to be applauded, but that *in spite of* and not because of the ethical violation, God still worked in that situation.

Paul Eshleman: But this distresses me much more than your answer last year, because this year it's like, "Hey, listen, we don't know anything about this." Last year it was, "We admit it's been in the one-hundred-twenty-day training manual. I'm sure some of our trainers have done it in the past."**

Anthony Guerra: No, I don't remember that.

Paul Eshleman: Maybe we'd better bring them out again.

Jonathan Wells: While you're looking, let me say that I was the State Director of the Unification church in Vermont a few years back when this whole thing became a very intense issue, and the State Legislature was called upon to investigate us on several points. The State Attorney General in Vermont investigated and concluded that there was no fundraising deception.

---

*Harvey Cox, "Myths Sanctioning Religious Persecution," *A Time for Consideration*, New York and Toronto: The Edwin Mellen Press, 1978.

**Ed Note: The reader can check the earlier discussion, p. 90.

There is no policy in the church to deceive people in fundraising, and I've heard Rev. Moon say numerous times that you must be honest in fundraising. Tell people who you are and who you're with. I've heard the president of the American Unification church say that, and I've heard the director of fundraising say that. And I've always said that in my capacity as a leader. I've never tolerated any kind of deception. Now, that's one thing. O.K.?

The other thing that concerns us more this weekend, I think, is whether you are going to get honest answers from us, because we're not asking for money. (laughter) O.K.? Now, on that issue, I would just like to distinguish two separate issues. One is, are you asking us for clarification of Unification theology, or are you asking us for a personal confession of faith? Now, our position is that we will really do our best to give you complete and candid answers on Unification theology, which in fact does *not* say that Rev. Moon is the Lord of the Second Advent; and, when it comes to confessions of faith, well, every individual is free to say whatever he wants; but I'm not sure that will get you anywhere. I mean, that's not really the issue, is it?

Rod Sawatsky: Though, Jonathan, you have on a couple of occasions given your confession, where you have said very straightforwardly that he is the Lord of the Second Advent. That is *your* confession of faith—and that's the differentiation you want to make.

(END OF SESSION)

Rod Sawatsky: We started with a rather hard-hitting session last night, which is good. I would hope we would continue being very frank and open. Having spent one weekend together earlier, I think we really know each other sufficiently so that we can really get down to basics. I think people should challenge each other fairly solidly and strongly. If we don't allow that to happen, then we are going to get charged with a cover-up, and we dare not allow that. So let's be prepared for frank, open discussion.

We were talking about "heavenly deception," and I don't think we concluded that discussion. I doubt if we can really conclude that discussion until we talk about the question of the Lord of the Second Advent, and are clear in our minds what Unification people mean by that idea. Let's turn to that now.

JESUS CHRIST AND
REV. SUN MYUNG MOON

Rod Sawatsky: Who's going to start us off on the subject of Jesus Christ and Rev. Moon?

Don Deffner: I'll start with an illustration. The story is of a little boy on a downtown street with his father. There were skyscrapers around. Another building was going up and the little boy saw figures etched against the sky high above them, and he said, "Daddy, what are those little boys doing up there?" And the father said, "Those aren't little boys; they are grown-up men." And the boy said, "Well, why do they look so small?" He said, "Well, because they are up so high." The little boy thought for a moment, and he said, "You know, when we get up to heaven there won't be very much of us left, will there?" (laughter)

To me, the heart of the Christian life and faith, and growing in grace, after conversion, is God working in me. I'm *His* workmanship; I don't "cooperate" with God; I don't "help Him out," but it is totally *God* at work in me. To paraphrase, "our life lived in this world is actually His life lived in us." (I John 4:6, 13, 17)

And one of the earlier questions I have raised with some of you Unificationists is that although I hear agreement on the fall, on the parousia, on the family, and on God being Father, I find a real disparity on Christ, His work, His mission, and then the whole question of His "failure" or "success." And for me, this is the crucial point about my conversion: I have the freedom to reject God, but I cannot *choose* God, because I am spiritually dead. As Scripture says: "You have not chosen Me, but I have chosen you." It was God who called me in baptism, it is *God* who works in me. The Scripture says "...work out your own salvation..." (Phil. 2:12) But the next verse says for God is at work in us.

Just to start it off...certainly as a Christian I have a "responsibility," but we must remember that "*I* am the vine, you are the branches. He who abides in me, and I in him, he it is that bears much fruit," says Christ, "for apart from me you can do nothing." (John 15:5) I think the question is whether one is saved by grace alone or saved by what one does.

Paul Eshleman: Are you asking also for who is Jesus?

Rod Sawatsky: I think that is one of the critical issues.

Paul Eshleman: We would believe that Jesus is wholly God and wholly man, the second person of the Trinity. He existed absolutely before the foundation of the world. When God said, "Let us make man," He was referring to the involvement of the Trinity in the creation of the universe. We believe that He came into the world to die. The Scripture states that it is for this cause that He came into the world. The Son of God came to give His life as ransom for many. We believe that Jesus Christ came in the form of man to pay the penalty for man's sin so that man might be reconciled to God, fulfilling the Scripture, for "without the shedding of blood, there is no forgiveness of sin." (Hebrews 9:22) Jesus was, in effect, the sacrifice that was offered for our sins that secures our salvation; He was raised bodily from the dead and appeared to more than five hundred after His resurrection from the dead. It was not merely a spiritual resurrection; He actually ate with His disciples. He ascended into heaven and at the present time sits at the right hand of the Father, and will again return to this earth in another time. That's a start.

Mark Branson: There are a couple of key Old Testament passages. In Isaiah 42:1-4, "Behold, my servant, whom I uphold, my chosen, in whom my soul delights; I have put my Spirit upon him, he will bring forth justice to the nations. He will not cry or lift up his voice, or make it heard in the street; a bruised reed, he will not break, and a dimly burning wick he will not quench; he will faithfully bring forth justice. He will not fail or be discouraged till he has established justice in the earth; and the coastlands wait for his law." And then Isaiah 53:1-12, "Who has believed what we have heard? And to whom has the arm of the Lord been revealed? For he grew up before him like a young plant, and like a root out of the dry ground; he had no form or comeliness that we should look at him, and no beauty that we should desire him. He was despised and rejected by men; a man of sorrows, and acquainted with grief, and as one from whom men hide their faces he was despised, and we esteemed him not." And the rest of the passage goes on, "He was oppressed, and he was afflicted, yet he opened not his mouth; like a lamb that is led to the slaughter, and like a sheep that before its shearers is dumb, so he opened not his mouth. By oppression and judgment he was taken away; and as for his generation, who considered that he was cut off out of the land of the living, stricken for the transgression of my people? And they made his grave with the wicked and with a rich man in his death, although he had done no violence, and there was no deceit in his mouth. Yet it was the will of the Lord to bruise him; he has put him to grief; when he makes himself an offering for sin, he shall see his offspring, he shall prolong his days; the will of the Lord shall prosper in his hand; he shall see the fruit of the travail of his soul and be satisfied; by his knowledge shall the righteous one, my servant, make many to be accounted righteous; and he shall bear their iniquities...he bore the sin of many, and made intercession for the transgressors."

The whole theme of the suffering servant is one that is key in the gospel writers, and in Jesus' own self-understanding. As the Gospel of Mark states, (Mark 1:2-3) "...Behold, I send my messenger before thy face, who shall prepare thy way; the voice of one crying in the wilderness: Prepare the way of the Lord, make his paths straight..." After this reference Mark goes on to John the Baptist and then to showing Jesus carrying out the last of what it meant to be God, God incarnate. He began to reveal, to act, to say who He was. All of His activity, everything He did and said was simply God.

Luke 4:18-19 is probably the key to understanding how Jesus understood His task when He preached in Nazareth. He read the Scripture: "The Spirit of the Lord is upon me, because he has anointed me to preach good news to the poor. He has sent me to proclaim release to the captives and recovering of sight to the blind, to set at liberty those who are oppressed, to proclaim the acceptable year of the Lord." Now this plainly sets out what it means to be proclaiming the kingdom, what it means to have God here. God is here to proclaim release, to give freedom and eyesight, help of all kinds, complete salvation. Salvation includes one's body, one's soul, one's economics, etc. That idea of Messiahship, then, came to be seen by the disciples who were with Him.

Finally, when Peter confessed, "You are the Christ," Jesus was worried that although he had the right title, he still somehow had the wrong concept. Peter's concept of messiah was still a second David, a new kingdom, and his key question was, "Is this the time to throw Rome out?" Jesus continually refused to be made into that kind of king, a welfare king or political king, and taught them to know that the messiah had one task—the messiah must suffer and die, and then be raised from the dead. Of course, they never quite caught that last line, either. His whole theme, from the way that He first revealed His identity by His actions and preached the Good News, was that the messiah must suffer and die—die at the hands of those very ones whom He ought to be ruling. Finally that is what happened, and even at that time, people wanted Him to be king, and He rejected that urging and preached just things that were true. This truth is what would get Him crucified, because there was no other way for salvation. The world had to have salvation in a complete way and this included the sacrifice that was both physical and spiritual, and it included a resurrection that is both. Finally He was raised, and His spirit now works inside us.

The overall thrust is that Jesus is God, and that as He lived, He lived as God. We are then called to live similarly, except we do not provide atonement. There had to be a substitution for our own sinfulness, otherwise we would have to make that sacrifice ourselves, and that still would not be complete. So Jesus' death on the cross was the sacrifice that was required by the Old Testament prophecy and by God's righteousness so that we might not have to die that death. In Jesus, the substitution was made for us. The resurrection said the power is going to continue with us as mentioned, so that now, simply by God, I might begin that pilgrimage.

Virgil Cruz: There's relatively little to be added to what has been said, and I might mention my agreement with what has been said. As Paul (Eshleman) said, we believe in the two natures of Christ. We would maintain that it is a case of the divine Son taking on humanity, not that the earthly Jesus acquired deity. Let me speak to another point raised by our sister Gonzales which I have found very valuable. I think we would say that Jesus Christ was killed. We would have no problem with that. I would not have any problem with that. However, I would want to add that Jesus was not powerless to alter that situation. As He has said, He could have summoned legions of angels from heaven to have prevented His crucifixion, but He was killed. He was killed by sinful and evil men, and I believe that I participated in that as I participate in sin. We would disagree with Schweitzer and others who have said that Jesus, by virtue of being killed, ended as a defeated, disillusioned figure. In the Gospel of John 18:4-5, we see that as Christ faced death and when the soldiers came looking for Him, He quickly went forward eagerly and offered Himself: "'Whom do you seek?' 'Jesus of Nazareth?' He said, 'I am he.'" John tells that in such a dramatic way, Jesus presented Himself with such force. I think He was understood by those individuals to be a supernatural figure to the extent that the people fell back on themselves, nearly a domino effect, and the soldiers fell on the ground. So Jesus virtually embraced this death, which was His mission.

Also in the Gospel of John, in Chapter 13, there is the fascinating discussion of the foot washing; and in John's Gospel, if you recall, there is not any real mention of a sacramental element in the Last Supper. There is the Last Supper, but the sacramental nature of the meal is not mentioned, and the foot washing episode is included, about which Carl Martin in particular says that the foot washing in and of itself says the same sort of thing that the sacramental meal says: namely, that Jesus comes to serve men and the highest service that He will perform is that of washing them from their sins. And that comes by virtue of His death.

In the Reformed tradition in particular, there is great discussion of the necessity of the death of Christ, and that had to come under a kind of juridical, judicial sentence in order that Christ could be counted with the transgressors. He had to be considered a kind of criminal, and that sentence would have had to be pronounced, or at least was pronounced in the context of a trial during which the innocence of Jesus could actually be discerned. He had to die a horrible death. He had to become cursed for us. Only in this way could the demands of the law be met. Subsequently, following the death and resurrection of Jesus Christ, comes the exaltation by God, and this seems to be the announcement by God of the approval of that which His Son, Jesus Christ, has done. This seems to be saying that He has indeed completed the mission which was ordained for Him. Revelation 3:21 is one reference to that sort of thing where Christ says, "He who conquers,

I will grant him to sit with me on my throne, as I myself conquered and sat down with my Father on his throne."

I could mention one other thing in this context, in response to what Warren was saying. I don't know whether I agree with you or differ with you, Warren, and you'll have to help me interpret what you did say on the point of the second coming of Christ. I know of only one Lord of the Second Advent, only one, and that is Jesus Christ. I know of only one central figure, to use the terminology of the Unificationists, and that is Jesus Christ, and one point at which this is presented to me is in Acts 1:11 where at the time of the ascension of Christ the angel asks why the disciples stand gazing into the heavens. But then the crucial words are these: "This Jesus, who was taken up from you into heaven, will come in the same way as you saw him go into heaven." That is a rather clear explication of this situation as far as the person of the second advent. As we know, Bultmann and those in his school wanted to separate the historical Jesus from the figure mentioned also by Jesus in His eschatological Son of man sayings. Bultmann at one point said that Jesus was prophesying about another when He mentioned the Son of man. To a degree some Unificationists say something of that same thing, but again I want to add that this same Jesus will return; the historical Jesus will return. There is not any room for another figure in my understanding.

I am extremely interested in and feel quite a bit of sympathy for—maybe I'll be considered a heretic at this point by my colleagues—your position of cooperating with God in His work in the world. Using the verses in Luke 4:18 which you mentioned, (Jesus' address at Nazareth where He used words from Isaiah): "The Spirit of the Lord is upon me, because he has anointed me to preach good news to the poor..." etc. I would contend that as the body of Christ now, we may say the spirit of the Lord is upon *us* because He has anointed us to preach to the poor, to help bring about release for the captives, and so on.

Once again the Book of Revelation helps me understand that we do work *with* God and *for* God in the cosmic confrontation with the anti-God forces. And I think that the Book of Revelation was clear that we can achieve, with God's help and in our allegiance with God, temporal provisional victories. I think with God's strength we can resist the work, the machinations of the anti-God forces. You have to understand what victory means, however, in the biblical sense. I would say that to be victorious means holding out against evil and being faithful to God even when to do so might mean death. And to be defeated in the biblical sense would be giving in, even if that might well mean the continuance of earthly life. Later I'd like to pursue further the question of our working with God in achieving temporal, provisional victories.

Rod Sawatsky: Do you want to add anything?

Pete Sommer: Only to refer very briefly to the *kenosis* passage, Philippians 2:5-7, which bears out what Virgil said about Jesus as the divine Son of God taking on human flesh instead of the reverse—the human Jesus taking on divinity. I'm sure this passage is familiar to everyone: "Have this mind among yourselves, which is yours in Christ Jesus, who, though he was in the form of God, did not count equality with God a thing to be grasped, but emptied himself, taking the form of a servant, being born in the likeness of men." And going on to verse 8, "And being found in human form he humbled himself and became obedient unto death, even death on a cross." And then the exaltation of Christ follows in the next verse through verse 11. And then another great christological passage...

Rod Sawatsky: Why don't you read that; because I think it's central to what we're saying.

Pete Sommer: It really is. I didn't want to take too much time, but it is very important. Philippians 2:9-11, "Therefore God has highly exalted him and bestowed on him the name which is above every name, that at the name of Jesus every knee should bow, in heaven and on earth and under the earth, and every tongue confess that Jesus Christ is Lord, to the glory of God the Father." And then another very important christological passage is Colossians 1, beginning at verse 12—really verse 15 gets into it; I'll read part of that: "...giving thanks to the Father, who has qualified us to share in the inheritance of the saints in light. He has delivered us from the dominion of darkness and transferred us to the kingdom of his beloved Son, in whom we have redemption, the forgiveness of sins. He is the image of the invisible God, the first-born of all creation; for in him all things were created, in heaven and on earth, visible and invisible, whether thrones or dominions or principalities or authorities—all things were created through him and for him. He is before all things, and in him all things hold together. He is the head of the body, the church; he is the beginning, the first-born from the dead, that in everything he might be pre-eminent." I think those passages really speak for themselves.

Paul Eshleman: I would just add a couple of other verses. John 1:18 says, "No one has ever seen God..." John 1:12 says, "But to all who received him, who believed in his name, he gave power to become children of God." And then verse 18 says, "No one has ever seen God; the only Son, who is in the bosom of the Father, he has made him known." So we would say that everything we know about God, basically we know because of Jesus Christ.

Mark Branson: Another focus concerns lordship—Jesus as Lord of the church as well as of the cosmos: His word is powerful, is authoritative; it is the final thing. To take it seriously in His own words: "Every one then who hears these words of mine and does them will be like a wise man who built his house on the rock." (Matthew 7:24) And He talks about the sands and the storm: "And every one who hears these words of mine and does not do them will be like a foolish man who built his house upon the sand; and the rain fell, and the floods came, winds blew and beat against that house, and it fell..." (Matthew 7:26-27) And now through the Scriptures and the church the authority of Jesus' word continues.

Rod Sawatsky: Do all the guests agree with what the other people were saying? I guess it's difficult to disagree when they were reading directly from the Scripture. (laughter)

Virgil Cruz: Just to have some attempt at disagreement, let me say to Paul (Eshleman), I probably would not want to phrase it just the way you did—that everything we know about God we know through Christ.

Paul Eshleman: You are right. We also know Him through personal revelation, through the cosmos, and creation.

Virgil Cruz: And through the Old Testament.

Rod Sawatsky: I wonder if something could have been added about the issue of revelation, which I think contrasts with Unification thought, particularly as to what ultimately is victorious—the victory in the lamb and not in the lion. I think there's some contrast in ideas of the nature of the victor.

Paul Eshleman: We would just say that the nature of the victory was in the sacrifice, not in the re-establishment of the kingdom, at that particular time.

Virgil Cruz: Now there again, I have some difference of

opinion. I think it's a mistake to understand the terminology of "lamb" in the Book of Revelation through the symbolism of Isaiah. Isaiah's lamb was a meek and innocent offering, pure and so forth. Christ, as recorded in the Book of Revelation, is meek and pure, but the lamb of the Old Testament does not do justice to the new and powerful lamb. In the symbolism in the Book of Revelation that lamb has not two horns but seven horns, which would symbolize power, and it's a wild thing to see in other literature of the period. In the testimonies of the twelve patriarchs, I believe in the testimonies of Joseph, there's a story about a vision which the writer had. He saw a virgin, and on the crown of the virgin there was a lamb, and there were many animals there, reptiles, and other ferocious beasts, and they all rushed against the lamb. The lamb overcame them. Now that seems to refer to the life or the symbol of the powerful lamb. So I want to qualify this seeing the lamb of Revelation only as a sacrificial lamb, because I think that's really the might and power of God at work. And that fits in with the other imageries of Christ in the Book of Revelation.

Irving Hexham: A second addition with reference to Christ's kingdom coming. In terms of traditional theology, it would be important to emphasize Christ's role as prophet, priest, and king. His kingship being kingship not simply in the future, but now. Christ is Lord; Christ is Lord of all: Christ is Lord of all areas of life now. I know here some Evangelicals might disagree and simply say Christ saved your soul, but I would want to say very strongly that He doesn't simply save one's soul. The redemption affects every aspect of life, including politics, art and literature, whatever. That is, the gospel must work itself out, throughout the whole of the world. Yet at the same time, even as Christ was the suffering servant in some ways, the church may be called to suffering.

Pete Sommer: Revelation 13:7 where it says the beast will be allowed to make war on the saints to conquer them indicates that the final restoration is ultimately the effort of God, not the effort of man.

Paul Eshleman: There is no doubt that Jesus claimed to be God. In John 10:30, He says, "I and the Father are one." The Jews took up stones to stone him, and he said, "For which works do you stone me?" and they said, "It is not for a good work that we stone you but for blasphemy; because you, being a man, make yourself God." There's no doubt that He was saying, "I and the Father are the same. When you've seen me you've seen the Father." I think one of the things that really concerns us is to hear you, or the Moonies, suggest that Rev. Moon is the Lord of the Second Advent. That flies right in the face of Matthew 24:4-5, 23-24, where Christ says, "...Take heed that no one leads you astray. For many will come in my name, saying, 'I am the Christ,' and they will lead many astray...Then if anyone says to you,'Lo, here is the Christ' or 'There he is,' do not believe it. For false Christs and false prophets will arise and show great signs and wonders so as to lead astray, if possible, even the elect." Well, we would say that Rev. Moon's being proclaimed the Lord of the Second Advent is simply fulfulling what Christ said.

Rod Sawatsky: Well, that sets us up very nicely. Now let's switch sides for a moment. I gather several of you are prepared to say something about the Unification view of christology. I wonder, though, if somebody needs to say something about creation, fall, and restoration, since I don't think your christology is going to make too much sense if we aren't all aware of what those initial doctrines are all about.

Tirza Shilgi: One of the first or fundamental principles of the Divine Principle is that through observing creation you can understand the nature of God. Then it goes down the line and tries to categorize phenomena in nature including man. One of the very first principles it points out is that everything in creation can be divided into two basic sets of dualities. The first set of dual characteristics is subjectivity and objectivity, or positivity and negativity, which are complete opposites. For example, you see male and female, stamen and pistil, and so forth. When we say positive and negative, we don't mean in terms of value, but rather in terms of their characteristics as complementary units, as in electronics, where positivity and negativity are different yet complementary.

The second kind of categorization we talk about is that of the internal and external manifestation of things, or in the original Korean, *sung sang* and *hyung sang,* but I think internal and external will be sufficient. That would be, for example, seen in the mind and body relationship. Mind is the internal and the body is the external. Internal is invisible, and we also believe that internal is the subject. In other words, it gives the direction. The body is the visible and the responsive. Now if there is oneness in the relations between mind and body, and the body indeed responds to the mind's direction, then there is harmony, action, productivity, purpose, and so forth. An ideal can be fulfilled. If there isn't oneness, then disharmony comes about.

Another major notion in the Divine Principle is "give-and-take." The purpose of the mentioned dualities is to allow give-and-take between them, and this give-and-take action is the source of all existence, growth and multiplication. That explains the dynamics of creation, so all dynamics are based on this polarity. That is why we need male and female. They allow multiplication and growth among all creation. From there comes the ideal: the four-position foundation as a reciprocal base of God's love. For the four-position foundation, an example would be God, (if you want I can show you a diagram), God at the top, man and woman, and man and woman as a unit form a new object, or child. A perfect give-and-take between all of these participants of the four-position foundation establishes a base for God's love, a stable foundation for God's love, and God's love flows between the different points of the four-position foundation.

As the basic purpose for the creation of man, the *Divine Principle* points to the verse from Genesis which we interpret as the "three major blessings," when God told Adam and Eve, "Be fruitful and multiply, and have dominion." The *Divine Principle* explains that "Be fruitful," is one blessing, "multiply," is another, and "have dominion," is the third. To be fruitful is taken as meaning to be fruitful as an individual, to achieve individual perfection. That means, basically, if you achieve a perfect give-and-take with God, and acquire an ability to love unconditionally then you would see things from God's point of view, would feel things from God's heart and you would be able to relate to people as God does. The second blessing is to multiply; that has to do not with the individual alone, but with individuals in a marriage relationship and in social interaction. To multiply means to establish a family; with this you establish the four-position foundation. And it also relates to all social interaction, so it's not man and God alone, but it's man in more horizontal relationships, man in his family and man in relation to others. And the third major blessing is to have dominion over the creation, but only based on these two previous achievements: an ability to love as God, and to be a true parent. With these kinds of qualifications, God gives you the permission to have dominion over the creation.

That means that at that point you will be able to dominate creation with perfect Godly love and a parental heart. These are the three major blessings that we see as the purpose of man.

A blessing is something that is given to you. However, we talk about a blessing being *fulfilled*. Whether we see the fulfillment of these blessings depends on both God and man. In other words, God can give us the potential to actualize these blessings, but it depends on us whether it is going to be realized in our lives or not. In other words, our bodies grow automatically, but whether our spirits grow is up to us. I can choose whether I want to accept Christ or not. I can choose whether I want to become a true Christian or not. I can choose which way of life I want to follow. So these blessings are available, but whether they become a part of my life, or realized in my life, is up to me. This is my portion of responsibility. This is why we see that the realization of God's ideal and God's own hope and desire, involves both God's responsibility and man's responsibility. And we put it symbolically in percentages: God put 95% into the creation of the world and of ourselves, and we are asked to complete the last 5%; but actually this 5% is our own 100% effort. Our own 100% effort compared to God's investment is like 5% and 95%; basically we are required to give 100% of ourselves in order to realize it. With our effort and God's grace together, these blessings will come, and they should be realized in our lives.

The last point in the Principle of Creation that I will mention is the question of the spirit world. Again, as we have a mind and a body, we have a spirit and a body. There is a constant give and take between our spirit and our body. The give and take is such that, by doing things that follow our mind and our ideals according to God's desire, we can gain vitality for our spirit, and in that way our spirit develops. This is why we do need to have a physical body, even though our eternal life is in the spirit world. This is the indispensibility of our physical body. By having a physical body, by investing ourselves in the world by doing good deeds, we create "vitality elements" which come to our spirit and grow and raise our spirit. And there is another element our spirit grows by—the "life element" which comes from God. This would be God's word, God's love, God's atmosphere, or God surrounding us. So basically our spirit grows by these two things—by that which comes from God—His word, love, His atmosphere surrounding us, and by that which comes from us, by investing ourselves, by giving ourselves for others, by serving, by living in God's way.

After we leave our life here on earth, our spirit goes to the spirit world, and in the spirit world are different levels, different realms. Basically, people are going to the level of spirit world which is equal to the level at which they lived their lives here. If they lived a very sinful life or a very selfish life, they will most probably go to a similar level in spirit world, and would be in what we say is a low spirit world, a low realm of spirit world. People who live a spiritually high life, living very close to God's ideal, would exist in spirit world in a higher realm. So the levels of the spirit world are similar to our mental or spiritual level. I think that is sufficient for now.

Rod Sawatsky: Would somebody pick up the fall?

Nora Spurgin: This, of course, is the ideal of God; man is God's creation, a beautiful reflection of God, yet we have to deal with the reality, that is, a man with fallen nature, or sinful nature. The concept of original sin explains how evil came into existence, even though God is a loving God. Where did evil come into existence? According to the *Divine Principle,* we take the story of Adam and Eve in the Bible, the Genesis story, and see it as a story which describes something which happened, the details of which are not all there. We see Adam and Eve, God's children, being created, not as perfect beings, but as potentially perfect beings, people who could have the opportunity to grow to maturity by following God's commandment. On the foundation of that oneness with God, they could establish what Tirza was saying—a family which can multiply God's goodness throughout all of creation and have dominion over creation.

However, we have the story that Adam and Eve, as they were growing, were tempted by the serpent, and ate the fruit. So, we take the story and look at it in terms of all the ramifications that are in the Bible and see Adam and Eve as two beings. There are also several symbolic statements, like the tree of life, and the tree of knowledge of good and evil. If you look at various references throughout the Bible to the tree of life, it could be said that the tree of life actually represents a certain hope, a certain ideal of perfection. I could use a lot of references but I don't want to take the time; I'll just say that we would say that the tree of life represents perfect man. The tree of knowledge of good and evil represents woman. So to eat the fruit of the tree of knowledge of good and evil, we would say, is to have a sexual relationship. I want to mention also the identity of the serpent. We see this as not a literal serpent, but as a being who obviously had a lot of spiritual power, who had the ability to entice; we see this as the archangel Lucifer who was God's servant, the angelic messenger to mankind, and who led Eve astray by enticing her into a relationship with himself. This relationship served to open her sexual awareness prematurely, and as a result of that her eyes were open, she sensed that something new had happened, and she was afraid. She saw that Adam still was in a pure relationship with God, and she desired to come back into that relationship with God, and so she in turn united with Adam. She taught him, or opened up his sexual awareness, and through a sexual relationship then, they united as a couple, and produced children at that point in time. We see that first production of children as being without God's blessing, not that it wasn't intended eventually, but it was without man reaching a point of maturity.

There's so much I'd like to say that it's hard to make a short synopsis. But the basic point was that mankind came into being after Adam and Eve multiplied while immature spiritually, and so the way to the tree of life was closed, until such point that it would again be open. Therefore, all of mankind has been affected; their immaturity has affected our relationships with each other, and even internally, we still fight within ourselves because of something that's not in harmony within ourselves, because our way to the tree of life has been cut off. There are so many things affected.

We believe in the concept of free will. God allowed this to happen. He could have stopped it, but if He had stopped it He would have violated His own principle, because man was created as a co-creator. Man has the responsibility of freedom to develop his spirit. So if God had stopped it at that point, then He would have been treating man as a puppet. And man would have become programmed by God to do certain things. So, we see that God was respecting man's free will in allowing this to happen, and instead, then, began to work to find a way of salvation for mankind, or to prepare a way of salvation for fallen mankind. Is there anything you'd like to add, or anything else? I know I skipped a lot of things, trying to get the essence of it.

Rod Sawatsky: Just continue on into the restoration and the role of Christ. Who's going to pick that up for us?

Patricia Zulkosky: I think that God's providence from the time of the fall was to try to create some kind of foundation or condition of faith whereby He could send His Son as the Messiah to all of mankind. So, in the principles of restoration, we start with Adam and Eve's family. We see how, if Adam and Eve, or more specifically, Cain and Abel had been able to unite with each other instead of continuing to multiply sinful mankind, some kind of condition could have been laid so that God's Son could come right then at the early stages of history and at that point wipe out the suffering of mankind and of God. But we find, just briefly speaking, that the principle of restoration did not work in Adam's family, and was transferred to Noah's family. If Noah's family could get it together, then very clearly the task of restoration would be relatively simple and God could send His Son. But Ham failed to unite with Noah. And finally, as we go through Abraham's family, through Abraham, Isaac, and Jacob there was some kind of "foundation of faith" and "foundation of substance" set up so that God's Son could come. By a foundation of faith I mean that the things that man failed to accomplish in the beginning—such as obedience and pure offering—could be accomplished. By foundation of substance I mean that the things man destroyed at the time of the fall were somehow restored in a symbolic sense. Adam and Eve didn't view things from God's point of view, but were stimulated on a horizontal plane. Through different biblical events, especially the story of Jacob and Esau, unity was restored. (This is a very long section of Principle; it would take a very long time to explain the details. I think that the interpretation of Old Testament history is extremely interesting and would suggest reading that section if you haven't read it so far, because I think you'll find it fascinating.)

It suffices to say that after Adam and Eve left their position as children of God and became sinners, multiplying evil, all of this was somehow symbolically reversed through the course of Abraham, Isaac, and Jacob. So, because the foundation was set up, it cleared the path for Jesus to come. So we look at the Old Testament as a very necessary aspect of God's continuing to work with mankind, whereby a foundation was laid for Jesus' coming. We see that Jesus' coming was not just at an arbitrary point in history, but was based on a foundation that was laid by the central figures in the Old Testament.

Ulrich Tuente: As Patricia just mentioned, the preparation for Jesus Christ to come among the Israelite people started with Abraham, Isaac and Jacob. Besides, we also see that the people of Israel had been prepared through the prophets and through the life of faith centered on the temple. They had been prepared to receive Jesus Christ. I come now to this very crucial question which Dr. Deffner also was asking: Did Jesus Christ come among the Israelite people in order to die?

First of all, in the whole history of the providence, we see that God prepared the Israelite people to receive the Messiah. When the disciples asked Jesus, "What must we do, to be doing the works of God?" Jesus said very simply, "This is the work of God, that you believe in him whom he has sent." And there are many other instances; I think I need only tell you the Bible verses and you will know what I mean. Jesus said, "Oh, Jerusalem, Jerusalem,...How often would I have gathered your children together as a hen gathers her brood under her wings, and you would not. Because you did not know the time of your visitation." So Jesus was trying very, very hard to make the Israelite people believe in Him, and even He knew that they didn't understand Him completely. For instance, once He said to His disciples, "If I have told you earthly things and you do not believe, how can you believe if I tell you heavenly things?" He was very much aware that his disciples couldn't understand Him, and the people of Israel could understand Him even less, but He still called the people of Israel to follow Him completely, to unite with Him completely. He said, "You search the Scriptures, because you think that in them you have eternal life; and it is they that bear witness to me; yet you refuse to come to me that you may have life."

I think there are so many instances where we see in the Bible that Jesus was asking for people to believe in Him because He knew He was sent by God to bring salvation to the Israelite people and that it was His desire to unite the Israelite people with Himself.

Richard Quebedeaux: Spiritually, or...?

Ulrich Tuente: To follow Him, just to follow Him completely. When He called for repentance, He said, "Repent, for the kingdom of heaven is at hand." When He spoke in parables and in the beatitudes, He was asking the Israelite people to change their lives and to follow Him.

In the Garden of Gethsemene, Jesus said, "My Father, if it

be possible, let this cup pass from me; nevertheless, not as I will, but as thou wilt." I think the traditional interpretation is that this revealed some kind of human weakness in Jesus, that He feared the suffering He would go through on the cross. But Jesus Christ was definitely not less than other human beings. Many of the martyrs in the Roman Empire, in Asia Minor and Greece have easily gone the way of suffering. They went to the arena of the lions, went to the death of crucifixion, and knew that when they would be dying for God, for Jesus Christ, it was no problem for them at all.

But we think that Jesus anticipated a different course for the people of Israel. Jesus knew that there was originally something different planned by God, because as we see in the Old Testament, there are two prophetic traditions. There is one prophecy about the suffering servant which Dr. Cruz just mentioned and Mark was reading these verses from Isaiah 53. But we see another emphasis in the Old Testament, that of a glorious messiah. Many now see this emphasis as something which Jesus Christ meant only spiritually and not physically. But I think this is the issue: God created both spirit and body. As Tirza said this duality is a unity, so salvation and restoration is something that should take place both spiritually and physically, and God wanted to work with the Israelite people centered on Jesus Christ to accomplish complete restoration. So that God gave these two kinds of prophecies, both of which are actually a victory. Therefore I think it's very wrong to say, and many times it has been said that Moonies believe that Jesus failed His mission. I think this is very wrong, because actually both prophecies indicate a victory. Through the way that Jesus Christ has gone, He has accomplished a victory over death, because He was resurrected, He established a personal community at Pentecost, and we received the whole Christian tradition. No other religion has spread from such a small country all over the entire world. I think that there are many indications that there is a victory, but what would have happened if the people of Israel had responded to Jesus Christ and understood Him immediately?

A last thing, which I want to emphasize as strongly as possible, concerns a reason for the misunderstanding of the Israelite people. I think the way Jesus was preaching was misunderstood. For instance, He said He had authority to forgive sins, when, according to the Israelites, forgiveness came through the

Law. Only the Law was actually the channel for forgiving sins, according to the Israelites. Or, when He said to His disciples, "He who loves father or mother more than me is not worthy of me; and he who loves son or daughter more than me is not worthy of me," Jesus seemed to be the destroyer of morality.

Jesus also seemed to be blaspheming against God, saying, "...How can you say, 'Show us the Father?' Do you not believe that I am in the Father and the Father in me?" So all the things that Jesus did appeared very, very dubious to the Jewish people.

On the other side, John the Baptist, whom we know was to prepare the way for Jesus Christ, was a highly respected figure. For instance, at the time that he was born, there were many miraculous signs. I think you all know the story that John's father became dumb, when he doubted that his wife ever would bear a child. Then afterwards John was leading an ascetic life, and encouraging the people to repent for the kingdom of heaven. John was very well recognized. Now, in one instance, priests and Levites came up to John (John 1:19-21) and asked him, "Who are you?" and John said, "I am not the Christ." Another question was, "Are you Elijah?" and John the Baptist denied he was Elijah. And also when he was asked, "Are you the prophet?" he said, "No." So John the Baptist denied that he was Elijah, but we know from Malachi that in one of the last prophecies, actually, one of the last verses of the Old Testament, the coming of Elijah was announced: (Malachi 4:5) "Behold, I will send you Elijah..." The Jewish people were anticipating the coming of Elijah before the coming of Christ, before the coming of the Messiah. So John the Baptist denied that he was Elijah, but in two instances Jesus affirmed that actually John the Baptist was Elijah. I think one is Matthew 17:10-11 where the disciples asked Him, "Then why do the scribes say that first Elijah must come?" and Jesus answered them, "'Elijah does come, and he is to restore all things; but I tell you that Elijah has already come, and they did not know him...' Then the disciples understood that he was speaking to them of John the Baptist." In another instance, Matthew 11:14, it says that Jesus said very explicitly, "...and if you are willing to accept it, he is Elijah who is to come."

So then, there are two statements, one from Jesus who says John the Baptist is Elijah, and the other from John the Baptist who denies being Elijah. And we see what kind of position Jesus had in Jewish society and what kind of position John the Baptist had. I think it is clear who was more trustworthy, who was accepted more. We see this as one of the major reasons, or one of the important reasons that Jesus was not accepted by the Israelite people. Because the prophecy had not been fulfilled, Elijah had not yet come, Jesus was seen as a blasphemer. Jewish people were even willing to release Barabbas rather than Jesus from the court. I don't know if anyone else wants to add something, but I think that's basically it.

Johnny Sonneborn: According to the *Divine Principle,* Jesus is the man towards whom all post-lapsarian history pointed, for whom God and man prepared in that history, who was prophesied in olden times. Jesus is the fruit of that history, especially Israelite history, and He came on that foundation, to consummate it. Jesus is God in the flesh, the first-begotten Son of God, so that finally God Himself, the Creator, the Father, could be seen through seeing the Son, Jesus Christ. Jesus is the perfect man, uniquely conceived and born without the original sin and destined to be the King of Kings who took responsibility for the sins of the world. He ransomed us by His blood on the cross. Jesus is the Lord, the head of the Church, king in His spiritual kingdom, our Saviour, who was raised from the dead to the right hand of God, the Father of Christians, bestowing with the Holy Spirit rebirth and new life to those who receive Him in faith, and being the necessary and irreplaceable mediator for the adoption into sonhood of those who have been the children of Satan, the children of Satan's children.

Jesus is the central figure, who, with the Holy Spirit, took responsibility for the divine providence of restoration, who has actively been directing His family, His body, His subject, His attenders, Christians, in carrying out the providence of the New Testament age, and entering into and participating in the providence of the new age. Jesus is the judge whose word of love is to judge all in the last days, and to slay evil.

Moving beyond the *Divine Principle,* Jesus, because of the preceding, is the one who personally initiated the providence of the new age, (He appeared to Sun Myung Moon) and who directly and continually participates in the unfolding providence. According to Sun Myung Moon, "Jesus has absolute power to resurrect everyone and everything." We believe that God has in these Last Days sent Christ on earth, and that Christ stands on earth as a man with a new name (as prophesied in the Book of

Revelation), that is, a person distinct from the man Jesus, intelligible only through Jesus. We believe that God has destined us to find and be with that person, and attend him in the completing of the providence of restoration. We do not believe that Jesus will "physically" come on literal clouds, and physically walk the earth again—we think that is not necessary.

It is not clear to me Jesus' exact role in the final providence. But since I trust the Father, the Son Jesus, and the Holy Spirit, and trust all the saints on earth whom the Father has raised up to be responsible for the new age, I'm curious but not worried about relationships among them—after all, they know the truth. We just take this from Divine Principle and then beyond that.

Virgil Cruz: Could I ask just one question? Did you say that Jesus was God, Himself?

Johnny Sonneborn: Jesus is God in the flesh. The quotation was not "Jesus was God Himself, the Father" but "Jesus was God in the flesh, the first begotten Son of God, so that finally God Himself, the Creator, God the Father, could be seen through seeing the Son, Jesus Christ." The Son is not the Father.

Virgil Cruz: Does He partake of the divine essence in any way?

Johnny Sonneborn: Divine essence is not discussed this way in Unification theology.

Virgil Cruz: I don't quite understand what "God in the flesh" is.

Anthony Guerra: Well, first of all, you don't find the concept of essence in the Bible, either. It is a Greek category, a Greek philosophical category. The way the Principle gets at the concept of how Jesus is related to God is as heart and love, to use the central categories of Unification thought. That is, there's a complete oneness of feeling between God and Jesus and also there's a complete oneness of will between God and Jesus, and therefore in their activity.

Virgil Cruz: Could that oneness be duplicated by me, if I am totally submitted to the will of God?

Anthony Guerra: No. You'd have to submit totally to the will of Jesus. You could only establish this relationship through Jesus; that is, Jesus is not only first in a temporal sense, but also in a salvific or a valuational sense. Jesus is without sin, and all humanity is born with the propensity to sin. So we can only reconnect with God through Jesus Christ, through the salvation

He offers.

Virgil Cruz: But no one else could ever approximate that position?

Anthony Guerra: By receiving the salvation of Jesus Christ, one could establish a relationship of love which is unique, that is different from Jesus because we're all unique. But nevertheless it could be a full relationship with God. So that you would be completely united with the heart of God and with the will and activity of God, in that sense equal to Jesus' relationship to God, but also unique. Is that clear to you?

Virgil Cruz: We'll come back to it.

Rod Sawatsky: I think I'd like to ask two more questions of the Unificationists before we open the discussion. One is, I don't think it's been clarified to the Evangelicals which prophecy Jesus didn't quite fulfill. If you don't want to talk about it as a failure, let's not, but that other side that was not fulfilled, we need to have that clarified. Then I would like somebody else to say a little more than Johnny did about Rev. Moon particularly.

Ulrich Tuente: Tirza has already covered the three blessings. Jesus came to fulfill the original ideal which God had destined for Adam. For instance, I don't know where I read this in Paul, but it says in one place, "If, because of one man's trespass, death reigned through that one man, much more will those who receive the abundance of grace and the free gift of righteousness reign in life through the one man Jesus Christ." So St. Paul has this concept of restoration. Through one man comes sin; therefore, through one man sin is overcome and man is restored to the original position.

The question then is what is the physical kingdom like? I think it's the realization of the three blessings on the individual level, family level, even up to the national level. Jesus not only wanted to establish the spiritual kingdom and spiritual salvation, He also wanted to establish physically and socially, God's kingdom and God's ideal in this world. Is this enough?

Rod Sawatsky: Keep on going. How is that to be done? In what way didn't the physical kingdom come? Was there a missing of the mark in Jesus' time? It didn't come in the first century, did it? Why not?

Ulrich Tuente: It didn't come, because Jesus was crucified at thirty-three years.

Anthony Guerra: The prophecies we're referring to we see

in Isaiah 9, where it says that Jesus will come as King of Kings, Prince of Peace, Mighty Counselor, etc., and it's these we interpret literally in the same way that the suffering servant is interpreted literally. Jesus was to establish the reign of peace. He would not have been a temporal ruler. He didn't want to become a king of any particular realm, not even king of the entire world in a political sense. Rather, He wanted to give spiritual direction to the rulers of nations such that they would receive the word of God and abide by it. Sovereignties and principalities of the world would then come under the sovereignty of God, the sovereignty of God's will, and there would be a completion of political, economic, cultural restoration, as well as spiritual restoration. But this is something which obviously we have not achieved to this day. This has become a vital category for discussion not only in Unification thought but in most contemporary theologies, which we believe are in accord with the providence of the age.

Ulrich Tuente: Originally in the creation, God created man in His image, male and female, He created them. I think it is the mission of Jesus to manifest God's ideal, but Jesus was male. We think that God is beyond human nature; God is beyond male and female, but both male and female are part of God. Did I make this at all clear? God is not somehow male and female, (I don't know how to say it in English) but He contains within Himself masculinity and femininity. So we believe that Jesus, if He had completed the restoration, would have established a marriage, would have established a family. This family as a nucleus, could have manifested all ideal relationships between husband and wife, parents and children, and would have been carried on further from the family level, to the national level, world-wide level, and would have set an example of what God wants to see realized, not only for the justificaton of the individual person but also for the proper relationship in the social realm. As Nora explained, the fall involved not only individuals, but also relationships, the distortion of relationships. Jesus came not only to justify the individual person before God, but also to restore relationships among people before God. In this way the kingdom of heaven was to be established.

Rod Sawatsky: I think we're ready for the Lord of the Second Advent now. Are you going to tell us about the Lord of the Second Advent, Whitney?

Whitney Shiner: I'll try to explain the necessity for the

mission of the Lord of the Second Advent, as well as his relationship to Jesus. We see Jesus in the role of the second Adam. I don't think our idea of perfected man has been clarified exactly. Perfected man, according to the principle of creation, is an ontological unit with God. We say that the relationship between God and perfected man is like that between mind and body. So, in fact, all perfected men, according to the original ideal of creation, can say that "I am in the Father and the Father is in me." What we receive from Jesus are spiritual salvation, justification, and a certain amount of sanctification. But still man has original sin. The reason that original sin is not removed by Jesus, we believe, is that restoration occurs through reversing the process of the fall. (I think the process of indemnity hasn't been explained very clearly either.) So, since the process of the fall involved family relationships—we can look at the fall as setting up a family that is centered on Satan rather than on God—in order to remove original sin, one of the conditions is the creation of a family centered on God's will. Before original sin is removed, no man can grow to perfection. So even Christians, with the salvation they have, can't grow to perfection, that is, to ontological oneness with God, complete moral oneness with God, oneness with heart and will that Adam and Eve should have had. So, in that sense, Jesus is unique up to this time, but the Lord of the Second Advent, the third Adam, is to complete the process that was not completed at the time of Jesus.

God keeps sending sinless men to become His sons, to be in the position of Adam, to set up the kingdom of God which is to fulfill the blessings which God gave to mankind in the beginning, but which were not fulfilled because of the fall. These are perfected individuality, perfected families and perfected creation. These have to be set up with the physical body. Therefore, the Lord of the Second Advent must come as a man to set up the perfected family. In order to set it up, there have to be certain spiritual conditions involving people uniting with the messiah. Once the perfected family is set up through the messiah, then God can allow the same for fallen men. Actually, in a sense, the messiah is both Adam and Eve, for only through them can there be the establishment of justified families. At that time, original sin can be forgiven and it will be possible for man to grow to perfection and complete sanctification.

Paul Eshleman: Just to clear up a fine point. What sin did

Christ then forgive? If His death on the cross is necessary for spiritual life, but He did not forgive original sin, what does His death on the cross mean?

Whitney Shiner: I think forgiveness of all other sin, personal, collective and ancestral sin.

Anthony Guerra: That's not right. Original sin is forgiven.

Warren Lewis: Isn't there a difference between "forgiveness" and "removal."?

Anthony Guerra: Right, justification and sanctification.

Whitney Shiner: That's right. There is a distinction. We say that when Jesus said He would come again, that He was talking about the mission. It's like saying Elijah will come again, and yet Elijah does not come again, but John the Baptist comes in the role of Elijah. So the third Adam is in the role of Jesus. They have oneness of mission, just as Abraham, Isaac, and Jacob had similar oneness.

Jonathan Wells: Can I comment about a Scriptural verse that was mentioned earlier? Acts 1:11. There are two divergent interpretations of that. One, which Virgil gave, emphasizes this *same* Jesus. Another way to read it, and the way it is read in *The Divine Principle Study Guide,** is that when the disciples are looking into the sky and the angels say to them, "Why are you looking into the sky?" the clear indication is that they are looking in the wrong direction and that Christ "will return in the same way you saw him go into heaven." And the Divine Principle interprets that to mean that the sky is the wrong place, that the Lord of the Second Advent comes in the same manner as Jesus came, which is to be born and to grow up as a human being and lead men to salvation here on earth.

Anthony Guerra: Isn't there a Scriptural passage in Revelations that says He's born of a woman?

Jonathan Wells: With a new name.

Anthony Guerra: Yes. With a new name.

Irving Hexham: Could we hear some more about the Lord of the Second Advent? What do you understand? Who or what is the Lord of the Second Advent?

Jonathan Wells: Well, according to Principle, the kingdom of heaven is the fulfillment of the three blessings, so the purpose of the messiah is to fulfill the three blessings and to accomplish

---

**The Divine Principle Study Guide,* New York, N.Y.: The Holy Spirit Association for the Unification of World Christianity, 1973-75. 2 volumes.

the kingdom of heaven on earth as well as in the spirit world, just as Adam and Eve should have done if they hadn't fallen. And just as Jesus was on His way to doing when He was murdered.

Many, but not all, members of the Unification church, consider Sun Myung Moon the Lord of the Second Advent. I'm not sure it's fruitful to debate whether he is or isn't, but there are passages in the *Divine Principle* that try to show that the second coming will occur in the Far East, and specifically, Korea. There are those of us who view those passages with varying degrees of skepticism. I mean, the hermeneutical aspects of them.

Rod Sawatsky: Do you believe it?

Jonathan Wells: Well, do I believe in those passages?

Rod Sawatsky: No, do you believe that...

Jonathan Wells: That Sun Myung Moon is the Lord of the Second Advent? I think there's a good possibility, and I'm giving you my honest answer.

Rod Sawatsky: Why do you say it's a good possibility? I think that's an important category that you're using that needs to be explained.

Jonathan Wells: Let me emphasize that you could ask anyone in this room and you'd get slightly different answers, so I'm not claiming this for the whole membership of the church. I think the ultimate answer is only going to come through history, but my own reasons are these: First of all, I'm convinced that we are in the last days, for a whole lot of reasons, among which is the fact that the human race may be destroyed very shortly if something doesn't happen. Second of all, as I look at history and the Bible, everything seems to point towards this time, the time that we're living in. When I read the Bible, when I pray and when I look at the world situation, it seems very logical and very much like God's way for Christ to come again as a man. The question is, what man? I don't think it's necessary that Jesus comes down from the sky on a cloud. In fact, I fail to see how that would solve the problem. Instead, I see us as being in the position to restore the failure of the human race 2,000 years ago.

In other words, when Jesus comes again, or when Christ comes again, I expect to be confronted with the same dilemma that the Jews were confronted with 2,000 years ago. It is not going to be some dramatic celestial event that cannot be denied. It's going to be something much more difficult than that. Just as those in the first century were expected to trust a carpenter from a poverty-stricken family, who appeared in the eyes of everybody to be a blasphemer, and a disreputable character, so our challenge is going to be to find the man who is most united with God's will, regardless of the worldly trappings that he comes with. And I see it as just the way God would work for that man to be an oriental. For one thing, this man has to unite all the races of the earth, and frankly, I don't think a white man could do it. I don't think a Jew could do it at this point. So I like the idea of an oriental man being the messiah. You can take that seriously or not, it's up to you. I think Rev. Moon might be the messiah because I've worked with him, and I've grown to know him and I trust him, and I've come to him from a very skeptical standpoint, looking for things to find wrong: such as hypocrisy, failings, egotism, selfishness. I know some of the things he says are taken out of context to make him appear that way, but my own experience of him is quite the contrary. So that's the best I can do. The Bible, prayer life, history, personal contact with the man, I'm not quite sure what else I can add to that.

Irving Hexham: You're saying the Lord of the Second Advent is a man. In the *Divine Principle* some questions of interpretation are raised about the Scripture, who Elijah was, and so forth. Could the Lord of the Second Advent be other than a man? Could the Lord of the Second Advent be the Divine Principle? Or could the Divine Principle be identified as a man? Or could the Divine Principle or the Lord of the Second Advent be the community which comes into existence through the Divine Principle?

Rod Sawatsky: Maybe Jan can speak first. Let him add a little bit.

Jan Weido: I'm going to step out of the Moonie bag, put on an evangelical mask and act as an advisor. The Lord of the Second Advent is not the Divine Principle. We believe that the messiah is one that you're grafted onto. You're part of that family. It has to be a man and a woman, and a family has to be set up as the basis. The messiah has to be a real person. It can't be a community of people, because we're all sinners. O.K.? Does that answer your question? Maybe this will get at it another way: if I were an Evangelical sitting here, I would ask the Moonies, "If Jesus didn't bring full salvation, then does Rev. Moon have the power to remove original sin? Has that been set up, or is it happening? How does the Unification church bring a higher salvation or sufficient or complete salvation?"

Irving Hexham: Good question, but can we get back to my question with your permission? You seem to be using the model of the family, of the western nuclear family. Now...

Jan Weido: It's Confucian. Rev. Moon is Confucian.

Irving Hexham: Confucian families were far more extended.

Jan Weido: That's true. God is also a grandfather. (laughter)

Irving Hexham: We're all related, yes, that's it, good point, but with two individuals, then you're individualizing. You say you've got this one family, and when you talk about this one family you're not talking about Confucius. I mean, you're talking about a man and a woman who are the basis of the nuclear family in the Western sense.

Rod Sawatsky: Let's not dispute it. Let's just leave it at that point for now. Can we leave it there?

Irving Hexham: Yes, but I'm wondering what goes with that.

Warren Lewis: Are you? Adam and Eve are the head of the race. If they had not fallen, their nuclear family would have been the nucleus of a divine race; but they fell. Jesus should have found His perfect bride and restored that Edenic situation, but He was crucified untimely. Now, the Lord of the Second Advent, who is the third Adam, with his second Eve and their nuclear family are the nucleus of this extended family. The vision is of a single Adamic family extended throughout the entire world.

Anthony Guerra: It's the kingdom of God.

Richard Quebedeaux: Nobody mentioned the fact that your understanding of the messiah is more Jewish than Christian. It's a messianic age, and we as Evangelicals are coming with a more traditionally Christian understanding of a focus on a person, and although you may focus on Rev. Moon, it's much larger than Rev. Moon, and I think that's why the position of Rev. Moon is somewhat up in the air, because the focus is the age, the messianic age, rather than the person.

Anthony Guerra: In terms of whether the Divine Principle is a person or a book, I think we see the *Divine Principle* book as an expression of the Divine Principle. Divine Principle is in a sense the ideal of God, the Logos which we say is God's original ideal which is the pattern of the entire cosmos. The most perfect expression of this ideal would be the perfect man and woman. In other words, the fullest manifestation of God would be in the persons of a male and a female, and the whole cosmos was patterned after that model. The first Adam didn't fulfill on the individual level the perfection of the masculine logos. Divine Principle is most fully embodied, not in the book, but in the individual man and the individual woman who are fully united with God. That's the most perfect expression that one will find of the Divine Principle. The Divine Principle would in a sense be an autobiography or a biography of the person who is united with the will of God.

Irving Hexham: Is this person reflected in a communal person? Does the person represent the community? Is it a cosmic person?

Anthony Guerra: No, it is an individual; however, this individual has the mission to create a true family. The Lord of the Second Advent has been commissioned to fulfill the second and third blessings on earth. Therefore, people uniting with the Lord of the Second Advent, unite with Jesus who has the same purpose as God.

Dan Davies: I think of the messiah in terms of a community. Yet, it is important to understand how God begins and spreads the messianic community.

God begins at one central point by sending a man, a messiah. The messiah takes a bride and forms a family. The messianic family grafts other families into it and forms the messianic tribe. The messianic concept in Unification theology is a community concept and, in this respect, it is similar to Judaism.

The *Divine Principle* speaks of the community and the nation being restored to God. It was God's intention to restore a nation at the time of Jesus, and it is also His intention to work that way now. Once the nation is restored and becomes a messianic nation, God can graft other nations into His nation and establish the kingdom of God among all nations on the earth.

To summarize: The messianic community starts from one man and develops into a family; families are grafted into the messianic family and this brings about the messianic community on the tribal level. The tribe becomes a nation and works with other nations to establish the kingdom of God over the whole earth.

Tirza Shilgi: I just want to comment on what Richard (Quebedeaux) was saying about the messiah being an age rather than a person. I agree half-heartedly. More than an age, I see the messiah as an office—which means that, if the age is right and the time is right but the qualification of the office is not met, the kingdom cannot come about. We can see what happened in Jesus' time. Even though the time was right and the foundation that was needed was all prepared and the nation was prepared by the proper qualification, the role of the messiah was not fulfilled, the people did not believe. What Ulrich was saying was that Jesus asked the people to believe in and follow Him; but because this qualification was not met, the messianic role, which was to save the people, could not be fulfilled. If the people did not want to be saved, then Jesus, the messiah, could not save the people. So "messiah" implies a certain role and a certain mission to be accomplished, and if this mission is not accomplished then the kingdom obviously is not coming about. Therefore, it ties in with what Jonathan was saying: History will prove whether Rev. Moon was or was not the messiah; and that will be decided if those qualifications of saving the world or laying the conditions to save the world, are met or not.

Jonathan Wells: I just want to make sure that the impression has not been given that we feel Jesus failed. Jesus fulfilled the qualifications of the messianic office. The salvation Jesus offered was complete salvation. The failure 2,000 years ago was not with Jesus; the failure was with us, the sinful people who failed to accept Jesus. I just want to clarify that.

Anthony Guerra: I think it's really critical what you're saying. The reason the Lord of the Second Advent has to come on the earth is not to correct a failure of Jesus but rather to complete in a sense the mission of Jesus. It is to give humanity the opportunity, the chance to restore its past failure. It is mankind who failed to fulfill its portion of the responsibility.

Jonathan Wells: I'd like to speak to the notion that there had to be the requirement of Jesus' death for the forgiveness of sins, and I would like to use Scripture. Before Jesus died, He said, "Your sins are forgiven," and in Matthew 9:2 it says, "And behold, they brought to him a paralytic, lying on his bed; and when Jesus saw their faith he said to the paralytic, 'Take heart, my son; your sins are forgiven.'" And two other places in the Bible it is written that Jesus forgives sins, before He died. So I think that there is biblical evidence that Jesus had forgiven sins before His death. It wasn't necessary that He die.

Pete Sommer: I misunderstand your eschaton—the prophecies of the messiah in the Old Testament imply immortality, e.g., He shall reign forever and ever. From the yellow book* I gather, though, that some day Moon is going to die. Do you then envision a Second Advent with an absent Lord of the Second Advent?

Dan Davies: Can I answer that? I look at him as a door opener; that is, he is opening the way for mankind. The Lord of the Second Advent will give man the means to establish the kingdom of God on the earth and then will no longer be needed. What he has to offer will be passed on to mankind.

Pete Sommer: So how will he reign after his death?

Dan Davies: He will be in the spiritual world at that time. The office will have been fulfilled. What he will have done will always be recognized—the mission he will have accomplished of opening the door for mankind to establish the kingdom of God. He can open the door, but then it is up to us to go through it.

Pete Sommer: So you do see in the second advent and in the messianic age that physical death continues to occur, and that it will forever.

Dan Davies: Yes. Right.

Pete Sommer: So in that sense, we would not have salvation from the physical experience of death?

Dan Davies: Yes. Right.

Pete Sommer: Is it Eastern and cyclical? Hit me if I am wrong.

Jonathan Wells: You die physically, but you live forever in the spiritual world.

Pete Sommer: This duality, then, is perpetuated in physical and spiritual worlds?

Ulrich Tuente: I have the feeling that you point to one place in Revelation when John said that there would be no more death. Is that right?

Pete Sommer: Yes.

Ulrich Tuente: I think the understanding of Divine Principle is that man exists both as a spiritual being and as a physical being. In Acts 2 it says—if I'm not wrong—that people will have visions and dreams, old men will have dreams and sons and daughters shall prophesy; so man's spirituality, man's ability to perceive spiritual phenomena becomes more and more developed as a

---

*Reference is to *Exploring Unification Theology,* M. Darrol Bryant and Susan Hodges, eds. New York, N. Y.: Distributed by the Rose of Sharon Press, 1978.

sign of the spiritual growth, prophesied for the last days. And then man, whether he is in the body, or whether he lives already in the spirit world, the more he spiritually advances, the more he is able to come into communication with those people who already have died. Because he is aware of the spiritual world, he is more aware, not only of how to dominate the physical world, but also of how to dominate the spiritual world, to communicate with the spiritual world. This is one of the signs of spiritual growth which indicates that the separation which comes through death will not be any more, because man can overcome the separation. So physical death does not mean any more the same thing that it meant before, when man was not aware of the spiritual world and did not know anything about it.

Pete Sommer: Then what is the continued function of physical existence in the messianic age?

Ulrich Tuente: This is what Tirza explained when discussing this physical life. To use an analogy, I would say that a tree grows on the foundation of the earth. It takes nourishment from the earth and also from the air and the sun to produce the fruit. Then in the very same way, man, in his physical life, develops not only his physical dominion but even his spiritual perception of things. This is the soil on which he develops his spirit. Physical death has nothing to do with the fall—the body is no longer needed. Man's spirit will continue to live in eternity.

Patricia Zulkosky: I would say that before the fall of man there were to be three great celebrations in man's life: first would be his birth into the physical world, whereby he could share in the creation of God; the second celebration would be his marriage, the second blessing. The purpose of the physical body is really to be married and have children, and in this way to share in the creativity of God. I mean, God is the creator of man, then man is the visible manifestation of God, and could be considered in the position of God to His children. So in that sense parenting intensifies our relationship to God and our experience of a feeling shared with God.

Irving Hexham: I have a question of qualification. When children are born, are they born physical, but with a spirituality? Does the physical create the spiritual, or is the spiritual implanted by God at birth?

Patricia Zulkosky: I think we would say the spirit is created by God at birth. I've heard different opinions on that. I don't think there's a dogmatic statement on this, but the spirit has its beginning point at the same time as the physical body. Then the spirit lives eternally thereafter, which brings us to the third great celebration in man's life, which would, of course, be death. So going from the physical world, having had the experience of marriage and child-bearing and raising and having the joy of receiving love from children, a joy such as God would experience in a love relationship with man, then we would go into the spiritual world where we would dwell eternally with God.

Pete Sommer: So that experience is your chance to participate in the divine nature.

Patricia Zulkosky: You mean our physical life?

Pete Sommer: ...marriage, family, and the male-female experience, which is inherent in the nature of God, which cannot occur in the spirit world.

Patricia Zulkosky: Yes. You can't have children in the spirit world. You have to be physical...

Pete Sommer: So the goal is a population boom in heaven. (laughter)

Patricia Zulkosky: Something like that.

Dan Davies: There's lots of room.

Patricia Zulkosky: I guess my favorite analogy of the kingdom of heaven is a ball of love. You have God, man, and woman and through the give and take of man and woman centered on God, they create a child, so there are four positions and there's a dynamic relationship between God and man and God and woman and man and woman and God and child and if you mapped them all out there are twelve relationships. When you start putting them in motion and set your imagination spinning it comes out to be a ball. Then, this ball from Adam and Eve in the very beginning is very small, but as they have more children it grows and it expands and it expands. So the kingdom of heaven is, in a sense, a ball of love. That would be inclusive of all mankind, and even though children would not be born perfect—they'd be born without sin and they would have to grow to maturity. But having lived in the sphere of this kind of love, they could never really step out of it. Or if they did step out of it, the lack of this love would be so obvious that they'd come dashing right back into it, with extremely repentant hearts. Therefore once the ball of love was set in motion, it could never be the same.

Irving Hexham: To go back to Pete's initial question about the messiah, and Jesus' failing, the prophecies for the messiah were that He would be Lord of Lords, King of Kings forever on earth. Here you have a messiah that does not die. But Jesus didn't live forever with a physical body.

Patricia Zulkosky: The question is what are life and death. There are physical life and death and there are also spiritual life and death. So if man was originally created to be born and to die then literal death could not be the result of the fall of man. But if by the fall of man there came a spiritual death, meaning we fell out of God's grace and away from God's love, then when you say that Jesus had eternal life, that He never died, it means that He was born in the love of God; He became perfect, fulfilled this relationship, and eternally it can never end. It is spiritual life that has no end. He never leaves the realm of God's love.

Irving Hexham: Isn't that then spiritualizing prophecies about Jesus' first coming? You're taking parts of the prophecies and then spiritualizing them.

Patricia Zulkosky: Well, the whole question of life and death comes up so many times, and we know that Jesus, Himself, for instance, talked about death in different senses. When He said, "Let the dead bury their dead," He didn't mean literally dead people should bury literally dead people. It doesn't make any sense. He meant the people who could not understand God's will should go out and bury the people who died, but those who understood God's will, who had the possibility for life should not bother themselves with this trivial thing. So if you go back and you think over and reread the whole thing from the point of view of spiritual life and death, rather than literal physical life and death, then it comes out a cohesive understanding, I think.

Irving Hexham: Where, then, did Jesus fail except in that He didn't marry, and where in Scripture do you find that He should have married? Can you give anything on that?

Patricia Zulkosky: Well, I can say that Jesus spoke many, many times of being a bridegroom and we thought that they were parables. Even changing the water into wine, Jesus said to His mother, "O woman, what have you to do with me? My hour has not yet come." Some would interpret it as being, "My time hasn't come yet for my marriage—don't get me involved in these kinds of things." But there are many passages where He talks about the parable of the bridegroom, or the wedding feast, that get interpreted symbolically, but mightn't they also be interpreted literally, that Jesus did in fact come to take a bride and was referring to the time of His own banquet, His own wedding feast? It's a possibility. All we can do, really, is raise these possibilities and these questions, and then you can sit down and read the New Testament again and think about plugging in spiritual life and spiritual death, think about plugging in the possibility that Jesus came to get married and to begin this kind of sinless family, and to actually achieve in His lifetime, the kingdom that He proclaimed. It's a possibility—you have to sit down and read it.

Paul Eshleman: I have a small question. What do you do with Matthew 24:25-29, when it states that we won't know exactly when he comes? It says there, "Lo, I have told you beforehand. So if they say to you, 'Lo, he is in the inner rooms,' do not believe it. For as the lightning comes from the east and shines as far as the west, so will be the coming of the Son of Man.... Immediately after the tribulation of those days the sun will be darkened, and the moon will not give its light, and the stars will fall from heaven, and the powers of the heavens will be shaken." It will seem that we will have some evidence that He is coming. That's my first question.

Jonathan Wells: What was the question at the end of your comment there?

Paul Eshleman: My comment is that you said, "I'm not sure that Sun Moon is the messiah or not, because we will just have to wait and see." I'm saying that you'll know dramatically when the messiah comes because stars are going to fall out of the sky. It will be pretty evident. The moon won't give light and the sun will be darkened, the sign of the Son of Man will come on the clouds in the sky with power and great glory. The angels with the great trumpet will gather together the elect with the four winds...So that's question number one.

Question number two is, what is your Scriptural justification for your interpretation of, "Let this cup pass from me"? You say He was hoping rather that He would have a chance to be married. I firmly believe that He was looking toward the time when God would turn His back on Him, and He would cry out, "My God, my God, why has Thou forsaken me?" He was looking ahead toward that time, and that's why He did not want to go through with it.

The third thing is, if He was looking to establish His kingdom, then when He met with Pilate and Pilate began to talk to Him, why did He say, "My kingdom is not of this world"? If my kingdom were of this world then all of my followers would come out to fight for me—to paraphrase. I have all these problems plus the ones of the interpretation of the sexual fall, and the need to bring man back to God through another family re-enacting what should have been enacted in the first place.

Joseph Hopkins: May I go back to Acts 1:11 and point out that Jonathan's interpretation does violence to the text as I read it: "Men of Galilee, why do you stand looking into heaven? This Jesus, who was taken up from you into heaven, will come the same way as you saw him go into heaven."

Warren Lewis: That's the point. It doesn't say that "the Christ" will come, but that "this Jesus" will arrive.

Jonathan Wells: . . . it also says Elijah will come.

Warren Lewis: The Unificationist point is that "Christ" comes again, but Jesus stays in the spirit world all along.

Rod Sawatsky: Let's go on to another one or two questions and then we can get a bundle of answers.

Mark Branson: I really didn't make my main point and I'd like to just make this comment. It seems to me that in this discussion, the Evangelicals are talking from the assumption of final revelation in Scripture, whereas the Unification people are talking from the assumption of continuing revelation through the interpretations and new insights of Rev. Moon. And it seems to me what we have here is something that's very similar to Mary Baker Eddy's *Key to the Scriptures.* You have here somebody who has come along, a latter day prophet with the key to proper Scripture interpretation, so we have all these allegorical explanations of things that traditionally have not been so interpreted. Plus you have something like Joseph Smith's special revelation which is the basis for the theology of the Church of Jesus Christ of the Latter Day Saints. This is the way it strikes me. And so, it seems to me, we're talking in two different circles here and never the twain shall meet because it gets back to the fundamental issue of authority.

Rod Sawatsky: I think that may be right. What I'm concerned with here, primarily, is that we all understand exactly what is being said. The interpretation, and then the question of the basis for that interpretation are, I think, separate questions. First, we want to simply understand what is being said.

Mark Branson: A couple of things. On the Elijah statement, no one has dealt with the transfiguration as fulfillment. Secondly, in Mark 4:13, there's another place where this whole dramatic second coming and Jesus coming in the clouds is predicted by Jesus, Himself. I won't take time to read that but it's a very powerful one and very dramatic.

Now a couple of questions: one is in the creation of the new family. In the Unification church, do I understand it that the children, in receiving the Lord of the Second Advent's blessing and receiving the Father's blessing, are receiving one that is spiritual and not physical? How is it physical when it is only non-material? Secondly, are those families and the offspring of those families any less evil? Are they more obedient? Is that then the establishment of a perfect family, a perfect kingdom? Do we find this in practice? Is this a reality within the church?

Rod Sawatsky: Now we had a set of questions over here. This last one was a matter of different interpretations. For the moment, we're still trying to get clarification of what Unificationists are saying, so I'd like to have these questions addressed. Do you want to toss one in first, Virgil? Let's hang on to Mark's question.

Virgil Cruz: I'm sure some detractor has put this sort of question to the Unification church, but is it possible that the wrong tests are being applied to Rev. Moon? As I understand what you folks have said, you've said that he has manifested great spiritual insight. I can accept that. He has manifested extraordinary leadership. That might well be provable. He has demonstrated personal piety, and I think you could clearly support that conclusion, but should you consider applying to him the same tests which were applied to Jesus Christ? There are various witnesses to Jesus' extraordinary personhood, one of which is the virgin birth. Another would be the performance of miracles; another would be the power that He manifested over death. One dramatic instance of that was the raising of Lazarus. He was Lord over death, even in life. Have you discussed these kinds of things on other occasions?

Rod Sawatsky: I think both of these are very worthy of discussion. Let's work with Mark's first, and then let's not forget Virgil.

Dan Davies: I'd like to address Mark on the dramatic second coming. It's interesting to note that at Jesus' time the Jews were expecting many signs. They were expecting what has been called the "Woes of the Messiah." There were to be stars falling from heaven, the sun darkening, the moon turning to blood, etc. This prophecy underlies one of the reasons that they weren't able to recognize Jesus; there were no such signs, so they did not believe it was the time of the messiah. It seems to be a phenomenon in the last days that those who are most waiting for the messiah wait for signs, too. However, the messiah will not give signs but, rather, the word of God.

Paul Eshleman: Are you saying that because those prophecies were not fulfilled for Jesus, they were inaccurate? Or that there are stars falling? I'm not seeing them.

Dan Davies: No, I'm saying that at the time of Jesus, the rabbis expected the "Woes of the Messiah," stars falling from heaven...

Paul Eshleman: But that did not happen because that had to do with the second coming, in our understanding.

Dan Davies: The people of Israel were expecting many signs. They probably got this expectation from a passage in the Book of Daniel that mentions the Son of man coming on the clouds. The Jewish people saw no signs and, therefore, they could not accept their time as the time of the messiah. Jesus became angry with the Pharisees who continually demanded a sign and told them only an evil and adulterous generation seeks after a sign. He told them they should believe in Him by what He said, and if not by what He said, then by His work.

Anthony Guerra: I'd like to say that what Dan is talking about is apocalyptic literature which was a form of Jewish literature that began about 200 B.C. and lasted until about 100 A.D. The Jews were talking about a catastrophic event which would coincide with the time of the messiah whom they were awaiting. And the Book of Revelation is very much in this mode; it's the New Testament version of this type of literature which was quite popular at the time of Jesus.

Mark Branson: So you're saying those are not to be taken literally, including the angel's comments about Jesus coming in the clouds?

Anthony Guerra: Right. We agree with Bultmann here—one of the few places we do agree with Bultmann.

Warren Lewis: The Unificationists are in bad trouble when it comes to biblical hermeneutics, and they know it; we talk about it here. But so are the Evangelicals in trouble. You know very well that the New Testament plays fast and loose with its quotations of the Old Testament because it's interpreting the Old

Testament through christological spectacles. A previous conclusion had been arrived at—that Jesus is the messiah; therefore, one could use the Old Testament to prove Jesus' messiahship when one needed to. One could find a virgin birth, where the Old Testament doesn't teach it. Joel prophesies that the stars will fall from heaven; Peter on the day of Pentecost says, "This is that." But I presume the moon did not turn to blood that day. So you both need to wage a hermeneutical battle against one another—or work hermeneutical love—because you're both in trouble. How do you folks make your decisions about the Bible, you Evangelicals, about which of these metaphorical forms to take literally, and which to leave metaphorical? This is how: you make those decisions on the basis of certain *a priori* christological decisions, just like the Unificationists and the first-century Christians. I'd love to see you get together on your hermeneutics. You really might make some progress. But since you're both so embarrassed by it, maybe in your common embarrassment, you might acknowledge one another's humanity and start there afresh. I suggest, and I'm siding with Joe here in a way, that some hermeneutical clarity should come into this conversation. We are going to chase this thing into Robin Hood's barn and get nowhere.

Anthony Guerra: What we're saying is that Jesus provided justification for the forgiveness of sins, so that man could individually unite with God. The Lord of the Second Advent similarly provides justification for families; that is, to achieve what we call the second blessing. This accounts for our interpretation of what Paul and Jesus say: "It would be better not to marry, for in heaven you will be like the angels, i.e., not married." In the Christian tradition marriage is "til death do you part." We believe that is because the family itself is not justified, although the individual is justified. The Lord of the Second Advent is coming specifically to grant to man this blessing which humanity has been deprived of by the fall. So, therefore, by receiving the blessing of the Lord of the Second Advent you are given the possibility of achieving a perfect marriage in God's sight. Just as when you receive justification from Jesus, it does not mean that you become perfected as an individual, right? You must actually lead a Christ-like life. So likewise, although you receive justification through the Lord of the Second Advent to have a family approved by God, that's only a possible condition. Given the principle of growth which Tirza talked about, man's responsibility must be fulfilled in order that the opportunity which God has given may be realized. So the Lord of the Second Advent gives justification but not sanctification on the family level.

Rod Sawatsky: Do we need more clarification on that?

Johnny Sonneborn: I want to put this in more practical terms. Let's consider the fall of man. We want there to be ultimately a situation in which people will never fall, so let's find what was missing then that will be present in the future. We note first that Adam and Eve were spiritually children, because if they had been perfected they couldn't have fallen. But they had no parents to guide them on earth; or as St. Irenaeus said, the Word was walking about the garden but He was invisible. Jesus came on earth and Word was visible. People had a standard to go on.

Therefore, when a tradition has been established with people who actively practice true parenthood on earth, then people can begin to learn the way of raising children and the children will have a situation for growth, and as the community is expanded, as we've been mentioning, then this can be developed so that ultimately when the kingdom is completely fulfilled we'll live under good family life, and there will never be falling away. It has to begin somewhere. This is how this linking up the spiritual with the physical happens that you're asking about.

Mark Branson: But there is no physical, tangible, material link between the Lord of the Second Advent and those whom he blesses?

Nora Spurgin: Well, basically, it is a spiritual thing in order to reverse the fall. Ever since Satan pulled man to his side, man has been responding to him. Satan has a claim over man because of this response. Therefore, the way to reverse this is for man to have that unity with the messiah. Now, the fall took place through the misuse of love. In reversal, we must unite our hearts—a spiritual unity in obedience to the messiah. It is not a sexual unity, as some of our opponents would lead people to believe.

Pete Sommer: But Rev. Moon encourages romantic feelings toward himself and his wife.

Jonathan Wells: Not sexual.

Pete Sommer: The word "romantic" is used in *Master Speaks...*

Virgil Cruz: I don't want to be crude, but why couldn't there be, theoretically, sexual relations with the messiah? Many religions have the holy sexual thing. Wouldn't that be reversing the fall totally?

Anthony Guerra: I think we are missing a central category in Unification theology: namely, the concept of the heart of God. In Unification theology, God is best imagined as a loving parent who created humanity as His children for whom He had great expectations. These expectations are expressed in the notion of the three blessings as: individual perfection, family perfection, and proper dominion over the rest of the created order. The failure to achieve these ends designed by God causes grief to the heart of God. The messiah's task is to realize God's ideal and by doing this he gains the authority to forgive others, and, most importantly, the Lord of the Second Advent and his bride may ask forgiveness from God for other couples. So the Lord of the Second Advent and his bride say to God, "Please forgive this couple," and they receive forgiveness. This is the same way that I John talks about Jesus as interceding for us as individuals, as advocating our cause.

Mark Branson: The forgiveness of a couple cannot be given by Jesus?

Anthony Guerra: That's right. He gives forgiveness to individuals and potentially to every individual, but not to a couple, and that's precisely why Paul says it's better that one does not marry.

Johnny Sonneborn: We have to say why that's the case, and why the theory didn't come a long time ago. If it was just a question of setting up a family, then why couldn't God have sent the Messiah the next day and set up a family? It's because the Lord comes again when all the nations unite, when there is a widespread foundation. Jesus came to open up the providence on a worldwide level, whereas before Jesus, God moved through nations. Therefore, there has to be a certain development of the social sphere at the time of the return of the Lord. Then, this will open up the final level in which people will be able to live on this earth in harmony. Therefore, this means that people who are married in the time of the new age have a new kind of hope, not just a sureness that the end will come somehow or other, but the hope they're actually living in a time when the purpose of life is going to be fulfilled. They actually are participating in establishing the kingdom of heaven on earth substantially. So this creates a whole new aspect. They're free to marry as something that's really going to be part of the substantial foundation for restoration, rather than just perpetuating the vale of tears. This changes the whole relationship between body and spirit as well. It's very important that this family aspect be seen in the context of the third blessing.

Mark Branson: I'm hearing another eschaton and I want to get back to that later. First, in the Unification church marriage ceremony, a major part of the sacrament is the wine. Is it true that of the twenty-one ingredients in the wine, one of the ingredients is the blood of Moon?* Is that a physical link?

Nora Spurgin: I never heard the actual ingredients. As far as I know, we've never been told. The Wine Ceremony to me was like a communion, with, of course, a different value than that, because it was a once-in-a-lifetime experience in our lives. In terms of something which you might be familiar with, it was like being served communion—a similar quality of spiritual transcendence.

One more thing—you mentioned something about romance, or a romantic relationship. Maybe what you are talking about is something like what Rev. Moon has sometimes said, that we as blessed couples are like the bride of the Messiah. The reference to the bride is symbolic, such as a nun who considers herself married to Jesus, or the references in Revelation, which are interpreted generally as the Church being the Bride.

Warren Lewis: You're right. You're absolutely right. It's all through *Master Speaks.* In context, what it's all about is an offer of imitation of the perfect marriage. He's saying, "Mrs. Moon and I have got this great thing going; and now, all of you sisters, if you are really lucky, you'll get a guy as good as I am." (laughter) "And you ought to prepare yourself to be married to the Messiah. And all of you brothers, if you could marry a woman like Mother, then you would be the luckiest guy around." In his speeches he frequently plays with that theme; what he's trying to say is, "Look for the kind of person who carries out his own messianic role. Since you can't have the real Messiah, get the next best thing."

Irving Hexham: Now I know that he very clearly repudiates adultery, and fornication would seem to be your ultimate sin;

---

*It was erroneously reported in the *Blessing Quarterly,* Vol. I, No. 2, pg. 46, that Mr. Sudo had said the wine "...contains...the blood of Father and Mother." This was an inaccurate presentation of Mr. Sudo's views on the meaning of the wine. There is no blood in the wine. The Holy Wine Ceremony is symbolic and Mr. Sudo's views were accurately presented in the *Blessing Quarterly,* Vol. II, No. 2.

does that place sexuality under a cloud?

Jonathan Wells: Fornication is sinful, but love isn't.

Rod Sawatsky: It is almost eleven o'clock and I think we'll have to cut it off at this point. There's much, much unfinished here obviously. I think one of the places we were left with was Virgil's question on tests of the messiah. Some of those questions are also related to personal testimonies in terms of how various people experience and have experienced the Rev. Moon. Jonathan began his testimony, and my impression is that if we went around the circle we would have many different kinds of testimonies of relationships with Rev. Moon. Maybe we will have occasion to do that. If we don't, that might be something we could pursue at mealtimes.

It seems to me that we ought to begin tomorrow morning with these questions of hermeneutics, of authority, of new Scriptures, and the like. Again, this needs to be dialogical; I think the Evangelicals need to tell the Moonies what their hermeneutical principles are, and how they interpret the Scriptures, and vice versa. We'll see who's in with Lindsell and who's out. That should be fun in itself. We will begin with that and see where we go after lunch.

Paul Eshleman: Maybe into salvation; at what point do you become assured of eternal life, and at what point do you see the perfection of the body; at what point can you be assured of your relationship with God? If everybody in the room dies tonight, what happens?

Richard Quebedeaux: Although the whole issue of salvation has been discussed there are still things that require clarification.

Dan Davies: I'd like to hear the Evangelical view of salvation too.

Rod Sawatsky: O.K., so first thing tomorrow morning is "authority" and then "salvation." O.K.?

[Editor's Note: The second seminar dealt with the question of Jesus Christ, Rev. Moon and their relationship again. This interchange follows in the text below before the discussion on authority and salvation.]

Roy Carlisle: I think the most succinct statement in the New Testament about who Jesus is, is in Philippians 2:5-11. I think it is very powerful because it contains both the elements of divinity and humanity, which are critical to the Evangelical understanding of Christ. I want to read just a couple of verses in that passage: "Have this mind among yourselves, which is yours in Christ Jesus, who, though he was in the form of God, did not count equality with God a thing to be grasped, but emptied himself, taking the form of a servant, being born in the likeness of men. And being found in human form he humbled himself and became obedient unto death, even death on a cross. Therefore God has highly exalted him and bestowed on him the name which is above every name, that at the name of Jesus every knee should bow, in heaven and on earth, and under the earth, and every tongue confess that Jesus Christ is Lord, to the glory of God the Father."

I don't think there's a more clear, powerful, christological statement in the New Testament, and the thing that's so important is that all the elements are there—first, that He is in the form of God, that somehow He was divine, whatever that really means, also that He was a man, that He died on the cross, that He was exalted. This is where Unification and evangelical theology really crunch. There's the sense in that passage that nothing else is needed. Christ was everything, did everything, was everything that we need. He is now Lord, and there is no need for another Lord of the Second Advent, or somebody else to fulfill the whole salvific purpose in Scripture. Now we can take off from that in different directions; but for an Evangelical, somehow we have to be convinced, based on Scripture, that there is a need for something more than this passage. This is where we have to dig into it. So to get started, let's talk about the elements of this.

Jonathan Wells: If we assume, which I do, that Jesus was speaking God's Word, His command to people was "Believe in Me." Of all the messages in the Bible, that one comes through the clearest—"Believe in Me"—it is clear as a bell. Now, for Jesus to die meant that people—it's a question—had to disbelieve in Him? Is God's will then contradictory? I mean, was Jesus giving us a commandment that God knew we couldn't fulfill, or didn't even want us to fulfill? How does that fit, logically?

Rod Sawatsky: Clarify that a little more. I don't think we're all with you.

Jonathan Wells: O.K., God's will was that people believe in Jesus. Jesus died because people didn't believe in Jesus. It wasn't the people who believed in Jesus who crucified Him. So on the one hand, Jesus is saying, "Believe in Me," and yet the evangelical position seems to be that God really wanted Jesus to die.

Paul Eshleman: See, it's exactly that point right now that's the crucial point of Christianity, and that is: why do you believe or trust in Jesus Christ? There are a lot of people who talk about Jesus today; but the evangelical position is this: we don't trust or believe in Jesus Christ as a hero, as a good man, as a great liberator, but we trust and believe in Him as a salvation and satisfaction and propitiation for our sins. Jesus made the payment. So when Jesus said, "Believe in Me," it was "trust and follow Me, not only for your salvation from sin, but total salvation in the whole remaking of your life."

Mark Branson: Paul (Eshleman) properly emphasized Jesus' role of propitiation. In achieving a way of forgiveness and providing reconciliation with God, Jesus deals effectively and finally with sin. Without downplaying that, I also want to say that He is the liberator, that there are other ramifications than forgiveness. Otherwise His *life* makes no sense. He didn't just come, say, "I'm the Messiah," and get arrested. But He lived a life for several years, and that is what we have to follow. Belief in Jesus, therefore, includes not only my personal reconciliation with God but also belief in His methodology for building the kingdom.

Jonathan Wells: None of those are my question.

Joseph Hopkins: In answer to your question, I find the distinction between God's will of purpose and His will of desire helpful, and also His will of command. God "desires not the death of a sinner, but that every man turn from his wickedness and life." It was His will of *desire* that people believe in Jesus, but it was His will of *purpose* that Jesus be sacrificed for our sins.

Evangelical X: In Matthew 16, it says that from that time Jesus began to show His disciples that He must go to Jerusalem and suffer many things from the elders and the chief priests and scribes and be killed, and on the third day be raised. And Peter took Him and rebuked Him, saying, "God forbid, Lord! This shall never happen to you." But Jesus said to him, "Get behind me, Satan! You are a hindrance to me; for you are not on the side of God, but of men." He made it very plain to His very choice group of twelve people: don't try to resist what I've come to try to do.

Sharon Gallagher: I'd like to answer you in another way. I perceive the role of Jesus as fulfilling the suffering servant role that is foreordained in the whole Old Testament. So, for me, there are three levels in Isaiah: One would be the nation of Israel, the suffering servant for the world at that time; another would be the suffering prophet role in Israel; and the third one would be the role that Jesus fulfilled, as the suffering servant for Israel.

Jonathan Wells: I will try to phrase it as a question again, since I'm still on the questioning side. Can we distinguish Jesus' command, "Believe in Me," from what is more in the nature of a prediction, namely, "I will be crucified," which He could clearly see coming? Now, objectively speaking, can there be a distinction between His command and His prediction of what would actually happen?

Patrick Means: Can I raise a question for clarification first? An honest clarification, because I don't know—I gather that you of the Unification movement give higher authority to the words of Jesus in Scripture than other words in Scripture, and that His words are evidently more authoritative than others that came after, and I'd like to have someone clarify that for me, if that's true or not.

Jonathan Wells: I didn't exactly say that, if I can clarify it. I'm saying that the least disputable message, and you can certainly debate me on this one, but I would say the least disputable message in the New Testament is Jesus' message, "Believe in Me." There's nobody who disputes that, right?

Patrick Means: Paul is as authoritative as Jesus on any of these questions.

Jonathan Wells: I won't comment on that.

Warren Lewis: Your answer is that St. Paul also said "Believe in Jesus," right?

Jonathan Wells: That's true in Paul, and in all the New Testament.

Mark Branson: Jesus is saying, "Believe in Me," but He's also aware that His message is going to cause opposition, and I don't see the conflict between the two things you're bringing up. You see it as a conflict, but I don't see it as a conflict, because while He commands "Believe in Me," He is also making a realistic prediction of the future—anyone who tries to live the kind of life I intend to live, might get himself crucified. That is also true, but the statement that this kind of lifestyle will lead to confrontation and eventually persecution doesn't change the command—My desire is that people believe in Me.

Jonathan Wells: Right, but the question we're trying to get at is what was God's will.

Mark Branson: God's will was that people believe in Jesus.

Jonathan Wells: That's my point.

Mark Branson: But that doesn't take away from the other one at all, the realistic statement that a lifestyle of love and giving for the people will produce a conflict.

Jonathan Wells: It's contrary to God's will, that's all, O.K. . . .

Mark Branson: But given the nature of men and the way the world is set up, that doesn't happen.

Jonathan Wells: The way the world is set up by God?

Mark Branson: No, the way the world is with sin in it.

Jonathan Wells: O.K., but is that the will of God?

Mark Branson: Once that incorporates the bigger picture, I'd say yes. That there really is a world and a dimension and a reality that incorporates this as well as much more, and . . .

Pete Sommer: It's your own moral choice as a free moral agent, not God's will . . .

Anthony Guerra: I just wanted to highlight the point you were making concerning the distinction between God's will and human possibilities. It seems to me that if you say on the one hand, that you understand God's will at the time of Jesus to be that people believe in Him, and that on the other hand it is impossible to fulfill the will, you have conceived of an absurd God.

Mark Branson: I didn't say impossible—I didn't say impossible, it's just going to get you into trouble . . .

Anthony Guerra: Was it the desire of God to have His will realized? This is the question. If people had believed in Jesus as the Messiah, then they would not have crucified Him, since Christ could only be crucified at the hands of disbelievers.

Evangelical Y: Hypothetical questions are impossible to answer . . .

Anthony Guerra: Well, I'm just asking you to follow the reasoning . . .

Evangelical Y: In philosophy, you don't ask contrary-to-fact questions. They're meaningless questions.

Rod Sawatsky: Not necessarily. On the basis of certain theological options given a particular view of the nature of creation, nature of God, the world, what may His will have been? This is

Anthony's question. I don't think that's out of hand, theologically, at all.

Evangelical Y: It can only be dealt with speculatively...

Rod Sawatsky: Yes, for sure, it's a speculative question...

Anthony Guerra: We're speculating at this point...

Jonathan Wells: It's equally speculative to say that God wanted Jesus to die—that would be my claim. It is clear that God foresaw the likelihood of the crucifixion, but I wouldn't say God *wanted* that to happen...

Paul Eshleman: That's not what Jesus said in Mark...

Johnny Sonneborn: It seems to me there's a rational evangelical position that's developing, although it's not one that I necessarily agree with. God wants everyone to believe in Jesus, and knew at that time, given the nature of the sinful realities, that they wouldn't. This is my understanding of foreknowledge. Under those circumstances there would be no salvation without blood. I think this is a rational position, even though many of us would like it some other way. Nevertheless, God would ask people to believe in Him under those circumstances, so that after the propitiation there would be this kind of belief. This is not saying it was God's will that Jesus die—His basic will was the belief of the people—but He knew it would happen as it did. It seems like a rational, logical position. However, it raises a question now as to God's foreknowledge. Does God know everything that's going to happen? Where does man's free will come in? It must be more rational than to say that God wanted some people to believe in Jesus and follow Him and other people to crucify Him and cause this great delay...

Richard Quebedeaux: Some Christians do believe that...

Joseph Hopkins: Well, again, there's the distinction between God's will of purpose and His will of desire, and with regard to the statement "Believe in God, believe also in Me," I don't see that as a command but as an appeal, because Jesus is dealing with free moral agents—He's not forcing His will upon people.

Anthony Guerra: Don't you have a freeing God, not a contradictory God; a freeing God who creates life itself—we must see it. He gives us forgiveness in Christ, and even gives us the third gift—freedom to reject Him.

Franz Feige: To me, it's very obvious that it was very strange to His disciples that Jesus suddenly said He would have to go and die. It means that Jesus must have somehow given support to the assumption in the disciples that He would come to live — otherwise they would not have turned against Jesus' desire of going out to die. So the question is: Don't you think there's a possibility that Jesus wanted to live to build God's kingdom on the earth, but because of the incredible rejection of Jesus by His own people He had to alter His will? Isn't it possible that through His death He brought in a temporary state, and promised a second coming for the fulfillment of the kingdom?

Rod Sawatsky: That would be a position held by many Evangelicals — that's a basic dispensationalist point of view...

Franz Feige: So God altered His will because...

Rod Sawatsky: Well, not necessarily God altering His will, but a change in plan...

Franz Feige: Because man rejected God, by rejecting Jesus. This would be the Unification church position, too...

Roy Carlisle: I think I would take exception to the fact that Jesus did somehow bolster their enthusiasm for Him to live, and somehow gave them fuel for those kinds of assumptions. I think that they were Jewish, and as messianic Jews their expectation was that Jesus, the Messiah, would be a messianic king, a political king. Jesus, however, never ever in His ministry gave any inkling, of anything that would have helped them continue to believe that at all. I mean, it's so critical that even after the resurrection they say to Him, "Well, now you've been resurrected, Lord, let's set up this kingdom." And He says, "You still don't understand what I've been doing all my life, and that is trying to teach you that I had to die..." He never said to them, "I'm going to become a political figure." He never gave them the basis for assuming that somehow He would not have to die. Never, there's no place in the New Testament...

Franz Feige: He somehow didn't make it clear in the beginning, right?

Roy Carlisle: No, I'm saying that He did make it clear, but because they were Jews who had a Messianic expectation, they didn't even get it after the resurrection — that's how strong their Messianic expectation was for a political king. It wasn't that Jesus didn't make it clear — it's just that it didn't sink in. It never sank in — it didn't even sink in after the resurrection — it didn't sink in until Pentecost, so it wasn't Jesus not making it clear — He made it clear all along the line.

Sharon Gallagher: I just wanted to say that in fact I think what Jesus was doing was trying to prepare them for His death and burial. Take the instance of Mary as an example. She poured ointment over His body, and some of the disciples were critical of this, but Jesus said, "Let her alone." I think He's affirming the fact that she has understood what His ministry was, that He came to die.

Franz Feige: The question is, why would Jesus have to wait for a few years to die? Why isn't it enough for Him to say, O.K., I've come to die, crucify me as soon as possible, so you might have salvation as soon as possible. Why wouldn't God have sent Jesus already 4,000 years ago, when the circumstances for rejection were even more probable. Why did God go and set up a nation of people?

Jonathan Wells: That they might have made the mistake of accepting him? (laughter)

Franz Feige: Was there a need for God to set up a nation to receive Him?

Sharon Gallagher: Because God didn't set that up. I mean, I hear you asking what is the necessity for human history—why did God bother with Abraham and the patriarchs—why didn't He just set up the kingdom of God right after the fall...

Franz Feige: Right, that's our question, too...

Johnny Sonneborn: That can be answered by Dr. Hopkins' notion of reform theology. Just say that God in His infinite wisdom and omniscience foreordained these activities.

Paul Eshleman: Scripturally, it says in the fullness of time. That's all it says.

Joseph Hopkins: But Jesus came not only to die: "...and the Word became flesh and dwelt among us, full of grace and truth; we have beheld His glory, glory as of the only Son from the Father."

He came to reveal the Father, so that we might know the beautiful and glorious holiness of God, in order that we might model our lives after Him and enter into His fellowship with comprehension of who our Creator is.

Dan Davies: Then why was He so angry when people refused Him? Why didn't He always calmly and peacefully take the accusations that He got from the Pharisees? And rejection? Why did He often viciously strike out?

Joseph Hopkins: Because they were rejecting the Father...

Dan Davies: But that was God's will...

Joseph Hopkins: No.

Frank Kaufmann: I'd like to suggest that you are making an assumption when you say that the necessary murder of Jesus for the forgiveness of sins, is a divine principle, especially in light of the fact that Jesus forgave sins during His life prior to His crucifixion; could some of the Evangelicals address this?

Evangelical X: Because He knew what He came to do, which was to pay the penalty for sin; somebody has to pay, and He knew He was going to pay. Therefore, on the basis of that, He could forgive. I also would like to say, although I don't know if I'm answering you or not, that *this* Evangelical believes that although Jesus died, He was not defeated; it's just the opposite. He won there, and the whole message of the New Testament church was the resurrection, and for some reason or another we're not giving that message clearly anymore. That's all they talked about in the early days of the church—the resurrection—that was the mark of the Christian Church—the resurrection, indicative of the fact that the victory has come. Just as it was said here by our friend, this victory is put off, and I don't like it, as you don't like it, and I don't think God likes it being put off this long. By His life, Jesus showed us the Father—that's what He came to do, and therefore we, as His people, are to do the same. But there's that ever-present conflict within us: having been born into the kingdom of this world, we Christians do not fulfill what He redeemed us to fulfill. All of us will have to admit that there are two poles within all of us somewhere along the line on some issues—not all issues, but some issues. One pole says this and one pole says that, and we have to find out what God's will is, and the only way to do this is to seek Christ, and then we know what God's will is. Just do what He did, by the grace of God, and then we'll be fulfilling the will of God, modeling it as He modeled it, in front of a world that needs to hear. The world needs to feel that dignity from us, and when we don't give that dignity, there's something wrong in the way we're living our Christian life. The death of Christ is the reason we're able to do that, because that freed us from all that guilt and penalty—that's why He could forgive—He knew He was going to pay for it.

Frank Kaufmann: But at that point we weren't forgiven? Was it a guarantee...following His crucifixion?

Rod Sawatsky: I think we should switch gears here a little bit. I'd like now to move to the other side, and have the Unificationists tell the story; but before doing that, I'd like some of the Unification people to list some of the areas which they feel are the most problematic about the answers they received from the Evangelicals. Where, in your minds, are the problems?

Jonathan Wells: Well, I will just list one, because it was the one that was addressed a bit earlier: When does that forgiveness take effect, or how? I don't think that question was answered, because we heard talk about going forth as models of God, and yet I think no Evangelical would claim to be sinless.

Dan Davies: I'd like to deal with the issue of how Christians will deal with other religions upon the return of Jesus.

Tirza Shilgi: I suppose one of the things I wanted to mention from the beginning of this discussion was that, during most of Jesus' ministry He kept trying to explain what the kingdom was rather than explain how He was going to be crucified. It's like the quote brought out earlier: From this time on, He started to talk about going to Jerusalem. When He said this He was already very close to the end of His ministry and His life—only a few days away from the crucifixion. Time-wise, and quantity-wise, in the gospels, the major part of Jesus' ministry deals with explaining the kingdom, *not* explaining His death; and I don't understand how you explain "from that time on" in light of the fact that most of His teaching was spent speaking of a totally different topic—the kingdom of God.

Thomas Carter: I have a question: Is Jesus representing the kind of God that can foreordain human suffering, and human damnation? My question is, how do you view the nature of God?

Franz Feige: I have another question. What is the act of salvation on Jesus' part, that would reconcile man back to God? I think you have to explain that a little bit more.

Rod Sawatsky: I think that what we will do, is talk about Jesus and the second coming from the Unification point of view, and then we'll go on to the question of salvation.

Paul Eshleman: I didn't quite get the last question.

Franz Feige: What is the necessary or reconciling act from God's point of view that Jesus would have to do to reconcile man to God? What is the actual act that effects salvation?

Johnny Sonneborn: One more problem concerns what seems to be a lack of clarity on the second coming, its nature and effect.

Anthony Guerra: I have a hermeneutical question. I am

intrigued by the way people are quoting Scripture. For instance, someone exegeted Mark to say that the kingdom is to have definite economic, political implications, and then somebody disagreed with that interpretation. I was wondering how you resolve such disagreements. What are the criteria by which you allow for some interpretations of Scripture and also disallow other interpretations?

Warren Lewis: That's been our problem for four hundred years. (laughter)

Rod Sawatsky: Yes, I think that's a fair enough question. I think someplace we need to address that one, too.

Johnny Sonneborn: I have one more problem with the eschatology that was mentioned by at least a couple of persons. It was emphasized that God always works by trying to persuade humans freely to accept Him and Jesus Christ; on the other hand one person said the eschaton will be a supernatural work of God, and it seemed to imply a forcible act. Isn't that contradictory?

Paul Eshleman: Excuse my question, Rod, but will these questions be answered at some time, or do we just hope they will, or what? For what purpose are we bringing up the questions?

Rod Sawatsky: To raise the things that are left unclear in the minds of Unificationists, so that the Evangelicals can speak to these questions during the process of the next day if possible. If we try to answer all of these now, we won't get to any other questions, I'm sure.

Mark Branson: It might help if we had clarification concerning the second coming of Christ to the nations. However, Unificationists probably have more consensus than would Evangelicals. Evangelicals would say that's just not spelled out clearly in the Scriptures. You'd probably get as many opinions as people on that particular question, and to pursue that is not going to be particularly helpful.

Dan Davies: But it's quite important.

Mark Branson: That may be, but you're still going to get as many answers as people.

Dan Davies: That's all right—we're here for dialogue.

Mark Branson: Well, if you're looking for a consensus, there are some areas where Evangelicals are going to have a real consensus, and there are going to be others where they won't.

Richard Quebedeaux: The second coming in Unification theology is of a different character than it is in evangelical theology. It is a more earthly kind of thing. Evangelicals, however, just assume that *everything* works out fine at the second coming, everything is taken care of by God, so the issue of what happens to the different cultures, and other things—that's all sort of resolved. As you say, there could be many interpretations, whereas in Unification theology, it's quite a different story.

Mark Branson: And the clarification of that in Unification theology is important. In Evangelical thought, I don't think it *is* important, because Evangelical thought tends to focus on the present, and says what God is doing, what is the responsibility of God, etc.

Dan Davies: From my perspective, I think that is a lack—one the Evangelicals have to confront every day in the world.

Warren Lewis: Let me underline what I think he means by that. Methodologically, for the Unificationists, it's important to raise the questions for which Evangelicals don't have answers, and indicate the points at which they are not united. Unificationists understand that Rev. Moon has brought the answers. In an attempt to appeal to you, they want to say: "You don't have the answer; we do; here it is." Strategically, they have to keep pushing you in the areas where they think you are weak.

Anthony Guerra: I want to punctuate that point. To say that we should be concerned with only the present moment is derived from a certain philosophical perspective—existentialism. On the other hand, to say that the *eschaton* or the final goal is decisive also rests on certain philosophical assumptions. But these are philosophical assumptions and not necessarily scriptural insights. Now returning to my original point: what is your hermeneutic? These kinds of questions are important to raise even if definitive answers cannot be given, for they keep us humble.

BREAK

Rod Sawatsky: Jonathan is going to start us off by talking about Jesus in the context of Unification's understanding, and then also move on to the second coming, the Lord of the Second Advent in that context. Then he'll speak to the question of the potential relationship of Jesus and Moon. After that Johnny Sonneborn is going to add some further things, and then we'll have some questions of clarification.

Jonathan Wells: I'll start off by saying that in Unification theology, Jesus comes as the Second Adam. For that reason, I'm going to go back and comment briefly on the first Adam. God's original desire in creating the world was for mankind to be His children, so Adam and Eve were supposed to be God's son and daughter, and were originally created sinless. God's desire for them was to grow up and become perfect; in other words, there is a distinction between sinlessness and perfection. This is similar to the thinking of Iranaeus, for those of you that are into historical theology. God gave the commandment to Adam and Eve, allowing them to choose whether to obey or not. As we know, they disobeyed the commandment and did not reach perfection, but fell away from sinlessness into sin and so human history became the story of God's continual efforts to prepare man for another attempt—that is, the second Adam. Man couldn't raise himself out of his sinfulness by his own effort, but instead God had to send another sinless man, and that man was Jesus, who was one with God, and perfect. Jesus said, "...if you knew me, you would know my Father also," meaning, therefore, to connect with Him and thereby connect with God. That would restore the relationship which Adam and Eve failed to establish.

And this is the solution to sin—that is, the origin of sin was the abuse of man's free will in the first place, so to restore that, man had to use his free will to accept Jesus. This is the point I was making earlier: to believe in Jesus was a kind of alternative commandment which fulfilled the function of the one that was violated in the garden.

Now, Jesus offered mankind complete salvation, that is, the kingdom of Heaven on earth, sinlessness, perfection, unity with God, and this would have fulfilled the purpose of God's original creation. Unfortunately, mankind did not accept Jesus, specifically because certain key people in Israel failed to believe in Him. Jesus could see that these people were turning away from Him, and that even His own followers weren't connected closely enough with Him. People followed Jesus, but actually we know that when they were challenged, everybody fell away, so Jesus was really without followers in the deepest sense of the word. Since God, through Jesus, could see this situation, He knew that mankind was rejecting Jesus, and that the only solution was for Jesus to go the way of the cross. Now, in that sense, the *Divine Principle* says the crucifixion was the will of God, but as Franz mentioned earlier, the secondary will, because man opposed God's primary will.

So even though complete salvation was offered at the time of Jesus, the crucifixion, in effect, was man's rejection of that offer, and the salvation that we experience in Christianity is somehow incomplete—not because of any failure of Jesus, but because of sinful man's rejection of Him. Therefore, the second coming is necessary in order for God's will to be accomplished.

Christianity does, however, offer a spiritual salvation. Jesus said He came to give His life as a ransom, and in fact, that is the result of the crucifixion—He ransoms our soul through His body—He gives His body to the cross, and thereby enables those people who turn to Him to be saved spiritually. So, in Christianity the most common understanding is that there's a heavenly kingdom to come—that is, in a spiritual sense, after we die. But the *Divine Principle* maintains that God's will was that the whole creation be restored, that is, physically as well as spiritually. For this reason Christ will come again in the same manner as He came the first time. The first coming, that is, Jesus, was completely adequate—it wasn't Jesus who failed, but man who rejected Him, and so the second coming, in effect, is like another opportunity from God for man to respond to His will. It occurs in a very similar manner to the first coming, and I'm not sure how much farther I want to press that, but it implies the second coming is a man born of woman, who walks the earth, preaches the kingdom of heaven, is accepted by some, rejected by others. For God's overture to be accepted means that the second coming must be accepted by people in the way that the first coming was not. The *Divine Principle* challenges us to fulfill what the people of 2,000 years ago failed to fulfill.

Rod Sawatsky: O.K., we'll let Johnny Sonneborn speak for a minute.

Johnny Sonneborn: The major point that I want to get to is that it seems that the evangelical folks here, with the exception of Mark, and possibly one other, have emphasized Jesus' present kingdom, which is now what we call a spiritual kingdom, or eternal kingdom; or as Sharon pointed out, there had been a temporal kingdom, and that had been changed through the advent of Christ, and later on, after the second coming, comes the substantial kingdom anew. This is the Divine Principle position on Jesus—He *is* the king of the spiritual kingdom.

Now, what does it mean—a spiritual kingdom? It means perhaps citizens, or subjects or whatever one calls followers of a king; and therefore, what the church does right *is* the kingdom. What the church does wrong in not following is *not:* the kingdom must be enacted as one is doing it. The kingdom is spreading and Jesus as the Lord is directing the spiritual spread of Christianity as the Evangelicals have described. Therefore, the kingdom now is greater all the time the more people are added. Jesus must have a plan for spreading this, a plan of going from a society to a nation, to other nations and so forth. In the Unification church, some understanding of this is given.

It also means that Jesus, as Mark said, is the king because He tears down the barriers to His rule. The question then is, are these barriers being broken down, and is the kingdom spreading in some terrestrial sense because barriers were broken down, or is it only spiritual, as Mark and others seem to be saying? Unificationists are saying that the kingdom of God in the spiritual and physical sense means God with people who are sinless, who have integrity. God is not designing His kingdom for sinners. Christians, according to Unification church, if they really have one hundred percent faith and are united with Jesus, can be spiritually sinless, reborn into living hope, can be freed from that accusation of thoughts, feelings, and so forth. That appears to be theoretically attainable; but in our actual actions, we know, as St. Paul and others have said, that we continue to sin. In a substantial sense, there has not been even one follower of Christ who could say, "I am really a true child of the kingdom." Rather one can only say, "I have the spirit of adoption, and am still waiting for the adoption as a child here." Much less, even, can be said about the redemption of our physical relationships. Because there haven't been any true individuals in the Christian Church in that sense, there haven't been any true marriages, much less further elaborations of the kingdom in a substantial, social sense. This is why we say that at this point the kingdom has been but a spiritual one, and why the second coming of Christ means it must be transformed or built, or be made more glorified and more concrete as Roy has said.

Now, I'd just like to refer to the quotation where Jesus said His kingdom is not of this world. This is obviously a true statement. He did not have a kingdom of this world. But that statement does not have to be taken to mean the kingdom should not then be or will not be of this world. It is clearly in the evangelical view that when Jesus comes back He *will* establish the kingdom on this earth; so it was not necessarily an indication or prediction as to what was going to happen back at that time.

As far as the Christian salvation that has been accomplished goes, I must emphasize again that there is not a substantial difference between the Unification church and Evangelicals or any other Christian group as regards what has been accomplished— what salvation has been accomplished by Jesus. The only question is what more needs to be done, and do we call this salvation or not. I would like to call attention to the two different meanings of the word "salvation": salvation as a rescue—propitiation, and salvation as restoration to health. I think it's not quite enough to say that God sent the perfect man to earth, and He said, "Here I am, perfect," and people just reached out to follow Him. Unification teaching tells us that this is not enough because people are so far short of that. Christ must come down from His status as a perfect person, and come down to what we call the top of the growth stage (it's explained in Unification teachings), and become the servant and really serve people and eventually be exalted by the people. When the people did exalt Jesus and did prepare at risk in the upper room, then He was able to send the Holy Spirit, not just rescuing them, as it were, but restoring them to health.

Rod Sawatsky: We're beginning to get into the area of salvation and the Holy Spirit—that's fine, but let's make sure we're clear on the questions of Jesus and the second coming first. Whitney wants to add something.

Whitney Shiner: Yes, I want to clarify part of Jonathan's statement, because I thought it sounded as though we saw the crucifixion as the problem, but actually it's not the crucifixion that is the problem, but the rejection of Jesus by the people which we see as defeating God's purpose. At that point, then, the crucifixion was a ransom that Jesus paid so that the spiritual kingdom would be possible if people united with Jesus after the resurrection; I think this is essentially the evangelical position, that Jesus goes to the cross as a ransom so that the spiritual kingdom can be established.

And this, I think, is very close to the position I was hearing the Evangelicals state, that God's will would be for people to unite with Jesus; but because He knew that they wouldn't, He would use the cross to establish the spiritual kingdom. We're saying that God didn't know whether man would unite or not because man does have free will. God, of course, had a plan in the event that people would unite with Jesus, and that would be the full establishment of the kingdom.

Rod Sawatsky: I think we need a little clarification on what Jesus would have done in order to fully initiate the kingdom had He not died on the cross.

Paul Eshleman: Let me add to that, then. How would sins have been propitiated and satisfied if He had not died? We agreed that Jesus Christ was sinless, but should He have kept on living, where would the sacrifice have come in?

Tirza Shilgi: Our view of overall salvation and Jesus' role is directly connected with the way we view sin. Essentially, the way we view sin is as concupiscence or disordered love. That means it is self-centered and misused love, as opposed to God-centered love. Thus, we don't see the redemption in the renunciation of love, and maintaining chastity, but rather, we see salvation in the establishment of the right order of love; namely, a God-centered family.

So, in the process of salvation, the function of a God-centered family as the redemptive element is essential. In other words, the salvation process goes beyond the sacrifice and into the establishment of a right-ordered love. What we want is the restoration of the God-centered family; such a family and its God-centered children are the redemptive unit from which later on the "second mankind," or the visible church will come about. It actually means not the sacramental or the Christian Church only, but rather a family of God which would start from that family and would grow on as a way of establishing the kingdom. So this unit is essential—this is why we see a need for a messianic figure to fulfill this step and establish a family. This is why we feel that Jesus did not come to die, but He came to lead us, or establish that first redemptive unit, which was the first perfected family, and from that, to build this visible new humanity. Since He was not able to do that, we see the need for somebody else coming in a physical body to do that, and that's also explained in our understanding of Christ as an office rather than a last name. We don't see the word "Christ" as related to one specific person, but rather as an office or a mission that has to be fulfilled. And the coming about of the kingdom is connected to the fulfillment of this office rather than to one specific individual. Before we have this unit established, we can't have the kingdom. That's why we need somebody who will come and will establish that initial unit and from there on, we can have the kingdom, namely, God-centered family, clan, tribe, society, and world.

Patricia Zulkosky: I think, to carry on where we left off, this means that Jesus would have had a bride and they would have had sinless children. Then, because of His oneness with God, Jesus could intercede for the forgiveness of sins of all people who united with Jesus through faith. Then, sinlessness would expand, and the kingdom itself would be spread throughout the world. About four hundred years before Jesus, there were great spiritual revivals in the Far East and in Rome and Greece. Because of these revivals, many religions came into being, raising the standard of people to such a level that they could easily unite with Jesus when knowledge of His teachings came to them. God intended that Jesus' message be poured out on the world very quickly at that time, so He sent spiritual leaders to raise the people, either in an ethical sense or a doctrinal sense, to help bridge the gap between where they were and where Jesus was to bring them. Salvation, as we see it, was not only for Israel, but was to spread quickly throughout the whole existing world.

Dan Davies: I'd like to answer Paul Eshleman's question: What would happen if Jesus wasn't crucified, and how, then, would the propitiation of our sins take place? Our view of Christian rebirth is that it comes through faith in the resurrected Jesus and through the work of the Holy Spirit.

We see the concept of true parents as being extremely important. Because Jesus did not gain the following that He needed, He was crucified. He didn't have the foundation to establish the physical kingdom of God, so instead of having a physical bride, the Holy Spirit took the position of His bride, spiritually. They became the True Parents, spiritually, for all mankind. It is not by physical true parents, but by spiritual true parents that Christians are reborn spiritually. The messiah will come again, he'll take a bride, and they will become the True Parents, physically and spiritually for all mankind. They will be God's means to remove original sin from the world.

How could that be possible? The blessing of grace that comes through the spiritual rebirth that transforms our nature is a miracle, and it is impossible to explain to people who don't see it from a spiritual point of view. Also, the total restoration, physical and spiritual, that takes place through the Blessing of the True Parents is a miracle, difficult to explain for the same reason.

It has to be understood from a spiritual point of view.

Frank Kaufmann: I'd like to follow up what Tirza said. This responds to Paul's question as well. If Jesus was able to forgive sin without dying, then we must ask: wherein lies the power of Jesus to lead us out of sin? If the wages of sin is death, that being the state of those who do not live in love, then we must realize that the power Satan holds over mankind is that he is capable of leading us to distort our love, to cause us to use our love wrongly. Jesus Christ as a man was the first man to conquer Satan. Satan could not cause Jesus to change His love, God's love. The power of the Messiah is to lead mankind out of sin so that he can conquer Satan, conquer him who has dominated man since Adam. The first man who was *never* dominated by Satan was Jesus. By His victory, He knows and becomes the way and the truth and the life. He can provide us the way to come out of the bondage of sin, out of the clutches of Satan. Because He conquered in a direct battle, in a direct confrontation, He was not defeated by the power of sin. He exalts the supremacy of man. Are we not to judge the angels?

Johnny Sonneborn: But I think we still aren't speaking to Paul's question. To a certain extent, I'm trying to make it more concrete, and there is a very important dimension we need to bring into this. Jesus *did* come to give His life as ransom—there had to be a sacrifice, but that doesn't necessarily mean to us a physical sacrifice, being murdered or killed. You can give your life to God; this is a dedication of your life to all other people for God. Now, what does it really mean to give your life to other people? In Unification teaching, (this is not a direct quotation from the *Principle,* but I think it very clearly follows), Jesus came to participate in a marriage of perfected persons, but He would not do this outside of the context of ransoming everyone, saving everyone, universal salvation. This has been a problem, that people have married for themselves or just for their children, something of this sort, and salvation has been an individual matter. But Jesus came to give Himself, and He wanted to offer the whole nation of Israel with Him, for the sake of the whole world; and thus, instead of enjoying His perfect relationship with God, a perfect home, He concerned Himself with the salvation of all mankind. This was really giving up everything that He could. This was the model, the sacrificial model. It is a difficult path, and yet the resurrection proves this is the way of hope.

Paul Eshleman: But the way you respond to the resurrection doesn't make any sense without a physical death. You tell me that God is satisfied that Jesus gave His life in service, but there's no resurrection from service.

Johnny Sonneborn: There is a resurrection from service, because you descend in the form of a *servant* and you serve and you get persecuted. You risk your life leading people in the nation on an evangelical crusade into Rome. You may get killed, but if you don't get killed, you still have come out by giving everything, by refusing to use the way of force. As has been eloquently stated by the Evangelicals, you refuse to use anything but love; you put your life in the hands of those enemies, and you come out from it, physically murdered or not, it doesn't matter, for you are elevated as Lord.

Paul Eshleman: How do you deal with the passage: "...without the shedding of blood there is no forgiveness of sins." How do you deal with that?

Johnny Sonneborn: The argument I've heard most often in the Unification church makes sense: in the Old Testament, everything is done on the physical level—this is physical blood. In the New Testament, this is on the spiritual level. I'm not so sure just what spiritual blood is, perhaps the circulation of blood implies something to do with relationships. It certainly doesn't have to be physical death. Many external requirements don't apply in the New Testament Age, because, of course, the dispensation is not the same. We are dispensationalists in this way.

Patricia Zulkosky: Unification theology considers two meanings of death. There is the literal, physical death, and also the spiritual death, which means that we're cut off from God. The kind of death that took place at the fall of man was the spiritual death, whereby we cut ourselves off from the love of God; so for us, resurrection means to revive the spiritual connection of this love relationship with God. Therefore, it is possible for spiritual resurrection to take place by reconnecting the essential bond that was cut by the fall. One need not speak of physical death and physical ressurection. So we're not looking for the eternal physical body. We assume that man is born and that man dies, and that he has an eternal spiritual life in the spiritual world, and that this was God's plan from the beginning. Jesus came to restore spiritual life and our relationship with God. And that could be done without a physical death and resurrection.

Jonathan Wells: The question of sacrifice is also an issue here. Unification theology says the meaning of Jesus' sacrifice is, as Johnny explained, that Jesus sacrificed Himself by disregarding His own pleasure and safety, and going out to save the world. But there is a common misconception that the crucifixion is an example of an Old Testament sacrifice. It's actually the opposite of that—I'll explain briefly. In the Old Testament, for a person to receive some blessing from God, or fulfill his duty, he had to sacrifice an animal, and then the person who offered the sacrifice received the blessing, right? So it's the person who does the sacrifice who receives the benefit. (Paul: With the right attitude ...) Yes, with the right attitude. The crucifixion of Jesus was committed by people who were going against God's will, and they didn't receive the blessing—you see—it was a Satanic sacrifice—actually the exact reverse of all the Old Testament sacrifices.

Paul Eshleman: It was Christ who offered up Himself as the sacrifice, so Christ received the blessing, thus being able to reconcile man to God through His own sacrifice. He was our high priest, laying His own life down as the sacrifice.

Johnny Sonneborn: I think we agree with that. And as Christians, in order to participate in the benefit, we have to offer up the sacrifice in our own offerings of love.

Paul Eshleman: Could anybody have done it? Not just Christ, but anybody in Christ's place?

Johnny Sonneborn: A perfect man, the only begotten Son of the Father.

Paul Eshleman: Why, if He was just coming...

Johnny Sonneborn: Nobody else could have made, nobody else would have made that sacrifice—you have to have the wholeness in order to transcend the national scope of love.

Franz Feige: I think it's important to realize the Divine Principle point of view of salvation as restoration. Now we see salvation taking place as reversing what took place at the fall of man. This is restoration, the reversing of the process of the fall of man. So, without a proper understanding of the fall of man, we will not be able to understand the mission of Jesus, His salvation. At the fall, Satan was able to deceive Eve, and Eve finally deceived Adam; Satan deceived Adam through Eve. For restoration, these three positions are the most important. That means, the messiah alone cannot bring salvation. He requires a woman in the position of Eve, and somebody in the position of Lucifer, who is restored. That's what it boils down to—that's why I asked the question before we made the break—what is needed to reconcile God with man? When would God forgive man? What is sufficient for man to do so that God can accept him again as a son?

According to the Divine Principle point of view, the reconciling act of man must involve the domination of Satan. Man at the beginning got subjugated by Satan, or by Lucifer. Now, the reconciling act before God must be man in the position of Adam, woman in the position of Eve, dominating Satan, subjugating Satan. Concerning Jesus, He was able to subjugate Satan in the desert, by resisting the temptation of Satan *three* times. Thus, on an individual level, He dominated Satan. Satan could not invade Him anymore after that, because of His faith in God; therefore, He Himself fulfilled on an individual level His position as Messiah.

Now, that was not enough. An Eve is necessary, a woman in the position of Eve, and also a man in the position of Lucifer. This precisely was the problem at Jesus' time. There were not a woman and man able to completely unite with Christ, to restore these three positions, to restore the fall of man.

What should have happened? Jesus should have found an Eve, a bride, who had complete faith in Him, and a man, like Peter, or John the Baptist originally, who had complete faith in Him. If He had found those two, then the kingdom of heaven would have come into being. Jesus with His bride would have given children without original sin to mankind. This is the point of view of restoration, according to the Divine Principle.

Jesus' act of dying was not enough to reconcile God's heart to man. It was a reconciling act to a certain degree, because Jesus showed complete loyalty to God by keeping His faith. Actually, the victory in Jesus' crucifixion was not brought about by His death, but by His faith. Through His faith in God, Jesus was able to reconcile on a spiritual level man to God, but not substantially, physically. There was also the necessity for a woman of complete faith, and a man in Lucifer's position, showing complete faith, and that was the problem.

Patricia Zulkosky: To address your question, why couldn't just anybody do it, we need to note that God is pure and man is impure, and purity and impurity don't have any foundation to relate to each other. So, when the messiah comes, in order to relate, to bring man back to God, he also must be pure. But it's still the same problem because man is impure and the messiah is pure, and there is still no foundation of connecting there. Therefore, before the messiah can be sent, mankind must fulfill a fundamental condition to become symbolically pure. This doesn't mean that we can purify ourselves; we can't, we're sinners. Nor can we really understand purity, but there are certain imbalances created during the fall that have to be restored. The stories of Cain and Abel, of Noah, and Abraham are instances in the Scriptures, where God was trying to give man the chance to symbolically reverse the things that happened at the fall, so that man could become symbolically pure. The minimum foundation for purity was accomplished through Abraham, Isaac, and Jacob; so technically speaking, that's the point in history when the messiah could have been able to come, but at that time the foundation was confined to a family level, while surrounding this family, great nations grew up without such a foundation. We feel that God wanted to save the world and not just a family. Therefore, God wanted that family foundation to be expanded so that when His Son came, He would have a fair chance to be able to reach the whole world.

The messiah can't be just anyone—in fact, the messiah couldn't even come until mankind, represented by certain central figures, had laid conditions for his coming. Even then the messiah could only appear through God's will and intervention. Based on these foundations, or symbolic conditions, if you will, that man had fulfilled, God could intervene in history through one sinless man. That sinless man is in the same position as Adam was before he fell; he has the responsibility to grow and to become what Adam should have become, perfect man, establishing his oneness with God beyond a possibility of falling. Jesus became the Messiah at that point, and only He can intercede for man's salvation, and it's only His sacrifice that can mediate man to God.

Mark Branson: So you're saying that spiritual salvation can be achieved without the cross.

Jonathan Wells: Complete salvation.

Patricia Zulkosky: Complete salvation should have been achieved without the cross.

Jonathan Wells: But not without sacrifice.

Whitney Shiner: The reason that the messiah is the only one who can offer sacrifice is the position that he's in as true parent. The actual point of restoration, the removal of sin, is the change of lineage. Original sin means that, because of the fall, Satan is in a position to claim all men as his children, and because we're in that position, no matter how much we work to overcome this sin, and no matter what God does, as long as Satan has that condition to claim us, then we can't be pure. So the point of restoration is changing from Satanic lineage to God's pure lineage, which means that there has to be somebody in the position of parent. True Parents, the pure man and woman, claim a person into their lineage.

Now, before that, there have to be conditions set by the messiah, and set by the people so that the True Parents can claim the people into their lineage. But, it has to be a pure son of God who does it. No matter what I do, I can't ever make the sacrifice. So Jesus and the Holy Spirit are in the position of True Parents.

Paul Eshleman: I understand True Parents in terms of restoration. You're saying to me that you look at the cross only as the representation of Christ's sacrifice, and that we need somebody else for complete restoration, because the cross ended with His death. If He hadn't died, Jesus could have gone forward and His sacrifice would have been His service, which would have been a reconciling factor of man to God, and then total restoration would have occurred as the new family would develop...

Patricia Zulkosky: Only supported by the faith of people.

Whitney Shiner: Already in Jesus' life there was the condition that if Jesus had been accepted, and then could have a bride in that position...

Paul Eshleman: But wouldn't He have had to sacrifice something in order to reconcile man to God?

Whitney Shiner: Sacrifice of His heart, it's always heart that God accepts as a sacrifice. Even on the cross, it wasn't the death that God accepted, but the offering of Jesus' heart—it was the attitude of Jesus' heart on the cross which made spiritual salvation possible. All His previous sacrifice was lost when people rejected Jesus, so the cross indemnified all that, all at once, providing another chance, spiritually.

Anthony Guerra: In line with the concept of sacrifice as a change of heart is the Unification notion of the failure of John the Baptist in his mission as the forerunner of Christ. I think that we need to understand the role of John the Baptist if the Unification position that Jesus could have built the kingdom of heaven

on earth 2,000 years ago is to be at all plausible. As an acknow-
ledged spiritual leader of his time, John the Baptist was supposed
to prepare the people to accept Jesus and to point to Him as the
Messiah. Although John recognized Jesus as the Christ through
his spiritual experience with Jesus at the Jordan River, he did not
carry out his tasks of bringing his own disciples to follow Jesus,
nor did he ever humble himself to the extent of becoming a
disciple. He failed to do these things. We point to several passages
in Scripture which accord with this perspective. For instance, we
find that after John the Baptist was imprisoned because of his
involvement in court affairs, he sent some of his own disciples to
Jesus in order to ask Him, "Are you he who is to come, or shall
we look for another?" (Mathew 11:3). The contradiction appears
between his earlier acknowledgement of Jesus and his asking the
question of Jesus if He is indeed the Messiah. We understand the
contradiction to be explained by the fact that John the Baptist
did not wholeheartedly accept Jesus as his master and fully unite
with Him in heart and action, (i.e., follow Him as His disciple). It
was this failure of John that made it very difficult for Jesus to accomplish His mission.

In Unification terms, the practical work of restoration entailed
bringing the people of Israel to repentance, so that the Israelites
could then go forth as a nation of priests to meet the spiritual
leaders of other nations and religions. They, together, would
establish a world family embodying the ideals of love and justice.
God had already established a world-wide foundation to accept
the Messiah, and various spiritual leaders existed throughout the
world capable of responding to the call of the times. Along with
such religious preparation, we look also at the socio-political
circumstances at the time of Jesus as conducive to the establishment of the kingdom of heaven on earth. This was the time of the
Pax Romana of the Roman Empire with its great system of transportation, and of the tremendous Hellenistic scientific and cultural
achievements. We believe that this external preparation was also
important for the fulfillment of the full messianic mission.

Yet, the critical factor remained the response of the people
of Israel to their new spiritual leader. It was at this moment that
the contribution of John the Baptist, as a revered prophet of the
Jewish people, in affirming Jesus and inspiring the loyalty of a
sizeable portion of Israel to Him, would have been essential to
the success of the mission of Jesus. God had worked throughout

a long history with the Jewish people to prepare them to accept the messiah. Had God wanted Jesus merely to be neglected and crucified then we would have had no reason for this lengthy period of special providence for the Israelite people. That is, the entire Old Testament age was to have culminated with John the Baptist connecting the Jews to the messiah. John the Baptist was the key factor in the final scene.

Let me make one more remark, and I hope this is not too confessional. When we as Unification church members consider the crucifixion, we look on it with great sorrow, and feel that at that moment God was deeply grieved over the crucifixion of His only Son. But He could also rejoice in the willingness of Jesus to sacrifice Himself for the love of God and the world, and particularly because Jesus was able to say, "Father, forgive them; for they know not what they do." This act of love was a victory; the expression of love was the sacrifice, a sacrifice which has redemptive value. Further, we must add that it would have been far better if "they knew what they were supposed to do," and did it!

Dan Davies: I'd like to add a comment to what Anthony is saying. We understand and experience the sorrow of the crucifixion very deeply. But, also, we experience and understand the joy of the resurrection.

Secondly, I think Christians have lost touch with the potential of each man to become a restored person because they have narrowed their theological focus solely on the crucifixion and the resulting spiritual salvation. Christianity would do well to learn the Buddhist understanding of the true man. The Buddhist focus is upon man on the earth. The Christian focus is upon man in the spiritual kingdom. Christianity would do well to bring its spirituality down to earth.

Tirza Shilgi: I just wanted to relate to one more thing Paul (Eshleman) was saying about sacrifice. I don't want you to get the idea that we deny the value of sacrifice. Actually, we don't see salvation without sacrifice. Also, we don't deny that once people rejected Jesus and the original disciples fell away, His death on the cross was the only way. We don't deny that.

And I think Jesus, Himself, gave us the formula for sacrifice when He said to the people, "The one who is willing to lose his life will gain his life, and the one who is not willing to lose his life will lose it." I'm sure He didn't mean people would literally commit suicide for His sake, but He was telling us actually that the way of salvation is through sacrifice. Jesus advised that the rich man give up his belongings, that he be willing to lose that for Jesus' sake in order to gain salvation. He showed that the way of sacrifice was the way of salvation, but not that physical death was indispensible.

Patrick Means: I've dialogued with a number of Buddhists who have tried to tell me that they believed in the concept of the Saviour as much as we do in Christianity. Of course they mean the concept of *bodhisattva,* with the prime example being Buddha, who turned away from the path he could have taken right on into Nirvana, and instead led a sacrifical life of giving himself to service here on earth. Now, in what sense is your concept of Christ's sacrifice different from the Buddhist concept of *bodhisattva*?

Dan Davies: It takes a true man, a person without original sin, a true Adam, to lead man into true manhood. Buddha showed people how to go a distance along the path to becoming a true man, but he didn't have the special mission to bear the burden of mankind's sins. His mission was to elevate the spirituality of the eastern part of the world in preparation to receive Christ. He took people as far as he could by way of the eightfold path, but he did not have the mission, the responsibility, or the capacity to pay for the sins of mankind.

Jonathan Wells: He was more comparable to John the Baptist than to Jesus.

Johnny Sonneborn: Yes, and from our view Jesus' whole purpose was to restore the individual, the family, the nation, the world, and the whole cosmos. Buddha, on the other hand, really came as a teacher, to show people about purified relationships without any answer on the world scope. He didn't have the heart of a parent, but the heart of a teacher. Now what are really being sacrificed, it seems to me, are undeniably relationships, because Satan and God work through relationships depending upon which condition you make, according to the Divine Principle. Jesus sacrificed His potential marriage relationship, and other kinds of relationships, and that is what we still need to do as Christians. Before the time of Jesus, and still now, unfortunately, people want to marry for themselves, have children for themselves, or for their image, rather than for the whole world and for God. That's why the family has been the crux of the battleground between God and Satan in this way.

This explains much of the Unification church view of marriage, which is that one must marry for the sake of the whole world; we are ready, for example, to marry interracially, for the providence, because we don't see the barriers anymore. The eschatological prophet, we've mentioned has to be able to do the work that John the Baptist was doing before, which was purifying the Israelites at that particular level of individual sacrifice. Now the coming eschatological prophet has to prepare the way for the coming third Adam, coming Christ, by warning Christians of falling short of the standard of Jesus, and trying to encourage people to live the full Christian sacrifice. As families, we can participate in this, and when enough people do this, and there is a nation based upon some morality of sacrifice, then the messiah, who, as you know, we believe stands on earth someplace, can stand as a messiah who performs the work.

Rod Sawatsky: Can I ask a question about a nuance here that I haven't caught before? There needs to be a new John the Baptist, a new Elijah, before there can be a third Adam? Is that Elijah present in the world?

Johnny Sonneborn: I think it's very clear that Rev. Moon is at least that eschatological prophet.

Rod Sawatsky: At least Elijah. He is the second coming?

Johnny Sonneborn: As we explained, the actual John the Baptist did not complete his mission, he did not deliver all the Israelites purified to Jesus as a sacrifice for the whole world. Therefore, Jesus—all His mission, actually—after the time of the temptation until His exaltation at Pentecost, was in the position of John the Baptist. He was doing that work; He was always speaking on a national level. He wasn't even talking about international liberation. He was always speaking only to the Jews, and He was speaking prophetically. Even His first words after the temptations were the same words John the Baptist used. It is very clear to us and in structural exegesis as well, that He was acting in the John the Baptist position because He had to do that before He could be elevated to resume His role as messiah; namely giving rebirth, physical and spiritual. Therefore, it is possible in that frame of reference that there could have been a John the Baptist person now who may have failed, and that the one who is carrying on that role could actually be that person who God intends to be the messiah; but that's not certain.

Rod Sawatsky: Can you have a person ultimately claim both

roles, both John the Baptist and the second coming?

Franz Feige: Before we go on, I think we should explain something about the nature of the messiah—who can be a messiah?

I think both the Christian and the Jewish concepts of the messiah come from biblical prophecy, but our concept of the messiah is not only from the Bible, but from our doctrine of creation and doctrine of the fall, and there is a very clear difference. At the fall of man, Adam could have remained intact if he had not given in to Eve's temptation. If he had remained separated from Satan, and had grown to perfection, into oneness with God, he would have become a true man, a perfect man. God, at that time, would have used Adam as the messiah, to first bring Eve back to God, and then to bring Lucifer back to God. That explains the position of the messiah.

It means the messiah cannot be God Himself. He must be a man. Therefore, a man is necessary to restore the sin of the fall. It doesn't have to be God Himself. Why? Because the nature of man is to be like unto God, is to be of even higher potential than the angels, higher than Lucifer. Man is to judge the angels, as St. Paul said, meaning that man is capable of subjugating Satan, of freeing man from the dominion of Satan and reconciling him with God. It is very important to understand that. This enables us to understand Jesus' nature. Was Jesus God Himself, or was He true man? We derive that from our concept of the messiah, which lies in our concept of the creation and the fall. It does not come from the tradition of biblical prophecy, but it could be reconciled with it.

Paul Eshleman: To go back earlier, where in Scripture does it say there is a need for Jesus Christ to have married and to have had a family?

Johnny Sonneborn: That's a very good question. Well, of course there is talk of the second coming, about the Lamb and His bride, which can be interpreted in different ways. We have given the Unification interpretation. Besides, Scripture doesn't necessarily always point to the details of what's coming. Jesus said, to paraphrase, I have told you many things, but you cannot bear everything now, I will reveal more things to you; the hour will come when I will speak plainly of the Father. In order to understand, therefore, it is wise to find the theological principles revealed in the Scripture. We look at how God has operated in the past, how His intention was revealed in Genesis. We note the mode of God's operation, how He always calls upon man to take greater responsibility, to have more faith. He has progressively given us more of His power and asked us to do more on the basis of that. Now, Adam was a totally special creation—no human parents; then the second Adam—of human parents, the way it is usually told, therefore, the third Adam doesn't have to have a mysterious birth in this way.

Patricia Zulkosky: We often point to different parables where Jesus refers to Himself as the bridegroom, such as in the parable about the marriage feast. I understand the modern interpretation is that Jesus is the bridegroom and the church is the bride. However, if we assume He is speaking literally, not allegorically, then we can go back and read the Scripture from the point of view that perhaps Jesus did come to take a bride, and establish an earthly kingdom. Then the total message of the ideal for man, the fall, and the process of restoration becomes clear.

Jonathan Wells: I get the feeling that we are going to break for lunch soon, and yet Paul has brought up what actually is one of the principal questions on our agenda: the relationship between the *Divine Principle* and Scripture. I want to make a brief comment on that, which won't be the last word, but can at least put something in perspective. As Franz pointed out, there are aspects of the *Divine Principle* which are not strictly deducible from Scripture—that is an observable fact. Nevertheless, we see the *Divine Principle* as thoroughly compatible with Scripture when read as a whole. In the same sense, Jesus' teachings are thoroughly compatible with the Old Testament, although not strictly deducible from it. That is a very superficial statement on a very complex subject, and I know we will try to do it more thoroughly after lunch.

Irving Hexham: You're affirming progressive revelation, though?

Jonathan Wells: Yes.

Rod Sawatsky: Time is virtually up. Can we have quick statements on what is on your minds now, and then we can pick up after lunch?

Joseph Hopkins: May I just observe from the Evangelical viewpoint that the Unification church is just one among many groups which claim to have a latter-day revelation to explain the Bible—the Mormon religion, Mary Baker Eddy's *Key to the Scriptures,* and so on. This is a dangerous precedent, because if the Scriptures don't mean what they say, then we're in trouble. Jude 1:3 warns, "...contend for the faith which was once for all delivered to the saints." This seems to indicate that the Bible is sufficient in itself for our faith and lives.

Mark Branson: There's another question I'd like clarified after lunch: I've been picking up a pretty strong inference that Adam had the same potential as Christ, and I'd like to have someone state simply what the Unification position is on the pre-incarnation existence of Jesus Christ.

Johnny Sonneborn: I think that Evangelicals have not answered satisfactorily on the area of the second coming. There are many different viewpoints that were given, many of them are conflicting. Unification also has a viewpoint on the second coming. It is one of the things that brings us together. And supposing we're wrong. What will it mean if we're wrong? I'd like to speak about that.

Whitney Shiner: It can be clearly deduced from the Bible that Jesus should have married. Paul said that Jesus came as the second Adam, and therefore as second Adam He should fulfill the purpose of the first Adam, and God's commandment to the first Adam was to be fruitful, multiply, and have dominion.

Rod Sawatsky: Before we conclude this discussion, would someone address briefly the pre-incarnation existence of Christ?

Anthony Guerra: The concept of Logos in Unification thought is that the Logos is the ideal of creation which exists as an attribute of God and as such exists eternally in the Godhead. The highest expression of the ideal is a person, or more correctly, the perfected family. Adam and Eve represented the first attempt to realize this ideal in the temporal order. This ideal was not fulfilled because of their disordered love. A dimension of becoming or self-actualizing is operative. The second opportunity to realize the Logos in the historical realm occurred with Jesus, and it is in this sense that Unification theology speaks of Jesus as the Logos. Jesus fulfilled the ideal as an individual, but the next level of the ideal—family perfection—was not realized.

Irving Hexham: Is the Lord of the Second Advent, then, also to be a perfect incarnation of the Logos?

Johnny Sonneborn: Yes, ultimately, all people...

Irving Hexham: Then there's nothing fundamentally distinctive about Jesus, who was the incarnation of the Logos, if all men are intended...

Johnny Sonneborn: We are to be like Him...

Irving Hexham: So He is not the only Begotten Son?

Johnny Sonneborn: At that time ...He was begotten in a

special way...

Irving Hexham: You believe in the virgin birth?

Johnny Sonneborn: There is no teaching in the *Divine Principle* that affirms the virgin birth. There is the fact that Jesus is born without original sin, and it says that through evil parents one can't be born without original sin. If fallen parents with original sin cannot have children without original sin, then Jesus had to come from heaven; and that mystery is left at that point in the *Divine Principle.*

Patrick Means: Jesus comes from heaven you said...

Johnny Sonneborn: But He came from heaven by being born of Mary on earth...

Patrick Means: And an earthly father as some would teach it...

Johnny Sonneborn: It doesn't say that in the *Divine Principle.*

Patrick Means: He came from heaven, but He didn't pre-exist? Except as an impersonal attribute of God?

Johnny Sonneborn: According to our understanding, we don't say that Jesus of Nazareth, that particular person, pre-existed His birth...pre-existed and became incarnate. The *Divine Principle* says at one point that "Jesus is God in the flesh," which is a way of saying God incarnate...

Jonathan Wells: Which is the same thing as Christian doctrine, basically. The physical man, Jesus of Nazareth, did not pre-exist His birth.

Patrick Means: Was there a person, an eternally begotten Son of God, co-existing with the Father from all eternity?

Jonathan Wells: In the sense of Logos, yes.

Patrick Means: You mean an impersonal idea...

Jonathan Wells: No, a personality...

Patrick Means: A separate personality? God the Father personality, God the Son personality...

Johnny Sonneborn: God also has the idea, called the individual image, of each creature, before it's created. His idea of the man Adam is distinct from His idea of the man, Jesus, and so whether He had all of these individual ideas of everybody from the beginning is one interpretation, whether they developed as things went on is another. The point is that God's idea of perfect man pre-existed; this is the Word. It is not that Jesus became flesh, but that the Word became flesh...

Patrick Means: Did He pre-exist as an idea, or as a person;

that's the distinction I would like to make.

Johnny Sonneborn: We don't speak of the Trinity as persons within God. That's not our category.

Paul Eshleman: When God said let us make man in our image, it sort of connotes a plurality of the Godhead...

Johnny Sonneborn: It might, or God might be speaking to the angels. Some people think He was speaking in majestic We—we happen to believe, as revealed through Rev. Moon, that He is speaking to the angels.

Paul Eshleman: There are Evangelicals who would agree with the heavenly courts concept.

Jonathan Wells: There are differences. Our notion of the Trinity is different—certainly not the traditional Christian notion, and we do speak of dual aspects of God.

Paul Eshleman: We've quoted the word Logos here out of John 1:1: "In the beginning was the Word, and the Word was with God, and the Word was God...all things were made through him, and without him was not anything made that was made." Who does that Him refer to?

Johnny Sonneborn: It refers to the Word, Logos.

Paul Eshleman: And all things were made by Him, and you're saying that that idea...

Jonathan Wells: The blueprint, so to speak...

Johnny Sonneborn: The idea of man. "Word" is a masculine noun in Greek so it becomes Him...

Jonathan Wells: So in a sense the entire creation reflects symbolically different aspects which in perfect man become the image of God.

Johnny Sonneborn: The Word that was made flesh—nothing was made except through this Word because a perfect man was this Word; and this Word became flesh.

AUTHORITY, WORD AND SPIRIT

Rod Sawatsky: Our agenda speaks to questions of authority, questions of revelation, questions of the relationship of the Divine Principle to Scripture, and so on. The issue of continuing revelation and possibly also the work of the Holy Spirit will probably come in here as well. So, let's begin and see where we go, and hopefully we'll not lose sight of discussion of the spirit world later this morning if our conversation moves that way. Do you have a question?

Anthony Guerra: Could we pray before we begin?

Rod Sawatsky: Would you like to pray?

Whitney Shiner: Dear Heavenly Father, we're so grateful for this time that we can spend together, and we look forward to the remaining part of the conference. We feel so much that Your spirit has been here, and we would wish it to be here in even deeper and more blessed ways so that we could really feel Your Holy Spirit, the spirit of Jesus, and spirit of all the saints and martyrs of history who have given their lives, Father. Father, we're grateful that You're working; we pray that we can always be obedient and humble to Your will. We pray this prayer in the most beloved name of Jesus Christ, Amen.

Everyone: Amen.

Rod Sawatsky: O.K., where shall we begin?

Johnny Sonneborn: Well, we are dealing with this whole question of the authority of Scripture. I think maybe the easiest place to begin is the interpretation of Scripture. Then we can move from there to the more complicated question of new revelation and new authority and then to the *Divine Principle* and the interpretation of Scripture in works such as Mary Baker Eddy's *Key to the Scriptures.* I have observed that all Christian groups must interpret Scripture, whether in a creed or a confession, unless they use direct quotations of Scripture only, and even then it's really a compilation. It seems to me that if a particular interpretation of Scripture helps all unite as Christians...

Rod Sawatsky: I'm wondering if we can get going on this by simply asking somebody to talk about *Divine Principle,* the book, the basic document, and tell us how you perceive that work. Is it a theology text, is it in some way new Scripture, what is it? Would that be a fairly tangible place to begin? I'm not arguing with you, Johnny; I think you're right. I'm just trying to think of something that is not too abstract but fairly concrete, because our minds need to get moving this early in the morning, and maybe this is one way to do it, to take something fairly concrete—a book—and begin to talk and see where we go from there. Jan, you had a counterproposal?

Jan Weido: I just thought it would be good to begin with the Bible, since the common denominator between the Unificationists and the Evangelicals is the Bible. If the Evangelicals' view on the Bible could be explained, then we could speak about *Divine Principle* and the relationship between the two.

Don Deffner: I don't think our common denominator is the Bible. I wonder if I could comment on that briefly? I heard a lot about *Divine Principle* last night, and I've read a lot in it. I think the question of its *place,* rather than of hearing more *about* it, is the question to me. For example, I feel that I heard last night and in individual conversations, that the ultimate criterion of truth for Unification persons is the *Divine Principle.* I find it as the ultimate authority; I find it superimposed upon Scripture and the Christian heritage and tradition. I find, for example in reference to Jude 1:6-7 in *Divine Principle* p. 71, and to the dead being raised on Good Friday, *Divine Principle* p. 183, a completely subjective point of view. I find it in *contradiction* to Scripture. Now I'm going to be very brief. And this again is "subjective," but I believe it's from Scripture nevertheless. The keystone in the Christian faith, (in Ephesians 2, 8, 9, and 10, and so on) is being "justified"—this is my hermeneutical principle—that is, "being made right" in God's eyes by *grace,* solely a gift of God through faith. This is the work of the *Holy Spirit* in me, not *my* choosing God. Faith in itself is not a good work; this is a *gift* of God, imputed righteousness through Christ's death and resurrection and the work of the Holy Spirit. But, granted, faith without works is dead. This does not eliminate a life of social justice, social action, that flows from the faith of men and women of the Holy Spirit. So that's my belief. Scripture is solely my guide, and I don't superimpose *my* point of view upon being justified by grace. I find from Unification persons that the *Divine Principle* is the hermeneutic which interprets Scripture, perverts it, and is superimposed upon the Christian tradition.

Rod Sawatsky: I'm a little concerned that we are going to just run with this without having somebody speak more systematically about the *Divine Principle* and its role. Are you going to do that?

Ulrich Tuente: I'll try.

Rod Sawatsky: O.K., so we're going to begin there.

Ulrich Tuente: In one place in the *Divine Principle* in the section about the Last Days, it speaks about false and progressive revelation. For instance, why is there a distinction between the Old Testament and the New Testament? The Old Testament was for the particular spiritual level of the Jewish people at that time to give particular spiritual guidance in order to advance a particular spiritual center. Then, when Jesus Himself came, Jesus said very clearly, "I did not come to abolish the law but to fulfill the law." So Jesus said, "I come to fulfill." He did not abandon that which had been said in the Old Testament, but said very clearly that He came in order to fulfill it. On this foundation of the Old Testament, the New Testament became, then, the most valued scriptural authority for the New Testament age. So we think that in this present time we are in a very similar situation. Jesus Christ has brought His gospel in His time. In this present time, man has advanced to a certain spiritual understanding which doesn't either abolish the Old Testament or the New Testament, but which brings both Old and New Testaments to their completion and to a further understanding. Just as, in this way, Jesus took His own word as the authority to advance mankind more, at this present time, we likewise take the *Divine Principle* as an authority, without abolishing at all the Old and New Testaments.

Anthony Guerra: I'd like to raise the historical point of how the Divine Principle came about. I think that this will throw light on the whole issue. *The Divine Principle,* as a textbook which is there before you, was not used or did not even exist when Rev.

Moon began his ministry. As I understand it, while matriculating at college, he would have three Bibles open in his room all the time, different Japanese and Korean translations. He read the Scriptures scrupulously and prayed about them. After seven years of this, he began to teach people by explaining passages of the Old and New Testaments in a kind of systematic way. There was not a *Divine Principle* book; there were no lectures at that point. He was doing exegesis in a way similar to how Martin Luther did his exegesis. Later, a *Divine Principle* textbook was developed as a way of systematizing his interpretation of the Scriptures. And it was used as a textbook, as a guide for people who wanted to communicate those insights. For me, the central point is that it's an interpretation of the Scriptures much in the same way as Martin Luther's works or Calvin's *Institutes* are interpretations of the Scriptures. We differ with the biblical doctrine of inerrancy. We don't believe in propositional revelation. The people who wrote the Bible certainly were inspired and were conveying the message of God, but they were conveying it in human language and in a cultural situation, at a historical point in time, communicating to people likewise bound. Their purpose was to communicate with people who were bound in historical situations. That does not mean that the meaning is limited but certainly means that the expression of that meaning is limited.

Irving Hexham: Divine Principle, then, is not the book; the Divine Principle is a transcendent, cosmic thing.

Anthony Guerra: Well, basically it's God's principle; it's within God. It's a metaphysical truth, and it's not anything that's written in the book.

Irving Hexham: It's not.

Anthony Guerra: Yes, it's not.

Pete Sommer: Maybe I misunderstood. This written *Divine Principle* is the fruit of Rev. Moon's Bible study? Or was it mediated through additional editions and revelations?

Anthony Guerra: You see, that's what I'm saying. The process of revelation for us, in a sense, is his reading the Scriptures, praying about what the Scriptures mean and receiving insight. The whole process is one of interacting with the Scriptures and the Holy Spirit.

Pete Sommer: But you don't have confidence that the average man reading the book and reading the Scripture would come up with any or near the same conclusions that he has here?

Anthony Guerra: No, that's not it at all. Many people have come up with very similar conclusions. Someone mentioned Bultmann in terms of similarity on one point of interpretation. If you study various other interpretations, you will find similarities with the Divine Principle interpretation, so the Holy Spirit had been working in many ways. We believe that the Divine Principle is the fullest explanation of the Scriptures. All the books of the Old Testament, all the books of the New Testament are inspired by God. One thing that's very important to us is finding an interpretation of the Scriptures which makes sense of the entirety of the Scriptures and doesn't concentrate, say, on one book or only on some passages. We need an interpretation that reconciles contradictions rather than saying, "Well, we just don't want to deal with that passage," or, "We don't want to deal with the book of James." We want to deal with the whole Scripture, and we believe that this interpretation presents the most comprehensive, consistent explanation of Scripture.

Irving Hexham: Is that an inspired explanation?

Rod Sawatsky: Let Dan speak; Mr. Davies has been wanting to get in here.

Dan Davies: This is something we have talked about before among ourselves. We are by no means in agreement on these things at all. I believe that all the Divine Principle is not in the book. The *Divine Principle* book comes on the foundation of the Bible. However, not everything that's in the *Divine Principle* is in the Bible or can be supported by the Bible. But the *Divine Principle* has a way of bringing together the biblical truth that I hold dear with science and world religions. I love the Principle. It brings me joy in the same way the Bible does and even deeper, because I find a deeper truth there. I find an explanation of the Bible that makes sense. The purpose for history is explained. I often wondered about the value of the stories of the Old Testament. They were nice, but they didn't mean anything to me. But through the Divine Principle I can now understand the whole purpose of the Old Testament history, and I can also understand the purpose of New Testament history. It answered important questions for me, such as why God has waited so long to restore the world.

Virgil Cruz: Just a very quick question directed to Anthony. The textbook in which Rev. Moon gives some explanation of the

Divine Principle—is that to be compared to the writings of Martin Luther as you said, or is it to be compared in stature and significance to the writings of the Gospel of Mark? Which of those?

Anthony Guerra: It's certainly not to be compared to the Gospel of Mark in the sense that I think you would say that one cannot change the Gospel of Mark. You wouldn't say that you could rewrite the Gospel of Mark, but Rev. Moon can say that he is going to rewrite this book. So that means that this book, as it stands, is not equated with the absolute truth. We do not affirm the tenet of propositional revelation.

Paul Eshleman: Can he alter the Principle? Change a few parts of it?

Anthony Guerra: No, the Divine Principle again is a metaphysical reality; it's an attribute of God, you might say, and it cannot be expressed in any words. It can't be fully expressed.

Warren Lewis: Let me work on this a little bit. As a teacher here, I have the pleasant opportunity of giving final examinations. On my final exams I always give the students a chance to express themselves theologically on some issue that was critical for the period of church history that we had just studied. So one time I raised the question with them, what is *Divine Principle*? Is it the 28th book of the New Testament? Is it a third testament? And I gave them a spread of options from something that you ought to bind in black leather and print in India ink on this paper with gold edges all the way over, to a book of theology, and a lot of things in between. And I got a spread of opinions. There are people who think that that Black Book is inerrant and infallible, just the way Lindsell thinks the Bible is, and there are people who know that Rev. Moon didn't write it. It's a committee product and some would frankly admit that it's simply riddled with historical and scientific inaccuracy, but who would still argue that the principles which it contains, which you can reduce to a handful, are metaphysical statements about the nature of God and reality. So I don't think any one Unificationist can ever answer your question because there is a variety.

Virgil Cruz: One more question of clarification. I still haven't gotten a handle on what it is which commends the textbook and the Divine Principle itself to a Unificationist. For example, as far as canonical Scriptures are concerned, we say there are principles of canonicity. The books have some contact with the apostles.

We say that the books were used in the Christian Church. We say that the books show an internal consistency with one as compared with another. Now, is it correct for me to deduce that this is a two-pronged affair? The basis of authority for one is that the authority of Rev. Moon himself is given to the *Divine Principle,* which therefore commends it to his followers. Secondly, is there some more subjective proof somewhat similar to that which Calvin used when he said, "How do you know that sugar is sweet? Taste it." How do you know by reading this Scripture that it commends itself? Is there something like that?

Johnny Sonneborn: I think that we should look at what the book says about itself. And the book says it is an attempt by the followers of Rev. Moon to write down parts of the new truth, the new expression of truth to be precise, which he has been speaking about, as they understood it. What were Rev. Moon's credentials for bringing this new truth? He studied the Scriptures. He also had spiritual encounters with many great spiritual leaders from the past and had other revelations. He spoke to Buddha, with Mary and other persons. He also went through a period of suffering and struggling, overcoming billions of satans in the way; the text describes this, that he really wrestled with the questions, and sorrows, of God and mankind this way. Also, in connection with the other prong of your questions, the expression of truth is set forth as an hypothesis. In other words, it is suggested that the book begins to express the principles which will solve the fundamental questions of man and the universe. It sets forth an hypothesis which we're asking people to study, to look at, to see and to pray about—and to accept—as a theorem on the grounds that as a new truth it brings a fundamental solution to followers of religion and science.

Anthony Guerra: To answer your question, why do we consider this book authoritative? Why do we accept it? And, well I don't know about anyone else here, but I didn't even know Rev. Moon or anything about Rev. Moon when I heard and accepted. The reason I accepted was that I thought that it was very reasonable. It sounded true by my own rational judgment; this was the original basis on which I said it was true. Others accepted it because they thought it best explained the Scriptures. Some may have found other interpretations, maybe the Lutheran inter- pretation or the Papal interpretation or the Calvinist interpretation, to be inadequate or unsatisfying. Other people pray to Jesus or pray to God and were directed or were told this is true. These are various ways in which people here encountered the teaching. We're not told, "Look, Rev. Moon received it and he was given a revelation by God, so believe it." They're not told that when they confront this. In these various ways an individual decides that he or she is going to commit himself/herself to this way of life.

Don Deffner: And each of these is very subjective.

Anthony Guerra: Sure.

Don Deffner: What I see then is a broad spectrum that Dr. Lewis was speaking of in terms of Unification students' view of the *Divine Principle.* I nevertheless have heard from students here a common assumption that the Bible is seen in the light of the *Divine Principle.*

Anthony Guerra: That's true.

Don Deffner: Whereas for me, I believe with my brethren here, it is Scripture in light of Scripture; the Bible interprets itself.

Irving Hexham: Can I ask for a clarification? It seems that what's going on is a misunderstanding between the Evangelicals and the Unification church people which could be put in one of two ways. I'll give them both. One would be that Unification is post-Guttenberg whereas Evangelicals are still Guttenberg. (laughter) We look to Scripture; they're working on something which is beyond a written document. It is cool communication; we are hot communicators. The other way of putting it would be David Riesman's model. We, the Evangelicals, are working with an inner-directedness in terms of an inner-directed Puritan society, a Puritan mind; they, members of the Unification church, are working with something which is closer to the tradition of the other-directed personality. And the other-directed personality, is, in McLuhan's terms, a post-Guttenberg thing. This discussion of Scripture isn't important because you have a different type of communication going on. Now I wonder if that is of any help or if someone would like to comment on it.

Mark Branson: Maybe we could focus on that by asking what happens to *Divine Principle* as a written text after Rev. Moon dies.

Whitney Shiner: I have a comment from several questions back. There are two aspects of the Divine Principle: one is a metaphysical system which is most of the "Principle of Creation," and the other is the rest of it as an interpretation of the Bible and of history based on that system. And, if you take the system and you look at the Bible, then that is a natural interpretation of the Bible. At some point Rev. Moon said that he gave us too much; he should have just given us the "Principle of Creation" and let us find the rest. Everybody takes to the Bible some metaphysical system from which he interprets it. Things like the spirit world or the ontology don't come from the Bible; they come from Rev. Moon's own understanding of the spirit world. Our own understanding of the relationship between God and man is something that one can test out in his own spiritual life. One can assume they're true and act as if they're true and see what results one gets. With the spirit world, many people have experiences with it directly. I consider it to be scientific truth that that has nothing to do with revelation or interpretation. Once you test that, then you take it to the Bible.

Warren Lewis: But it's still up for grabs as far as he's concerned on a lot of points. And this is where it's really different from what we people from traditional Christian backgrounds have experienced. This is a wide-open theological situation which is why I find it interesting as a historian of Christian thought and a practicing Christian theologian. If you can ever get off the confessional agony of deciding whether they're right or we're right, you can just appreciate it as a theological novelty. It's wide open, and what's happening here is that oriental categories—Buddhism, Shintoism, Confucianism—all those things are being wedded to the Christian Gospel.

Athanasius wedded Christianity to Greek thought. When I ask you whether you believe that Jesus Christ is of the same substance as the Father, you confess that He is and you confess Greek philosophy. You don't confess the Gospel, yet it's in the creed of Nicea. Now, what we're getting here is a step in the acute orientalization of the Gospel. The Greeks did it, the Latins did it, Thomas did it with Aristotle, Luther did it, Calvin did it, the Americans have done it, and now the Koreans are taking their turn. So, what's interesting about it from a theological perspective is that it's wide open and these people don't think that they already know what every verse of the Bible means, the way you and I do. Don, I respect you, but there are many interpretations of what that passage means about the dead saints being raised on Good Friday. You know you can't just sort of pull that one on us. But you're right when you say that these folk are reading the

Bible through the perspective of Divine Principle. Just as Rev. Moon, who has an oriental mind and heart, is looking at the Christian Gospel through the spectacles of his oriental perspective and coming up therefore with a completely new system of Christian thought.

Virgil Cruz: Just one quickie here. I don't understand your impression that the field is wide open to creative theologizing. Johnny and I talked about that, and there are certain givens, aren't there? There are certain immutable principles, it would seem. It would be very helpful for me if someone would lay on me a few of them.

Warren Lewis: What the Divine Principles really are?

Virgil Cruz: Yes. Because I just cannot believe that tomorrow you could be going off with it in another firm direction and reverse yourself in any way. I just can't believe that. I think you're spelling out the implications of certain givens, and I don't yet know all the givens.

Irving Hexham: Before we turn to this question, could we have a response to the question I asked about hot and cold communication? I would like to know if I was on the right track.

Anthony Guerra: If I understood you right, I think I agree that we don't consider any written word or expression to be the equivalent of absolute truth. The written word is an expression of truth, and the written word does not have the same kind of ultimate authority in itself. I wasn't sure about the second point regarding cool and hot media.

Irving Hexham: It's a feeling about where the communication comes from. The Divine Principle seems to float around and land on people, and people in the community share it. You share in it and it's not something that you point to. I don't know whether you can discuss it as we are doing, because I don't think you operate in that way. You're operating with a different model of communication.

Rod Sawatsky: Well, let's test it out. I think we can talk about the canon. I think we can have somebody spell out what Divine Principle is. Who is going to do it? I think Jonathan could probably do a good job with it.

Jonathan Wells: Yes, I'd like to suggest a few basic principles and also, by way of tying it in with these other comments, set it in an historical situation. First of all, God is unchanging, absolute and eternal and is the Creator of the world. God created man,

Adam and Eve, to be His children. Because of the position of
man in creation, man is given free will. So, unlike the rest of the
creation, man is capable of turning against God. As a guide to
fulfilling their responsibility, God gave Adam and Eve the commandment in the Garden of Eden, which they violated. Because
of the violation of the commandment then, rather than abandoning
His fallen children, God has worked His providence of restoration
ever since and tried to bring mankind back to Him, to be His true
children. The history of Israel was a preparation for the coming
of Jesus, who came as the second Adam and who, in His own life,
fulfilled what Adam failed to fulfill. But, in order to save the rest
of mankind, it was necessary for mankind to reverse the fall by
following Jesus. We know that mankind failed to do this. Even
Jesus' closest disciples ultimately deserted Him at the critical
time. So, before Jesus was crucified, He Himself said that a new
truth would come, and the whole prediction of the second
coming implies that there is more. So, since Jesus died, the
history of Christianity actually has been a preparation for the
second coming. These times that we're living in now are the last
days that Jesus spoke about. And, therefore, this is the time of
the second coming.

We have a wide-open theological situation. Christian dogma
went through some very serious dislocations when the parousia
failed 2,000 years ago. Jesus said He'd come again before the
disciples went throughout Israel, but He didn't. So Christian
dogma became frozen to various hybridizations with Greek
philosophy and other doctrines, and we're looking back on this
kind of frozen situation. But, at the time of the second coming,
new truth comes. And, we must avoid the same mistake that was
made two thousand years ago, which was to adhere too literally
to an accepted notion of what the Scripture meant. Because of
their literal adherence to their own ideas of the Scripture, people
rejected Jesus. So, one basic distinction I feel here, between
Evangelicals and Unification people, is that Unification people
feel that the historical context now justifies a re-evaluation of our
ideas of Scripture.

Rod Sawatsky: Now, just a minute before we move on. What
you have said is that the Divine Principle is immutable. Even Rev.
Moon couldn't change what you have said, and everybody would
have to agree with what Jonathan said. Right?

Jonathan Wells: Well, up to the point where I discussed the present situation. Even that, it's a basic outline.

Jan Weido: I agree with him, but I would use different expressions. I think we speak to more than just the Judeo-Christian tradition. Take the law of indemnity, for example; it works for Hindus, and for Muslims. Call it karma, or whatever, but it works. The whole thing about dual essentialities works for a Taoist, just as it works for me. For the thing about misuse of love, you don't have to talk about the serpent seducing Eve, just about the misuse of love and the destruction of the four-position foundation without talking about Adam and Eve and Cain and Abel. Those are universal principles.

Rod Sawatsky: We've got to get clarity on this one before we move on. On the one hand we have basically a Judeo-Christian interpretation, insisting that the Judeo-Christian tradition is necessary for the Divine Principle, and you are saying no, you don't need that.

Jan Weido: A final thing I would say is that the principle of restoration also talks about God's having to work from one point—the family, the tribe, the nation. There's a principle of chosen religion which makes the Judeo-Christian religion, as a tradition, important; but it also means that all other traditions have some role to play in the restoration of the world. The whole world is evolving and is converging in some way. We have not spelled it out yet; but the traditions are all important.

Irving Hexham: A question directed to Jonathan: is the outline you've given history or myth? You were talking about Adam and all this sort of thing—is it history or myth?

Jonathan Wells: History.

Nora Spurgin: One of the earlier versions of the Divine Principle in English was entitled: *The Divine Principle and Its Application.** Actually, this Divine Principle is basically contained in the first chapter. If you read that first chapter, it describes the basic Divine Principle—The Principle of Creation— including the principles of growth, the principles of the four-position foundation, etc. Then, the rest of it is history, applying those basic principles to the history of man. Beginning with man's deviation, the fall, you then find how things were restored by

---

*Young Oon Kim, *Divine Principle and its Application,* various editions, Washington, D.C.: Holy Spirit Association for the Unification of World Christianity, 1960-1972.

using the basic principles in the first section. So, actually Rev. Moon has said that, if we only have the very first chapter, we can figure out all the rest, even though it would take quite a lot to figure out the second part. That was a real key to his being able to give mankind a key to life. I feel that's the real key, that he gave mankind something additional—an understanding of evil and the way to overcome it—but basically the Divine Principle is contained in the first chapter.

Johnny Sonneborn: As I understand it, the question we're trying to answer is: what is it that most Unification church members believe? Everything Nora says is absolutely true, but it's a question of what is the Divine Principle, or Principle of Creation. Everything that Jonathan said, every member of the Unification church believes. We all believe the additional things that Jan said. We also all believe that God develops His providence leading up to the time of Jesus through events such as are accounted for by the stories of Noah and all the others. Now some people in the church might believe that the stories didn't happen exactly the way they are told, but may be representations of stories; these steps of development had to be gone through on the family level, tribal level, up to today. God did work centering through Israel. These are historical facts, not a myth. There was first a man and a woman, wherever it was, whatever the circumstances were. It's not a myth; this must have happened. We will all agree on that. We will all agree on there being a John the Baptist, and these things happening, there being disciples of Jesus, as reported in the *Divine Principle* textbook. We would all agree on what happened with Jesus and certain key figures in Christendom. We would all agree that God is working in other religions, but we don't have any agreement as to how or where. We might disagree as to how God is working in Hinduism, but He must work by the same principle—that we would agree with.

Rod Sawatsky: We have explored this quite thoroughly. I would like to turn the tables for awhile. I'd like for some people now, from the Evangelical side, to talk about the authority of Scriptures as they understand it.

Mark Branson: Could anyone answer, or at least give me an idea on my question about canonicity, especially in reference to Rev. Moon's death?

Jonathan Wells: I'm not sure anybody knows how to answer.

Anthony Guerra: One of the things we believe about the

Principle is that what is contained in that book is really a guide to one's life, and, most importantly, it's a guide for perfection. Once the purpose of creation is accomplished, each one of us is going to be in perfect relationship with God. So, as we express truth, it'll be the Divine Principle, it'll be an expression of God's truth. What the book is trying to do is create a way of life, a tradition of the kingdom of God which we believe to be the consummation of the ideal of God in humanity. So that, in a sense, all the truths up to this time—the Bible, and interpretations of it—are given for what purpose, for the salvation of mankind. Right? Once the salvation of mankind is accomplished, truth, or expressions of truth, will have a totally different meaning. In other words, the function or purpose of Scriptures then changes; in a sense, it doesn't have the central soteriological purpose which it now has.

Johnny Sonneborn: Since man's spiritual and intellectual standards still have a way to go, there are going to have to be higher expressions of truth; in other words, the *Divine Principle* book in the present form cannot be the last word. If Rev. Moon were to die tomorrow, that still would not change the fact that this book would have to be rewritten. It has errors in it, and the book itself is only a part of what Rev. Moon himself is teaching. It is bound to have to be supplemented by his own testimony in this way. It might be the first word of the last truth prior to the ultimate kingdom of heaven.

Patrica Zulkosky: I think there's a difference between principles and doctrine. Principles are things that can't be changed, no matter what. They come from God. They are the principles working behind the creation of the world and the continued maintenance of the world, etc., as opposed to doctrine, which is man's viewpoint of how things are developing or the applications of truth to this or that. Doctrine can change, but principles cannot. This understanding may be valuable when we enter into the evangelical discussion.

Irving Hexham: I wonder if it is possible that, if Rev. Moon were to die tomorrow, his "spirit man" would enter or be in communication with his son or someone else and therefore provide ongoing continuity.

Jan Weido: One thing I think will happen is that when Rev. Moon goes into the spirit world, Mrs. Moon, barring any unforeseen accident, will probably live for another forty years, and she will continue the tradition. After that, a family inheritance process, like a monarchy, will allow the next son to follow in Father's footsteps. Even if the next son spaced out and became an American hippy—he can space out—I think it would still continue within the family. There's a heavenly hierarchy, Mr. Kim likes to say. I also think Rev. Moon is putting the responsibility on us, too, especially the graduate students. We are supposed to tighten this up, to work it out, to get it together.

Rod Sawatsky: What Jan just said is highly significant. For most of us from traditional groups, everything is finished more or less, and we know what it is. The Unification people here are in the process of forming a new theology; there's a creative possibility here which many of us are not a part of in the same way. This is not only very interesting, it also changes the dynamic, too, as we communicate with each other. One is more defensive, and one is more open.

Warren Lewis: I just have to tell one of my favorite stories here. On one occasion, Rev. Moon—the clairvoyant shaman who visits the spirit world and talks with people there—told us professors: "If you want to become rich and famous, ask me questions for which nobody knows the answers; I'll get the answers for you from the spirit world; you can write a book and make a lot of money." (laughter) One evening when we were seated at high table in Camelot, I raised the issue with Rev. Moon that I would like to write a book on the Resurrection. The doctrine of ongoing resurrection in *Divine Principle* is one of the most theologically creative notions, although, from my evangelical perspective, short-shrift unfortunately is paid to the physical resurrection of the body of Jesus. So I decided to debate the point with the Reverend. I said, "In terms of your own teaching, because you're a spiritual materialist, there's a built-in reverence for matter. Therefore, somewhere along the line, you have come to terms with the physical resurrection of the body of Jesus. It's only consistent with your point of view on the venerability of matter." I was very gratified when he replied, "You've got a point there; at least you've read the Divine Principle carefully." That made me feel good; so I said, "Now I'm going to collect on your promise. Everybody wants to know what really happened on Easter Sunday morning. So please tell me, so that I can write a book and become rich and famous. Ask Jesus, or whomever, what really happened on Easter morning." He grinned a little bit and said, "Well, I'm not at liberty to tell everything I know, and some things have not yet been revealed." We went back and forth a couple of times more, and finally I pressed him and said, "But you promised to give me the inside info so I could become rich and famous. If you won't tell me, how can I write this book?" He said, "Go ahead and use your own theological imagination. What do you think I do?" (laughter)

Johnny Sonneborn: This is related to the point that was just made, and to a point that Dr. Quebedeaux made at some time; that what is critical is the messianic age and not just a messianic person. In the Divine Principle, whereas God took responsibility for making Satan surrender in the Old Testament age, whereas Jesus and the Holy Spirit have been fulfilling their responsibilities in the New Testament age, the responsibility in the Completed Testament age, the new age, falls upon all of the saints. Therefore, we have to be developing, working at using our imaginations.

Anthony Guerra: Incidentally, the point you're making, it's basically Acts 2:17—that "in the last days it shall be, . . . that I will pour out my spirit upon all flesh, and your sons and your daughters shall prophesy, and your young men shall see visions, and your old men shall dream dreams." So as a young man you should do some prophesying.

Beatriz Gonzales: I would like to say something to what Johnny has said, relating to the earlier mention that when Rev. Moon dies his spirit will be working through someone in our movement. It's true that Rev. Moon will give direction to us. But what's important, and this is the reason why I follow Rev. Moon, is that I recognize that the power behind Rev. Moon is the power of God. Rev. Moon has made himself such a perfect tool for God to work through that the living God can speak to us, can give direction to us, through this man. But Rev. Moon is always saying, "I want you to become Rev. Moons so that when I die, there will be thousands of Rev. Moons." And this is possible. We come to realize this. And this is also why I follow him, because he can bring me to such a relationship with God. God can be a living God in me so that I can serve as a direct tool for God. Maybe not me, maybe I have too much fallen nature, but, as our lineages are purified, maybe several generations from now God will work very directly through man, much more directly than He can work through us.

Pete Sommer: That you're on your way to becoming...

Warren Lewis: Heavenly, potentially divine, divinizable.

Because they are the expression of the Logos and the Holy Spirit, if they had gone on to the perfection intended for Adam and Eve, according to the Divine Principle, then they would have formed a trinity with the Father.

Pete Sommer: Have you ever decided whether your view of creation is really a transcendental model or is it an emanationist ...

Jonathan Wells: Oh, we've been around that one many times!

Pete Sommer: Which is it?...I was interested in Henry Vander Goot's excellent pursuit of this issue in *Exploring Unification Theology.**

Warren Lewis: I think that, after all of the words have been defined and all the points have been pressed, they are finally emanationists. There is no "wholly other" understanding of God as the one, between whom and us there is a great gulf fixed. There is, rather, an infinite number of steps and stages. These people are Platonists, believers in the great chain of being.

Pete Sommer: And that's where an Evangelical would differ on the work of the mediator.

Warren Lewis: Or you can understand the mediator as the missing link.

Mark Branson: Already you're dealing with a pantheistic model; everything is already there.

Warren Lewis: And that's why, ultimately, on the pattern of their originism, which is neo-platonism in and of itself, everything will ultimately return to God. It is entirely a theology of creation— it starts and ends with creation.

Joseph Hopkins: Warren, you said Adam and Eve *are* potentially divine; you didn't say *were,* is that correct?

Warren Lewis: Because they fell, the first pair lost their possibility...

Joseph Hopkins: Yes, I understand that, but are they still potentially divine through restoration?

Warren Lewis: The third Adam and the second Eve are eschatological figures.

Joseph Hopkins: All right, then. How is this different from the Mormon and Armstrong doctrine that God is a family, and

---

*M. Darrol Bryant and Susan Hodges, eds., *Exploring Unification Theology,* New York, N.Y.: Distributed by the Rose of Sharon Press, 1978.

that all mankind are potentially gods?

Warren Lewis: I understand the Mormon teaching a lot less than I understand the Unificationists, but I think there are real points of similarity.

Jonathan Wells: At the same time, though, I think the Mormons say that God is evolving, whereas the Unification position is that God is absolute, eternal, and unchanging...

Anthony Guerra: The Mormons also teach that the fall was intended.

Johnny Sonneborn: In *Unification Thought,** which is more philosophical, God is the original being, and all other beings are created beings, but the first elements were projected from God. I don't think that's emanationist. In this way, God is the being who stands beyond all. Mr. Sudo always speaks of Him as being transcendent and infinite, and *Unification Thought* speaks about the infinite being in the finite...God is infinite. Otherwise, we end up with a model of the universe as all complete, and then what keeps it going? There has to be something which has to be constantly initiating—an original being, an original force, original love, constantly coming into the creation—otherwise it couldn't expand. And there must always be God to harvest, to get joy at the other end. So, as I understand the teaching, especially from Korean writers, and also from Mr. Sudo, there's definitely a concept of a transcendent God who is immanent in the typical Christian sense that He came into the world. The gulf that came between God and man came with the fall, wherein that which was created became unwhole. But God remained, and man lost the commandments, and then a mediator had to come in place of Adam to bring man back to the holy person.

Pete Sommer: I still think that sounds like Brahma breathing out and breathing in.

Tirza Shilgi: I just wanted to make a brief comment about what I find in *Divine Principle.* There seems to be the consistent principle of the book—the way it works. But this often makes it hard for people outside to categorize or classify it as one thing or another. Many times the Divine Principle is not this or that, but many times it is somewhere in between or both. It really works that way quite often. Let me illustrate in relation to the creation

---

Unification Thought, New York, N.Y.: Unification Thought Institute, 1973. Unification Thought is the philosophical expression of the Divine Principle.

question. It is not emanationist and it's not transcendental; it's somewhere in between. That's why it's so hard, even for ourselves, to classify it as this or that, because it is not only this or that, but it's somewhere in between. It's the same thing with faith and works—it's not only faith and it's not only works, it's somewhere in between. It's the combination of both which should bring about God's will. It may be helpful to look at things in this way rather than to classify them as this or that; a lot of times Divine Principle will be somewhere in between.

Irving Hexham: I want to ask about this developing theology and the way in which things work out. You've said that Rev. Moon visits the spirit world and talks with the spirits. To what extent in the development of your theology do you have experiences with people or beings from the spirit world which help develop your individual theology? Now, yesterday, some people talked about experiences of Christ or Moon, but I'm sure these things are much more common than have so far been mentioned, and I'd like to hear something on that.

John Wiemann: I'd like to say something that answers your question a little bit. As a regular guy growing up, I didn't understand very much about the Bible, and I didn't understand anything about salvation. I was about as spiritual as a turnip and I'm still not very spiritual. I haven't had any spiritual experiences; that is not the way I receive understanding. Sometimes I have inspirational prayer about something which may be true or may not be true. I received a lot of understanding about the Bible—at least I was given the opportunity to think more deeply about it—when I joined the Unification church. I started to understand things which I'd always wondered about—what's Cain-Abel, what's the Jacob story where he deceives his brother with the help of his mother. These all made perfectly good sense to me. Now I find that the Unification church needs to understand more about the Christian understanding of salvation, because it seems to me that this is the foundation upon which Rev. Moon, upon which the Lord of the Second Advent, comes. Rev. Moon himself says, "You cannot understand me one iota unless you have a relationship with Jesus, unless you really can experience through going through the history of all that's taken place. If you can't do that, you just can't understand anything."

Irving Hexham: That's a rationalist explanation. When I asked my question, I noticed that a lot of people nodded and responded and I would like to hear from some of them.

Johnny Sonneborn: There are many people in our movement who have very direct experiences with the spiritual world. In my case, before I joined the movement, I was always taught to have dialogue with authors of books. I always wondered why. Now I believe that it's dangerous for me to see the spirits that are guiding me. I am very aware of being guided but fear that I'll end up forming an unhealthy relationship with the spirits, so I carefully don't keep spiritually open. But I'm aware of being guided.

Don Deffner: I'd like to get some reflection on how Rev. Moon knows that, when he talks to spirits, they're not lying to him? That they are not *demonic* spirits? Satan tempts me, and the prince of liars is trying to trap me all the time. What is the criterion? I see some trouble with both of us there. What is the place of the demonic, satanic, and the evil spirits which could well be behind all this?

Warren Lewis: Are God and Satan the only spirits in the spirit world that we have give-and-take with?

Several voices: No.

Warren Lewis: A lot of us Evangelicals are aware of the presence of evil spiritual powers, but, because we are not very good Catholics, we don't know about the "communio sanctorum," the angels and the spirits of the just ones made perfect.

Don Deffner: No, Satan and his evil hosts...I'd just like to hear that.

Rod Sawatsky: O.K., Jan.

Jan Weido: Well, I can't speak for Rev. Moon, but I can speak for myself. I know the difference when I'm sleeping at night, and I'm awakened, and there's a wild-looking spirit trying to choke me, or I can't get out of bed because I have to exorcise that spirit in the name of Christ. The difference between that and the difference between a very high spirit that comes and brings comfort is clear in the night. Sometimes it's an experience of a dream that will help me understand something about God or something about Divine Principle. It's intuitive; you can tell the difference. You just don't want to be around those lower spirits, because they're very heavy, they're very ugly, and they're very terrible.

Whitney Shiner: I'd like to speak about the authority of the spirit world. We really don't consider anything that we've received from the spirit world as authoritative in any way—that's made very clear. Rev. Moon says that even high spirits in the spirit world generally do what they're doing without understanding probably as much as we do, and that certainly anything we receive from the spirit world should be taken with circumspection. But I'd also like to say this on distinguishing spirits in the spirit world: one's spiritual body reflects one's spiritual state, so you can spiritually see what kind of spirit you're dealing with. For example, high spirits give off a very bright light, and low spirits are very dark.

Helen Subrenat: I know from my evangelical background that many Evangelicals consider any give-and-take with the spirit world as satanic. So I'd like to know what the evangelical side of it is. On the other side, I'd like to say that since I joined the church, there has been an emphasis of not having give-and-take with the spirit world. The Spirit that we want to deepen and increase our relationship with is God, through His mediator, Jesus Christ. So, if we do have a spiritual experience or if we do tend to be more intuitive or more spiritual, we are taught to test the spirits, to challenge them to testify to Jesus Christ, to the truth of God. We don't accept as true just any experience we have.

Virgil Cruz: A couple of things. You wanted us to have just an explicit concentrated discussion of the spirit world. I must say I need something like that. I need a profile of the spirit world. I am very confused as to who those inhabitants are. I had the feeling, I think now incorrectly, that Jesus would be considered as an inhabitant of the spirit world and the Holy Spirit would also be involved in that dimension, and, if those two *are* tax-paying inhabitants, (laughter) how can one say that we should not take anything as authoritative which comes from the spirit world?

Rod Sawatsky: It seems to me that we're going in that direction. I had hoped we were going to get some Evangelical comments on authority first. We seem to be losing that end, and I'm a little worried about that. I think it's running too much in a one-way stream here, and it's not being dialogical. But I think we'd better do what Virgil is asking for now, because if we want to go into this discussion, we'd better have some data on the spirit world. I hope we can get back to having some elaboration in the other direction as well. So let's do this, very quickly and then...

Warren Lewis: Just by way of footnoting a response to what you've said: you're right, but we are still really talking about authority, aren't we? (Yes.) Because you're convinced that Rev. Moon has talked to God the Father, Jesus Christ the Son, and Satan himself, and has, in good shamanistic fashion, wrestled with the spirits and has triumphed in the spirit world, then you don't really have too many problems with biblical authority.

Rod Sawatsky: Good point. Would somebody outline the spirit world for us?

Johnny Sonneborn: This is from the *Divine Principle Study Guide* by Young Whi Kim. He summarizes that good spiritual beings include God (He's not in the spiritual world but is a spiritual being beyond it), good angels, good spirit men, good souls—and the evil spirits include Satan and the spirit people of evil people, or evil spirits. That's who is in the spiritual world. To the other question very succinctly; according to the *Divine Principle* or the *Study Guide* you test the spirits as follows: it's not just a light or dark question; at the beginning they look alike. Unless you have the Divine Principle and have a good spiritual master, you can't be secure in judging spirits. Of course, a good spiritual master is helpful because he's got a higher spiritual standard than you do, and the Divine Principle is the standard of truth by which you judge whether or not the spirit is on God's side or Satan's side.

Irving Hexham: A simple point of clarification. What do you mean by a spiritual master?

Johnny Sonneborn: It means somebody who can give you guidance, who has a higher spiritual level than you, who has a wider and less conditional perspective. Rev. Moon would be a great, very high spiritual master.

Irving Hexham: But there could be other spiritual masters?

Johnny Sonneborn: Yes, anybody who is spiritual might be a good spiritual master.

Beatriz Gonzales: I'd like to share something about my experience in living with medicine people because I think that this was my foundation for being able to accept the Divine Principle and getting into this idea of a spiritual master. I was raised with medicine people, and, because of my native Indian background, my way of life was shaped by trying to be in harmony with the universe. Being in harmony with the universe meant being in harmony with things in the physical world, being in harmony with people and with the creation as well as with things in the spiritual world. So to me I often have difficulty understanding how they are separated in people's minds. When we're talking about what the Divine Principle is, it is just an understanding of very basic universal principles that operate in our daily lives, whether we are aware of them or not. And, we may violate them or we may go in accordance with them and that determines what state we are in, how much we are able to grow, and what conflicts we go through. These principles operate for us as human beings as well as for all creation. The Indians, for example, in order to know how to relate to each other, spend hours and hours watching the insects and animals and seeing how they interrelate with each other, and then the Indians imitate these patterns and inter-relationships because they recognize that the animals are living in accordance with the harmony of the universe. They recognize that they, as men, are not living in accordance with this harmony, and that is why they have conflicts. The Indians will sit and watch ants for hours and hours and see how the ant works, and then they shape their community life after the community life of the ant, and it works out great. So, this is an understanding of very basic universal principles and how they operate, and I think this is the Divine Principle.

Another thing is the idea of the Divine Master. The medicine people have a tradition that has been passed on through history that God works through one central person, someone to connect the people to God, and this person is in the position of a prophet or a prophetess, or in the position of a spiritual leader, in the position of a healer, of a counselor and advisor, everything. This person represents God to the community. He or she is like a messiah to the community. I grew up with a woman who was in this position, and she lived right next to my house. This woman had a spiritual master, and the spiritual master was a man who died in 1943 in Texas, and his name was Don Juanito Jaramillo. This man was a very short man in stature and he had a long white beard. He is recognized in the Southwest, in South Texas especially, as a saint, even if he is not recognized in the church as a Christian. The priests wouldn't even let him go into the church, because, according to the Scriptures, as Pat was saying, according to doctrine, this man was not going to confession, was not making his communion. This man was dealing with spirits, and therefore this man, according to the Scriptures and according to the teachings of Jesus, was evil. But God was working very directly through him and he had a very deep relationship with Jesus. He was opening the way for the people to live in harmony, and they were growing in their relationship with God. He was healing and performing miracles, just as Jesus was performing miracles, and just as Oral Roberts does in America today.

The point is that this man, before he died, passed on his medicine powers to a certain number of people, depending on the foundation of his accomplishment and theirs. One of these people was the woman that I knew. And, of course, one of the qualifications for a medicine person is that this person must lead a totally selfless life, that he or she believe in God and believe in a life centered on God, that is, in harmony with creation and in harmony with people. After this medicine man has died, he works from the spiritual world to guide the people that he has passed his medicine powers to. When they examine a sick person, they go to God, directly to God in prayer, and then the medicine man—Don Juanito for example—comes to give them guidance. This is the concept of a spiritual master. When I heard the Divine Principle, I could understand Rev. Moon's position as a spiritual master through whom I could be able to connect with God and learn how to serve both God and mankind. This impressed me very much about the Unification church.

Rod Sawatsky: Let me ask Virgil, have we covered the area of spirit world sufficiently by way of how it works or how it's populated?

Virgil Cruz: I think I have a bit of a handle on it now. There are other personal things that I would pursue with Jan, without asking for an answer. I am extremely thankful to God that I haven't been visited by these spirits who would choke one. I sometimes have a bit of an inferiority complex there; I wonder if I'm not worth choking. (laughter)

Rod Sawatsky: If anyone else has anything to add by way of clarification of the spiritual world, let's hear you now. O.K.?

Ulrich Tuente: One basic principle which is explained in the principle of creation is the principle of give-and-take. I think one very essential aspect of give-and-take is that, in order to have give-and-take, you need to have at least something in common. For instance, if I were to speak in German, I think few people would understand me, and so, at least we need a common language in order to talk to each other. And I think the same thing is true concerning the spirit world. What Jan said, for example—that all religions have some truth, that these medicine men about whom Beatriz was speaking have some truth—is true, but actually that which reveals most of God's heart and through which God can most clearly communicate and work in the human community is what has been revealed in the Old and New Testaments through the prophets and through Jesus Christ. God has had His greatest basis there to work with men and in relationship with them, and this then is a foundation through which God could work with Christianity as the central religion. All the other religions contain good things but could not communicate much of God's nature and heart to man. So there was not this basis to work for God. This principle of give-and-take is also in the spirit world. There must be a common foundation, so that something can be communicated from the spirit world to the physical world.

Rod Sawatsky: Let's have two more comments on this whole thing.

Nora Spurgin: Here we're putting a lot of emphasis on the spiritual world. It's not important in light of the total Principle, although it permeates throughout because it's a fact of life. There is life after death; we believe that one's spirit goes on living. In that sense it's important. What is more important is what God is doing on earth (Amen) and *that* we must understand— it's not what is going on up there (Amen), but it's what's happening here that is important. The spiritual world, we feel, is very active here because they know what is going on and are helping bring in the dispensation. They're just like people and may be as confused as people on earth. Many are learning the Divine Principle through us. Therefore, we do test the spirits by the Divine Principle.

Pete Sommer: You've tested it yourself? Correct me if I'm misunderstanding. You are inhabited by a good spirit woman? When we got into your eschatology last night, it seemed that the spiritual world was critical. Is that right?

Nora Spurgin: I'm not that sensitive, maybe intuitive, but not that open; so I've never seen a spirit. However, I have had the experience many, many times of speaking in tongues. I'm sure that that's a spirit speaking through me. I do believe that there are spiritual guides and that I probably receive spiritual help, but I don't know their names; I don't know if they're ancestors of mine.

Patricia Zulkosky: We see that our spiritual growing is a

function not only of God's grace but also of man's effort; so, to the extent we cooperate in our spiritual growing and grow our spirits, then, when we die, our spirits will go to the identical level in the spiritual world. It's not heaven or hell—if you're 99 and above you go here, and 99 and under you go there. You go to exactly the same level you grew your spirit to while you were here on earth. The essential thing about the relationship between the spirit world and the physical world is that the spirits in the spirit world are still aiming at oneness with God, and they must still cooperate with man on earth. In the sense that they inspire me to serve my brothers and sisters, and I follow that inspiration, then I get a blessing for doing that, and they also get a blessing for inspiring me. (They move up?) Yes, in a sense, so that they can resurrect. This is what we call the continuing resurrection of spirit men, so that eventually every spirit would come back to God, but the process may take a long, long, time. A spirit can inspire me, but I can say, "I don't want to," so that they're stuck, they can't do anything without my cooperation, without my conscious decision.

Pete Sommer: Some similarity to purgatory?

Patricia Zulkosky: Yes.

Joseph Hopkins: What about all the biblical warnings and prohibitions against necromancy and communicating with the dead? What about that?

Patricia Zulkosky: Exactly. In our church, too, we don't encourage it. Time and time again, we've been told: don't try to have give-and-take with the spirit world; it's dangerous; you don't know what you're getting into. If your will is weak and the will of the spirit is especially strong, you might end up possessed and in some mental hospital.

Mark Branson: But, you just said you wanted their guidance.

Patricia Zulkosky: No. I'm saying that you might get the inspiration to serve someone, or you might get the inspiration to kick me and run out of the room. Now, it's up to you to say, "Now, that's ridiculous!"

Mark Branson: So you are encouraged to have that kind of communication?

Patricia Zulkosky: No. You have inspirations coming to you all the time. Western man thinks, "This is just me. I have all these great inspirations floating around." We would say the spirit world is inspiring us, but we're in the driver's seat...

Mark Branson: But you are doing that.

Patricia Zulkosky: However many back-seat drivers there are, you have the steering wheel, and you decide whether you are going to go straight or whether you are going to turn, or whatever you may do.

Mark Branson: So you are encouraged to have communication with the spirit world?

Patricia Zulkosky: No.

Dan Davies: That's not what she said.

Patricia Zulkosky: I am saying you decide the course of your life and even though people are telling you, do this or do that, you decide.

Dan Davies: It happens whether you want it to happen or not; just by sitting here it happens. So you have to decide what you are going to accept or not.

Mark Branson: So why the admonition not to have influence from the spirit world?

Lloyd Howell: I was going to say that it's a matter of how you live your life. Now, if you live a holy life, you separate from evil and wrongdoing and come into the position to receive grace, guidance, and the Holy Spirit, and have good spirits work with you. The kind of person you are is often what you attract to you. If you're a low spirit selling drugs, you'll attract evil spirits to you. You'll get into all those things according to how you live your life, but, if you start living a holy life, then you receive guidance and inspiration from a higher level. It is most desirable to receive guidance and inspiration through those closest to God, which would be the sinless man, the Messiah; and we do receive other inspirations.

I've been out witnessing and I have prayed, "God, lead me to the person who is looking for You. Don't lead me to some girl—I don't want to be lustful. That's not the kind of spiritual guidance I'm seeking." Then I've said, "Lead me to the person that's looking for You on the street right now, right this hour; help me to say the words to him so that he'll feel Your Presence with me." I've walked down the street, and at times someone says to me, "Who are we going to witness to now? There are so many people on the street." And I've felt inspiration: "Go to the corner." And then I've been told (this happened to me once), "There's somebody who is going to come off the bus." There's a crowd of people; I said, "Who in this crowd am I supposed to witness to?" I didn't know; I had to make myself the clay in the potter's hand. Then I thought, "That person," and I went over to that person and talked to him. These things happen commonly in our church.

Another example occurred when I met a person who lived a few miles down the road from me but who decided to take a walk back home instead of taking a bus back. He didn't know why he was walking; he just did it. I had an inspiration not to go into my home that day; instead, I turned around and came to where he was and met him. The person had prayed that morning to hear something from God. That's how you come to realize there is a spirit world.

Rod Sawatsky: I think we also need to understand that we're also dealing with certain kinds of definitions of psychology. Given western psychology, we might say that this is your id, superego, or whatever; whereas, you have a sense that these are all spirits...

Mark Branson: Evangelical Christianity has a mix of those spirits...

Anthony Guerra: I think we need to hear from the other side. (Amen)

Tirza Shilgi: It's true about our inspirations from the spirit world, but I think that we have to make it very clear that our ideal is not to be led and guided and driven by the spirit world. We hope to establish connections with God and Christ, to live our lives according to Divine Principle. We are aware that there are influences from the spirit world, and we want to choose and select those according to the Divine Principle, so that the primary guidance of our lives should be the Divine Principle. However, when spiritual influence comes, we don't say it doesn't exist; we say it does, but we should be selective according to the Principle and according to God's providence. God and Christ are primary over the spirit world, and our own choice—not the spirit world— will eventually raise us up.

Rod Sawatsky: Can we hear now from the Evangelicals concerning their understanding of the spirit world?

Roy Carlisle: I'll state the case by asking a very basic question. I'm not so sure that the case hasn't been stated in some form or another, but the real point is that we've heard the Unification people saying that they test the spirits by the Divine Principle. That's not the evangelical position. None of us will deny that there are spirits, angels, demons, whatever, but the real question

is how you know what's what. The biblical issue is the passage in
I John, where it says you test the spirits by seeing whether they
confess that Jesus Christ came in the body, not whether they
allow the Divine Principle to be the guiding light. Here we really
disconnect. We don't disconnect on our understanding of the
population of the spirit world.

Rod Sawatsky: Before you answer that, and I'm sure you
can, I would like for one of the Evangelicals to give a more
systematic statement of your position. I think that's the only fair
thing to do for the sake of the Unification people here. Somebody
should systematically speak to the notion of the authority of the
Scriptures, and, if you will, the first canon.

Warren Lewis: Are we not going to let the Evangelicals
speak about the spirit world? It's in Scripture, but is it in your
experience?

Richard Quebedeaux: I just have two statements. One is that
there is the spiritual gift of the discernment of spirits, which
obviously not every Christian has, but some do. Secondly, you
Unification people remember that we all tend to be rather Calvin-
istic Evangelicals. If we were classical Wesleyan, Holiness Pentecostal people, you would get an awful lot of different feeling
about the answers; so don't think that what we say is definitive
for the whole evangelical movement, because there is absent
from this group a whole bunch of people who would have a very
different kind of answer, including the issue of Scripture. Remember, Pentecostals believe in the gift of prophecy and really, I
think, believe in continuing revelation, although they would always
step aside and say they shouldn't contradict Scripture, but quite
often they do.

Virgil Cruz: Let me make just a few comments which circle
around both the authority of Scripture and how we use Scripture,
and I hope that will get some discussion from members of our
team.

The initial statement that I'd like to make as a Reformed
individual is this: the Bible is the only infallible rule of faith and
practice. Now that's our fundamental principle, and you might
have to draw conclusions from that later.

After having made that statement, I think we have to decide
what we do with the Scripture, after having posited its authority.
It's been fascinating for me to notice that the historical critical
method—and all that it entails—has now been widely accepted

in the evangelical wing of the church. This is the method which has been used for the interpretation of Scripture at Fuller Seminary, at Gordon-Conwell and at Wheaton College. It's used, I think, throughout the evangelical wing—with the exception of certain Bible colleges. That means, therefore, that when we come to the study of the synoptic gospels, we believe that we should approach that material through the insights given to us by source criticism, and we would accept the modified two-source theory. We will accept the insight from form criticism that Scripture circulated first in an oral medium. We would also accept the main conclusions of redaction criticism to the extent that there was an editor who, by virtue of following his own agenda, would have had a special way of arranging the available materials, and his arrangement, his editing, might well differ from that of another author.

Now, after having said that, I think we in the evangelical world would be on guard against certain excesses which are claimed by proponents of the historical critical method. For example, there are certain form critics who would say that if the materials in the Scriptures, in the synoptic gospels, do not clearly fall in one of those patterns, that material is inauthentic, and they wouldn't accept it. We would say that every bit of Scripture was finely polished in order to evolve into one of those clearly defined units.

Another thing that I believe has to do with our interpretation of Scripture: after having given it all authority, we would say that we operate by the christological key. Christ is the central figure of the New Testament. In addition to that, we believe that we can also understand the Old Testament through the christological material that is given us in the newer Testament. That is not to say that the Old Testament cannot stand on its own legs or does not have a bona fide contribution to our theology. At an earlier point, some of us in the evangelical wing of the church looked upon the Old Testament as filled with stories that were used as sermon illustrations; there were morals to be found: for example, Isaac portrayed the proper filial attitude toward his father, Abraham, by virtue of being obedient. We didn't see the theology there. Now, I think we're open to that. We can say that the christological key is significant for the interpretation of the Old Testament because we think that the Old Testament aids us to believe in fulfillment—that there will be more coming.

Another point, and this will be the last one that I'll make, is the following: as we work with Scripture, I think we're quite concerned to steer clear of allegorical interpretation of Scripture. There has been that struggle going on in the churches throughout history, perhaps particularly symbolized in the struggle between the Alexandrian way of interpreting Scripture—the allegorical way—and the Antioch way—the more literal way. I believe that we would feel close to Martin Luther, who said to accept, whenever possible, the literal interpretation, the plain meaning of Scripture. That would not preclude interpreting certain passages symbolically when the Scriptures themselves push for that kind of interpretation. Let me stop there.

Rod Sawatsky: What about the question of continuing revelation?

Virgil Cruz: As far as I am concerned, I indeed believe that the canon is closed, on the basis of those tests of canonicity to which I referred earlier. We believe, however, that God continually reveals new insight to us. In my circles, we term that illumination of Scripture. This is vital, this is extremely significant, this is terribly important. Just one illustration which I think would be attractive to Unificationists: I believe that in our day two new illuminations have come to me, one of which is the necessity for being concerned with ecumenism. That's an illumination for my day, for me. I think it was in Scripture, but we weren't open to seeing that, to hearing that. Another insight, which has come to me, and I share here this illumination with many other persons, is the necessity—not the option, but the necessity—of every child of God to be concerned for responsible social action. That was *in* Scripture, it was *in* the Prophets, it was *in* the words of Jesus.

Warren Lewis: Was it inside where we couldn't see it?

Virgil Cruz: Pardon? (laughter) I think it can be found in Scripture, but that's a long debate. I don't think we would settle that here, Warren. I would say it could be found there, yes.

Warren Lewis: We Southerners didn't think it could be!

Virgil Cruz: Absolutely not. Some Northerners who went south to preach to the children and the slaves didn't see it there either. Permit me one illustration. You've heard some discussion of Black theology; now, there are those who are trying to compile White theology, and that's a pejorative term. One attempt has been made by Gaylord Wilmore (he's an historian as well as a theologian). One of the things he has done is to look at historical documents of the period, in particular catechisms which were used among the slaves, and there is real perversity there. One question-and-answer thing, patterned on the Westminster confession or catechism, would be this: Why did God make man? The answer slaves were to learn was this: To make crops. But the one that really makes me first cry and then fight is this: What does it mean when it says in Scripture, "Thou shalt not commit adultery?" The answer which the slaves were supposed to learn was this: The commandment, "Thou shalt not commit adultery," means that thou shalt not fail to obey thy earthly master in every command that is given. That's perversion, really...

Warren Lewis: That's adultery!

Virgil Cruz: To get back to the main point. I don't think that this has been any new revelation, the fact that we should be concerned about social issues.

Warren Lewis: What about political revolution? What about de-throning the king? If we believe in propositional revelation, then don't you think we ought to obey "the powers that be" and not topple George III? After all, St. Paul does say...

Virgil Cruz: No, he doesn't. In Romans he doesn't say obey the powers in an unqualified sense. He says obey the powers as they work in that province given to them by God in which to work.

Warren Lewis: Which is precisely the political realm...

Virgil Cruz: Yes, but when they are tyrannical they move into the realm of trespassing on the will of God. When they become for us, or want to become for us, the highest allegiance, then we have the right to disobey them. I think we would all agree.

Warren Lewis: It makes sense in America, but I don't think it made sense in Canada.

Paul Eshleman: Revelation 13—I think it does.

Warren Lewis: Patmos is not in Rome.

Paul Eshleman: Revelation says, "I warn every one who hears the words of prophecy of this book; if anyone adds to them, God will add to him the plagues described in this book, and if anyone takes away from the words of the book of this prophecy, God will take away his share in the tree of life and in the holy city, which are described in this book." Therefore, we feel very strongly about things added that are in direct violation to the Scriptures—and to add a few new insights such as are contained in the Divine Principle would be, in a sense, trying to add to the words already completed in the book.

Here's an approach I found helpful. The Bible is important to me because of Jesus Christ. I have an encounter with Jesus Christ, then I discover the Word of Christ. He, as my Lord, is my authority. His endorsement of the Old Testament stands for me; therefore, I take the Old Testament seriously and I read it through His eyes, insofar as I am able. But, I would want to say it stands on its own and contributes positively to my theology. The exegesis, for instance, of Genesis 22, of Abraham and Isaac, is the story of the atonement. The New Testament is important because I can relate it in some way to the Apostles or closely to the person of Jesus Christ. When that event is over, Jesus Christ is my decisive word from God; then I need no more words. And there is that mood through the entire New Testament. Now that God has spoken, it does not mean that God does not continue to speak, but that the spirit of God speaks through what we understand as the Word of God which we can understand fairly directly through the perspective of the person of Jesus Christ. Wouldn't that be the major test of canonicity? So, very simply, the Bible stands in relation to our view of Jesus Christ.

Pete Sommer: If we devalue our view of Jesus, then we would change—we would revise our view of Scripture. I can still engage in all sorts of textual criticism, but I am committed to being engaged in this study because Jesus Christ Himself engaged me in His Word.

Warren Lewis: What does Jesus have to say about whether or not women ought to pray and prophesy in church, and whether or not they ought to have their heads covered, and whether or not you will ordain them?

Pete Sommer: Well, His servant, Paul, instructed when and how they were to perform the preaching function in the church.

Warren Lewis: Do your women cover their heads when they pray and prophesy?

Pete Sommer: Since they're not the first-century Corinthians they don't, but they do observe the principles of modesty appropriate to their culture.

Warren Lewis: So, you have a hermeneutical principle that if something in Scripture doesn't happen to fit our culture, then we are not bound by it. Is that right?

Pete Sommer: Not externally, but internally they are bound by it.

Warren Lewis: There's no rule that just because it's in the Bible we have to abide by it, according to you. We'll adopt the modesty appropriate in the twentieth century and think that we have thereby fulfilled the requirements of Scripture.

Pete Sommer: We would repudiate any levelling of the Scripture to say that everything is as important as everything else.

Warren Lewis: But, how do you decide which cultural things are important and which cultural things are not? What's your canon within the canon?

Mark Branson: It comes about as a matter of how congruent the issues in the Scriptures themselves are. You look at Paul's life and his words, and you see there is some variety. There is a sense of Paul struggling with these tensions: his traditions, his pastoral tasks, his words. When we see variation on an issue, we can often at least see a direction. That direction, when affirmed by Jesus' words or actions, provides a hermeneutical key.

Warren Lewis: The male domination that runs throughout the New Testament, which is consistent there, but which is inconsistent with our culture, you simply excuse?

Mark Branson: I'd say that in the New Testament you're dealing with a cultural male domination that is on different planes. Then there's the illumination of the life of Jesus, as well as the behavior of the church, saying, "This is something that is not in accord with creation." So the kingdom, salvation, begins to effect changes toward equality.

Warren Lewis: Paul precisely argues that accord with creation requires male domination: God is on top, then Christ, then the male, and then the female.

Mark Branson: You'd have to get into specific passages.

Warren Lewis: That's exactly what we need to do, because that's what you're doing to the Moonies, though they're no good at proof-texting back at you. By the way, I just quoted you a specific text—I Corinthians 11:3.

Virgil Cruz: This question, which has troubled the church for centuries, is not going to be settled in fifteen minutes. But I think, in agreement with what has just been said, that many of us would think that at certain points in the Pauline corpus, Paul is giving theological statements—not propositional theology necessarily—but he's "doing theology." And we would say, on the man-woman thing, that when he says there's neither Jew nor Greek

and so forth, that's theology. At other points, I think many of us
would hold to the idea that Paul is attempting to apply theological
principles in his own situation. And Paul tells us of his struggle at
certain dramatic points. He says, I don't have a word from God,
but I'll do what I jolly well want to: and, at other points, even
when he doesn't say that, I think he's working at applying those
principles. I think everybody here can understand our being
ready to grasp that way of looking at Paul, because you're saying
you're doing that with your theology.

Warren Lewis: That's a very sensitive and responsible statement, Virgil, but that kind of statement doesn't accord with the
kind of fundamentalist generalizing we started out with a moment
ago, where the drift was: "By God, we believe the word of God,
and we'll use it against you if you happen to disagree with us on
this point, but if we find ourselves in trouble on some other point,
then, well, the church has had this problem for thousands of
years!"

Mark Branson: Continuity is there that is not being realized.
I think there is a continuity in seeking congruence and direction.

Warren Lewis: Now we see continuity. Help me see why
some things that were culturally conditioned are not the word of
God, but other things that were culturally conditioned are the
word of God. We Church of Christ people, for example, would
insist on adult believers' baptism, which none of you people
believe in, and yet I can prove it to you from every book in the
Bible. What are you going to do about that? (laughter)

Mark Branson: That's true, but none of us would believe in
baptismal regeneration.

Rod Sawatsky: But it's not true that everyone does not
believe in believers' baptism.

Warren Lewis: Well, the Presbyterians, then!

Mark Branson: Not true about Presbyterians either. I'm a
Presbyterian and I believe in adult baptism.

Warren Lewis: Maybe there's hope, after all! (laughter) Let
me retract the emotion of my statement and just urge the point.
How do you deal with that? Is your theological system open-
ended, too, like the Unificationist system?

Irving Hexham: You've got to raise questions about interpretations of Scripture, which holds them together, and I'd like to
ask them about the role they ascribe to the Lutheran confessions.
As I understand it, all Lutherans adhere to certain statements

stated in confession, and I know that, if they seriously disagree, then they wouldn't be Lutherans, though they might be Christians. Luther probably has some ideas of a group of statements that you probably have to reinterpret as Christian, and these are not only quotations from the Bible, but also readings and abstractions from it. Another group will have its own statements and these tend to supplement the Scriptures in the same way.

Don Deffner: I do not interpret the Scriptures in the light of Lutheran confessions. I believe the confessions are a clear explication of the Scripture, and I feel a loyalty to them because they are a clear exposition of Scripture, but I do not superimpose them on the Scripture.

Mark Branson: In fact, you have to live by Luther's statement that, "If you can show me in the Scriptures where I've erred, I will repent."

Johnny Sonneborn: How did you decide that these confessions are a clear interpretation of Scriptures, as opposed to someone else's? Is this each person's decision?

Paul Eshleman: I would say that you, Warren, have tried to put everything in the Scriptures on the same level, and I think the Scriptures are very clear internally in matters that have to do with eternal salvation and less specifically clear on matters of Christian etiquette. We're not wrestling with whether it's right to eat meat offered to idols—we're not wrestling with that today, but that is an application of how the Christian should act in the light of that culture. I think there is no dispute among the Evangelicals here on the forgiveness of sin and the role of Christ, and that's why you can even go to almost every confession of every denomination and see that those confessionals overlap and lay one on top of the other with the essence of what it means to come to know God through Jesus Christ.

You go from one denomination to the next and say that here is the out-working of the Christian faith in everyday life, and you'll find much disparity and opinion in that particular area.

Warren Lewis: Three million members of the Church of Christ teach that your sins have not been forgiven until you have immersed in the waters of baptism, and we, too, are Bible-believing Evangelicals. Now, somewhere along the line we've got a hermeneutical problem, and it doesn't have to do with peripheral questions.

Paul Eshleman: Then I would say we have a very central

disagreement.

Mark Branson: ...and that's why a lot of us would say therefore the Church of Christ is cultic! (laughter)

Richard Quebedeaux: That's why the Church of Christ has never been really accepted by Evangelicals...

Pete Sommer: Nor have they accepted us.

Warren Lewis: How can we? If you won't be baptized, as scripture teaches, how can we accept you as Christians? (laughter)

Rod Sawatsky: We could play out the same thing in reference to Mennonite non-resistance.

Don Deffner: I think this point is crucial. There are *sedes doctrinae,* seats of doctrine, the foundation or cardinal principles, or you might say, primary in contrast to secondary doctrines. But, in the primary category, there's the *forgiveness of sins.* Luke 24:47: this is the message: "...repentance and forgiveness of sins should be preached in His name to all nations..."

Paul Eshleman: Could we spend some time on the forgiveness of sins? I feel as though we continually move to the restoration side of things, and I don't know if everybody here in the Unification church considers his sins forgiven continually day by day. It seems to be less important whether one's sins are forgiven than whether we get people into the restoration process, and I would like to explore that at some point with the whole group.

Rod Sawatsky: In the next time session, we'll discuss the question of conversion, the gospel, and forgiveness. But first, I think some of the Unification people ought to respond to the questions that have been raised by way of testing the validity of this ongoing revelation in reference to biblical materials. It has been said, a number of times, that you are different because you don't test the spirits against the Bible.

Lloyd Howell: I just want to speak to one point Paul brought up. There's a lot I want to say, but I'll just mention one point in Revelation he's quoting, about adding to and subtracting from. I think it says specifically *this* book of prophecy, so maybe we can assume that he's just talking about Revelation. But even if he were talking about the whole New Testament, I know it also says in Deuteronomy 4:2 and 12:32: Do not add onto or subtract from these commandments. Yet that's what Jesus did. He came to illuminate the point that the Old Testament should be a testimony to Him, the life of suffering, and blood, sweat and tears—that it was to establish the foundation for Him to come. He was not

adding or subtracting. In my understanding, the New Testament
records the history of blood, sweat and tears for God's work from
Christ to St. Paul. Laboring, sweating, getting whipped, having
sleepless nights are a testimony, I think, to the life of who will be
the Lord of the Second Advent. I think that if you do live at the
foot of the cross, feeling sin, knowing that we are sinners, receiving
forgiveness from day to day—if you live in that place, and you
don't wander away, and just go glory, glory hallelujah, but you're
aware, all the time, that you're a sinner, a forgiven sinner—and
you've lived in recognition of the sweat, the blood, and the tears
that Christ shed going up to that cross, then you will, I think,
recognize the Lord when He comes. I'm speaking of the Lord of
the Second Advent, who, according at least to the Principle,
doesn't go to the cross—he is to make this family and multiply.
But it doesn't mean that such a person would not suffer; it
doesn't mean that such a person would not shed his tears, his
blood, his sweat, and that he wouldn't be in this tradition of the
Bible. I think there are principles there that carry over and do
witness and testify as to how God works.

Dan Davies: I'd like to speak to the question Paul brought
up about continuing revelation and also to what Lloyd was just
speaking to. When John received the Book of Revelation in 90-95
A.D. or so, he wrote it down. He received those words, said by
the angel Gabriel, that no words should be added to this book.
When, I'm wondering, did the council put together the entire
Bible? I'm asking the question: was the Bible already canonized
at the time that Gabriel said those words to John?

Paul Eshleman: Not at all.

Dan Davies: So John could only be referring to the revelation
that he received. He was considering *that* the book.

Mark Branson: I think there would be some of us who would
agree with that, that the passage does refer to Revelation, although
I think I would also say that the spirit of it applies to the whole
New Testament.

Virgil Cruz: And there are other passages in Paul which
could serve the same purpose: "If anyone speaks another gospel..."
for example.

John Wiemann: But I don't think we speak another gospel.
Rev. Moon says that you cannot understand the Divine Principle
unless you understand and experience Jesus Christ. He says it
time and time again. When he came here in 1971 he had to bring

the whole American movement to an understanding of Christ.

Mark Branson: He said, basically, Christ didn't accomplish anything.

John Wiemann: That's out of context.

Don Deffner: When he said Christ didn't come to die, page 134 of Sontag's book*...

Whitney Shiner: I want to respond to something Pete said. He said that one of his tests for interpreting Scripture is whether it in any way devalues Jesus; and I want to make it clear that, when I deal with Evangelicals, I often have to control my anger because, from my point of view, your doctrine devalues both the value of Jesus and of God the Father. I think you don't understand our position. I want to make it clear that that feeling works on both sides.

Pete Sommer: Help me with that. Could you give me an example?

Whitney Shiner: Well, I think it's a way of understanding. For one example, by making what Jesus is doing predetermined, it devalues His sacrifice and His love and His accomplishment.

Anthony Guerra: The idea that He came to die makes Him sound like a robot.

Mark Branson: We think Jesus, in the passage that Joe read yesterday, had choice, He was obedient. The obedience is there; even if ahead of time He knew from the Father that there was a task to be done, this does not at all belittle the reality of his obedience.

Virgil Cruz: But even before the foundation of the world, according to the Book of Revelation, Chapter 3, God the Father knew the Son would be obedient. It was not forced upon Him—He chose that ministry, that mission.

Ulrich Tuente: If Jesus really were predestined to die, why did He make all this effort to find disciples from the people around Him? He asked people to believe in Him, and He was constantly met with disbelief. If He was predestined, from before, to be crucified, to be sent to the cross, why then did He ask them to believe in Him?

Don Deffner: He said, "I'm going to be crucified and I'm going to be raised..."

---

*Frederick Sontag, *Sun Myung Moon and the Unification Church*, Nashville, Tenn.: Abingdon Press, 1977.

Ulrich Tuente: Then he wouldn't have to make this effort of preaching and doing many things.

Whitney Shiner: I think we interpret His life as much more important. You're saying, primarily, that His death and resurrection are important, but we view His whole life as important!

Pete Sommer: Our christology emphasizes not only the role of Jesus of Nazareth in redemption, but also in creation. In John 1, Colossians 1, and Hebrews 1, and I noticed in all the explication of creation last night, there's no view of christology in the creation.

Whitney Shiner: We believe that the creation is only completed through a perfect man, through Jesus; Jesus completed creation. God created with an image of perfect man, His Son, as His starting point and then, all things were created through Him and for Him.

Pete Sommer: We see Him also as agent in creation.

Johnny Sonneborn: This is a terminological problem. In *Unification Thought,* the doctrine of the Logos in creation is clearly elaborated.

Pete Sommer: But you say that God created Christ. Right?

Johnny Sonneborn: No, the Word is an aspect of God, an attribute of God.

Pete Sommer: That's where your emanationist thing works.

Johnny Sonneborn: The Word is God's Word. Now the only difference, which is a terminological difference, is with the term Jesus. We say this is a name of a human being; this is not the name of the pre-existent Logos. The Logos was pre-existent. It became flesh as Jesus. So the Logos, the Son of God, in that sense the ideal man—the whole thing was created according to a Logos, but it became flesh in Jesus...

Warren Lewis: Unification teaches that God's Logos, or plan, was most fully expressed in Jesus. There is no idea of a pre-existent "person" of the Logos or eternally begotten Son of God. Unification christology is very far from Chalcedon, with a functionally Nestorian emphasis on the human Jesus, and predicated on a Unitarianism of the Father. Adam could have been the incarnate Logos as easily as Jesus, if he had only lived up to the Father's expectation.

Johnny Sonneborn: What's your justification for calling the Word that existed before creation Jesus?

Pete Sommer: I read in Hebrews that, when he's talking

about the Son, he is talking about Christ active in creation. All things were created through Him and for Him. Paul could not mean anybody else other than the Jesus of Nazareth. For Paul, there's no distinction between the Christ of Faith and the Jesus of history.

Rod Sawatsky: Let's allow Nora a last word, and then we'll decide where we'll go from here.

Nora Spurgin: I just wanted to make some comments about the historical process within the Unification church which might be helpful in terms of defining historical continuity as opposed to the separation of Unification church and Christianity. Rev. Moon has said that he never intended to establish the Unification church. He never intended to establish a new church; he came as a reformer to Christianity, or as a person to bring enlightenment or illumination to Christianity itself. So, just as Jesus came to fulfill the Old Testament, and His people did not accept Him, the teachings of Jesus became a New Testament, a new church. Because Christianity did not accept Rev. Moon, (this is our conviction, very honestly) his teachings went to others around the world, and many people who are not Christians have joined the Unification church. Therefore, we strive very hard to fill the gap; we teach the New Testament to the people who are not Christians when they join Unification church. Recently I visited some of our missionaries who are teaching the Divine Principle to Moslems. They felt that they could make a new principle of the Koran rather than the Bible. Immediately, I had to inform them that that's not what we're doing at all. In Japan, some people felt that the Divine Principle could be modified to fit Buddhist teachings, but Rev. Moon said, "Absolutely not," because no one can fully understand salvation if we do not include the clear lineage through Jesus Christ. So I want to make that clear, that we really see it as a continuous line; there is no break, no new church.

Jonathan Wells: All morning I've been thinking of Virgil's question of yesterday that was never answered, namely, how do we decide whether Sun Myung Moon is the messiah? Miracles, healing, raising from the dead, I believe, were the points you raised, and this morning we've been talking about authority and how we know what to believe. Do we believe spiritual advice? Well, lots of people get spiritual advice, and some of it is wrong. Do we believe miracles? Lots of people perform miracles, and they're not necessarily the messiah. Do we believe gurus? A guru is not the messiah. Buddha was not the messiah. Do we believe a literal interpretation of Scripture? This mistake was made 2,000 years ago. Israel rejected Jesus because Jesus didn't fit their conception of Scripture, to which nothing was supposed to be added, as Lloyd pointed out. That was a terrible disaster. We can't just rely on reason. But what is revelation? I mean, I can say I just received a revelation that I'm the messiah. Would you follow me? (laughter) I wouldn't follow someone who said that. There are thousands of people who have said that, and they're obviously not the messiah. When I listened to Virgil's description of certain aspects of the evangelical view of Scripture, I found myself agreeing with everything you said; specifically and most importantly, I think that the key point is Christ, and, in the New Testament, Jesus is Christ. We view the New Testament and the Old Testament through a christological perspective. That was the key point that I got from Virgil's explanation.

In the Unification church, I have to say, we see things the same way, with this distinction: As I said before, we believe that these are the last days—these are the days when Christ comes again, and I don't think all Evangelicals agree on *how* Christ is coming again; in fact, I know they don't. The Unification church believes that it is possible, even likely, that Christ comes as a man, just as Jesus did 2,000 years ago. Now, I'm not saying *any* man—he must be very special, obviously—maybe it's Jesus Himself, again; maybe it's someone with a different name. It's something to be discussed. And the key point is still, "How do we tell who Christ is?" and then through that person we can gain our perspective on all these other things. And, having said that, I'd like to make the comment that I think the key point is sonship—before Jesus, nobody talked about being the Son of God in a believable way. Jesus was the *Son* of God. Nobody in the Unification church will deny that. To a man and woman, everybody believes that Jesus was the Son of God and is the Son of God, unlike Buddha or any others.

Virgil Cruz: I do have to say that we're not in agreement. You are not remembering what we've said on previous points about Jesus Christ. You're using Christ in quite another sense when you're saying you use a christological interpretation as the key, and we say *Jesus* Christ, linking those two inseparably. Therefore, we would have no room for another one who comes, other than Jesus.

Jonathan Wells: I realize that, and that's the starting point of our disagreement. I mean, that's really the basic thing. The point is: is it possible that God could have another son? Is God limited to one son? And if God has another son, then what will teach us that this is the Son of God?

Paul Eshleman: So your whole case rests on the credibility of the person of Sun Myung Moon? Without him there is nothing in my Scriptures that can tell me to look further?

Jonathan Wells: Well, when I read the Scriptures before, I knew that Christ was coming again, and I felt that Christ would come as a man before I ever heard of the Unification church.

Virgil Cruz: Jesus Christ, or Christ?

Jonathan Wells: I didn't know. I tried to have an open mind about it. Many missed Jesus because of their rigid conception of how He was supposed to come.

Virgil Cruz: Another point: the reason why we think the Second Advent will only issue in triumph is that, in the first coming of Christ, it was in a state of humility, whereas, subsequent to that, Christ comes in a state of exaltation. He will not be in the state of humility. He will be revealed for that which He is—King of Kings, and Lord of Glory.

Jonathan Wells: I agree with that.

Johnny Sonneborn: According to the evangelical position, He will come immediately, in a flash, from East to West. Everyone will immediately know Him and He will have a new name; they'll quickly know what it is. Whereas, in the Unificationist understanding, this is not the way God has ever worked, and it is not likely, from our viewpoint, that God will make it that easy for anybody at that time. He's always giving man a chance to respond to that which is even more difficult and to widen our own love, our faith, in this way.

Richard Quebedeaux: There is an evangelical position that really believes in two second comings—the dispensationalists believe in a secret rapture and then a coming visible to everyone. Remember that.

Irving Hexham: But they do believe in the Day of the Lord.

Pete Sommer: They do believe in the Day of the Lord. I think our eschatology as Evangelicals is far more together than many realize.

Anthony Guerra: The belief in the Unification church is that

Jesus passed the mission on or commissioned Rev. Moon to seek after the insights of the Principle, and that he's doing it with the grace of God and commission of Jesus; he's accomplishing something with the approval of God and Jesus. Jesus could have accomplished possibly both what you see as happening at the parousia as well as that which He did accomplish 2,000 years ago. Everything could have been accomplished at that time, and the kingdom of heaven would have been established. Because we believe that Jesus and God are united in purpose to restore the whole cosmos to its original plan, so we believe that God and Jesus approve of what the Lord of the Second Advent will do, and if that's the case, I don't see that as displacing Jesus. It may displace your concept of Jesus!

Pete Sommer: That's Rev. Moon's word, though.

Anthony Guerra: No. It's based on a relationship with Jesus. You could ask Jesus! Asking the question presupposes that you have an open mind. If you already have an answer to that question, then you haven't asked the question. One of the key points about Scripture, as we see it, is that Jesus is admonishing us to take a humble attitude, and He's asking, "When I come back, will there be faith on earth?"

Irving Hexham: What do you say to the Mormons who say, "You must ask if Joseph Smith is the Prophet"? They say exactly the same thing—you pray with an open mind to God, because you've got the three figures that appeared to Joseph, and said, "Here is my beloved son; hear him." Exactly the same as you've just said.

Anthony Guerra: O.K., the point is that, when I read the Mormon scriptures and, for instance, their view of God as being material, I couldn't go on.

Warren Lewis: That's because you're not prayerfully asking the question! (laughter)

Irving Hexham: There's more unity between you and the Evangelicals than I thought. (laughter)

Lloyd Howell: The way I see it, God intended for all people to become sons and daughters, in the fullest perfection, in complete love. As far as we're concerned, Jesus achieved that relationship of oneness and a complete image of God, and nothing could destroy or shake Him in any way. It is the will of God that all men become that, so it is the will of Jesus that all men become that, and it is the will of the Lord of the Second Advent, too. It is the same will, so we are all serving God. Of course, Jesus wants the will of God to be done. He certainly doesn't want something else done. So, we see two similar people, or two perfected Adams. We don't see one pushing the other out of the way. It's not, "I'm top dog and you're not—push Jesus down."

Virgil Cruz: One little bit of evangelical concern: when I pushed the question of the significance of Rev. Moon earlier today, I think if you had said to me that Rev. Moon *is* a spiritual leader, an extraordinary spiritual leader on the level of Martin Luther, on the level of John Calvin, I would say, I'll check this out. If you had even said—and I would have had more problems with it, but I would have accepted it—Rev. Moon is a central figure in the way that the prophets of the Old Testament are central figures, I would have more difficulty, but I would have said, well, you know, I'll look at it. But when you say he is the Lord of the Second Advent, and when you say he's the second Adam or third Adam then I can't go any farther.

Lloyd Howell: It's not something you say. If such a person exists, then you have to find him in another way; he's not going to have a label on his forehead: "Second Coming."

Warren Lewis: I have a second point. In terms of the dynamics of the conversation, we speak of the dialogical nature of what we're doing here. But in proceeding always and ever on that model of conversation, we're perpetuating the Protestant debacle: "Here I am, here I stand; I will not agree with you, God damn you, God help me!" We don't think *towards* one another. As a good Anabaptist, I want to see us work towards one another. I want to see us personally indwell one another. I want to see us get past this stage of ego-critical consciousness where everybody is sticking up for his side and see if anybody can learn from the other side, if anybody can love as they communicate.

Rod Sawatsky: What is interesting in this is that we're working with two models of truth: one in which truth is complete and now must be defended, and the other in which truth is unfolding, it is in process. I think the very nature of the two positions makes dialogue virtually impossible, because we're not dealing with equal partners. We're dealing with unequal partners because of certain assumptions.

Paul Eshleman: There's a level of personal life that we each have in our own individual relationships with God, and I would hope our individual desires are to know God in a closer way. This comes not just through theological interpretations of passages of Scripture or the *Divine Principle,* but in some of those areas of our personal prayer life and in devotion. Perhaps we could share ways in which we have gotten to know God in a more personal way as an encouragement to one another.

Jonathan Wells: That would be good for tonight?

|Editorial note: The following conversation occurred in the second conference.|

Rod Sawatsky: I'd like to have one or two of the Unification people here talk about their own experiences with the spirit world and also their relationship to Rev. Moon. And I want some Evangelicals to talk about their relationship to the spirit world and Jesus. Who wants to start us off?

Nora Spurgin: Maybe I'll say something. I'm not a particularly spiritually open or spiritually sensitive person. I don't see spirits or anything like this, but I do have an intuitive sense of being inspired. Prior to hearing the Divine Principle, I was a Charismatic and I had experiences of speaking in tongues and similar kinds of experiences. At the time, it was a very emotional experience for me. I couldn't deny what was happening and the fact that it brought me to an even closer experience with God. I felt a lot of spiritual aliveness which I had not felt before. Fortunately I was very carefully *receptive* in these experiences, so that I didn't have bad experiences, and they were all very good.

After I heard the Divine Principle for the first time, it gave me an intellectual understanding of what was happening. And I realized that it wasn't necessarily God or the Holy Spirit who was talking through me, but it actually could be any spirit in the spiritual world. By opening up myself, I was allowing my own body to be used, and, if I had the right motivation, the right thought, the right kind of connection with God, it could be a very high experience, it could be a good experience, but it *could* also be a bad experience. So that was my one validation of actually relating with the spiritual world in a tangible kind of way, and after I heard the Divine Principle, it gave me a lot of clarity about life after death and what heaven is like. So, to me, it's a fact of life.

It's not a big thing which rules my whole life, and I think many times when we start talking about the spirit world, people begin feeling that we're really caught up in spiritual things. We have certain basic rules. One is that what is bound on earth is bound in heaven and what is loosed on earth is loosed in heaven. So earth is where things are happening. The second is that heaven may be helping to influence it, but the result is going to be here. Therefore, what's happening here is important, and we must be in control of our own lives. Aside from deliberately giving our own will to God, we don't just allow ourselves to be led all over the place. So, for me, understanding the Divine Principle gave me a much clearer understanding of how to guide my own spiritual life by testing it with the truth. So I think the truth is a guideline to test the spirit.

Sharon Gallagher: I think that, at one point, when asked would you have another physical body, you said no, the spirits don't need that, because they could communicate through people who did have bodies. And I wondered to what extent you feel the need to mediate in some way for disembodied spirits.

Patricia Zulkosky: We would say that we have a physical body and a physical brain and a spiritual body and a spiritual mind. Our physical body and our physical brain are more on the instinctual level: intuition and rationality and imagination are attributes of the spirit mind. And our spirit body has the same processes that our physical body has. So, in spiritual literature, you often hear of terms like clairvoyance and clairaudience, of spiritual experiences going right along with physical experiences.

So, our view of how spirits can grow in the spiritual world is that they cooperate with people on earth. So many ideas go through our heads, and we think, "I'm the master of all of these ideas, or I thought them all up myself." Sometimes they're great ideas and sometimes they're like, "Kick the lady and run down the street." (laughter) And some you want to overcome and some you don't.

So we're saying, because we have a spirit and a spirit mind and spirit body, that there's a spiritual communication that we're not concretely aware of because man fell. Without the fall, we'd be able to relate to the spirit world equally, maybe like tuning in a different channel on the television set, so it would be very clear what's going on. In this case, then, however many influences or suggestions the spirit world gives, you're the one who decides what you're going to act on and what you're not going to act on.

We note that many major medical discoveries or scientific inventions seem to occur simultaneously around the world. We can say that one possible explanation of that might be that the spirit would inspired a hundred thousand people with a cure for cancer, and, out of those hundred thousand people, maybe one thousand people say, "Oh, yeah, that's a good idea. Maybe I should do something with it." And, out of those, maybe one hundred people start to do some kind of elementary research, but then perhaps five or ten become very serious, and then they're the ones that make the breakthrough. So it's as though lots of people got the inspiration but just a few people followed through, and it's up to us to decide what kind of inspiration we want to follow. The same analogy might be used in robbing a bank. Understanding these things, we can take dominion over our life in a much stronger way than people who don't realize that the spirit world influences us.

Frank Kaufmann: Pat explained the dynamics. I'd like to add perhaps the motivation behind the activities of the people in the spiritual world. According to the Divine Principle, we need our physical bodies in order to love. The designs of our heart are manifested by the way we live and the way we treat others; we can cause our spiritual man or being to grow ever higher and brighter in love as we continue to exhibit sacrificial love. Once you die physically you no longer have a physical body with which to love people, yet the motivation of spirits in the spiritual world is to continue to grow in love, though they're not capable of physically doing anything for someone, carrying somebody's luggage or bringing somebody a bunch of flowers. So, through working on the earth, by influencing circumstances and earthly people, they are seeking to grow their own spirits. This is the tremendous benefit of having our physical life. If you are inspired to find a cure for cancer while you have your physical body, you are in complete control of the situation and can work for the sake of mankind with all your heart and soul. But a spirit with the same deep desire can inspire someone, and then all he can do is hope. This, perhaps, might clarify what Pat was describing. It's much more difficult for spirits to bring an act of love to fruition because the spirit is dependent on the free will of the earthly person with whom he is trying to work.

Richard Quebedeaux: Are you saying that when you lose your body and become a spirit you're incomplete? This is one reason I think that the Christian doctrine of the bodily resurrection isn't incomplete. I wonder, how in the world can you think of an eternal spirit state where you are less capable of loving or doing things than you were in your physical body that you have had for forty, fifty, seventy years?

Frank Kaufmann: The level of our incompleteness is that we are not fully grown in God's love. If you're fully grown in God's love, you don't need to act toward developing maturity. Our purpose is to mature in God's love.

Nora Spurgin: Actually, the problem is the fall of man. If man had never fallen, then he would have, in his physical life, grown to completeness with God, and, therefore, at the point of death he would be moving into a new life. It's almost as though you're born prematurely without quite having all your respiratory system developed or something like that, so you end up a little bit handicapped. But you work with that handicap until you get yourself out of it.

Richard Quebedeaux: Also, eventually in the spirit world you continue to grow?

Nora Spurgin: Yes.

Richard Quebedeaux: And then, do you ever arrive ultimately at some—I don't want to say Nirvana—blessed state?

Nora Spurgin: We say that growth continues forever. It's never a plateau that one can never go beyond, because God is always a little further beyond, but at the same time you reach the point of perfect oneness with God. Some people may disagree with that, I'm not sure.

Jonathan Wells: Well, the model was Jesus. He was one with God, and that's the ideal, but His oneness with God didn't mean that He didn't change during His life or say different things in different situations.

Anthony Guerra: There is a certain point where you no longer want to or are capable of sinning, and that is what we call perfection. However, that does not mean that you will not deepen your way of life and experiences of love. These will continue to grow eternally, but, when we talk about a period of growth, we mean that one passes through that threshold after which one is no longer able to sin.

Franz Feige: In the spirit world, you can't multiply physiological bodies. You can't have children anymore. To fulfill the three blessings is to become perfect on the individual level and to become perfect on a family level—meaning to become a true mother or a true father—and then to become perfect on the level of completely uniting with the creation and nature. To have that experience on earth serves as a foundation to grow even higher in the spirit world.

Jack Harford: One thing we talk about in regard to this period of growth is being in indirect dominion and direct dominion. In the period of growth, we say there are three stages: formation, growth, and perfection. When you're going through these growth stages you're in a period of indirect dominion, indirect relationship with God, but, when you reach perfection, then you have direct relationship with God. So, when you have that direct relationship with God and make that oneness, like Christ's relationship to Him, then at that point your heart grows deeper.

Jonathan Wells: I'm going to tell a story, and it may sound strange, because many stories about spiritual experiences sound strange. And I want you to know that I'm generally skeptical about spiritual experiences. But on this one occasion, I was the Unification church director in Vermont in 1976, and one of our goals in 1976 was to turn the bicentennial into something centered on God. I found out that January 21st was Ethan Allan's birthday. He was a revolutionary war hero from Vermont, and I decided that Vermont was going to have the first God-Bless-America parade in 1976. So we arranged a parade with the National Guard and some local groups.

To prepare for it I decided to pray on a hillside where there was a monument to Ethan Allan. And my prayer was for guidance and the success of the venture, and, also, I was aware that I was making contact with the spiritual world. In other words, I believe that Ethan Allan exists in the spiritual world. So I prayed and, when the prayer ended, I had an impression of somebody in front of me, and it was a figure with a large cape and a big high-collar revolutionary war costume, three-cornered hat, and I could make out the major facial features. He looked somewhat like Napoleon, only this guy was big, and the face was rather dark, and sad. The vision lasted just an instant, and I put it out of my mind because I figured it was just my imagination.

Then I went back to town and got a book out of the library, the biography of Ethan Allan. When I turned to the first page, there was a picture of him. I had never seen a picture of Ethan Allan before, but he was the guy I had seen up on the hilltop. When I saw that picture, chills just went up and down my spine because I realized that I had had a spiritual experience up there. I found out that he was an atheist, and that explained why he looked so sad, because, in the spiritual world, an atheist has little relationship with God, the source of joy. Well, we had our parade. We had arranged to have all the traffic stop on the main street in Burlington, Vermont, for this parade, and just as we got everybody assembled at the north end of the street, the police said, "The guy that you arranged the parade with is out of town, and we have no authority to stop the traffic on the street. You're going to have to go down the sidewalk." A parade threading its way past the shoppers on the sidewalk! So I said, "That's ridiculous! We've got to use the street." There were some radio calls back and forth to the station, and, somehow, somebody, somewhere said, "Oh, go ahead and let them use the street." They stopped the traffic and we had our parade. A few nights later I was again praying and had another very fleeting vision of Ethan Allan, and this time he was smiling. Now, according to Unification theology, if he was instrumental in bringing about the success of that parade, and thereby contributing to God's providence, he was raising himself closer to God in the spiritual world. Now you can make what you want of the story. I'm telling you the way it was.

Anthony Guerra: As I understand our spirituality, we emphasize prayer very much, and that is directed towards God, Heavenly Father. We don't emphasize spiritual experiences, although they may happen as a by-product of one's coming closer to the Father. Before I joined the Unification church I was agnostic, and that meant I refused to kneel to someone I thought might exist or might not exist. At points I would have liked to pray, but felt it would somehow violate my integrity if I did so. When I heard the Divine Principle, coming from that pagan perspective, I was given the confidence that it was possible, even likely, that God existed, that He loved me, and that I should pray to Him and find out if, in fact, I could begin some communication.

After I heard the Divine Principle, I began praying on my own — I lived for several months apart from the church while going to school. There was no doubt from my experiences in prayer that there was a living God who loved me and who loved everyone else. I felt tremendous gratitude. I went for a period of three or four months in which I felt tremendous gratitude towards the living God, who is not to be identified with the spirit world. He is the Creator of the spirit world, the physical world, of all beings physical and spiritual. I felt such tremendous gratitude because, in my own life, I was a person who had denied His existence, who had even talked other people out of religion, and yet He loved me. It was this kind of validating spiritual experience with God that allowed me to take the Divine Principle very seriously.

Also, as I began to study the words of Rev. Moon, I realized that Rev. Moon is always talking about Jesus Christ. He's always relating his mission to the work of Jesus and yet, in my own life, in my own understanding of Divine Principle, I rarely did that. In our church, seven years ago when I first joined, the members did not. But, somehow Rev. Moon was always relating his work and his mission to Jesus Christ. And so I thought that maybe I would have to deal with the question of where Jesus fit into this spirituality.

I had had this experience: Rev. Moon had written a rather lengthy statement, called "Forgive, Love and Unite," that was published in newspapers during the Watergate crisis. The essence of it was that the legal system should take care of the wrongs that Nixon may have committed, but that our hearts be ones of forgiveness, with love towards everyone, and, as Jesus said, including our enemies. At the time I was going through a difficult time spiritually; God was distant from me. I felt I was letting God down. This was in 1974; I was in New Orleans at the time, and I had to take the statement that Rev. Moon had written to the *Picayune Times* in New Orleans. I happened to read it before I took it up there. And I realized that those words of forgiveness in the statement were meant not only for Richard Nixon but also for me. They were meant for all of us. I felt the forgiveness of Jesus Christ very directly and the concurrence of Rev. Moon in that forgiveness. I felt no separation between the two, no contradictions. As a result, two years later I was baptized—I was immersed fully—and that was a genuine religious experience.

Later, during the Washington Monument campaign, I was talking to Christians and inviting them to come to hear Rev. Moon speak. Several of the people I was speaking to, who had close relationships with Jesus, felt confirmed when they prayed to Jesus, to go and hear Rev. Moon speak. So, in my own life, in my own spirituality, I have found that there is one living God, the Father, who is the Creator of us all, and that the Son, Jesus Christ, is united with the Father's will. They are the same in will, in purpose, and in love.

My spiritual experience has testified to that. So when a Christian comes and says, "How can I know if this is heretical or not?" I always ask him to pray to Jesus—and many who have taken this advice have received confirmation that they should join.

Beatriz Gonzales: We're always asked by the Evangelicals what kind of spiritual experiences we've had with Rev. Moon, and I'd like to share one which I had last year, which I feel has resolved something for me. Actually it's not only something for me, but I think it's something for the Mexican-American people, or my ancestors, Indians, American Indians, and Spanish. So, as a result, a lot of resentment that is carried by the Mexican-American people can be dealt with.

I know that in 1975 and 1976 Rev. Moon made many conditions when he was fishing off the coast in the Atlantic Ocean and he made certain ceremonies or conditions that tried to take away the resentment the Indian people have toward the white people because of the way the white people treated them. I was very moved to realize how serious he was and how much he really felt responsibility to take away that resentment, because of the suffering of the Indian people.

But anyway, I, at that point, realized something very strong. I'd been in the movement about three years, and I realized that I had something inside me that I could not overcome. It was a certain kind of resentment, but I had buried it and didn't want to face it, even though I was working so much in this movement. I used to be very involved in the civil rights movement, the Chicano movement, and I'd completely left those to work in this movement.

But, last summer, after being in this church now for over four years, I had an experience where I was completely immobilized—I was so sick that I couldn't work anymore. I had worked very, very hard in this movement. All of a sudden, I was completely immobilized and I couldn't work because of my physical condition, and no one could figure out what was wrong. The doctors couldn't figure out anything, nobody could figure it out, and I couldn't do anything.

Then, one night, I had a dream, and in that dream I was talking with Rev. Moon. He had walked up to me, and there was no one else in a huge building. It was like one of the buildings we have and use for publications. He walked up to me and asked me a question and I started to answer him and, in answering him, my tongue got twisted. I couldn't talk, and he asked me the question again, and I knew what I wanted to say and I tried to say it but I couldn't move my tongue. It just got twisted. So I just said,

"Father, why can't I say what I want to say to you," and, in a very firm way, he pointed to me and said, "You must repent." And I was really struck, because I felt so judged and I didn't know why. So I started to cry. No, I didn't actually cry, I was shocked instead. And then he walked away from me and into another room, and, in the process, somehow the lights went out and I got very scared. So I started to walk towards where I had seen him go into the room. I was afraid, and I bumped into him. As I bumped into him, I started to cry, and I said, "I'm sorry, I'm sorry." He put his arm around me and said, "That's O.K., don't worry." And I said, "I know that I'm wrong. Why am I wrong? I'm really sorry," and I was really crying.

I woke up that morning, and the dream was so real to me that I cried the whole day. And I cried and I cried and I prayed and I asked Heavenly Father, "What's wrong with me? Why must I repent? What have I done wrong?" And I knew something was wrong, because all of a sudden I was sick for a couple of months. And I cried and cried all day long. I couldn't work. I was just crying and I kept going to the prayer room and praying to find out why I must repent.

So that next night I had another dream, and in the dream again Rev. Moon came. And it was interesting. I was sitting in the Manhattan Center waiting for a performance to start—the Manhattan Center is a theater we own—and all of a sudden I realized that Rev. Moon's guard was sitting beside me, and I thought, "Oh, no. Here's the guard. Father must be somewhere around here and I don't want him to see me," because of the dream I had had the night before. I thought, "I don't want him to see me." And he was seated right in front of me. And he turned around, and, in a very fatherly way, he said, "Why do you work so hard? It is for me?" And so I realized, "He's questioning, he's questioning my work, why I work, my attitude, my heart." And I knew I was working hard. So I was really stuck.

So, of course, I woke up. I cried all day. I couldn't work. I kept going to the prayer room, and I searched, and he has always said, "If I come to you in dreams, it's because God uses my physical body to speak to you." In my prayers that day I was asking God, "Why do you question my work? Why do you question what I'm doing? I've worked very hard, with a sincere heart." And so, of course, this went on. The next night I was afraid to go to sleep, because it was the third night, and I knew that I was going to get an answer, but I was really afraid at the same time.

So, the third night I had another dream, and in this dream Rev. Moon was calling all the members of our movement for a blessing. I saw him call all these people who are in the church, this movement, yet they were younger than me in physical and spiritual age and had less accomplishments than me, and yet they were all being called to be matched, to be blessed. I was not called. And so I watched everybody being called and everybody being matched and I watched the whole blessing, all the sisters dressed in white dresses, and everything, and here I was, not included.

So I was crying, and I told God, "Heavenly Father, why not me? I am old enough physically and spiritually. I have worked hard, why not me?" And just then one of the blessed mothers, who was blessed at the same time Mrs. Spurgin was blessed, told me, "But look at the attitude of this other sister."The other sister that she pointed out was younger than me spiritually and physically and had never worked so much, but I was struck, because this sister was also a Mexican-American sister, but her heart was very good. She didn't have the resentment, she hadn't gone through what I had gone through actually, her family was very much more Spanish and more light-skinned, she was more middle class, but she had a very, very pure heart, and so, I realized, I was struck by that.

I woke up. I spent about half of the day in the prayer room, really trying to understand. I knew that God questioned my attitude. It did not mean anything to God that I had worked so hard in this movement, it didn't mean anything to God that I would keep working in this movement. God was questioning my heart, the attitude with which I was working. God could not accept my work because my heart was not right. And why was my heart not right? It had something to do with my attitude. So I spent several days praying and trying to understand. I went on a condition on the 22nd of June, 1977, and I told God, "I want to understand what is wrong with my heart, and I want to change my heart." It was such a struggle because I told God, "I cannot change my heart. You must change my heart. And You must show me what I am doing wrong."

During this time I was always reading Rev. Moon's speeches, and I kept praying that I would find some way that God would talk to me. I found a speech by Rev. Moon called "Human

Relationships" where he talked about how the greatest thing about Jesus, and the reason that even God was humble before Jesus, was that Jesus could not only forgive the people when He was crucified, but that He took complete responsibility for their sins, for their failure, for crucifying Him. This struck me very much and stuck to me throughout this time.

Eventually I came to the seminary and, on October 22nd, 1977, when I was praying in the chapel, God answered me. Here I'd been struggling for all these months, for four months, struggling with the same question why it was that God could not accept my work. It was exactly four months after I had started my condition, and four is a very significant number for us. But, that night, in that prayer, God spoke to me very directly and told me, "I cannot accept your work because you have so much resentment against the white people. You have so much resentment against your brothers and sisters, against the white people, and, until you can overcome that resentment, I cannot receive your work." And I was struck, and immediately I remembered the white people that had put me through hell while I was a farm worker and was going to segregated schools. In the fields the bosses had spit at us and had mistreated my parents. I just cried and cried.

But I felt it was not just me that was crying; I felt that the Mexican people, Indian people, they were crying through me, and I cried and cried and cried. And, as I was crying, God told me again, I felt very clearly, "The reason that you can be here in the Unification church, the reason that you are here to serve Me now, is that your heart has been deepened by the struggles that you have gone through under these people." In other words, because I had had to suffer so much under the oppression of white people, I could deepen my heart so that I could come into this movement.

So I realized then that the people who were responsible for deepening my heart, so that I could come to know the suffering heart of God and so that I could come to be in this movement, were the white people. And I made it a point to remember clearly in my heart, in my mind, the people that I felt the most resentment towards, the white people when I was growing up. I remembered each one, and I tried to remember all the children that they had. (I used to babysit sometimes for some of their children.) I remembered many of their children, everyone of them. Then I prayed for their children and I told God, "On the foundation of the work that I am doing right now, You must bless their children, because of what their parents put me through I am in this movement, and therefore these children must be blessed on the foundation of my merit in this movement." And, at that point, I completely changed.

I was totally liberated, and I could sincerely feel gratitude towards the people that I had had so much resentment for in my heart, for so long. And so, my life was completely changed, and completely liberated, and I felt I liberated some of my ancestors who had felt some resentment. But I also liberated the heart of God because even though we may suffer as people, God suffers the most, as our parent, at seeing how cruel we are to each other, how we cannot forgive each other. One of the greatest struggles of God, on the world-wide scale, is the resentment of people and of nations. It was a deep experience for me.

Rod Sawatsky: Do the Evangelical people want to speak about their own realization of the spirit world and the Holy Spirit?

Roy Carlisle: I have a sense that there's a lot that Evangelicals and Charismatics are just beginning to understand about the spirit world and about how the Holy Spirit does work. I have my own spiritual experience. It's been very dramatic, but I hesitate to generalize from that experience. I see things from your experiences that I resonate with and some other things that I feel have some very serious biblical problems. Four years ago I was in seminary and I was going through a rather serious career decision in my life. I was making a contract with God that, unless I could see the power of the Holy Spirit, I was going to leave the faith. It was a very serious decision and one that I felt tctally obligated to make and to keep. So I began my own personal search, and in the process of that search I came into contact with the only kind of people that you can come into contact with in southern California (laughter)...

Jonathan Wells: Well, I've had experience in that! (laughter)

Roy Carlisle: I guess the only word that I really think describes it is "bizarre." That's the only word. So I started to go to all kinds of different meetings and see different kinds of spiritual things happening. What they did was drive me back to the Bible. A passage in I John 4:1-3 was very critical for me at that time, "Beloved, do not believe in every spirit, but test the spirits to see whether they are of God; for many false prophets have gone out into the world. By this you know the Spirit of God: every spirit which confesses that Jesus Christ has come in the flesh is of God, and every spirit which does not confess Jesus is not of God." It goes on and talks about more. I was going to alleged Christian meetings of all different kinds, and I saw things happen and experienced things that made me realize that there is a large spirit world. This was something that I, as an Evangelical, had never really dealt with. At that time, I began to see that, to work yourself through the maze, you've got to have some test, and the Scripture gives us this test.

So I began to apply it very concretely. I would be in a meeting, home meetings where people would be. I don't want to make it sound too bizarre, but there would be certain kinds of prophecies and tongues and, after those things had happened, I would go up to them and say, "Do you confess, as a person and as a spirit person, that Jesus Christ came in the flesh?" And I got lots of answers, and not all of them affirmative. And many of them said, "I'm charismatic and I'm a Christian." And I would say, "But do you confess that Jesus came..." And they would say, "Welllll..." I found such multiplicity in the answers that I was really confused, and I finally just had to resort to a search on my own, listening to other people and getting the guidance that I could get. In that process, I got involved in probably one of the most dangerous and scary areas of the spirit world, and that was exorcism. That experience liberated me in terms of understanding the spirit world and in understanding my own spirituality. We definitely have to have a conference about the Unification understanding of the spirit world and the evangelical-charismatic understanding of the spirit world, because there are some serious differences.

But my confession now is that my life was radically changed by my moving into that dimension. Tongues and interpretation and all those things are a part of my experience, but I don't emphasize those. The central thing was that God revealed to me that there is power and that the Holy Spirit is a spirit of power and a spirit of freedom and a spirit that only exalts Jesus Christ. My career changed, I got married—everything good that could happen happened right at that time, and I felt confirmed in a lot of other ways. So personally I've had some bizarre experiences and I've had some very good experiences and, quite frankly, I'm working it out. I think it is significant that today, if I understand the biblical view of history, there is such an outpouring of spiritual life and beings, good and evil, that we dare not misunderstand and we dare not ignore it. We, as Evangelicals, have tended to ignore it, and Unificationists obviously have not ignored it. There are some things we can learn there, but I think there are some things that we have to wrestle with, too.

Jonathan Wells: Would it be getting into too much if we were to talk a little bit specifically about people's experiences with Rev. Moon and/or Jesus?

Rod Sawatsky: No. I'd be very happy to have some people speak to that. Also some stories about Rev. Moon. We know Jesus primarily from stories, too, don't we? We know stories of His life, and those are very important for Christian people. What about stories of Rev. Moon's life and relationships with him?

Jonathan Wells: I can start. This isn't my personal story, but this story of Rev. Moon's life plays a very large role in our acquaintance with him. And that's the story of his life in prison, which we have partly from his own comments and partly from descriptions by people who were in prison with him or connected with him at the time. He was actually in prison more than once, but the time I'm speaking of was his time in a communist labor camp in North Korea. He was put in prison for subverting the social order, namely, preaching about God in communist North Korea, preaching Divine Principle. He was sentenced to five years at the Hung Nam labor camp (I hope I get all these details straight, but the spirit will be accurate anyway), and the average life span of the prisoners there was about six months, because they were grossly overworked and grossly underfed. So, in effect, it was a sentence of death to be sent to that camp. Rev. Moon decided that he wasn't going to worry about his own survival, and he prayed to comfort God's heart at this time. That was the primary emphasis of his prayer; he prayed, "Heavenly Father, don't worry about me. I know You're aware of my situation, but You've got enough troubles because You've got the weight of the whole world on You, so don't worry about me." And he was praying for the rest of the world in effect.

When he saw that his food ration was inadequate, he decided that he would begin by cutting it in half. Actually, a fist-sized ball of rice constituted a meal, and, though others were starving with that, he decided he could survive on half of it. And so, at each meal, for the first three months, I believe, he cut his portion in half and gave that to various other prisoners. The situation was so desperate that people were dying. In the middle of meals they would die of exhaustion and starvation, and other prisoners would run over and take the rice out of the dead men's mouths. It was that desperate. And yet Rev. Moon was giving away half his food. So, after the three months, when he started eating the whole portion he could tell himself, "Well, now I'm getting twice as much as I really need."

And he took the attitude that, because people were suffering from over-work, he would do the toughest job. The job they were doing was loading fertilizer, and, on the work crew, he always took the toughest job, and so the prisoners always wanted to be on his crew. In fact, he won an award from the communists for being the best laborer in the camp. And the prisoners, as I understand it, never saw him sleep, because, when the other prisoners collapsed exhausted on their beds at night, he would be kneeling in prayer. And, when they woke up in the morning, he would be kneeling in prayer because he would get up before them. And his message to us that I hear over and over is, "If you want to be a leader, you have to eat less and sleep less and work harder than anybody else." And just as an aside, my personal experience with him verifies his own faithfulness to that principle.

While he was in prison, his friends would bring him things—clothing and extra food—and he always shared them with the other prisoners. Even though he couldn't teach anything in the camp, because if he said a word about God or the Bible or Divine Principle he would be executed, yet people were drawn to him, and he actually gathered a following in the camp. Finally, the time came when the allies were counter-attacking and the camp was being shelled or bombed, and the prisoners that were following him clung to him because they knew somehow that he wasn't going to be destroyed. And, in fact, he wasn't, so, after two years and ten months, he was freed from the camp by the allies. That's two years and four months longer than most people survived.

Anthony Guerra: I have a personal story which is shared by many of us concerning Rev. Moon's quite frequent visits to the seminary. In the two years that I was here, we got to know him very personally. I recall that, the year before last, he came quite a few times and spoke to us, and one time when he was speaking to us he said, "You know, really, I'd like to be doing things with you.

I'd like to go hunting with you, fishing... I know you are in classes all the time, but it would be nice to do something together, wouldn't it?"

So the following week, it was a Friday, he came up here, and some of us went outside to greet him. The first thing he did was to take large balls of nets and start laying them out right in front of the building, 3,000 yards of them. He began unrolling them with a few people helping him, and then he began running ropes along the top of one of the nets and also down along the bottom, and then he began fastening corks to the top rope. He was making the fishing nets that we used throughout the spring. As it was growing darker outside, he moved all these fishing nets, ropes, corks, and weights into the large hall downstairs. He was making the nets, a few people were helping him, and a lot of us were just standing around because we didn't know precisely what to do. We stayed up through the night, and Rev. Moon began teaching us how to make certain things. He taught us individually how to tie knots onto the corks and how to tie the weights onto the bottom of the net. Many of us went to sleep. We weren't sure if we were supposed to be there, but Rev. Moon stayed up the entire night making those nets. He arrived here at five o'clock, stayed up through the night until eight o'clock the next morning, and then he went to sleep for a few hours.

At eleven in the morning he came back and invited all of us to come out again, once more teaching us how to make the nets. We were astonished at his determination. But he wanted to finish the job quickly because, that Sunday, he wanted to go out fishing with us. He spent two days virtually without sleep making those nets so that he could go fishing with us, and, at the same time, he wanted to teach us how to make nets and how to fish, so that we would be able to survive under any circumstances and also gain some practical knowledge. Several times that spring Rev. Moon went fishing with us.

Many people who I talk to about Rev. Moon imagine him to be very distant from us, but our relationship to him is quite the opposite. We feel very close to him, and we feel him to be not only our spiritual leader, but also a very close friend who has sacrificed much of his personal time to share with us and talk with us and teach us how to make fishing nets. This is the Rev. Moon that we know. And I've been to dinner with him on several occasions when he was staying in Massachusetts. I was the director for a time in Massachusetts, and, as you mentioned, he was tuna fishing for a period of some forty days. He would go out early at three o'clock in the morning, before any other fishermen would go out, and come back at about eight o'clock at night, which is about three or four hours later than other fishermen. Incidentally, this is on the yacht that everyone talks about, that you've heard about in the newspapers. He uses it as a fishing vessel and not as a pleasure cruiser. He often brings out people, leaders of the movement, and teaches them how to fish for tuna with him.

I've also been to his mansion in Tarrytown because that mansion is used every month for state directors' conferences. He has seventy to one hundred people there at those conferences that last sometimes two or three days every month. We never slept there—the house is too small and all the bedrooms were usually occupied with guests who would come from Korea and other countries to consult on church matters. So knowing Rev. Moon and his life style and the purposefulness with which he carries out his mission as he sees it, I've always received inspiration that I'm following someone who lives his own ideals, someone who sincerely believes them. Apart from the question of whether what he believes is right, Rev. Moon believes in what he's doing with all his heart, all his mind, and all his strength, and he puts himself on the line to do it again and again.

Dan Davies: My first encounter with Rev. Moon was very important. I had just come back from Israel. I had met the movement in New York and had gone to a three-day workshop. I was profoundly affected by what I heard. Then, a few days later, I met Rev. Moon. One thing that had been a problem for me was that I'd never found anybody that I could share the depths of the joy in my heart with. There was a joy that I could only share with God. When I met Rev. Moon for the first time, at Belvedere, down the river about seventy miles from the Unification Seminary, he was sitting on the grass with fifty or sixty other people. I was feeling a depth of joy at that time that I couldn't really share with anyone. I mean that in a slight way I could, but to a deeper degree I couldn't. I caught his eye, and he caught mine. He smiled, not just smiled, but lit up with a kind of joy that hit me full force. My first experience with him was an experience of joy; that's the main reason, besides the truth that I find here, that I'm able to stay; that is, I find in him a source of joy.

When the seminary went to England this summer it was a

traumatic experience in a way. You're on an airplane and you go over there, and you don't know what you're going to find. You don't know what you're going to meet. Rev. Moon was waiting to meet us, but our plane was late. At midnight we all came into his room. He said, "What happened? Why are you late? I was waiting for you to come." It seemed that he was sorrowful. He had missed us so much that it hurt him when we didn't arrive.

After that I came to realize that, in a way, he is a weak man, because of his love for us. He really misses us, as a parent misses his children. He spoke with us that night for about four hours, late into the night, until four o'clock in the morning. I doubt very much if he had any sleep before. I know, from being with him, that he will often speak through the night, then get a couple of hours of sleep, and then go all day.

Besides finding the truth here, I also find a sense of love and joy that comes from him. But it's not just a joyful experience that I'm looking for from him. I don't really find just a joyful experience from him, because he really does care about me. He takes the responsibility to train me. He wants me to become so strong that there is no evil that can conquer me. So he'll put me in difficult situations that I have to work my way out of.

Rev. Moon wanted to send us right out into the streets of England to find a family to live with and establish a home church. Most of us didn't have any money. It was cold. We didn't know it would be cold when we came, so we didn't have any warm clothes. He wanted to send us out because he knew that would be the best training for us to go out without money, without warm clothes, but he didn't want people to misunderstand him. They would say, "Oh, Rev. Moon is an evil man; he sends these people out into the streets, without any money." So instead of doing that, which he would rather have done and I really rather he would've done, he gave us money to go out with to find a family to live with and carry out a witnessing program. I imagine many of the people here could share experiences that have been very important to them, like the first fishing experience we had with him.

Rev. Moon doesn't know everything right off the bat; it takes him a while to figure things out, but he learns. This was the first time we were fishing with a big net. We did a voluntary thing. He asked people if they wanted to go fishing in the cold water. "Are you sure you want to do this—go out into the cold water?" and we said, "Oh, yeah, we really want to do it." So we all went traipsing down there, and everybody was all excited. It was just great. We took the net across the lagoon. But we had to walk across, everybody one at a time, or two at a time would step into the water. Dagfinn and I were two of the first guys in (laughter) so we took the net across the water, and it took a long time to lay it out. As it ended up, we were in the water a total of three hours. No one died, but it was close. It was an experience that none of us will ever forget. I don't think we caught any fish (laughter) but we caught lots of fish after that, and we did work out a better system after that. We didn't use people to hold the net later, we used poles (*Jonathan:*...and the water got warmer) and our technique got better.

Rod Sawatsky: Do you want to let somebody from the Evangelical side talk first—did you want to add something?

Patricia Zulkosky: I just wanted to say that not everyone's experience with Rev. Moon is so joyful. I often become angry or negative, at least for a couple of hours. I've thought a lot about it—what in the world are you doing in a movement when almost every time you see the leader you get a little negative?

I remember very clearly one time I had been out pioneering, and I had a very difficult time. I didn't really feel I was making a good contribution to society because I was too caught up in my own fear and my own self. I couldn't really serve, and I really was trying to repent and trying to change, and I knew I wasn't really doing what God wanted. I was going to do a seven-day fast, as some effort towards having a repentance experience, and then I went to hear Rev. Moon speak that weekend. He knew that we were stuck by our own fear and weren't connected enough to God, so he was trying to push us more and exaggerating about what we should be willing to do in order to serve God. I didn't pick up on the spirit of sacrifice but reacted to the literal statements. And I remember walking off the estate and shaking my head violently, no, and walking with my friend, and I said, "No, no, no, I am not. I refuse. I am not going to eat out of garbage cans, I'm not going to sleep on the park bench, I'm not going to do my seven-day fast, either, so there." (laughter) I had this kind of feeling, and it took me a while to come back around to the place where I did do my seven-day fast. God did give me the gift of repentance that I wanted so much, and that was literally my rebirth.

And I thought a lot about why I often react so strongly to

Rev. Moon, and it may even surprise you to hear someone speak so candidly. I think a lot of it is that he wants us to confront our fallen nature, and he is always holding up the highest standard. So many times when I hear him speak, it comes down to: will I continue going the way I am going or do I change to a higher standard of love, a higher standard of serving, a deeper relationship with God? Will I put myself on the limb, or will I play it safe the way I always play it safe? Somehow he says something or does something that really helps me understand where I fall short of how Jesus would do it, of how God would have me do it. And then I have to work out, in my heart, in my prayer, and in my studying, a willingness to offer myself to God anew, and a willingness to put myself on what appears to be a limb that won't hold me, even though it is a great struggle for me to get to the point of making that offering. The greatness of God and His love for me and His love for people comes through again and again in a sense.

Jonathan Wells: We call that challenging our limitations.

Charles Barfoot: I just was thinking about stories about Rev. Moon and it flashed. Roy was talking about setting up a Pentecostal/ Charismatic Conference and Richard has been thinking about that—I would like to see more leaders here—Richard or whoever will do it—seriously consider inviting Dr. Cho. He has the world's largest Pentecostal church in Korea—he knew Rev. Moon—I think that would be an interesting dialogue. Dr. Cho comes to the States, he holds services in my father's church, which is always packed—the church seats about two thousand, and is jammed. I think that would be a very interesting kind of dialogue, especially if your movement is strong in Korea as well.

The other thing that I just wanted to reflect on is that I was struck today in the chapel. There was that last song or hymn, and it flashed in my mind that in my father's church, one time, we had a Latin-American Bible School there. They came to the church and sang, and they tried to do these things in English, and it wasn't full of life, and then they did Spanish, and were vibrant. I sensed some vibrancy in that last song or hymn or whatever. Then I walked downstairs and I saw somebody who had a real spark of life, so I guess I would say to you: I've seen some sparks, but I've also seen the weight of the world. Don't be afraid to have that vibrancy.

Joseph Hopkins: I don't want to be a wet blanket, but I've been studying religious movements in America over a number of

years and, as I said before, I see the Unification church as one
movement among many which have common characteristics.
You have a charismatic leader with the self-image of being God's
latter-day prophet, who imparts a new revelation, who attracts
followers and constitutes the "one true church" for these latter
days, whose teachings deviate from traditional doctrines held for
two thousand years by the mainstream of Christianity.

So I can't help being skeptical. I hear the same sort of
anecdotes related here about Rev. Moon which I have read about
in the annals of Joseph Smith, Mary Baker Eddy, and other
charismatic personalities who are held in awe by their faithful
disciples. In view of what Roy said, in quoting I John, we have all
these warnings in the New Testament about false prophets who
would arise in the latter days and deceive many people.

Frankly, I can't help but regard Moon in this way—as not
unique but just one of a *number* of latter-day prophets. Maybe
very sincere, but self-deceived into believing that he has a messianic
role to fulfill. A man with a strong personality and vivid imagination,
with spiritual sensitivity and dedication, who comes up with
these far-out doctrines about re-interpreting the fall, about his
being Lord of the Second Advent, and so on. When Jesus said to
Peter, "Get thee behind me, Satan," He didn't mean that Peter
was malicious or evil in his motivation. He merely meant that
Peter was trying to dissuade Him from the cross, from fulfilling
His destiny as our Redeemer. I can't help but wonder if Rev.
Moon, who comes across to you folks who know him as a very
sincere, gentle, humble man who has a burning concern for
uniting the world in love and peace and brotherhood, is being
unconsciously used by Satan. Through his high intelligence and
spiritual openness, he may have exposed himself to the manipulation
of Satan in believing these things about himself, in believing the
so-called revelations that are recorded in the *Divine Principle*.

Dan Davies: I'd like to point out that everything that Joseph
just said can be applied to Jesus, too. Why do you believe in
Jesus? He was called all those things.

Joseph Hopkins: But Jesus fulfilled prophecy. The Old and
New Testaments stand together, from Genesis 3:15 until the
fulfillment of the last of the messianic prophecies in Jesus. The
biblical scheme of redemption is complete, and we are warned
against adding to this faith "once and for all delivered"—in Jude
3, for example.

Anthony Guerra: There are a lot of rabbis who would disagree with you about how it hangs together.

Nora Spurgin: I was going to say the same thing that Anthony said, it's only in hindsight that they hang together, and two thousand years from now hindsight may...

Joseph Hopkins: But there's the resurrection...

Nora Spurgin: Yes, there's the resurrection...

Joseph Hopkins: But what do you define as the point of resurrection?

Frank Kaufmann: Well, one or two minor points—first, to say that we reinterpret the fall is to assume that traditional Christianity has a unified interpretation of the fall. Of course, it hasn't! Next, a test—I'm not so familiar with all the tests, but from those presented this morning, for false prophets, or for testing the spirits, one is to see whether or not it confesses that Jesus Christ came in the flesh, which the Divine Principle indisputably does. Finally, it is not Unification doctrine that Rev. Moon calls himself the messiah, but we do have a theology which interprets the nature of the second coming of the Christ, which is not contradictory to Scripture. Although it might be new to what traditional Christianity has decided upon, we found this weekend, in fact, that Christians do not agree on the doctrine of the second coming at all.

Anthony Guerra: But I have a much bigger problem with what you said, Joe, even if I were not a Unificationist. It's the way you write off the Mormons and Christian Scientists and people like Mary Baker Eddy. You fail to appreciate the way in which the Holy Spirit may in fact be manifesting itself in human history after the Scripture was canonized. In the Old Testament, you have the Scriptures recording God at work in human history, and then you have the New Testament, which reports perhaps a hundred years of the history of how the Holy Spirit was working. But, as to how the Holy Spirit is going to work after that time, i.e. during the last 1900 years, it's there where you seem to have made all the conclusions, whereas I would be forced to say that one has to be open to how that's done.

Thomas Bower: Could I raise a procedural question? I am just expressing my personal view. It seems to me that we're getting back into dialogue, and we can read this. I'm going to feel awfully cheated if in an hour we can't have had a bit more exposure to testimonials. We can just go back and forth here all day.

Jonathan Wells: I feel a lack of testimonials from the evangelical side...

Evangelical Y: It's not directly testimonial. It's why I am somewhat reticent to enter into that. Not that I am reticent to give testimony to Jesus Christ—it comes from another perspective. My officemate at the University of Hawaii taught Philosophy of Science, and he'd done a study of why people take particular perspectives in the philosophy of science. In the process of dialoguing with him for long periods of time, I found a very useful way for understanding Christian faith—to be talking about the importance of paradigms, and also paradigm shifts. This particular dissertation happened to be on how individual scientists shift from one paradigm to another. And it finally concluded that, fundamentally, it came down to a conversion experience, and that is usually what happens before a scientific revolution takes place. You have to wait a generation for one whole generation of scientists just to die. Very few of them make this paradigm shift—it has to wait for the younger generation coming up. It was somewhat amusing, because our Campus Crusade people will not be able to appreciate this comment, but a Campus Crusader gave him the book by Joshua Dell—the man's very interesting, but all that Josh took as evidence, he would not interpret as evidence, because it's your paradigm which determines the evidence pro or con. That's why the futility of the interaction here on how to interpret the Old Testament, because, what you would take as evidence of Jesus' understanding of the Old Testament, I don't read as evidence at all, and the stories about Rev. Moon leading you to see Him as having some importance, I don't view as evidence at all. It has significance on a personal level in the sense that, as a human being, you're experiencing Him (and values have importance), but, in terms of entering into understanding of the concepts, we're passing each other. The thing that struck me in terms of dialogue this weekend is in some ways the futility of dialogue, because what is really fundamental is a paradigm, the way you look at evidence, and, since we're not totally prepared to shift paradigms, it becomes an illuminating experience to understand another person's point of view. But you can never really hit head on because the paradigm is different.

Anthony Guerra: First of all, let me clarify, there is a Jewish interpretation in Scriptures, which is quite different from...

Evangelical Y: But there's a paradigm yet...

Anthony Guerra: I was addressing myself to a certain attitude. I think we have to be careful not to violate the spirit of the New Testament and merely abide by the letter.

Evangelical Y: Now what seems to be the spirit of the New Testament in your understanding is a new paradigm. I find an element of real rigor and intolerance in the New Testament—Jesus said, "I am the way." He didn't equivocate on that. "If anybody comes after me and says, 'I am the way,' then he preaches another gospel, let him be damned." Now that is also part of the New Testament, and to say that it isn't there is to say...

Jonathan Wells: The New Testament also includes passages such as: "I have yet many things to say to you, but you cannot bear them now. When the Spirit of truth comes, He will guide you into all truth...;" and "He who conquers,...I will write on Him...my own new name;" and "She brought forth a male child, one who is to rule all the nations with a rod of iron..." It seems to me that the fundamental issue here is whether a paradigm shift is possible in religion?

Evangelical Y: Once in a while, but not very often... more often it is a radical shift...it's a conversion experience. There is very little likelihood that I would become a member of the Unification church over a period of time. It is psychologically possible to have a paradigm shift, but, in that case, it is likely to take place in a rather short period of time...

Jonathan Wells: It is quite possible, and, conceding a point here, I would like to say with Joe that all of us are, I think, enjoined by the Scriptures to be skeptical, and I am. And I'm glad you are. But there is a difference between being skeptical and saying *a priori* they're all no good. I think that's the key issue here, isn't it? Are we open to a paradigm shift either way, from Unification back to the New Testament, or from New Testament to Unification, or Mormon? I mean, are we dedicated to the proposition that it's possible, even if unlikely?

Rod Sawatsky: I find it a little amazing that Joe would say, "I don't know if we should be listening to each other's testimonies." I find that very strange from an evangelical perspective, because surely the whole processs of witness is the process of telling what I have found to be true, and it requires the other person to make some paradigm shift. Correct? But, what else can you do? That's all we can do. And, what is meaningful and true for us is something that we need to tell others.

Evangelical Y: The thing that frustrates me, if I understand what I'm hearing from the Unification position, is that no matter what I say about Jesus Christ, it will be understood differently from what I intend it (*Dan:* Why?) because you believe in the Lord of the Second Advent. This gives a radically different perspective on the Lord who came first, because, to me, one of the essential elements of Christian faith is the finality of Jesus Christ, whereas you do not believe in the finality of Jesus Christ.

Anthony Guerra: It sounds as though you're afraid that we won't be able to receive what you have to offer...

Evangelical Y: It's not that you won't receive it—it will mean something very different. The translation problem is almost insurmountable here. The only way we start to understand each other's paradigms, even to be able to consider them as possibly viable for ourselves, is to hear them from a systematic theological perspective. You see, I can read your books, but I can't get nuances of the experiences without sitting in the room with you. And that's where then we can begin to compare.

Rod Sawatsky: I think it would be good if maybe another person from the evangelical group spoke a little bit about his own experience.

Thomas Bower: Let me do so, because mine is terribly undramatic. (laughter) It's a very short statement. I don't know how to say it. I haven't rehearsed this. I find my classical evangelical perspective to be adequate for my life. Period. And I presume there is no possibility of a paradigm shift for me unless a cataclysmic event occurs in my life, or in the life of the world, which is also my life, which would cause me to re-evaluate the adequacy of my own paradigm. Now, my paradigm, evangelical paradigm, speaks to me. It has always spoken to my experience. Why didn't it speak to you in your experience? Is it because of an inherent limitation of that paradigm, to continue using that word, or is it a caricature of it, to which you are exposed in your upbringing, or what? In other words, why hasn't the evangelical paradigm worked for you? I want to make one other comment, purely a sociological, psychological common sense comment. I think that one of the things I've appreciated is being in an environment which isn't blue with profanity. It's been very, very refreshing to be among young people who know something about hosting, and it has not been canned, I don't think, or intricately rehearsed. It seems to me to be a natural outflow of who you are and where you are. On the other hand I want to say—and I don't want to discuss this, because it would take some thought—that I miss, and for what reason I don't know, I miss sensuality in the environment. Maybe that's part of the brick and mortar of this particular piece of real estate, I don't know. There seems to be a dimension in my life that I haven't found here. I'm calling it sensuality, maybe it's color, a certain kind of spark in females' eyes—I don't know, I'm not sure—but something I miss, and maybe it's a reflection of the society here... (laughter)

Charles Barfoot: That's what I call vibrancy. I feel the same way. I saw evidence of that this morning, and it is refreshing... (talking at once; laughter)

Franz Feige: In the 2,000-year history of Christianity, I can see a certain shift taking place concerning the center of spiritual growth. In Catholicism, spiritual growth or spirituality was centered on symbols and images. In the Greek Orthodox Church an example would be the icons. With Luther, we see a shift taking place, where the center becomes the word. The people were able to read. The Bible became very important. It became a guide for their spiritual growth in their relationship with God, Jesus, and one another. Then, even in Protestantism, we observe another shift. Jesus Himself becomes the center, meaning your personal relationship with Jesus. Therefore, we are going beyond the word in the Bible—the word becomes a limitation. Wesley is an example—his relationships with Jesus, God and Holy Spirit. I want to ask you whether you are open enough to go beyond the Bible through your relationship with Jesus Christ. Can you let God speak to your heart, in your relationship with this world, and with the Bible? Can you be open to a new revelation, new insights—something that goes beyond the Bible? I believe that many people in the Unification church see the Scripture, whether *Divine Principle* or the Bible, as an expression of truth, but not the truth itself. The truth itself is Jesus Christ or the true man. Our relationship with Jesus is the real standard of truth; it determines our relationships in life.

Mark Branson: I just want to deal with this testimonially, rather than theologically. I came out of a very literal church, which had very little to say about the person of Jesus but a lot to do with ethics. It made sense and attracted me. It was during mid-high school that someone for the first time talked to me about Jesus as a person rather than as the head of the church, so that was something of a breakthrough for me. I started understanding and praying and building a relationship, and I had some spiritual experiences in prayer, but this has not been the major part of my life. I eventually came to the point of studying His word, and, as you can tell, it was concentrated in the Gospels, although I'm not at all limited to it. I don't have any higher respect for the Gospels than for the writings of Paul. But, what has happened is that I've seen more and more as I've gotten into the word—I've seen the vibrancy of it, I've seen the power of it, I've seen the consistency of it, and it doesn't mean I like it all—there are really some things that Jesus does and says that *I don't like*, and I've had to wrestle with them, and yet there are some things that ring so true as to be authentic and consistent.

Again I come down to this, as Charlie mentioned earlier: the resurrection is a very powerful attestation to the validity of what Christ has done. The authority and power of the Bible as it witnesses to Jesus Christ is what's made the difference in my own life. I've simply found that His word is trustworthy—when I hear this word and obey it, I am met by Him—and that anything which contradicts or goes beyond and changes that consistency witnesses to my spirit that it is false. If the Scriptures were not pointing to Jesus, I would have different questions, but I am simply finding that, as I get into the word, then my relationship with Him is fed and my own life becomes more the life that I think God has intended me to have.

Richard Quebedeaux: Could I ask a question of some Unificationists? Last time we didn't agree on anything, and yet most of us came back, and all of the people who didn't come back wanted to if they could. That's the first time in my life that I've ever seen that happen. Barrytown is nice, but it is not Hawaii, and a lot of people here are very, very busy, and made a sacrifice to come. Again, this time, we've been very direct with very little common agreement resulting. We Evangelicals keep saying over and over, and I think Donald Deffner preached it* in a way, that we're very determined about what we're saying. You're talking about paradigms. Someone said that I don't think you understand the nature of dialogue and taking the risk of conversion, and what that means in a dialogue; that's why nobody wants to dialogue, because they're afraid that they're going to be "converted"

---

*See Sermon, p. 365ff.

and have to change their minds.

Have *we* done anything specifically for you Unificationists to draw you in our direction? I think I have been drawn in your direction, though I don't think I know how to explain it because I have *not* been drawn in your direction doctrinally. What can you say to us about this?

Dan Davies: Maybe I can talk to you directly about that, because, after the first conference, I had already decided to go to Toronto, to the Institute of Christian Thought. But, after the conference, I decided to accept Perkins in Dallas. I had had no hope of having any kind of relationship with Evangelicals, but, because of our last conference, I gained the hope that we could. Not just a relationship for relationship's sake, but actually I can see that the Evangelicals are the hope for America. Frankly, it's the only place where Bible morality still exists in America, outside the Unification church and some other groups. I feel the Evangelicals have a great deal to offer, in living out the Christian way of life. This is what you have to offer to us.

Jack Harford: Most of my experience with Evangelicals has been when I was fundraising (laughter)—they didn't give a dime—(liberals are much better). We refer to them as parking lot Christians, and they're the kind you always meet in the parking lot. Although my brother is an evangelical Christian, and my parents are turning more evangelical, I had become resentful towards all Christianity, towards Christ, towards God—completely turned away. It's only been through Unification church that I've been able to start to repair that relationship. I just want to say that I really feel that a new relationship to Christ is developing in my life because of this weekend, in seeing how much you love Jesus. It's really helped me to grow in my relationship to Jesus and to realize that there is a love relationship to Jesus that Christians have that makes Christianity different from everything else; so I just want to thank you.

Don Deffner: I'd like to respond to that, too, in spite of the negative thing that I said about being frustrated... In a sense what I say is very much what Mark says. Jesus, to me, is the revelation of the Father, and in Jesus I see the one point in time and space where, in an ultimate way, the barrier between God and man has been crossed. When I see Jesus of Nazareth, Jesus the Christ, I come to an appreciation of the austere God of the Old Testament, of both God's love and God's wrath—it would be

easy to miss the love in the Old Testament—it has been historical—
and many people have missed that fact. When I see Jesus of
Nazareth, I see the austerity of God of the Old Testament, and I
also see the love of God. Austerity is easier to see in the Old
Testament, but the point is the same: He communicates to me
who God is, and that then becomes the pattern of what human
life should be. Life should be a reflection of Jesus of Nazareth,
and, as many others have said, I have a sense that this is a pattern
of life that makes sense to me; my relationship to Jesus Christ
flows out of that.

Also, by its very nature, then, a unique relationship results,
because I see in Jesus Christ the place where God has spoken
and said, "This is where I am, follow Me in this way." I find the
satisfaction in prayer and in being told that I can communicate
with the Father and in the sense of having been reconciled to the
Father through the work of Jesus Christ. That's all I want to say.

Franz Feige: We haven't said too much yet about the heart
of God, and what the real heart of the Unification church is. I
don't think that sensuality is the real heart of the Unification
church. What you see in the Unification church is many, many
young people eighteen, twenty-five and thirty years of age. I
think throughout the Unification church we feel responsible—that's
why we are in the Unification church—not only for our own life,
but for the life of our families and for this world and even for
God.

It is very difficult at times to bear the burden of this world
and to feel the heavy heart of God, to feel the struggle, this
infinite struggle of all the people of this world, that starve, that
lose their faith in God, in a world that moves more towards Satan
than towards God. One can't help but feel sometimes so deep
and heavy that you don't always see vibrancy in our eyes. But,
when you look deeper, you can really see that we sometimes cry
for one another because we feel responsible and that we sometimes
cry with God for this world and for Christianity. Whenever I read
the Bible, I feel the spirit of Jesus coming to me and crying,
crying and crying, and I can't help but cry along. This is the heart
of Jesus: this is the heart of God. Jesus told me many times that
He is terribly sad about the state of Christianity being split into so
many parts. He would like to see Christianity united into a vital
force in order to solve all the problems. So, what I feel through
this dialogue, too, is that responsibility to solve the problems

within Christianity and then, hopefully with Christianity, the problems of this world. It's a rather heavy feeling, I honestly admit, but there's also a spark of hope; otherwise this heavy weight and burden would kill me.

I also get out of this dialogue an incredible hope, because there is a willingness to cooperate, as much on our side, as on the side of you, the Evangelicals.

Joseph Hopkins: I suppose I have come across as being rather narrow and intolerant, and I hope you don't feel rejected, because certainly on a personal level—I've been here three times now—I want to reaffirm my increasing admiration, respect, and love for my friends in the Unification church. I am very grateful for your hospitality, once again, and feel this has been a very stimulating and rewarding conference. So thank you very much.

Rod Sawatsky: I don't think the conversation need stop, but four of us have to run off right now, and I must say, simply, as the one who has been moderating it, that I am very pleased at the forthrightness of this discussion—we have not been trying to hide behind any trees, but have been forthright and said what we thought, and that's been good, that's been necessary.

Obviously the differences are very, very deep—obviously the deepest difference is the relationship of Jesus to Rev. Moon. I think the process of conversation at least leads us to understanding, if not to agreement. I think we need to say, with Joseph, again, thank you very much to Unification people for their excellent hospitality; it has been very fine. That is also one of the marks of the spirit which is difficult for us to forget, just like love, and we appreciate that.

SALVATION

Conversion and Faith

Rod Sawatsky: To begin our discussion of conversion and of redemption, I wonder if it might be helpful to let the Evangelicals speak first. Maybe Paul Eshleman, since he was one of the ones to raise the question, might start by summarizing the evangelical view of conversion, and other people can add to that, and then we can have some questions and answers on that basis. Agreed?

Paul Eshleman: We believe that all men are sinful, and thus separated from God, and that the purpose for which Jesus Christ came was to pay the penalty for man's sin. The Scripture that we would use in conjunction with these statements would be John 3:16: "For God so loved the world that He gave His only Son, that whoever believes in Him should not perish, but have eternal life." In Romans it says, very specifically, that "The wages of sin is death," spiritual separation from God, and that Jesus Christ came to pay the penalty for sin. We believe that the response to Jesus Christ has to be basically an individual decision. There would probably be some disagreements among the Evangelicals on how much man is involved in that, whether it is totally of God and man doesn't even have the ability to respond, or whether he does have a free will to say yes or no. I think it would be mostly God seeking man out, and that man has ultimately the choice to say yes or no in that regard. That's a way of beginning.

Don Deffner: I would add that, if a person becomes a Christian, it is God at work in the person, not "my choosing God." Another way of putting it is that God gives us three gifts: first of all, He gives us life itself. "You are not your own"—you didn't make yourself—"it is He that hath made you, and not you, yourself." If I misuse this life, I play God. I need forgiveness. Then, the loving, incredibly loving God gives us Himself in His Son, Jesus Christ. He suffered and died for us on the cross, rose from the dead, and ascended into heaven. This incredible "God's kind of God," not *my* kind of God, not *my* confused conception of Him, this freeing, loving, giving God even gives me the freedom to throw away the first two gifts, to reject Him. If I am converted, it's God at work in me. Our life in this world is actually His life lived in us...(I John 4:17).

Paul Eshleman: I think of several Scriptures as corollaries: Romans 5:8: "But God shows His love for us even while we were yet sinners. Christ died for us." He could pay the price because He was supernatural; He rose from the dead. John 14:6: "Jesus said to him, 'I am the way and the truth and the life; no one comes to the Father but by me.'" John 1:12: "But to all who received him, (Jesus Christ) who believed his name, he gave power to become children of God." We would feel it's very important that a new family relationship—and we mean this, I'm sure, in a different way than you do—be established with God, the Heavenly Father, through spiritual rebirth, and that this birth comes through faith in Christ plus nothing, as has been quoted several times. Ephesians 2:8-9; "For by grace you have been saved through faith; and this is not of your own doing, it is the gift of God—not because of your works, lest any man should boast." We would feel that, on the basis of an individual making that kind of decision, he would be spiritually reborn into the family of God. Thus he would have the inheritance of an eternal relationship with God, and would begin as a baby in the family, and, through the empowering of the Holy Spirit within him, would progressively be conformed to the image of Christ. He would one day be completed when he would receive his new body, after resurrection.

Mark Branson: I guess I'd like to develop it just a little bit historically. When Jesus was first baptized, His command, the fifteen-word sermon that He was famous for, is "The time is fulfilled, and the kingdom of God is at hand, repent, and believe in the gospel." Time had reached a climax. Everything is done that needs to be done to this point. He says it is fulfilled. The kingdom of God is at hand. His task was to *introduce* the kingdom of God. By being "at hand," He simply means that if you reach out and touch it, it is attainable, it's available, it is at hand. Then, He says that the way you touch it is by repenting and believing.

Repenting means turning around, and believing, to "live in accordance with." Then He commenced to show what it means to repent and believe by His life, by His preaching, by His works. The kingdom, the gospel, focuses on Jesus as He shows He is Lord. The effects of the fall on nature and the perversion of the world are encountered. All of the different areas of brokenness— brokenness with nature, brokenness with emotion, brokenness with the spiritual world, brokenness with God (sin)—Jesus set out, in His life, to reconcile.

Then He healed, He raised the dead, He forgave sins, He cast out demons. So we say that the fall, the curse, is reversed. What God intended in creation, He now restores in the redemption. The Lord of the universe is here, setting about creation again. At that point He is not saying who He is. He is simply living it out, as king. Halfway into the gospel, after Jesus had been with the disciples for a while, He asked the question, "Who do you say that I am?" Peter has the right title; he says, "You are the Messiah." Jesus says, "Don't tell anybody." The reason, we all know, that he shouldn't tell anybody is because that word, although it is the right name, is totally misunderstood by that culture. They are expecting a zealot option, the overthrowing of Rome. If they were to say Jesus was the Messiah, it would have been a lie to the hearers, because their hearing was wrong. Jesus says, "O.K. You've got the right title, you've got some correct understandings, but I also want you to hear what it means." He says, "The Son of Man must suffer and die and be raised again from the dead. You've got to understand God's way of providing forgiveness, reconciliation, the kingdom, the new life, the gospel." Of course, the disciples couldn't hear this. They did, off and on, but the rest of the book is a struggle to understand what it means to be the suffering servant.

They still didn't even hear about His resurrection. He preached that all the time, too! The cross is not just a sidetrack—the cross is the kingdom come. His call is, "You must deny yourself, take up your cross." To them, this did not have deep spiritual significance. The cross simply meant that, as you repent, as you buy into the kingdom of God, then you're going to be in conflict with every other kingdom. You're going to be in conflict with every other authority, every other ruler, every other institution, every other principality, every other power. And that means automatically you might as well just plan on the crucifixion by the time you get halfway into the day, or whatever. So you've given up any thought of establishing your loyalty to any other force or any other power. You simply say, "I've got one Lord and one God." This means that, rather than demanding my rights and demanding to be equal to God, as I did in the fall, I say, "I give up my rights. I deny myself. I take up the cross and follow, or imitate, Jesus." And then I see salvation. If I understand being born again, if I understand Jesus' parable about new birth, that everything is provided by Him, I don't think there is any room for more than one Christ in Christianity. Even my behavior is that which has been given me by Jesus. The part of me that has to do with obedience, the part of me that has to do with the fact that I think obedience is a very necessary part of salvation, knows that even obedience is granted to me by my Lord through the Holy Spirit. Salvation, then, means following Jesus. Anything short of following Jesus is not salvation.

Irving Hexham: There are other theological ramifications and interpretations of the evangelical view. Salvation comes from God. God is the giver of salvation. But all would agree that salvation is the work of the Holy Spirit in our hearts. We are blind in sin, until the Holy Spirit works in us and brings us a knowledge of the truth; without the Spirit one cannot perceive the gospel. We are responsible to God, but we are unable, without the working of His spirit, to respond. That is salvation, a gift of God, and God is the Lord of all. Everything depends on God.

Richard Quebedeaux: Nobody mentioned the church. That, I think, is a real weakness in evangelical theology. There has been a feeling that once you get saved, you really ought to be part of the church, but it's almost optional. My feeling is that that's ridiculous, because the whole idea of rebirth means that you're a baby again. Well, you've got to be nurtured, and who nurtures you? Well, the church, historically, has been the nurturing organization, and I think the whole issue of Christian growth is in the context of the community of people of God, and it's inextricably bound with salvation. That may be a more high-church kind of thing, and I have still to wrestle with that, but I think it's very important.

Pete Sommer: I think that's the full weight of the term "kingdom of God" as a corporate metaphor. I think Mark would add to that, but we were talking more about Christian growth.

Most of us have tended not to come to Christ *en masse,* but as individuals.

Mark Branson: Galatians 5 and 6—the sign of the Christian spirit is not something I am doing, but something the Holy Spirit is doing in me—love, joy, patience, long-suffering, kindness—the joy of being the channel of God's work.

Warren Lewis: Do you make a distinction between justification, salvation, and sanctification, or are they all one act?

Mark Branson: There are certain distinctions, yes. Sanctification is a growing in grace, and even though I fall flat on my face, or rebel, God picks me up again. Justification would be the appropriation of Christ's propitiation by an individual. Baptism is an act of obedience that symbolizes justification.

Rod Sawatsky: What happens at baptism?

Mark Branson: Baptism is linked with justification. The Holy Spirit moves in; water symbolizes cleansing.

Rod Sawatsky: You were baptized as an infant? Does somebody want to clarify the different views here of baptism?

Don Deffner: I don't see it as a cleavage among us. We understand the sacrament differently. Some see it as symbolic. Others, including myself, see it as a "means of grace," an application of grace to sin. Some would say (about the Lord's Supper) this is only bread and wine. "It is symbolic," when you speak of the body and blood. I believe it is truly bread and wine, *and* truly Christ's body and blood for the forgiveness of sins. But, that does not in any way detract from the basic statement (that we Evangelicals agree on), the work of the Holy Spirit, the salvation through Christ.

Paul Eshleman: I believe we would affirm that it's the Holy Spirit that draws man to Christ and that He is in the process of drawing all men to Christ. We are born spiritually through the Holy Spirit. It is at that point that we are justified, we are forgiven, we are made pure in God's sight, and, once and for all, we are made perfect. For, by that one offering, He has made perfect forever, past tense. He made those that are sanctified, those whom He is in the process of making wholly perfect, by that one offering. At the moment Christ died, He paid for sins past, present, and future. But the role of the Holy Spirit in our lives, day by day and moment by moment, is now one of sanctification, that process of conforming us to the image of Christ, of making us pure and holy in His sight. That's why, in my life, the ministry of the Holy Spirit is so central—because, now that I have eternally been made right in God's sight, I want my whole life to reflect His life, and the only way my life can reflect His life is if the Holy Spirit works, dwells and lives in me and lives that life of Christ in my life. That's why I am continually, as I receive Christ by faith, walking in Him by faith, that He might express His life through me.

We would believe that, at the moment of salvation, a person is indwelled by the Father, the Son, and the Holy Spirit. But not all Christians are filled and controlled and directed by the spirit of God within them. So it's possible for a Christian to become carnal, as Paul explains in I Corinthians. He said, "I could not address you as spiritual men, but as men of the flesh, as babes in Christ...For while there is jealousy and strife among you, are you not of the flesh, and behaving as ordinary men?" There are Christians throughout the whole world that are carnal today. They are living their lives according to their own direction, instead of allowing Christ's direction.

Warren Lewis: Will they go to heaven?

Paul Eshleman: I believe they will go to heaven, but they've missed salvation in the fullest sense, because it's an escape-from-a-fiery-hell kind of salvation instead of the totality that God intended, which was to save the whole life. He intended to do that by implanting Himself in the individual, so He might be lived out.

Warren Lewis: Will there be time in heaven to make up for all lost time? What about the people who reject it out of hand?

Paul Eshleman: I believe that is the unpardonable sin the Scriptures speak about, the rejection of the Holy Spirit.

Warren Lewis: And they'll burn in hell forever?

Paul Eshleman: I believe that. I don't judge any individual person, but, in principle, the Scripture says, "Except you repent, you shall all likewise perish." So this is the way that I personally deal with, let's say, the Hindus, or the person who says, "What about the guys in Africa who have never heard, you mean to tell me that God damned them to hell?" My answer is this: First, it says that everyone in the world knows there is a God in two ways: instinctively and through creation. However, nowhere in the Scriptures does it say that everyone will know the name of Christ. It also says in Deuteronomy 4:29: "But from there you will seek the Lord your God, and you will find Him, if you search after Him with all your heart and all your soul." And yet I contrast that with, "Except a man repent, he'll perish." But, I come to the conclusion that here is the man in Africa, he has tried walking on coals, or whatever. He says, "God, I just don't know you. Whatever your way is, I accept it. I want you. I want to go your way." He has sought God with his whole heart, he's repented from his own way of life, and has chosen God's way. I believe that Jesus Christ is the only way. I believe God imputes to him the righteousness of Christ because he has sought it.

Warren Lewis: Really, then, it's humility before God that *really* saves?

Paul Eshleman: Jesus is still the one who saves, but my humility is a condition of repentance. It's me saying, "God, whatever your way is, I want it." That's repentance. "God, I throw myself on You." I think, then, that if a man comes to explain Christ to him, he'll respond. He'll recognize that. I also think there will be people who will say, "God, I want your way; whatever it is, I'm available." And some other person may come along and say, "Well, why don't you come over to the Hindu temple?" and he may go along, because he really sincerely wants to know. If that happens, I think his doctrine is going to be messed up for the rest of his life, but I won't say all Hindus are going to hell, or all Muslims are going to hell, or all Moonies.

Warren Lewis: When you, as a Christian missionary, convey both the gospel and your culture, and provide a heathen man with a doctrinal alternative which he rejects because it seems culturally quite foreign to him, does that jeopardize his situation before God?

Paul Eshleman: I don't think so, because my qualification— that he will automatically recognize it—is simply opinion, and there is no scriptural foundation that, if he is in another culture and you come and preach Christ, he will recognize it. I don't necessarily think there is a basis for that in Scripture.

Warren Lewis: My point is: why not just leave them alone? If it is really humility that counts, why don't we save our missionary fund and let them be saved by pagan humility rather than Christian humility?

Paul Eshleman: Because it is the command of God. I'm in direct disobedience to my Lord and Savior Jesus Christ if I don't take the gospel everywhere. He said to go into all the world, to go into every nation. The whole thing is that it's not on me, anyway.

My duty is just to share. I don't believe I have to worry about the rest.

Johnny Sonneborn: I've heard it said here that Jesus is Lord of every creature.

Paul Eshleman: I believe that, at the point in history when Christ comes again, every knee will bow.

Richard Quebedeaux: "In the last days, I will pour out my spirit on *all* flesh." Do you believe that?

Mark Branson: That's not automatically saying all will be saved. Paul and I will disagree there. I don't think humility before God is a key. I think the key is response to God's revelation, especially to God's word, and especially to God's living word, Jesus Christ.

Anthony Guerra: O.K. So that's a disagreement, because he just said you had to be humble before God.

Paul Eshleman: Not if you reject Christ. If I come to you, and I explain Christ to you, and you understand and reject, then the fact that you were humble doesn't make any difference.

Warren Lewis: So it's not humility after all; it's something else—a confession, an act of faith.

Virgil Cruz: Perhaps the word in Hebrews could be extended a bit to be of some help here. I think we would say, first of all, that God is sovereign over the whole universe. Paul said that he wouldn't go about judging whether or not a person would end up in hell or not, he wouldn't want to judge.

I think Paul and I would agree on another point, however, that first point being true. Our responsibility is to proclaim no other name, but alongside that is the acceptance of the sovereignty of God. And then, finally getting back to Hebrews, the opening verse seems to say that, in many and diverse ways, God spoke through the prophets, and maybe we're shoehorning too much in there to think that God spoke a natural revelation in creation and so forth. However, the last revelation is the clearest—Jesus Christ. Now, I think we feel an obligation to present that clearest revelation; however, we're not saying that another kind of revelation, perhaps less clear, is impossible, that another revelation could not be apprehended.

Paul Eshleman: And the reason we don't leave the others alone is that it's a direct command from God, and we're disobedient if we don't...

Pete Sommer: I have an answer that's not theological, but I think it invokes the heart of us as Evangelicals. In an anthropology class at Chico State during my college days, the professor was coming down hard on cultural imperialism—why were missionaries going to China, and why didn't they leave them alone, because they were happy in their own religion. And a Chinese girl put up her hand and said, "What if they're not happy?" She had become a Christian that year.

Warren Lewis: That's why a lot of Christians are becoming Hindus; they're looking for happiness.

Pete Sommer: The point is, without passing on the eternal question, our prediction is that the world is not getting on all right without Jesus Christ.

Johnny Sonneborn: That's our position, that you just cannot reach the same closeness to God and love for humanity and internal joy and happiness if you're a Hindu or Jew instead of a Christian with Jesus, because your vista is narrower. You see the world for the first time when you meet Jesus. But also, then, through Jesus and the Holy Spirit, you can become sanctified to a certain extent. But, still, there's more. There are depths of God's heart that we need to see, that we will only see at the parousia, however it may come out, and that will enable us to reach the fullness.

Mark Branson: This will be a key issue for me: salvation is in following Jesus. In my understanding of the claims of others, whether they are from a gifted one speaking prophecy in my own church group, or from an individual in the Moon family, I must be able to see that life as one that points toward *the* life, the lifestyle, the revelation of God that Jesus has given me.

Rod Sawatsky: Do you want to talk about that a little bit? About the charge being made here that Rev. Moon does not show the way Christ taught?

Don Deffner: I know this isn't an answer, because it is in response to an earlier question: "Why don't more Christians lead radiant lives?" For one reason, it's because we do have the power to resist. God didn't make us puppets, automatons. So this new life of which you are speaking is still a paradox. It's not an I've-got-it-made kind of thing. With Paul, as a Christian, by the grace of God, I say, "I know whom I have believed. I am persuaded..." But I also am *simul justus et peccator,* at once justified and a sinner. The old Donald Deffner, the old "man of sin," is still there and will be ticking away until they close the casket over me. The new creation, the new man in Christ Jesus, is there too, and tension between the two will always exist. So, again, "not that I have attained." I don't "have it made," but, by God's grace I pray, "I *know*," as a Christian, yet I *can* lose that faith when I don't follow Christ. But again, as I follow Christ, I don't just "have a feeling." I *know*...

Jan Weido: I plead ignorance, but I hear you saying: "We have the power to resist God." Then, why don't we have the power to seek after God?

Don Deffner: Rationally, you're right. That's why I cannot totally explain the miracle of conversion. "I have the power to reject God. I have the power to turn to Him." Logically, I know that makes sense, but faith is illogical. "I walk by faith, not by sight..." It is because God is working in me that I'm saved.

Virgil Cruz: The natural man doesn't groove on the things of God because he doesn't want to be in tune with God. We want to be gods ourselves, as Don has said.

John Wiemann: It's often brought up, and I don't think we've defined it, that the limits of salvation are in Jesus. I don't pretend to know what they are, and I would like to know if there are any. If there are, what are they? If there aren't, well, what is salvation?

Mark Branson: Sketching eschatology, take a straight line. Dub the left, "creation," and you end up on the right with consummation. God created a perfect world and humanity, and that was the way He intended it to be. At that point, because of the way man fell—by choosing to make himself out to be God—at that point, then, we enter the evil age. And that evil age will not be turned around, will not be halted, will not be totally conquered, until Jesus comes back in a way that sets up the kingdom. That's the consummation. But the surprise of history is that, in the cross, the future was invaded by the present. The last chapter has been written. The fall, Satan, the curse, were completely done away at the cross. The penalty has been paid. We have met the king. He has told us what the kingdom is like, and He has told us to live as if the kingdom were here. That has thrown us into an age between the cross and the consummation, where we are living both in the present evil age and in the kingdom of God. We, as God's people, the church, agents of the kingdom, live according to the kingdom. At the same time, we are caught in the time when Satan has been unloosed. There is a time when Christ will come in glory, no longer as the suffering servant. He's among us now; in the future, He will no longer be the suffering servant, but instead will be the reigning king. What has been completely victorious already at the cross becomes realized in the future.

John Wiemann: I think the question that we Unificationists have is how that final realization comes about. Does it come about in the individual? In the perfection of an individual? Is this in the spiritual world? Is it here?

Mark Branson: We're talking about physical resurrection, resurrected bodies, a new heaven and a new earth. That's not just spiritualized. We're talking about Jesus reigning as king in His glory.

Johnny Sonneborn: Is that pre- or post-millennium? Do you have a millenium?

Mark Branson: You'll probably get all three positions here. I don't know.

Johnny Sonneborn: But you also have a new physical world. Some people here wouldn't. I know that one person I was talking to here ultimately doesn't. He has a millenium in the physical world, but after that there's no more physical world. It's purely spiritual forever.

Mark Branson: O.K. I would say that the resurrected body is eternal.

Paul Eshleman: Like Christ's body.

Jan Weido: The difference is in our doctrines of creation, in the conception of the nature of man. You're saying we're totally depraved, that there's no part of us that has original goodness, that can respond to God. Whereas, we're saying that, even though man is a corrupt sinner, a slug in the pits of hell, that we still believe there's an original mind responding, looking for God, crying out for God. That's the freedom to go after God. But you're saying no, there's nothing. We're just totally corrupt, that it's only by God's grace that we are pulled out of the pits of hell.

Don Deffner: Basically, I'm saying I cannot, by my own reason or strength, believe in my Lord Jesus Christ, so I am dead and lost, without salvation through Jesus Christ. So, in that respect, yes, I am dead and, as "natural man," lost forever.

Rod Sawatsky: Let's see if everyone agrees with that.

Paul Eshleman: Let me say there would seem to be almost two conflicting Scriptures on the same point. David says, "My heart yearns after God; I seek after God." At the same time, it says, "No man seeketh after God." So you try to put these two together, and, simply, what you say is, "On my own power I cannot seek after God, because I don't naturally want to go after Him. *But* because the Holy Spirit is continually drawing me, He is engendering in me a heart's desire to move toward God that I don't naturally have. He is the one who is working, and He does it in a lot of different ways to draw me towards the cross."

Jan Weido: What part needs the drawing?

Paul Eshleman: My will, I believe.

Johnny Sonneborn: I believe Dr. Deffner's position is right, according to the Principle. We're given all good things. God is the subject to initiate it, and man is the responding object.

Don Deffner: But *after* conversion I still struggle with Tirza's "5%," which is *man's 100%*. For me, it is *100% God's work* — conversion, justification, *and* the process, which you're picking up again in sanctification.

Jan Weido: Then God is the "puppet master," not Rev. Moon. I mean, that's all that I hear and see. God and Jesus and the Holy Spirit. *We* should write a book on the "puppet master," you know. There's no freedom in what you say!

Don Deffner: I believe the origin of sin was man's misuse of his freedom. I can misuse my freedom, but that freedom is intrinsically a blessing, a gift, from a freeing, loving God who even frees me to reject Him. And that is not a capricious, fatalistic God. It is a freeing, loving God. He's not playing games with me.

Warren Lewis: Adam was free *not* to eat, so there's an ontological discontinuity between Adam and Eve and the rest of us. Is that right?

Don Deffner: I don't follow you completely.

Warren Lewis: They were free not only to sin, but also to do righteousness.

Don Deffner: I don't know if I equate Adam's situation with ours today completely.

Paul Eshleman: I don't think it is the same, because God is drawing him. I think the drawing part replaces what man has rejected, and thus, the choice is back again to man because of God initiating a drawing force to him.

Warren Lewis: So then there is no original sin that pervades the race...

Paul Eshleman: Absolutely there is original sin. Absolutely.

Evangelical X: That doesn't mean there's no choice.

Warren Lewis: Then where does that original sin come from? Does each one of us commit it again? Or have we inherited it from our first parents?

Paul Eshleman: We've inherited it.

Don Deffner: And we all commit the original sin all over again. It happens every day.

Warren Lewis: In that case, then, we are not in the exact same position that Adam and Eve were in before they sinned. There was a time when they had not sinned. But there is not a time when we have not sinned, because we inherit it from our mother's womb—our original sinful condition. And that's why Hindus will go to hell without the gospel.

Evangelical X: That's right.

Dan Davies: Now, wait a minute. Before, they were not going to hell. And now, they *are* going to hell.

Irving Hexham: What you said was that the Hindus would go to hell without the gospel, implying the preaching of the gospel. They will go to hell without the sacrifice of Christ. But how are they forgiven through Christ's sacrifice? It may be through something which we do not know. I think, in times of the past, God forgave the sin of Abraham and others. Abraham never heard the gospel preached as such, but God was able to forgive him through the sacrifice of Christ.

Warren Lewis: I bet that, if you were to ask a rabbi, he would not receive that saying.

Jonathan Wells: That's the catch. By faith, that person has to believe in Jesus first.

John Wiemann: Something more has to be said about the doctrine of the nature of man. In the Divine Principle, man can never be totally alienated from God, and the problem with man is that everything is in distortion, and everything is from the wrong point of view. It's from his own point of view. Therefore, he seeks love, which comes from God, although he does it in the wrong *way,* and I emphasize the word because, if you search for or seek God in the right way, if you go the right way, you can get to God. But we can't go *our* way, and we can't go *any* way, so we need Christ, *the* way to God. But what I'm trying to get at is that we all have the ability and we all do seek God in everything we do, *everything* we do. So I guess I am saying, 5%-95%, yet I don't like those terms. I'd like to know what exactly is the nature of man after the fall—is he *that* far from God, really?

Mark Branson: I think we say yes...

John Weimann: But the thing is that his nature is all distorted. It seems all jumbled up, but it's not *totally* alien—it's alien to God's way, but there are still things about man that God can relate to.

Irving Hexham: His will is totally distorted—his will is not seeking after God...

Johnny Sonneborn: There's very little that's related to God— just the heart, and that's the foundation on which God is working. Rev. Moon says, "These are not my words I'm giving you. These are God's words." He goes out of his way to remind us of this fact. It's God's initiative. And, in his book, Mr. Sudo said about Jesus, "God spoke through Him, His words were God's words, His love was God's love, His works were God's works through Him, so if you can see Jesus, you can see God."

Mark Branson: Does His death on the cross play a role in that?

Johnny Sonneborn: Yes, the *Divine Principle* speaks several times of the ransom of the blood of the cross.

Paul Eshleman: What I see in the Unification church is that Christ forgives your sins, but that you don't get rid of your original sin until some other kind of process occurs, until you receive the second blessing, until marriage occurs. And you can't get married in the church until you live a certain kind of lifestyle, and then somebody makes the decision and says, "Yes, you've attained." So, what comes across to me is that you've been forgiven your sins, but your sins have not been *washed away* until somebody makes a value decision on your life, and you get to receive the second blessing of marriage.

Johnny Sonneborn: Most of this is from what some Evangelicals here have said, that, although Christ has forgiven our sins, we still have original sin, that He made the sacrifice and in God's sight, it's quite sure that if we accept Jesus we're going to be saved.

Paul Eshleman: With this exception: I still retain original sin, but, if I were to die right now, I would stand in the presence of God, holy and blameless before Him. Now, it's my impression that, if *you* die right now, you don't stand holy and blameless before God, that, somehow, your original sin needs to be dealt with. Therefore, Christ couldn't quite do it all on the cross.

Richard Quebedeaux: I have to say that all the Evangelicals here are talking Calvinism. In my parents' Pentecostal church, he who sins is of the devil, and there is a cleansing of sin. But, if you sin again, you are unsaved, and you've got to get saved again. And some people get saved every week. There's an uncertainty of salvation, unless you pursue "holiness"—works—to the end. I would say that Arminian evangelical theology is much closer to Unificationist theology than Calvinist theology is—free will, choice, works, and the strong relationship of works to faith.

Paul Eshleman: Still, Richard, even the Arminian theologians would say that, if you live your life so to reflect what happened to you, then your salvation is assured; there is no other agent needed, such as Rev. Moon, and marriage.

Richard Quebedeaux: Yes, if you attain sanctification, i.e., perfection, you are saved. But there is very little assurance among good Arminians; that is, you'd say, "Are you saved?" "Well, I hope so." (laughter) And they say, "Yes, I am now." And then next week...

Irving Hexham: Richard, I think that's your particular Arminian theology.

Richard Quebedeaux: That's very true. But when we talk about Calvinism, we're not necessarily talking Calvin either. You know, we've often taught the Westminster Confesssion of Faith when we think we've taught "Calvin." In terms of who the Evangelicals are, the 40 or 50 million Evangelicals, a lot of these are Arminian—including the Pentecostals.

Warren Lewis: It's unfair to say that they are mostly Calvinist, just because you Evangelicals disagree with the Pentecostals and Wesleyans. They, too, are Evangelicals.

Paul Eshleman: Richard, you've studied all brands of Evangelicals. What would you say the breakdown is?

Richard Quebedeaux: Of Pentecostals who are Arminian?

Paul Eshleman: No. What percentage of all Evangelicals are Calvinist? Arminian?

Richard Quebedeaux: That's really hard to say. Evangelical has been a word that has been applied by certain people to include only Calvinists to the exclusion of basic Arminians, Pentecostals, certain kinds of Reformed people, and Anabaptists.

Warren Lewis: There are supposed to be 15 million Pentecostals...

Richard Quebedeaux: O.K., Pentecostals. Of that number,

the Assemblies of God, which have at least 1,400,000, would be more toward the Calvinist side, but almost with embarrassment, because this is a peculiar mixture of Presbyterianism and Baptist theology, whereas most Pentecostals, the Holiness people, are Arminians. Then you have the whole non-Pentecostal Holiness groups, the Wesleyan Church, the Salvation Army, the Church of God (Anderson, Indiana) and the Nazarenes.

Paul Eshleman: Could we say this, though—that, in essence, both Arminians and Calvinists come to the Lord in the same way and that the processes of salvation and forgiveness of sins are alike?

Richard Quebedeaux: Salvation *is* the same, but there is the qualification of how long it lasts.

Paul Eshleman: That's what I'm saying—there's the qualification of how long it lasts after that.

Warren Lewis: The point being made is that it's a faulty thing to divide Moonie versus Evangelical and put the Moonies over here in favor of some sort of Pelagian free will, whereas all true Evangelicals stick up for the sovereignty of God. There are as many Evangelicals who agree with Moonies on this point as there are Evangelicals who disagree.

Mark Branson: Except what happens at the cross? Is everything provided at the cross? The Evangelicals would say yes.

Dan Davies: I'd like to present a point of view on conversion, or better, rebirth. According to the Divine Principle, when Jesus came, He was to be accepted by Israel, and, in that acceptance, He could have taken a bride. With that bride, then, through the sacrament of the blessing, He could have given rebirth to all men, and the whole world would have become the kingdom of God. But, because of His crucifixion, that wasn't possible, and God had to work through the sacraments to give rebirth. So, I think you will find that, in the Catholic church, to begin with, rebirth was given through the sacrament of bread and wine and also baptism. That was essentially true up until the time of Luther. The Holy Spirit has been working in history these last 2,000 years, preparing mankind to receive the True Parents. So the first stage of history was through the bread and wine and water baptism. I think we'll find them right here, but at least in this country. They believe that's the way you gain salvation. But, what happened during the Reformation, and later in the Wesleyan revival, was that we had a new kind of rebirth that came through the word, the Bible—the primacy of the word of God, the Bible, plus (in the nineteenth-century Holiness movement) the baptism of the Holy Spirit. Those became the two sacraments, and it's my hunch that those things, those two sacraments, are a preparation for the True Parents. In other words, the word represented true Adam, the Holy Spirit represented true Eve. I'm trying to explain a progression of the Holy Spirit from the time of Jesus, whose crucifixion and resurrection brought about a rebirth, through to the True Parents, whose purpose is to give mankind full salvation on the earth.

Anthony Guerra: At the time of the mission of Jesus, we explain, there were two possibilities for salvation. Either way, salvation would come. But, a more complete salvation would have been possible had the people united with Jesus. Given the other alternative, that they rejected Jesus, He had to go the way of the cross, which we believe was God's will at that point, and by the cross Jesus brought salvation to the individual and forgiveness of sins—justification. We believe that rebirth happens through the trinity of God, Jesus and the Holy Spirit. Jesus and the Holy Spirit are in the role of parents. Together they generate a love force which recreates the Christian so that he is able to communicate with God the Father. Just as you were born through love of your father and mother, so you have to be born again through the love of Jesus and the Holy Spirit, and that's a different kind of love—it's a love which gives you the forgiveness of sins, a new heart, a new relationship with God, and a new relationship with your brothers and sisters. The salvation by Jesus' sacrifice on the cross is very real. Jesus didn't *have* to go the way of the cross—in the Garden of Gethsemane He could've said, "No"—but, because of His love for God and His desire to save humankind, He went the way of the cross. It's with great agony that we say Jesus wanted to give humankind a fuller salvation. But, nevertheless, He was willing to sacrifice His body on the cross to give the salvation which we call justification on the individual level—the forgiveness of sins that is absolutely essential for our life.

After hearing this lecture on the mission of Jesus, many people receive the Holy Spirit and accept Jesus as their Saviour. Many people have come up to me and said, "For the first time, I really accept Jesus, and I feel Jesus and I feel the Holy Spirit." Some were people who had been completely opposed to Jesus but, because this explanation made sense to them, opened their hearts and made the commitment to Jesus. Many of those people leave our workshops and they become Christians without joining the Unification church.

Paul Eshleman: Do you ask them to make a decision, an act of their will at that point?

Anthony Guerra: No.

Paul Eshleman: Well, why not?

Anthony Guerra: Because, as you've said, the major category for you is will, but the major category for us is heart. And we believe that once the person's heart is changed, and he turns his love and his feeling to God and to Jesus, that's it. That's the most important thing. That's what brings salvation.

Paul Eshleman: That's a little vague.

Anthony Guerra: Oh no, that's not vague. There are three categories that one can talk about in terms of the human spirit: emotion, reason, and will; I'm saying the central category is emotion or heart. Love as opposed to activity.

Warren Lewis: Charismatic Methodism strikes again!

Mark Branson: I don't think that Jesus got sidetracked in His mission. I think that is something which needs to be understood. Jesus lived and gave us a perfect revelation of what God is like, what His values were, what the kingdom of God is like, etc. God is not one to conquer evil with power. God is one to submit to it because He provides for us. He died so that we might be saved. His whole lifestyle, then, was one of poverty, was one of living in the world, with the poor, with the people who were needy. He said He came for those who are sick, not for those who are well. His entire lifestyle was one of humility—one that did not include riches. That is a very specific area that I'd have to investigate. He says you cannot serve God and mammon, and I see Moon attempting that. You have to consider the type of people with whom He spent His time. Consider the entirety of what He is doing in the Sermon on the Mount, whether He's dealing with the teachings about blessings or the whole significance of the cross. This includes not only the cross of salvation but the cross as a way of life. That's salvation. I can be saved *from* my materialism, I can be saved *from* my sin, I can be saved *from* all the different ways the fall has had an impact on me. My question, then, is whether the lifestyle of Rev. Moon reflects the lifestyle of Jesus.

Anthony Guerra: I have some reason first to clarify some of your motivation in asking this. Do you believe that poverty and sickness are part of God's original plan?

Mark Branson: No, but I believe that evil...

Anthony Guerra: And, therefore, you would say that the kingdom of God is one in which those elements are eliminated? Is that correct?

Mark Branson: No.

Anthony Guerra: You would say that, in the kingdom of God, sickness and poverty, etc., would still be present?

Irving Hexham: No, wait. Let him exegete what it means in Scripture by the kingdom of God.

Rod Sawatsky: Irving, you have something to say about that.

Irving Hexham: The kingdom of God in Scripture is the reign of God in the lives of many—not a physical kingdom; it is God's rule which comes with Christ. Jesus said, "Repent, the kingdom of heaven is at hand." And then He said, "The kingdom of God is in the midst of you." Jesus brought the kingdom of God in His person, and it is His rule on earth which has continued ever since.

Virgil Cruz: And the important thing is, as Irving is saying, that the emphasis is upon the fact that God's sovereignty, which has always been real, cannot be consummated and become totally explicit. The other item is that we are now fully in communion with God. The other things, such as the amount of material possessions we have, the degree of opulence, do not interest us so much.

Anthony Guerra: Well, of course it doesn't concern you, because you're not in the Third World and you're not oppressed and you're not poor.

Virgil Cruz: I don't think that's it. We say that oppression is a satanic thing that will, by definition, be removed when the sovereignty of God is consummated. But, when we hear your discussion of materialism, it's reminiscent of what my Muslim friend would describe to me.

Anthony Guerra: Well, first of all, the question was asked specifically with reference to Rev. Moon's lifestyle. In his early life, when he began his mission, he lived in extreme poverty. He was imprisoned in a communist prison camp in North Korea, in a camp where the average prisoner's life span was six months. They did heavy labor, eight hours a day, loading nitrate fertilizer into bags, filling them up to exactly eighty pounds, weighing them on a scale, and then loading them onto a truck. Without an adequate diet or gloves, the nitrate eats into the skin. Prisoners were dying of hunger. People would even fall dead while they were eating, and the others would be so hungry that they would take the rice out of the dead people's mouths and eat it. And, in that situation, Rev. Moon decided to give half his portion of food away to other prisoners—and then, he considered the other half as given to him by God. He was praised while he was in that prison camp as the best worker. Each of the teams had a certain quota, and, if they didn't fulfill the quota, there was certain punishment. The people always wanted to join his team because he worked so hard that they could all get the work done. Members of our church, then in North Korea, would bring food to him and they would bring clothes to him, but when they returned, they would always find that he was still wearing the same shoes. He was still wearing the same clothes, because he had always given the new clothes away to his fellow prisoners.

After the war, before coming to America, he lived in a one-room or two-room apartment house above the Korean church center—even though the members there many times offered to buy him a house. When Rev. Moon came to America in 1971, he lived in the very strict centers along with us. While he was in Korea in 1972, we purchased Belvedere, in his absence, and when he came back, we asked him to live in that house in Tarrytown, New York. The church leaders in America explained to him that America has a culture where, even if you have a great message of God, and especially if you feel your mission is not just to poor people but to *all* people (leaders of government as well as the man in Harlem), you need to live in a dignified fashion. He debated the issue, but we prevailed upon him to do it.

Paul Eshleman: That may have been a tactical error.

Anthony Guerra: Well, I don't think it is. The point I want to make is that none of the properties are in his own name. He doesn't have anything in his own name. And the house that everyone talks about Rev. Moon living in—I've been there several times because, as I explained before, I was a state director—holds many of our conferences. It's a public house. Rev. Moon has guests from Korea, Japan, from all around the world visiting there. His lifestyle is a very public one. Rev. Moon had begun many businesses in Korea before coming to America and was running a movement which had become fairly wealthy, yet he was living in a very impoverished situation in Korea. He never used the wealth for himself—only for the mission. And I believe that now, in the same way, he's using all that he has, just for the purpose of serving God. And I see that as the major category— What is your purpose? The creation is good—why are you using it? With what heart? And this is where I affirm fully that he is leading a God-centered, sacrificial life.

Pete Sommer: I don't want to lose the good will of anybody by saying what I do, but we're coming back to some things that I wanted to raise yesterday afternoon. I'm going to read—well, it's something that has been all too common to the evangelical world as well—the words of Ken Sudo on page 72 of the training manual. And you'll pardon us, I hope, if we giggle when we read this kind of stuff, because we've heard this cant from so many people, and it's hard not to believe that it does not have the blessing of Rev. Moon. The part that really made me laugh was—and pardon me if I'm offending anybody's piety here—

> Do you like to make green bills happy? When the green bills are in the hands of fallen man, can they be happy? Why don't you make them happy? So many green bills are crying. Have you ever heard them crying? Not yet? You must hear. They are all destined to go to Father. This is our responsibility, eventually, unless everything goes through Father, it cannot be happy. This is a heartistic understanding of the offering of things. When Jesus came, he could not fulfill the second blessing, so He wasn't fully qualified to have dominion over the creation and restore things [—which would be a fundamental disagreement—]...Christians think that the Messiah must be poor and miserable—he did not come for this. The Messiah must be the richest.

I could go on, but you'll pardon us if we think that is really funny.

Jonathan Wells: We laughed when we heard it, too.

(laughter)

Pete Sommer: Richard could give us a list of evangelical people who are saying roughly the same thing.

Tirza Shilgi: Anyway, I just wanted to read a section from Richard's book, *The Worldly Evangelicals.* "Today, however, it is not uncommon for pastors of large evangelical and charismatic congregations with multi-million-dollar facilities to earn as much as doctors and lawyers, dress in the height of fashion, live in very expensive homes, if not mansions, and drive the finest cars. A few of them even have their own airplanes."*

Irving Hexham: O.K., but we would attack them for that...

Lloyd Howell: There are some people here who are really getting into materialism; they're seeing the material things; they have to go beyond to see if there is a spiritual something behind this. Now, as I know Rev. Moon, he's not a fat cat. I don't think he's sipping cocktails. He only sleeps four or five hours a night. We could go on with testimonies. We're not here to lay a big, heavy testimony about Rev. Moon on you. But somebody's asking to know something about his personal life. We're trying to say a few things. We know this man goes way over the standard of anybody in the movement, and before that we are humbled.

Irving Hexham: I'd like to hear some testimonies.

Anthony Guerra: Could someone tell about the net-making last year?

Dan Davies: I could tell a little bit. I'm thirty years old. Pretty young, and strong for my age. I lasted with him one day at the pace he goes. He came up here last year for about two months, every day. I don't know how long other people lasted, but I couldn't keep up with him.

He would never begrudge talking to us if he was tired. Sometimes he hadn't slept for two or three days, and he would still talk to us. I can give an instance of this. A few years ago at Belvedere he had just returned from traveling to Korea and Japan. He hadn't slept for a couple of days, yet he talked to us for about four hours in the early morning, did many things during the day, and ended up singing and taking part in the entertainment that night.

Pete Sommer: Oh, we have these evangelical workaholics too.

Dan Davies: That's not what I'm pointing out here. It's not his work that's important. It's that he's doing it for others that's important. I've noticed that what he does is for others, and not for himself. I actually feel that he is trying to do as much for others as he possibly can. He is not holding anything back. He's giving away his time and his money—even income from his own inventions. He's teaching that you gain spiritual riches by giving.

Johnny Sonneborn: I think it's very obvious that the man is a genius, whatever you may think of his purpose, or whatever you

---

*Richard Quebedeaux, *The Worldly Evangelicals,* New York, N.Y.: Harper & Row, 1978.

think of his connections, and so forth. And he's the kind of genius who was there in Japan and in Korea at a time when he could've become an industrial tycoon, and could've moved only in high, intellectual Christian circles, surrounded by good people. He wouldn't have had to deal with Marxist scientists, he never would've had to work as a short-order cook, as a dock worker, he never would've lived in a cave, if he hadn't been concerned about people. And the equivalent is the case with Jesus. Jesus was accused, also, of sitting down at the table with tax collectors—those were the really wealthy people—yet He had fishermen as His disciples. Rev. Moon has us instead of high Christian people. He doesn't have Billy Graham for his disciple, and he doesn't have the *Sojourners.* He has some ex-drug addicts and he has self-centered people like me. Here he comes and spends time with us. He would probably have much greater joy amongst philosophers and great artists. But I think he is very much dedicating himself completely for all the people, in whatever circumstances he may find them, the way Jesus did. He used to go to our factory every day and work with the people; he wasn't just the director of the factory.

Don Deffner: Can I ask my question about Rev. Moon, and that's in terms of what we've been saying, about his sinful-sinless or perfectable nature. How does he vary from you? Not just in terms of degree, but could he fall away from being a Christian, lose his faith, and the relationship of that with his being the Lord of the Second Advent?

Tirza Shilgi: Well, I was going to say something about Rev. Moon in Japan. When we were in Japan, in Tokyo, we were taken to a little house near Waseda University, where Rev. Moon had stayed for four years, while he was studying there. They told us some stories about the time he was there. They were very good and special people. They were persecuted for having a Korean in their home, because at that time the Japanese hated Koreans. Anyway, they said that he used to get a check from Korea every month to cover his lodging and that, even though lodging included three meals a day, every day he used to leave the house so early that he would not have breakfast. Rather, he would come for lunch, and then, right after lunch, leave the house and stay away until late at night. This lasted the whole four years, and they never really understood why he was not there in the afternoon or evening, since he was going to school. Then, a year and a half later, they found out that he had spent all this time working down on the docks of Kawasaki in the most difficult jobs, carrying loads and removing cargo from ships. And, later on, they found out from the teachings of the Divine Principle that during this time he was searching for the motivation of the fall—what the nature of man's desire for happiness was. He associated with the hard laborers, with the beggars, and with the harlots to be able to understand where their hearts were, and why they were living the way they lived. Did they seek happiness? If they did, what did they do about it? So, for four years of his life, even though he did have money to come home every evening and spend time doing his homework, or whatever, and eat with the family, he never did. They found out that part of the money he had had, he had given to other students. Again, for years all his afternoons were spent on the docks, and he was always trying to understand the hearts of these people.

Rod Sawatsky: Jonathan, are you prepared to speak now to the question that Don raised?

Jonathan Wells: To the extent that it can be answered, which I think is a very limited one. You asked the extent of his sinlessness and also whether he can fall away, and I will just make a stab at an answer. A few years back, I was sent as a solitary missionary to, of all places, Stamford, Connecticut, and was supposed to start from scratch there and build up a church, very much like Rev. Moon has done on several different occasions. Within three weeks I was dramatically confronted with my own sinfulness and the difficulty of accomplishing what God wanted me to do there. That convinced me that Rev. Moon, if not being absolutely sinless, was pretty close, closer than anyone I had run into before. Now, as to whether he can fall away at some point, I think that remains to be seen. I know that when people have asked him or brought the subject up, his response is something like this. "Everybody else in the Unification church can leave, but not I, because I know God's heart, and I know it would break God's heart if I stopped giving everything I have to bring the kingdom of heaven on earth." That's the kind of response he gives.

Irving Hexham: There's a book, *No Man Knows My History,* by Fawn Brodie. She did a biography of Joseph Smith as a Mormon, and checked up on all the documents, and came to the conclusion that Joseph Smith was not what he claimed, and wrote her book. Now, suppose someone came along and had done research on Moon, and all these stories you're telling about him; suppose they came saying, "I have an affidavit here from people who knew him as a student. He didn't do these things you claim; he didn't get checks from Korea—we've checked the banks. He had to work." All these things, how would you react?

Dan Davies: I'm doing a study with Warren Lewis on Mother Ann Lee, the founder of the Shakers. I have carefully considered many sworn affidavits against the character of Mother Ann Lee and I have concluded them to be false. It is easy to find the falsehoods; the statements do not complement each other and many contradict each other. There is no consistent picture and the charges vary tremendously. She was accused of everything from starting wild orgies to murdering babies. But if she had been all that evil, her work, the fruits of her work, would have been evil. The Shakers have a reputation throughout time for being honest, hardworking, chaste. By their fruits ye shall know them.

Irving Hexham: I think you're not looking too closely at the idea of a sworn affidavit. The Mormons...

Dan Davies: Yes, they also have sworn affidavits.

Irving Hexham: It's not just affidavits. There is a lot of documentary evidence.

Dan Davies: Like what?

Irving Hexham: That's not the question.

Dan Davies: I think it's a question.

Irving Hexham: The original document of *The Pearl of Great Price* was discovered recently after Mormon scholars thought it had been destroyed in a fire. When it was translated, it didn't say what Joseph Smith claimed it said, and that's causing a major crisis in the Mormon church.

Beatriz Gonzales: I think the problem is that you are asking the wrong people the question, because most of us have been "in the family" four or five years, maybe more, and we've had the opportunity to be very close to Rev. Moon and his wife and their nine children. Rev. Moon spends a lot of time coming out here with us. We've also seen how he works. Most of us have been on tours across the country with him. Everything that we see him do and say is consistent. So it is, as Lloyd was saying, that our lives have been totally humbled before this man and this woman who live such sacrificial lives. It doesn't matter to me what anyone would tell me about his past life—I believe what he has said and what I have seen. I believe in this man.

Jan Weido: Just a little more about sinlessness. You referred to the 120-day training manual. The logic is Mr. Sudo's logic. He says only a sinless man could discover the cause of original sin. Is that what you are looking at?

Paul Eshleman: Yes, and it also says, "Father is sinless, mother is sinless, the children are sinless..."

Jan Weido: I think that, in some way or another, we Moonies would say we believe Rev. Moon is sinless; but we would also say...

Paul Eshleman: How did he choose the wrong wife, then? He's had a couple of wives, different children...

Jan Weido: Let me finish my point; maybe then we can get into that. In the messianic age, God prepares certain indemnity conditions, and a certain foundation is prepared. It's not just that one man is born sinless. God doesn't want to lay all His money on one person. There are maybe 120 sinless people who go through the course. The one who makes it through is the messiah. Not that Rev. Moon is the incarnation or whatever, but that he has to work it out. Anywhere along the line he could have blown it. In the prison camp, he was the next in line to be shot. If this story is true, he could have had a bullet in his head; if, for some reason, he had laid bad conditions, that could have happened, but he made it through all of this. Maybe there is some other guy walking around out in a mud hut in Africa somewhere, a guy who, if Rev. Moon blows it, will come up and take the mantle of the messiah and push the providence through. It's not going to stop. If Rev. Moon doesn't do it, then someone else will. There's a multiplicity of sinless people.

Mark Branson: By sinless, you mean he doesn't have original sin? He's never deviated from the will of God? What do you mean?

Jan Weido: He's born without original sin.

Mark Branson: And therefore he has never made a mistake, he's never...

Several voices: No, no. That's not true.

Anthony Guerra: One could be born sinless and still sin. In other words, in our view, Adam and Eve were born without sin, but they failed later on.

Mark Branson: He was born without original sin and he has never done anything against the will of God? Is that true? That's what I would say about Jesus, that He was born without original sin and never did anything against God's will.

Jonathan Wells: I'd like to respond to that and to an earlier question. I would say that Rev. Moon is sinless. Whether he's done anything against the will of God I think is an unanswered question, because in the Unification doctrine there's a growth period that everyone has to go through, during which time one is not under God's direct dominion.

I don't believe he has sinned, but—and that leads into this question over here—what if somebody were to discover some really serious problem? I think Unification church members have to say, if they are honest, that, if something like that were to come up and be validated, then it would seriously jeopardize Rev. Moon's credibility and perhaps even the credibility of the Divine Principle and our entire movement. Certainly it would destroy a lot of faith.

Irving Hexham: I'd like to get to the point directly: under what conditions would you leave the Unification church?

Jonathan Wells: That I won't even try to answer, because that varies from individual to individual, and people are leaving all the time for various reasons. But I have watched Rev. Moon because I'm a skeptical person by nature, and I haven't seen evidence of any wrongdoing. Professor Frederick Sontag, who, despite what some people may say about him, is really a pretty objective observer, has gone to Korea, and has talked to the people who originated some of these rumors that you hear about Rev. Moon's sex life, prison and corruption, and all this. He talked to those people, and he concluded that those rumors are unsubstantiated.

Warren Lewis: I asked Fred why he avoided the sex issue in his book, the one question that the prurient minds of all of us would like to see raised. He said he looked into every document that anybody has brought up anywhere—it never existed beyond the newspapers in Korea. There is no evidence against Rev. Moon.

Tirza Shilgi: I think that, even if Rev. Moon is sinless, and he has chosen the right wife, there is still the possibility that his wife will not fulfill her mission, and therefore will just walk away. And it's impossible for him to force his will on her just as much as it is impossible for God to force His own love on us. So it is possible that Jesus, who was sinless, could fulfill His mission from beginning to end, but the people would not fulfill their mission, which is to recognize Him and believe in Him, and therefore the office would not be fulfilled, and the kingdom would not come—God's will would not be realized. So there's always what God establishes, but then there's always an element that needs to respond—the restoration needs to take place in the people, which means that they have to change. They have to respond. It's not magic that falls on them; so, even if Jesus Himself is totally perfect and sinless, and everything else, the process of restoration still depends upon people's response and change.

Rod Sawatsky: We have moved rather a long way from our initial topic of conversation. We are going to break now for dinner and I would suggest that this evening we turn our attention to the issue of deprogramming.

Pete Sommer: I think that deprogramming is something that most of us would say is very wrong. It's tragic. I'm not sure I want to spend a lot of time on it. I think we're in agreement.

Virgil Cruz: I have not had the privilege of talking about deprogramming with Unification church members. I've been impressed by members of our team who have said deprogramming is indeed something that they would totally object to. I wish I could be converted to that view. And I think it would be very easy to do that. I think there is someone here who could give us a testimony that would make me a missionary to carry that word out to people I know. As an Evangelical, I think that I should feel close to that person. So, if it wouldn't take too much time, I would like some personal exposure to this topic.

Deprogramming

Rod Sawatsky: Mark Wilenchik is going to share his story with us.

Mark Wilenchik: All good stories have to begin somewhere, so let's start with my graduation in 1975 from the University of Connecticut. I graduated with a degree in economics and was a confirmed communist, having studied Marxism during my last three years at college. I was accepted into the New School for Social Research graduate school in New York City to study Marxist economics in a Masters program with a Ph.D. option. I was very serious. Upon completion of my undergraduate work, I traveled across the country with two other fellows and met the Unification church in Berkeley, California, sometime in August of 1975. The other thing of importance is that I am Jewish. So you have a Jewish Red. (laughter)

I traveled, as I said, and met the church and became involved. How I joined the church is a funny story, in that it reveals how I didn't want to go to the introductory dinner, I didn't want to go to the weekend workshop, and I didn't want to stay for the first week; but I had a friend who wanted to stay and, being somewhat loyal, I decided to stay, too. But then, as I began to spend my summer at the ranch in Oakland, I began to experience many things, I guess you would call it "true communism." I don't like to use that word. I'll put it in quotes.

In the California family I began to find people who were working for an ideal, people who were sacrificing for the good of mankind, people who were trying to share true values with each other. The California family provided a sharp contrast to other friends of mine who I'd thought were going to change the world. I saw, before I left the University of Connecticut, two of my professors, brilliant men, one from Cambridge, and one from Yale, Ph.D.s who were both involved with each other's lives, and wives! Their families ended up smashed apart. These people were not living lives that could be examples to others.

I remember one special day in California I would like to share. We heard a lecture on the mission of Jesus as it is taught in *Divine Principle.* In the middle of the lecture, I just started crying, and I realized that, in Jesus Christ, there was really something to be found. I was raised Jewish, and I always wondered why Christians believed what they did. I never could understand why, if people had so much love and faith, there was so much wrong in the world. I remember crying in that lecture to the point that I had to be led out. When I prayed afterwards, I saw myself at the crucifixion. And I also saw my father there. He and I were involved and I remember repenting for myself, and I repented for my father, and I repented for all Jewish people, and then I asked God to forgive me for being a communist, and then I became a Christian.

This morning I went into the chapel to figure out what I was going to say tonight. In the past, I've given this testimony but I've never had to explain about becoming a Christian, because that's not the point you start off with when you're in the family. Everybody wants to know the good details. Everybody wants to know: "How did you escape? How did you get away? Who did you fool? Who'd you trick? How did you do it?" But Heavenly Father really told me that you all should hear about my conversion as the first thing that happened to me: how a "Jewish Red" became a Christian.

The most important thing that I want to share tonight is that, when I was deprogrammed, when they locked me in the room, when they locked the windows, when they guarded the house, when they did all these things, they were trying to deprogram me from Christianity. That's my message tonight. My parents were there. I told them. I said right to their face: "Do you realize what you're doing to me?" And I had respect for them; I didn't have anger. They didn't understand. All the negative people were in a closed room less than one-fifth the size of this room, where all I heard was profanity, swearing, everything, you name it. Finally it got to a point where that was making me stronger, because I became disgusted by what they were saying. How could they be godly? How could their message be the truthful message? Could it be? It couldn't.

That Sunday morning when I was kidnapped by my parents, I was the one who had arranged to see them after I came to New York. I had been working with the church for three months at the time. I arranged our meeting with good faith! "Come see me, meet my friends." There was 100% trust on my part.

A funny thing happened that Sunday at morning service. A sister came over to me and said that a fellow named Peter

T———— had left the church. I said, "I don't even know him. What do you mean?" She shrugged her shoulders and walked away. That very afternoon, I was introduced to Peter T———— as the assistant deprogrammer. That God had told me ahead of time that Peter T———— was going to be there showed me clearly that He was with me. That foreshadowing kept my faith alive the whole day. Between that incident and that of being barraged with abuse helped to keep me strong the first day.

I mentioned at the beginning of my talk that I traveled out to California with three other people. One of these friends, Michael, was also kidnapped at the same time. He had joined for awhile and was kidnapped at the same time I was by Joe Alexander, Jr. (Joe Alexander is one of the leading deprogrammers.) They had Michael in New Haven, Connecticut, and they had me in Long Island. Michael was deprogrammed.

Each day was basically the same. I was forced to sit on a couch, three people sitting right in front of me just nailing me. They couldn't think of enough things to say; it was really terrible. One funny thing happened that I'll share with you. All my clothes that I was wearing were bought during my summer by the church. I was in New York—I had come from California, so I was wearing new winter clothes. The deprogrammers made me take off all my clothes and gave me new ones. This was to disassociate me from anything that had to do with the church. My socks, which the church had bought, I had to give away, my shoes I had to give away, everything. But then, a half hour later, who comes back in but Peter T———— wearing all my clothes! (laughter)

That night passed by and I didn't sleep. I remember I prayed all night. In fact, I was lying on a couch similar to this one, and someone was sleeping beside me. The windows were all nailed shut. I tried to figure out what to do, what to do! It was in the middle of one of their barrages that my strategy became, "I'm not going to answer them." But after a few hours I realized I couldn't do that because they had the hammers, they had the nails, they had the windows locked. So, eventually, I had enough and got up and just started screaming. But what I started screaming was rational, about the situation in the world. I started talking about communism, I guess because I had been a communist before. I spoke just to let it out—like a safety valve. And then the most amazing thing happened. Ironically, they started believing me. They started listening. Why? Because, if you think about it, if you're lecturing to your class for six hours straight, and then all of a sudden somebody else says something, pow, (laughter) it doesn't matter what they say! And also, because I don't think they knew what they were saying either. So they began to think that I was being deprogrammed, but all I was doing was telling them about the world. They didn't know what was going on, so bit by bit I began to realize that anything I said they were going to believe. But, it took a while to realize that. So that's how the first day passed. I realized that I was a captive, and I had to get away, but somehow there was little hope that anything I could do could free me.

The second day went a lot like the first, the same kind of barrage. Joe Alexander came that day, and he started talking to me about the Bible. That was very interesting, because I don't think I had read the New Testament prior to joining the Oakland family—perhaps not even once! So, all he kept doing was telling me these intricate Bible verses that he'd claim were contradictory to the *Divine Principle*. This strategy was totally ineffective because I didn't know what he was talking about anyway. And then my parents came in and they thought it was a little weird, since they are Jewish, to come in and hear these guys talking about the New Testament. They didn't dig that so much, either. (laughter)

That evening they started to move me to a new location. It's really dangerous to keep someone at the same place, because they never know if the police are going to come, so they moved me to the T———— house. What happened there was very amazing. The T————s are very wealthy people—their house had huge rugs, chandeliers, gold silverware, the whole bit. I went to their house, and, as we say sometimes in the church, God leaves you. God left. From the moment I walked into that house, the only thing that I could think of was, "This is the way Rev. Moon lives." We're out fundraising, we're out doing all this hard work, and this is the way Rev. Moon lives. You're crazy, kid. When you were a communist, you wouldn't even have walked into this house. These are the "pigs." These are the capitalists. These are the people that are causing all the problems. What are you doing here? And it came heavy, and it came really hard. And I have to admit I didn't know what to think. I really didn't. So I persuaded them to let me go to the bathroom alone. I got into the bathroom, I closed the door, and I locked it. And I started praying. I got down on my knees, and prayed so hard that my nose started to bleed. But no answer, no answer at all.

After a while they were worried about me, so they started knocking on the door. They made me open it, and they saw all the blood, so they didn't know what to think. Then they started really going after me because they could sense that something was happening. And, for the rest of the night, from maybe 12 o'clock at night to six in the morning, they were constantly at me, worse than the first day, worse than the second afternoon. And I was irrational because I didn't know what I believed anymore. When I reflect on that night I realize the reason for my confusion was that the two ideas or beliefs can't exist at the same place (in the same mind) at the same time—we've got only one brain—and that was what was happening to me. The way I finally started pulling out of it was that I made what we call a condition: I would scream at the top of my lungs with all of my heart and with all my soul. I said this to God before I did it. That night everything the deprogrammers said was directed against Rev. Moon. There was nothing else except Rev. Moon, Rev. Moon, Rev. Moon. The idea of trying to separate me from some kind of relationship with him was their strategy at the time. So, I thought, I'll just have to look the tiger in the mouth; and I just screamed with all my heart at the top of my lungs: "I claim this room for Rev. Moon." (laughter)

And, now that I look back on it, I can't think of anything that they would have hated more, but still I really don't know why I did it. And, also, I'd said to God before I did it that I would do it three times. By the third time, I was soaking wet with perspiration; this was six hours, remember, I'm not kidding. And I did it twice, and I had to do it a third time. And, because I didn't have enough faith, I did it a fourth time. (laughter) I'd told God I was going to do it three times but I did it four, just in case He didn't hear the first one! And then I just gave up. I said, O.K., forget it. Heavenly Father, I've done as much as I can. I can't do any more. It had been six hours! I couldn't do any more—I hadn't slept. So then that feeling that I had when I first walked into the house went away. The feeling that God was right there came to me. And, when they started asking questions, God just seemed to give all the answers. This was the beginning of their thinking I was deprogrammed. But, of course, that was just the beginning of my coming around to my faith again.

The next day, I began trying to talk them into letting me sow my own oats, and I started talking about how I hadn't seen any girls for three months and how it would be good to go out for a ride with a girl that was there. They started believing it. They didn't allow me to leave, but they did let me go into the back yard of the T— — — —s' house—if you remember, it was a very big house. When I was in the back yard talking with the girl, I started telling her about immorality; I started talking to her and talking to her. And I took off, running through the back yards. It was about four o'clock in the afternoon, and it was almost dusk. I ran about five hundred yards, saw a pile of leaves, and jumped in. They started running after me, but couldn't find me. Twenty minutes later they came walking through the leaves and stepped on me! (laughter) What do I do now? I'm supposed to be deprogrammed. Why would I run away? It's going to start all over again. What am I going to do now? Heavenly Father? He said, "Play dead. Play unconscious. Don't deal with them." So, when they tried to wake me up I wouldn't react. They slapped me in the face, but I wouldn't react. Somewhere in the back of my mind I knew (I don't know why, maybe I read it somewhere) that if I could get to a hospital I could tell the doctor, tell him I've been kidnapped. I'm over twenty-one. They've got to let me go. So that became my hope. To make a long story short, they took me into the house and couldn't revive me, so they drove me to a nearby hospital. There, I talked to the doctor about my situation. The doctor was amazed by what I told him, and left the room to speak to the people who'd brought me. The doctor then came back in and talked to me again. He couldn't believe it. We've got to realize the doctor's situation. This was the hospital emergency room. He didn't understand anything. After talking to him three times, I convinced him. He came back in and said, "O.K., no problem, you can go. You can call up the church, no problem." When the "deprogrammers" found out, along with my parents, they came back in and had terrible feelings toward me, but they couldn't do anything. Five minutes later they came storming back into the room, ten of them, picked me up in my underwear, dragged me out of the hospital, and threw me in a car!

It's ironic. Looking back now, I kept seeming to get away, to escape, but I never could accomplish it. Eventually I was to realize that God didn't want me to get away by running. I had "escaped" two times but I wasn't able to get free. So, through the process of the next three weeks of being with them, twenty-one days in all, I totally convinced them that I was normal. I went to a psychiatrist and the whole bit, because they couldn't figure me out. One day I was running away; one day I was deprogrammed. Never did they fully realize that I was just faking it. After twenty-one days, I had to sign a legal paper at a lawyer's office saying that, if I ever go back to the church, it's not of my own free will. I researched that action myself and found out it doesn't mean anything, because it's signed under duress; if you sign anything under duress, it means it is not legally binding. After three weeks I "arranged" to go back to visit the University of Connecticut to see my friends, and, instead of going east on Route 84 to Hartford, I went west to Tarrytown, New York, with my mom's car. That's how I finally got away. And, to add one really short postscript, as I was driving the car, I was really excited and happy and crying, and all of a sudden this sense came over me—a feeling, "What if they don't take you back?" What if they don't take me back into the Unification church? I can't be punished anymore. Where can I go—I'm not a communist anymore...my friends aren't living Christian lives. It was like saying, "What if God doesn't take me back?" But, they took me back, and the past three years have been deeply rewarding.

Paul Eshleman: Have you seen your folks?

Mark Wilenchik: Yes.

Paul Eshleman: How is it with them?

Mark Wilenchik: Mrs. Spurgin's helped me with this. The first year, I was always faithful to my parents. When I was on the different fundraising teams, I called them quite a bit. As I look back on that, it might not have been the best idea. I called them every other week, which is more than I was calling them when I was in college. I was faithful to them, because I wanted more than anything else to show them that I was doing what I believed in and that I understood what I was doing. So, I figured that, if I could do something "religiously," rationally, with them in mind, then they could begin to come around. Before I left for England in June, 1978, I visited with them, here at the Seminary. I also saw them about three weeks ago. I surprised them and went home, and it was a very good visit. Just a little note—my sister is a Hassidic Jew. She became a Hassidic and then married a Hassidic. So how do you put the pieces together? Prior to her conversion, she was not religious either.

Paul Eshleman: Aren't you afraid to go home, afraid that they might imprison you again?

Mark Wilenchik: Yes, actually, I was. That's why I dropped in on them about midnight. But now I'm beginning to trust them again, because they're displaying that they can be trusted. But I think I'll always have an eye open...

Paul Eshleman: Why did the other guy quit? Can you give some reasons about it?

Mark Wilenchik: Mike's nature was happy-go-lucky. He was the "spiritual" one of the original trio. I was the serious one, and the other guy was the "try-anything-once" type of guy. Michael's the one that wanted to go to the first dinner; he's the one who wanted to go for the weekend workshop and the one who wanted most to stay the week at Booneville. So I think Michael's problem was that he never got serious. He never committed himself; he never gave himself to God. He just gave himself to himself. He re-met an old girlfriend during his kidnapping, and that romantic situation helped to pull him out. One time during the three weeks I was held, I went out to dinner with Michael, after he'd been deprogrammed, with Sandy, the guy who helped pull him out, and with Debby, his girlfriend. And the whole evening I had to fake being deprogrammed. It's an incredible thing to speak 100% what you don't believe. Try it for a while.

Paul Eshleman: What are the experiences of the thousands who have been through the deprogramming process? What do they reject? If they have accepted Christ through their experience, do they reject Christ, or do they reject the church? What do most of them end up rejecting? Does anybody know?

Mark Wilenchik: I have one view. I think they reject the straight and narrow path, religious life; they feel that it's not necessary to walk the certain path that we talk about here.

Paul Eshleman: Was there any thought in your mind as you came back that, if the church rejected you, you still had Christ, or is it the Unification view that they're inextricable?

Mark Wilenchik: Personally, after being a Christian for three months, what I felt was that my religious relationship had always been more of one with God. Being raised in the Jewish tradition, it is just God without Jesus. That's just me. It's something I've got to work out in my life of faith. Yet today, in the chapel, I had the deepest experience of my life with Jesus, and it was clearly from God. I didn't know what I was going to say today. I have never given my testimony in this way before, trying to explain my conversion. When I got up from my chair in the chapel, I said to Heavenly Father something to the effect that "My life is for You." Those were my last words, and the spirit of that saying was so intense that all I could do was to sit down again and start praying. This is the kind of experience I had this morning with Christ.

Charles Barfoot: I guess a good evangelical question would be, if you left this organization, whether the centrality of Christ would still be there. I guess maybe that's what I would hope for you.

Mark Wilenchik: I don't think the Unification church would say anything else either. I don't think we'd say, if anyone left the church, that they could not find Christ.

Evangelical Y: I think that people pass through Campus Crusade, to use that as an example; that's perhaps a way station, it hits them at a right time. Certain churches have hit me at the right time, and I've gone on, but I don't see my commitment to Christ as any less strong.

Mark Wilenchik: If someone left Campus Crusade for Christ and joined the Unification church, Paul would probably say, "I hope someday they come back."

Paul Eshleman: The issue would not be whether they left the movement or not, but what their commitment to Christ is and what they are doing about it. If somebody left, and just wasted away his life, that would be too bad, but thousands come and go, and the question is, "How's your life with the Lord? Are you following Him and doing what He wants you to do?"

Patricia Zulkosky: I think unfortunately a lot of people who go through the deprogramming experience lose faith completely. Some have been forced to defecate on the Bible as proof that they are giving up all regard for such holy traditions.

In a similar way, there are a number of people in our generation who were very involved in the anti-war movement or civil rights movement. They put their whole heart and soul into the cause, but the movements fell apart, and their idealism was crushed. They became so disillusioned with trying to make a positive impact on the world that they just threw their hands up in despair and said, "What the heck. I'm just going to go off and lead my own selfish life and let the world suffer and do whatever it wants. I'm not going to do anything about it."

Deprogrammed members may be involved in deprogramming

activities for a while, because they have to prove that they are deprogrammed, but, once they get out of that circuit, they just become completely apathetic. Not only apathetic to the Unification church, but apathetic to Christ, apathetic to social involvement and commitment. With social movements, the purpose of life is taken away because the social movement loses its power, but, in the case of deprogramming, it's a forcible, actual brainwashing situation where your values are taken away but nothing is put back in their place.

Rod Sawatsky: I'd like to cut it off now.

Salvation and Restoration

Paul Eshleman: Is salvation a category for the Unification church?

Several voices: Yes, spiritual salvation and physical salvation...

Paul Eshleman: I would like to hear a definition of spiritual salvation and hear how a Moonie knows he has spiritual salvation.

Johnny Sonneborn: I knew before I came to the Unification church. I can define spiritual salvation in terms of being born into a living hope, I think that is the best expression. We know that God loves us and will always love us; therefore, we have hope in being free of accusation, being free of those who say, "Don't hope, God doesn't love you; He can't help you, you'll be eternally dead." We can repel these accusations and turn against Satan spiritually. Though we can't tell Satan entirely that we are free of sin, we can say we have faith, and so he can't separate us from the love of Christ Jesus.

Richard Quebedeaux: Would you agree with the four spiritual laws?

Johnny Sonneborn: I forget what the fourth is, but I remember that I originally had some problem with it...

Paul Eshleman: 1) God loves you and offers a wonderful plan for your life. 2) Man is sinful and separated from God, so he can't experience it. 3) Jesus Christ was God's only provision for man's sin through His death on the cross. 4) We must individually receive Jesus Christ as Saviour and Lord.

Evangelical X: Wait a minute. Explain your agreement with the third one. The word *only* there...

Johnny Sonneborn: This is a statement of present reality—Jesus. Having been resurrected, Jesus became the means of salvation that has been affirmed—that's exactly what God did.

Jonathan Wells: I know a professor who says the essence of Christianity is the affirmation that Jesus is unsurpassable. I affirmed that with him, and he challenged me, since he knows something about Unification theology. We finally narrowed it down to *finality;* in other words, as I explained earlier, the salvation brought by Jesus was complete—there was nothing lacking in it. However, according to Unification doctrine, that salvation was rejected by Jesus' contemporaries in a way that makes it necessary for it to be brought again at the second advent, which supercedes the first advent in this sense.

Paul Eshleman: Can we go back, then, to the question of the individual? How do you, at this point, have assurance of your spiritual salvation? I don't want necessarily to single you out, but how does the Unification theology have assurance of your personal salvation? What is necessary?

Dan Davies: Christian rebirth comes first by guidance from the Holy Spirit and second by acceptance of Jesus as Christ, as Lord. I was guided by the Holy Spirit to a knowledge and acceptance of Jesus Christ. As to how I have assurance of spiritual salvation, I think you're talking about the rebirth experience. I can only speak for myself: I was a Christian when I joined the Unification movement, and, when I had a rebirth experience, my whole heart changed. I turned from my sinful life. Not that I was sinless, but my attitude changed, my heart changed, the love I felt changed. In talking with members, I've found that there are different ways in which people experience change of heart. Some people are gradual; I can't speak for everybody, but I know members who have had gradual change. I think you know you're experiencing spiritual salvation by a change of heart, toward your own self and toward other people.

Anthony Guerra: Let me say that I think this is a real problem in Christian theology. Some people believe that in order to be saved you have to confess the Holy Spirit and Jesus, and there are other people who believe that confession is not necessary—in fact you might not be sure about your status, but that grace is administered through the sacraments, which are efficacious, independent of your attitude.

Evangelical X: I think Evangelicals would agree with that. I mean Luther would agree with what was just said, certainly evangelical Lutherans...

Paul Eshleman: I missed the last phrase...

Anthony Guerra: What I said was that one's personal view of assurance is irrelevant to the fact of salvation for some segments of Christianity, those which find efficacy through the sacraments, for instance.

Evangelical X: Yes, Luther was very much doubtful of feelings as the gauge of one's certainty...

Paul Eshleman: But what about the sacramental part of it?

Warren Lewis: If you want to talk about sacraments, you could talk about faith and not define it as a feeling...

Paul Eshleman: That was the essence of Luther's break—he said that salvation was by faith and not simply by the sacraments...

Richard Quebedeaux: Also, in Holiness and in some forms of pentecostal Christianity, which I call evangelical, there is *no* assurance of salvation, but there is a hope in my parents' Pentecostal Church of God. Most of the people literally say, "Well, I hope I'm going to make it. If I persevere." But there is no assurance, and this is very much akin to Catholicism, which is one reason why Catholicism and Pentecostalism have seemed to join together.

Charles Barfoot: Having grown up in the Assemblies of God, having six ministers of the Assemblies of God in the family (laughter) not I, no! (laughter)...I remember the testimonials, especially the standard phrase at the end, "And I want to go all the way with Him." It was that kind of thing; we really doubted if we were going to make it. But the other thing that I told Richard before is that there were a lot of problems, especially with the more far-out people—there were all sorts of stereotypes. We were just talking about A.A. Allen, for instance. He left many a piano player a gift after the revivals, but I think one of the reasons that one could keep functioning was speaking in tongues. It almost became an ethic: "You were saved because you could speak in tongues." That was your assurance. I do think there is an assurance...and I wanted to raise that in terms of the Holy Spirit. I almost wanted to take both sides today, sitting in the middle, maybe...what role does the Holy Spirit play?—and I really don't want to jump the gun on that, but you mentioned it—is it just a rational kind of thing, or do you feel glad, do you feel guided; I mean, are you moved?

Dan Davies: You can say the official name for the Unification church is the Holy Spirit Association...for me it is a real experience.

Evangelical X: But how does that experience function? I mean, I've looked at the *Divine Principle*, and I feel bored—I don't think I can get *moved* to read that kind of thing, but...

Dan Davies: Many people read the Bible and are bored, too...

Evangelical X: Yes, that's true of any spiritual discipline...

Charles Barfoot: If one converts—I'm more interested in

conversion, or joining—is one motivated by the Spirit—is there..?

Dan Davies: Yes, I would say it's like this. I can speak personally, and then I think other people can talk. I was in search of the truth. And I feel that my search was controlled by the Holy Spirit, and, in my search for truth, I was led to Jesus Christ because I considered all possibilities, so the Holy Spirit moves me and other people to God and to Jesus Christ.

Charles Barfoot: You said you were led by the Holy Spirit. I guess, Dan, you were talking about two women who were involved with Aimee Semple McPherson—sort of "old Moonies." Do you think that the motivation of being led by the Spirit can attract you to charismatic heights? Perhaps your allegiance, then, to God, Jesus, the Holy Spirit, somehow gets moved over to Rev. Moon? I think that, in "classical pentecostalism," Aimee Semple McPherson was undoubtedly a goddess to her followers; I mean, I'm sure that, when the roll is called up yonder, they'll want to see her up there—they'll want to see her just as much as, say, Jesus.

Dan Davies: Well, I think I see what you're saying...Frankly, in my life, I intuit the will of God, and I do that basically through prayer—I test things that way, and...

Evangelical Y: You said intuition. Would you say there is spiritual discernment?

Dan Davies: I don't know exactly how to say it in theological terms. I follow the will of the Holy Spirit as I sense it through intuition; and, in the course of following it, I was led to the Unification church. I had heard no negative things about the Unification church. I just looked at what was taught. I hadn't been brought up in any doctrine, so I didn't have to plow through all that.

Johnny Sonneborn: Herman ten Bokkel Huinink was an Evangelical who had a very close personal relationship with the Holy Spirit, and one of our sisters witnessed to him. He saw from the very beginning that our doctrine was not evangelical, and, at that point, he waited to hear her out so he could save her. Finally, she taught the whole thing; he was very patient and listened very carefully, as he really wanted to understand her. When she was finished, he prayed to the Holy Spirit about how he could save this girl, and the Holy Spirit said, "Herman, they're right, you must join them." So he did, and he was led by the voice of the Holy Spirit—that's an extreme case. There are those led to us by the Holy Spirit; there are others who come through the teachings, the truth; others through the way of life, the commitment.

We believe that people come led by the spirit and truth. I don't think you can make a case that all of us are spiritual people who are naturally attracted to a charismatic figure. Some people undoubtedly know him as a truth-teller.

Frank Kaufmann: I'd like to respond to Paul about our salvific relationship to Jesus Christ. People who join the Unification church don't necessarily have a conversion experience at that time. But, the way of life prescribed by the Unification church will lead all members to become aware of their sinfulness and also to know, with absolute conviction, that Jesus Christ died on the cross for the salvation of our sins. This is an unshakable faith. Now, there are members within the Unification church who may not have come to that realization yet, but the way of life and the teachings of the Unification church will lead each and every member to the absolute understanding of his own sinfulness and the fact that Jesus Christ, the Son of God, died for our sins.

Tom Carter: In our daily life, we have many experiences that we describe as experiences with God. From the way you described the movement of the Holy Spirit, I think it would be the same thing, only instead of saying "Holy Spirit," we say God. I think that in reading through the *Divine Principle* one notices a lack of definition of exactly who or what the Holy Spirit is, but, from the way you seem to describe what the Holy Spirit is, the way you view it in your life, and the way you respond to it, that's what I would call God moving in my life. I think it is the same.

Nora Spurgin: I just want to say that both the Holy Spirit and Jesus (the spirit of Jesus) are very present in our lives. And so, because we believe in the Divine Principle and in Rev. Moon as coming with a further understanding, this does not negate the spirit of Jesus and the Holy Spirit working in our lives. We believe very much that both are very present and very much leading us into the future kingdom.

Also, I just wanted to respond a little bit to something that we feel about the Holy Spirit. Because Jesus is the model for masculinity—for perfect masculinity—and because He brings to us an example of God's heart as a masculine parent, we need that feminine kind of parentage too which we see as a different kind of energy. So, we believe that the energy that comes through the Holy Spirit is a different kind of energy—it's nurturing, leading to truth, a kind of motherly spirit.

Warren Lewis: I came across the following question while putting my book on the Holy Spirit together.* It shows how the Rev. Moon puts his feminist doctrine of the Spirit together with current social notions: "The phenomenon of women being able to rise and entrench themselves in power is very recent, showing that the time has come when God will elevate one woman to be the physical Holy Spirit. This is the time for the birth of the true Eve. God is looking for the ideal woman who has the qualifications and potential to become a true wife and a true mother, eventually the true queen, or empress, of the universe. Every woman is a candidate for this position, which is why women in general have been given a chance to rise."**

Dan Davies: I would like to speak more of repentance as it relates to conversion. It seems to me that repentance plays the same role in conversion that it does in an experience of Jesus and of God at any time. I think it is necessary for a person to become painfully aware of his sin; I think that is the pre-condition for the Holy Spirit to come to work in the heart, and that doesn't just apply to conversion. I think that applies to any time we want to offer ourselves up to God; it's necessary to acknowledge our sin and be sorry for it. Then, on that pre-condition, the Holy Spirit can work in our hearts and lives.

Anthony Guerra: I just wanted to register my problem with evangelical, or maybe it's Campus Crusade, theology concerning this point of repentance. It seems to me you're looking for a very particular formula for people to confess, which marks them as saved. It strikes me that there are different ways of being saved and of living a Christian life. If there is an underlying assumption that all people must come to God in a certain way, I would be opposed to that. The Unification theology of the spiritual life cannot be classified as dogmatic. I would say that we find many ways in which one could have an experience with God, Jesus, and the Holy Spirit, and that the subjective manifestation of that experience may vary from person to person, and that it may have something to do with the person's background. For instance, if one comes from a Buddhist background, then the way one will experience salvation may be different from that of the person

---

*Warren Lewis, ed., *Witnesses to the Holy Spirit; an anthology,* Valley Forge, Pa.: Judson Press, 1978.
**Rev. Sun Myung Moon in an informal talk given on the 23rd Anniversary of the Unification Church, May 1, 1977.

who comes from a Christian family with six ministers in his lineage.

We talk about an economic trinity, where God, Jesus and the Holy Spirit communicate love to one another and then express that love to the believer who stands in the fourth position as the child, receiving the spiritual love that gives him a new vision and the possibility to live a life closer to God.

Don Deffner: There are many ways in which the Spirit works—providing varieties of gifts, spiritual gifts. Would you grant, however, that one's salvation is 100% the work of God? That even repentance is not my cooperating with God, but God at work in me. It's not 95% God and then 5% me; but I am saved solely by grace through faith, "not because of works, lest any man should boast." (Ephesians 2:9)

Johnny Sonneborn: Our faith is the condition by which we receive God's grace.

Franz Feige: I had different repentance experiences, similar to the experiences that the New Testament Christians had in the primitive church. At times, I felt God's Spirit entering me and showing me the purity of His love and, based on this, I could see the difference between His love, or the Holy Spirit's love, and the love in this fallen world. Feeling the greatness of His love, I would have a deep experience of repentance, with many tears. At other times repentance would come in a way that I first really felt at the rock bottom of hell, in my sin; then I would begin to repent, feeling more and more God's Spirit entering me. These are different types of experiences. But, I found out that repentance does not come at random. When I do a lot of works, when I show God through many tests of my perseverance and my faith, then that type of experience comes more often. So I realized that the number of repentance experiences depends very much on me, though I cannot predict when they will happen. When one happens, I realize that it is actually God's gift. Yet, I have more repentance experiences when I lead a better way of life. So, it acts on my works to a certain degree, but, finally, it is God's gift for me.

Also, I want to say that I don't think the traditional Christian notion of salvation and our concept of salvation are the same.

Rod Sawatsky: I'm glad you introduced that right at this point, because we need to push it harder. Right now it looks as if the two are pretty similar, but I wonder if that's so.

Jonathan Wells: The concept of salvation in traditional Chris-

tianity is like a switch in a railroad yard: after death, or at the
Last Judgment, you go one way or the other, either to heaven or
to hell, based on God's weighing of your good or bad deeds, or
predestination, or any criteria you want to name. There's a
discontinuity between heaven and hell that is not present in
Unification theology. In Unification theology, the spiritual world,
just like the physical world, is more of a continuum, and it's a
matter of distance from God. So, the highest realm of the
spiritual world is that realm which has the closest relationship to
God; the lowest realm would contain those spirits which are
furthest from God. Now, when a person dies and leaves his
physical body, his spirit continues in the same state as it was at
his death; that's a very important consideration. It means that
during my life the spiritual state which I attain becomes the
spiritual state in which I continue after my death. So salvation—
actually we tend not to use this word in Unification theology; we
talk more about restoration—becomes the work of the Holy
Spirit through my physical body here on earth. It's more like
sanctification. From the standpoint of Unification theology it
doesn't make much sense to ask somebody how he knows for
sure he is saved. When you have asked that, you may have
noticed a bit of a silence.

Richard Quebedeaux: That strikes me as a rather traditional
understanding that I could resonate with. Would other Evangelicals call that salvation?

Frank Kaufmann: Without Christ working in your life, you're
incapable of living or attaining a spiritual level beyond a certain
point. In other words, no matter how many good works you do,
your sinfulness will prevent you from ever going beyond a certain
spiritual level. It is from our sinful nature that we need the
salvation Christ has provided for us if we truly repent and recognize Him as our Saviour. But that is not the final consideration of
Unification, which is what Jonathan described; sanctification, or
restoration, is closer to the primary consideration for Unification.

Tirza Shilgi: I think there is an essential difference between
what we in the Unification church define as the goal of salvation
and the understanding of the goal of salvation in evangelical
Christianity, in that we see the goal of salvation as being perfected man, whereas Evangelicals would define their goal of salvation as forgiveness of sin. So the whole notion of salvation ties up
with the original purpose of creation, which is to be perfect, and

forgiveness is the means by which you attain that perfection.

Jonathan Wells: It may sound as though there is a contradiction between what I said and what Frank said. But there isn't. He's talking about the starting point, the moment of repentance. I'm stressing a later stage. And it's from that point on that Unification theology gets interesting.

Joseph Hopkins: Jonathan, did I hear you saying that we cross over into eternity on the same spiritual level as our attainment here on earth? You didn't say eternity, but that's what I assume you meant.

Jonathan Wells: Spiritual world. Our spirits are with us now, yours and mine, but they are eternal.

Joseph Hopkins: Do you not have a doctrine of glorification, as in Pauline theology, that instantly upon death the process of sanctification is completed and we are glorified?

Warren Lewis: Well, yes, they do, but it doesn't come out like that. The glorification process is a continuing, gradual process in the spirit world...

Tirza Shilgi: Ideally, though, it should happen here on earth. Ideally, it should be accomplished by the time you depart from this world. But, because of the fall, right now we can't, so unfortunately, we have to continue our process of salvation in the spirit world.

Evangelical X: In evangelical theology, except in the Holiness churches, the attainment of spiritual succession is so far from human possibility that we believe it simply can't be accomplished until death, and then it happens instantly.

Dan Davies: As long as you mention the Holiness movements, there is a different belief there, especially in Wesley. His concept was that, upon rebirth you were justified, and you were on the road to sanctification, and that your full sanctification or glorification could only come about through good works.

Rod Sawatsky: I would really like us to push on in the direction of restoration and Unification marriage. I think we have kept circling on this too long.

Johnny Sonneborn: Just to put plainly what was said here, salvation through Jesus or what we call spiritual salvation, is not enough. One goes to Paradise, but he is not completely happy since lots of other people are in hell. Therefore, one has only really reached the intermediate level—one has repented, one is now ready to die for God, but one doesn't have fulfillment, one can't marry for God, have children for God in this world, and see the world as one family. Therefore, we believe in physical salvation—salvation is quite often called physical rebirth—in which we are not only adopted children of God, but we become true children of God. That opens another door. Frank said one can only reach a certain level without Jesus. Then, having been spiritually saved by Jesus, your physical sinfulness—the law in our members which is at war with the law of God—prevents one from reaching a certain completion, fulfillment and satisfaction. God and Jesus are not completely happy and fulfilled, in our teachings, therefore how could Christian saints be? This cannot happen until there stands on earth the perfect couple, and salvation spreads.

Evangelical X: May I ask a question of clarification? Are you a spiritual being in Paradise, and then are you a glorified physical being at the second coming?

Johnny Sonneborn: We don't believe that one gets another physical body; one's spiritual mind and spiritual body are eternal, and one relates through these on earth with those who have both soul and body.

Rod Sawatsky: Would somebody tell us what restoration is first, then tell us what the Blessing is?

Nora Spurgin: We haven't really talked very deeply about original sin. I think that, for Evangelicals, there is an assumption that there is original sin, so we don't have to argue about that point. We basically believe that mankind, our lineage, is sinful, and therefore Satan has a claim over us—he can claim us as his children—we're the sons of Satan, although we are also the sons of God. So, there is a certain double claim on us, and we can't free ourselves from that double claim—that has to come through the mission of Christ, the messianic mission. That's what Jesus came to do, and, spiritually, He could do that, but, physically, we still pass on original sin to our children.

The value of the Blessing is that when a true parent or a set of true parents on earth are in this position, then we can be adopted into their family by receiving the Blessing from them. In the blessing of marriage, we are conditionally offered to God as if we were pure, as if we were without sin, even though we aren't, on their merit. It's a process of salvation, and, in so doing, then, we can start our own families, which are part of the new lineage and no longer pass on original sin. Now that doesn't mean that our children never sin, it doesn't mean that we can never sin, but it does mean that we're not passing that on, and that our children are more in the position of Adam and Eve: they don't inherit original sin, they don't inherit the claim of Satan over man, or the guilt that comes with that—the sort of universal guilt that has nothing to do with what they have done, just what they've inherited. So, to us, the Blessing is the most precious and the most valuable thing in our church. To accept Jesus is the beginning. Then to accept the Blessing is a whole new level of physical salvation on earth; the beginning of a whole new lineage—it's the beginning of the kingdom of heaven on earth. It's our hope. Our desire is to reflect God's nature as a totality, as husband and wife, who are free from Satan's claim as his sons and daughters—we are to be the reflection of God's nature, and we hope we can live out that kind of life. It doesn't mean we are perfect—it means that we are on our way to perfection, without Satan's claim over us.

Evangelical X: Nora, does it mean, then, that the hope is that you breed as many children as you possibly can, children who will then populate the earth with sinless nature? Is that the ultimate goal?

Nora Spurgin: We believe that the more children we have the better it would be for the whole world. That's our attitude.

Joseph Hopkins: This is a revelation to me that justification under the Divine Principle is accomplished this way. In effect, that's what you're saying, aren't you?

Jonathan Wells: Earlier, when I was leading up to Jesus, and skipped over the fall of man, I really left out the essential foundation for understanding this whole concept. At first glance, it's really strange to think about salvation in terms of a marriage and children; but in Unification theology, the fall of man becomes the key to understanding restoration and salvation. In Augustinian theology, we've got a serious problem because Adam and Eve are perfect, and it's very difficult to explain how two perfect people can commit sin. In the Unification doctrine of the fall, Adam and Eve start out as children, growing toward perfection. They were destined to be husband and wife, but God told them to refrain temporarily from marriage. Our interpretation of the commandment is that the fruit of the tree of knowledge of good and evil is a symbol for the love of an immature Eve.

Now, Lucifer was envious of Adam, who actually stood in a

position of being loved by God more than Lucifer, as God's son—I hope I'm not going too fast. What happened was that Lucifer and Eve became involved in a relationship which, little by little in the nature of intimate relationships, led to a situation in which the love between them was stronger than God's commandment, resulting in an adulterous relationship between Lucifer and Eve.

Eve, then, realizing Adam was to be her true mate, and desiring to return to God, entered into a premature sexual relationship with him. This is where we get the notion of Satan's lineage that Jesus talks about in the New Testament. Now, if that's the way the fall occurred, then the solution of sin has to be the reversal of that process. That's why the Blessing is preceded by a long period of celibacy in the Unification church, to purify this sexual contamination from the Garden of Eden.

Franz Feige: Salvation is a process of restoration. Hence, it doesn't necessarily have anything to do with Christianity or with our movement. It can work in everyone's life; even an atheist can participate in the *process* of restoration, even though he doesn't know it, through paying indemnity. What is indemnity? If something has lost its original status or position, for example a stone has fallen down, then that can be restored by bringing the stone back to its original position. Paying indemnity means paying back, reversing. The energy that I put into getting the stone back into position is called indemnity. Through that indemnity I am able to restore. Such restoration works in anybody's life. By obeying the law that Moses gave, you are restored to a higher level, you come closer to the original position. Then comes Christianity. Here I can go further by believing in Jesus Christ as my Saviour. Through that love of Jesus and the Holy Spirit, I can attain to a higher degree of restoration. This is restoration within Christianity, and can happen to us, too, in the Unification church. Now, restoration in the Unification church is not just entering into a relationship with Jesus and the Holy Spirit, but involves being engrafted into the second advent family. This engrafting is both spiritual and physical.

It can happen that I am restored spiritually by being engrafted into Jesus' lineage a long time before I am engrafted into the second advent's lineage. In this sense, there are two different aspects of restoration—they can take place at two different times—and we should not confuse them. The restoration I receive through the second advent will bring me to a higher state than that of the first advent since now I can reach complete perfection, I can become completely one with God.

Rod Sawatsky: Is it at the point of marriage that this incorporation into the lineage of the second advent occurs?

Nora Spurgin: First of all, the Blessing is on the basis of our dedication, our *belief.* You wouldn't want to be Blessed if you didn't believe in the Divine Principle, in Rev. Moon, in the Unification church. Secondly, it is on the basis of your having, through certain steps, proved yourself, on the basis of having met certain qualifications: having led a celibate life for a period of time, having taken a seven-day fast, which is a symbol of having purified yourself of the world, and having three spiritual children, which means you've taken a parental position in raising up new babes in Christ, raising them to a position also of being able to be Blessed. So those are the basic qualifications, but they are not absolute. It's giving whatever you have—if you've given 100%, if you've wholly given yourself and offered yourself, then you should qualify for the Blessing, no matter what your past life of sin was. After you've been exposed to the Divine Principle, once you've been exposed to this truth, then, if you've lived that to the best of your knowledge, and you offer yourself ultimately, you will receive this.

Rod Sawatsky: In order to hurry the process a little, Warren has been writing on this question. Do you want to say anything in further elaboration?

Warren Lewis: A blessed Unificationist is not twice born, but thrice born, and believes that if one is not born again, one won't ultimately be saved.

Evangelical Y: It almost sounds like the baptism of the Holy Spirit.

Warren Lewis: It certainly does. It is the equivalent of new birth in pentecostalism, or the second work of grace, or the "second blessing." This is perfectionism. When Rev. Moon left the Presbyterians he went towards his present Unificationist position by way of some Methodist charismatic types and picked up some Wesleyan Holiness along the way. The perfectionist element in Unificationist thought is very strong.

How does it work for them? It is not within the Blessing that one overcomes all sin. The original sin was fornication; one must therefore go through an indemnity process of three years of celibacy—though the time span varies—before receiving the Blessing. The Lord of the Second Advent is, for them, the second coming of Christ; they now belong, not just spiritually (which is what we get in Christianity) but also physically to the messiah. Jan Weido, whom a lot of you know, once tried to talk to my father about this. Dad was a Texas Church of Christ elder, and, when he came on with all of his Texas evangelical fundamentalism, Jan listened respectfully. Dad can get you up to about the day of Pentecost, but, after that, it doesn't matter for him any more. Jan said, "Well, Brother Lewis, that's the point at which we get interested. Justification is what Jesus gets you; the Blessing is what the Lord of the Second Advent gets you. Justification, salvation of your soul, spiritual salvation are what we get in Christianity. But that's just not enough. It has not been enough for 2000 years. That's why American divorce is more successful than American marriage; that's why sexism and racism and all the other corruptions of human society are still around. Rev. Moon speaks of the failure of Christianity. Spiritual salvation is what produces the kind of mullygrubbing around, where Evangelicals get together and say pious things to one another, while the Marxists make away with the world. We Unificationists are trying to say that Jesus is O.K. as far as He goes, but He doesn't go far enough." That's what Jan Weido said to my dad.

Translating this into Christian theology, I think we can talk about sanctification of the individual life in terms of the blessed couple, and sanctification of the social order in terms of establishing a theocratic socialism for the whole world. Also, unification of the world's religions is a part of the program. But these are parts of the physical salvation which the Lord of the Second Advent has wrought. Unificationism takes Christianity with it, but goes infinitely beyond what Christianity has accomplished. With Jesus, you get forgiveness of your sins; with Luther, you're still *simul peccator;* but, with the Lord of the Second Advent, the *fomas peccati* is rooted out. That root of sin which causes us to keep on sinning is removed through the indemnity process, so that once one has been blessed, one can achieve perfection, can give birth to sinless children, can grow up to the Edenic perfection of Adam and Eve originally intended by God.

Dan Davies: I'd like to make it clear that we do not view the fall as sexual. The cause of the fall was a selfish attitude, expressed sexually.

Whitney Shiner: It's not sex itself.

Warren Lewis: I don't think it's transmitted sexually. It's transmitted socially. Guilt, the fear of death, is a kind of existential claim Satan makes on all the descendants of Adam and Eve because of their sins. It's not an essential corruption of human nature: the "original mind" is still there, and it can be appealed to through free will. One can merit before God on the basis of getting out one's original mind, polishing it up, and using it.

Anthony Guerra: I was thinking that they should describe justification. The way I would put it is that, in the Christian tradition, the individual is justified—that is, he receives approval from God as an individual. Then, there is the process of sanctification, in which he becomes transformed into a perfected individual, realizing the ideal person.

Warren Lewis: Only the Wesleyans believe in that degree of perfection!

Anthony Guerra: But ultimately, there will be a moment of sanctification or glorification, even if it takes til the eschaton. In Unification theology the terms of the Blessing being talked about go back to the problem of the fall. The family itself comes under the disapproval of God because Adam and Eve turned away from the commandment and centered themselves around Satan. Because of this, no family can be approved by God. Now the Blessing is not a sanctification of the family, rather it is justification on the family level. Social justification in our theology occurs at the time of the Blessing, but there is the subsequent period in which one must work towards the perfection of the family. So, it seems to me that what the *Divine Principle* is speaking about in terms of the Lord of the Second Advent is a kind of social justification, which makes possible individual sanctification, because ultimately individuals themselves find their realization in the family unit. Therefore, instead of talking about sanctification, I would talk about the social and family level of justification.

Rod Sawatsky: So you want two justifications—individual and social?

Anthony Guerra: Right.

Jonathan Wells: But another point needs to be clarified. We are not Pelagian. Pelagius denied the doctrine of original sin, which we uphold. Because of original sin, it is impossible for people to become perfect by themselves; but, we are like Pelagius in affirming the power of free will. Even sinful people have enough original goodness to turn towards the good. As Johnny explained, that becomes the condition for God's grace.

Johnny Sonneborn: And also we must remember that it is only God who inspires our faith and calls us; we can never argue on that, but still it is our faith.

Don Deffner: To me Ephesians 2:8-9 would speak to this, "Not of works, lest any person boast."

Johnny Sonneborn: I think works can help put you in a position—works may sanctify your spiritual salvation from God, or something like that. I don't think we're going to come out with your terminology, that God does everything and man has no part of it. However, I think we're not very far apart. But I haven't found the test to prove that I'm as close as I say I am, so I'll hold it in abeyance.

Let me summarize our point. Due to "original" sin, Adam and Eve could not become true parents and therefore everybody else was born without true parents. So the remedy is to be reborn into the family of the True Parents and be able to start on the way to becoming true parents ourselves. Parents blessed by God, parents as the image of God is the key thing. And you can see that it follows from what is being said now that it is not just a question of us or Rev. Moon or anybody else—we're talking about the children. We were not born as Rev. Moon's children— we become engrafted into the family; therefore, many have to become engrafted, not just the children we have. Everyone here will be invited to become true parents through becoming true children.

Evangelical Y: Once these people get their original sinful nature removed, what are the practical implications? How do they behave? Do they sin at all? Do they know they sin? What do they do? How do they know that something has happened other than by doing the things you said? Do the people behave differently? Are these children different from other children?

Nora Spurgin: They're different from other children in that they don't have that inherited sin.

Evangelical Y: But how do you know that? Is this simply a faith statement you make? Is the behavior exactly the same? Do the parents, and the children of Blessed couples all behave exactly the same as people who haven't been Blessed?

Warren Lewis: They don't commit fornication—that's how

they know; that is the difference.

Evangelical Y: Is that the only way you know? What about other sins? What about greed or covetousness? Can you do all of those things as long as you don't commit sexual sin?

Rod Sawatsky: We haven't dealt with what happens to the perfected children.

Evangelical Y: Or the perfected parents—what do they do? The Wesleyans admit that they sin, and they get forgiveness again; so that's what is different here from the Wesleyan beliefs.

Nora Spurgin: We don't believe that these children and ourselves can't ever sin again. What it means is that we're in the position of not having the constant accusation of Satan that we're defiled, that we did this wrong, that we did that wrong—that kind of accusation. We're now God's children, but it doesn't mean we can never sin or fall away from that position.

Warren Lewis: But, of course, Christians believe that Jesus accomplished that for us. I always believed I received this through being immersed in the blood of Jesus according to the Church-of-Christ baptism. Now, Satan can no longer accuse me: I am home free.

Tirza Shilgi: I think it's good to mention here, when we talk about the Blessing, that it doesn't just mean marriage. The three blessings that God gave Adam and Eve must be considered. Be fruitful, multiply and have dominion. Being fruitful means to be perfect as an individual, to be God-centered in your love and in your life. Based on that, you will be qualified for the second blessing, which is sharing your life with your spouse, having children, and attaining a parental heart. You will then be qualified for the third blessing, which will be having dominion over creation, but having it with a parental heart of love, which means not abusing the creation, but treating it with love. I think it is important here because we see ourselves qualified for the blessing only after attaining the first blessing. And, when we say *blessing,* this is not something passively received, but something you work on, from both ends. You have to work on it, and then you receive it. Individual perfection is living your life as an individual centered on God, putting God ahead of your selfish desires. To remove this original sin within yourself, you have to put God ahead of your own desires, and that, we see, as encompassing three years of celibacy, or three years of working for other countries or for other people, whatever our responsibility is at that moment. Based on that, we will qualify for the second blessing. We actually think that it will take a few generations to practically cleanse ourselves of sin, so that means that we do have greed, and we do have jealousy, and we do have many other things, and we have to work on ourselves, but it's really like the idea of sanctification, where we have to work to cleanse ourselves for God. So it's not a question of either faith or works; we hold both.

Anthony Guerra: I really feel a lack of the dynamics which we enjoyed this morning, when you Evangelicals and then we Unificationists talked about Christ. This afternoon, since we've gotten onto salvation, the Unificationists have been doing all the talking. I feel as though we're preaching at this point, and that's probably the way you feel. From my point of view, the dialogue is missing something.

Rod Sawatsky: I think what's happened is that we're being introduced to something so novel that it has to filter through before we can really converse on the other end.

Patricia Zulkosky: I don't think at any point we are ever qualified for the Blessing. I think the Blessing is an act of grace from God, and that I can never pretend to earn it. The whole doctrine of salvation through grace is, in some sense, very important in my life, because I can never earn the Blessing—God's grace.

And the other thing is the Blessing—although it takes away original sin, it doesn't take away my fallen nature, which means that I've already grown up and been influenced by society and developed all of these bad vices and things that don't go away like that because of the Blessing.

Evangelical Y: Let me ask a point, then. What about your children's fallen nature?

Patricia Zulkosky: If, for instance, I work on my fallen nature, and it declines, then my way of raising my children is such that there is that much less fallen nature; but, we're still living in a sinful society, and we're still exposed to it in varying degrees, so sinless children without fallen nature are still two to three generations away.

Charles Barfoot: Is there an unpardonable sin? Would that be adultery?

Patricia Zulkosky: After the Blessing...

Johnny Sonneborn: Everything is pardonable...God will

save everybody.

Warren Lewis: I just can't let that one go by. In the Principle, nobody goes to a devil's fiery hell, according to Unificationists; but, if after the Blessing you commit adultery, for seventy generations following you, your descendants will accuse you before God, and you will remain forever further away from God than you otherwise would have been. Not in a devil's hell, not burning eternally forever with the worms and the maggots, like the Christians believe, but still you lose your status before God. In terms of the way theological dynamics work, since the Blessing is the highest good, then obviously it would be an "unpardonable sin" to violate it.

Sharon Gallagher: For clarification, when you were listing the sins of the modern world, you mentioned divorce, racism, and feminism or sexism (laughter)—I have to ask because it was said twice...

Warren Lewis: For the record...feminism is *not* a mortal sin. (laughter)

Sharon Gallagher: A couple of people have said that being reborn in the second advent is a higher stage, and I wanted to ask someone on a personal level—one, what is your daily relationship to Jesus Christ, and two, what is your daily relationship to Sun Myung Moon?

Franz Feige: I think there are different positions in the Unification church: some hold a more distinct personal relationship with Jesus because they were very strong Christians, and some hold a distinct personal relationship with Rev. Moon. My whole relationship to Rev. Moon is not with Rev. Moon as a person, but with him as a Messiah. Jesus and Rev. Moon come together—they are two persons—but they both hold the same position, so I don't distinguish between those two—they're one and the same. When I pray very deeply, then I feel God as my Father and I also experience Rev. Moon very easily. I experience the same thing with Jesus. He comes in the spirit, and they're both united with God, and they're one and the same to me.

Tom Carter: My perspective is that you can't understand Rev. Moon without understanding Jesus. For the first several years of my life in the Unification church, in order to understand Rev. Moon, I spent many hours praying, studying the New Testament, praying in Jesus' name, trying to understand Jesus.

I'd like to answer now, on a practical level, in terms of what the *Divine Principle* says. Moses didn't get to go into the land of Canaan, even though he was chosen by God. But, before he died in the wilderness, he chose his most faithful servant, Joshua, to take his people into the land of Canaan and Joshua accomplished that. So, in that sense, the relationship between Rev. Moon and Jesus is the same as the relationship between Joshua and Moses. In other words, Rev. Moon is Jesus' most faithful servant, commissioned by Jesus to bring the people out of the spiritual wilderness into the land of universal Canaan. So, it's impossible to understand Rev. Moon outside a relationship with Jesus—it can't be done.

Dan Davies: During my search for truth in life, I came into a relationship with Jesus and the Holy Spirit, about six months before I joined the Unification movement. The change was so real, my commitment so great...

Evangelical Y: How did that happen?

Dan Davies: It was through a search. It happened when I was in Israel. I didn't even believe that Jesus Christ was a reality until I took part in a movie, *Jesus Christ, Superstar.* While I was in that movie, three days after the crucifixion scene, Jesus appeared to me and told me He was the Son of God. About three or four months after that, I had a rebirth experience in Jesus through the Holy Spirit. I dedicated myself to Jesus Christ and the Holy Spirit and tried to live by the Bible at that time. That dedication has always remained a force in my life. Frankly, I won't do anything unless it is the will of Jesus and the Holy Spirit. I'm here because of them, and I continue to be here because of them. If I'm ever told, or moved by them not to be here, I won't be here. But I'm still here.

Evangelical Y: Could there be a potential conflict between their roles?

Dan Davies: I don't know—to this point...

Evangelical Y: Have you sinned since that time?

Dan Davies: What do you mean?

Evangelical Y: Have you committed any sin since the time you joined the church? And *who* has forgiven those sins you've committed since you joined—Rev. Moon or Jesus?

Dan Davies: When I repent I feel forgiveness.

Evangelical X: Who do you ask for forgiveness?

Dan Davies: I ask God for forgiveness; I feel forgiveness from God.

Patricia Zulkosky: I guess in my case it might be a little bit different, because my daily relationship is with God, and, for me, God means God the Father, and, for me, Jesus and Rev. Moon are mediators for me to know God the Father. Because of that I study the Bible, because of that I read *Divine Principle* to find inspiration how to know God, but my daily prayer is conversation with God. When I'm asking for direction when I'm looking for guidance, I go to God the way I do my Father. So I don't get all tangled up in Rev. Moon and Jesus. For me, they're both mediators that are bringing me the love of God, helping me to lead the life that I think God would have me lead if He had a physical body, and if He were here in this room. I think many Unificationists relate more to God as the focal point than they do to Rev. Moon and Jesus. We pray in the name of True Parents, which for me means the spiritual parents of Jesus and the Holy Spirit as well as Rev. Moon and Mrs. Moon. My daily life centers on a personal communication with God.

Mark Branson: Just to ask a pragmatic question: some of you go to churches in the area. Would there be one kind of church more of you would feel at home at?

Jack Harford: There are certain churches where we're received well and certain churches where we're rejected or where we are paid no attention at all. There are certain churches where they refuse to even talk to us...

Evangelical Y: Is there one church that you feel closer to the truth in, or more spiritually attuned?

Jack Harford: I'd like to relate a couple of experiences that I've had. Last summer, when I was in England, I went to a Catholic church, and, for a while, I was praying there a half hour to an hour every day. I had many deep experiences with Jesus and shed great tears, feeling His heart, because we were like pioneers on a mission, trying to feel the way Jesus felt by trying to build up our own neighborhood into a family of God and trying to find our own disciples. It was very difficult, and so, in that church I could feel Jesus very much, and I felt comfortable in that church. Also, now, I go to a Reformed Church in Kingston, and, when I go, I feel at home there, too...

Evangelical Y: One other thing I want to ask: What happens if somebody doesn't want to get Blessed?

Warren Lewis: Then they don't.

Evangelical Y: So they're missing the fullness of the Spirit, as we would say. We always had one or two in our churches...

Nora Spurgin: But they don't understand that until they get Blessed...

Evangelical Y: But I'm comparing it to the pentecostal belief, and we had people that wanted it, but never quite got it.

Rod Sawatsky: Can we shift gears now and move on to the question of heresy and orthodoxy? Would two of you do that task for us from the evangelical side?

Mark Branson: Well, you have heard of the four spiritual laws. I'd like to take a start with the question of Jesus' words. To those around Him within the Jewish community, His words were very basically, "Follow me, believe in me." Jesus gave the people around Him something to respond to in His life and in His words. As people would respond, He gave them more to respond to. His disciples had the opportunity to slip, and many of them did; many of them also returned later on. Jesus' words in the first part of the Gospel of Mark are, "The time is fulfilled; and the kingdom of God is at hand; repent, and believe in the gospel." This is the very crucial beginning point. Something has happened that has not happened before. The way has been paved. God is here. The kingdom of God is at hand, it is within reach; all its ramifications, not just spiritual, are present. Repent means you must turn around, for you're going in the wrong direction. You're going in that direction because you're living as part of the kingdom of this world, the kingdom of Satan. Now you can turn around and believe—you can live in accordance with the gospel, the Good News that Jesus Christ is here. This simply means Jesus Christ is Lord. It's not just a "sir" or a term of respect. It's a term of authority. As Jesus goes through Mark, He is God. He calls me then to follow Him. As I take that step, it is the Spirit who releases me. The Spirit is the one that works in me to take away my blindness. As I hear the words, the work of grace comes to me, and, as I respond in simple obedience, then that word becomes more powerful. I receive more words, and I keep responding—that's the way the kingdom is built, the way I enter into a relationship with God. It has other ramifications we can get into later concerning eternal life. For now, primarily, I wanted to see salvation as entering into the kingdom through hearing and responding to the words of Jesus.

Paul Eshleman: Several questions came up at the end which we didn't answer last time. For instance, when does forgiveness occur? I think of the passage in Hebrews 10 where it says, "For by a single offering He has perfected for all time those who are sanctified." We would say that, at the moment a person entrusts, he repents. Jesus says, "But unless you repent you will all likewise perish." So the man who says, "I repent in the way I am going now, I will follow Christ and go His way," (and that may or may not involve tears, but it involves change in mind and attitude, which should lead to change in action), that repentance then will lead him to say, "I do accept Christ and His blood atonement on the cross as the payment for my sins, problems, and my original sinful nature." At that point, when, by an act of his will, he has been energized by the Holy Spirit, when he responds, and, by faith, trusts that payment for his salvation, at that point we would say he has eternal life—his eternal life begins. Some would say, then, that he has to maintain it or he will fall away, but the majority would say that eternal life begins here for him, so he is justified at that moment—then, for the remainder of his physical life, he is in the process of sanctification. That sanctification does not take place through the struggle and strain of the Christian himself trying to clean up his life and get rid of sin here and there. The sanctification comes about primarily through the indwelling and controlling of the Holy Spirit—at the moment he accepts Christ as his payment, the Holy Spirit comes to indwell him. The process of sanctification, the life of the Christian, then, is one that is involved in allowing the Spirit of Christ—the Holy Spirit and Christ who are now within him—to have full and unhindered access and control in his life, so that in his life he is submitting moment by moment, and day by day, to the Holy Spirit's control of his life, to reflect the fruit of the spirit, a life of joy, peace, patience, and so forth.

He then looks forward to the second bodily return of Christ to this earth, which, in Matthew 24, is signaled by the trumpets blaring and Christ returning in the air, and he waits for that return, at which time his perfection and sanctification will be completed. Those who are alive will be caught up to meet Christ, those who are dead will be raised, and we, in a moment, in a twinkling of an eye, will have a new body which is like unto his own body at that particular time. That would be my addition.

Warren Lewis: I'm as moved to talk about your notion of salvation as I was moved to talk about the Blessing a while ago. Unificationist friends, I speak from a completely different evangelical point of view, and one more faithful to the Bible than anything that has been said. (laughter)

The question is how a person is saved. On the day of Pentecost, the apostle Peter, in very clear terms, told you exactly what you had to do to be saved. He said, "Repent, and be baptized, every one of you, in the name of Jesus Christ, for the forgiveness of your sins; and you shall receive the gift of the Holy Spirit." In every chapter of the Book of Acts, in all gospel records of the great commission, baptism is directly, intimately, bound up with the forgiveness of sin and salvation. What this Calvinist *kwatsch* (laughter) Paul [Eshleman] has just dished up is not historically accurate in either the Bible or the church. If you do not have your sins washed away in baptism, you are *still* in your sins. Apparently you have the idea that you will go to heaven carrying your sins with you! In the words of Ananias to Saul, "And now why do you wait? Rise and be baptized, and wash away your sins, calling on this name." These two gentlemen didn't mention the resurrection, didn't mention baptism, and yet they are going to tell you about salvation. (laughter)

Paul Eshleman: You very clearly place greater emphasis on baptism than I do. Both of us would agree that there needs to be an identification with Christ, and Warren thinks the water baptism is a part of that.

Warren Lewis: So did Ananias. (laughter)

Paul Eshleman: I don't think any Evangelicals would dispute the fact that baptism should be an occurrence in and around the point of salvation. There would be disputes over whether it was necessary for the actual salvation or whether it was a testimony to the commitment of faith.

Warren Lewis: But what's interesting is the rhetoric—when they ask you what you must do to be saved, you don't give Peter's answer, you give "four spiritual laws." You don't give the answer of Pentecost, the answer of Paul or the answer of the college of the apostles.

Evangelical Y: How about John 3:16—will that do?

Warren Lewis: For a start. "...that whoever believes in him..." (that's what John 3:16 says) "and is baptized" (that's what Matthew 28 says) "and is baptized, will be saved..." (that's what Mark 16 says).

This is no idle theology. Mark told us all about the gospel of Mark, but, in a very real sense, the gospels belong to the time before the cross, before the death, burial, and resurrection of Jesus—only after the resurrection of Jesus, the bodily, physical resurrection of Jesus which bespeaks our own bodily, physical resurrection in the day of His coming, can we begin to talk about salvation, forgiveness of sins, and so forth. The thief on the cross was saved the way anybody else was saved during the life of Jesus—He could save you on the spot because He was God; but, after the resurrection, and after the Apostles' doctrine becomes the way to come to God, then baptism is essential for salvation.

Rod Sawatsky: Would some Evangelicals like to speak to that question of Warren's reading of the Bible?

Warren Lewis: I agree with Catholicism, with the Orthodox, though I disagree with them about which specific individuals to baptize—they do it to babies, but Scripture says it ought to be done to believers. The teaching of the church for 2,000 years is clear; it's only you Johnny-come-lately Calvinists who have changed it. Speak up, Brother Luther. (laughter)

Don Deffner: I'll just quote Augustine, "It is not the lack of baptism, but the contempt of it, that damns."

Warren Lewis: Good, good.

Richard Quebedeaux: Pragmatically, that's been an evangelical problem. How do we regard the sacraments? It's not only baptism, but the Lord's Supper as well; they often seem totally unnecessary.

Warren Lewis: The Lord's Supper is the other side of my record. Shall I play it?

Richard Quebedeaux: And not only the lack of necessity of the sacraments or the ordinances, in fact, but also the lack of necessity of the institutional church—that's our real weakness. Campus Crusade's "four spiritual laws" are an example of that problem. Somehow that's enough, and, while it may in fact be that God's grace is enough (and I stand more over there than with you) it is a real lack in our Christian life. And though I would not stand with you on the absolute necessity of baptism, I think it *is* something that Evangelicals need to think about more.

Mark Branson: That hits one of my fears. If I might go back to the gospels, though, to the parable of the sower: some seeds fall on stony ground, and they spring up fast, and then wither away. The problem of those that are not faced with the issue of following Jesus when they're offered forgiveness is illustration here. I think Jesus very clearly teaches He doesn't just want people to come to Him for forgiveness—He teaches that He wants people to come to Him to follow Him. The problem of not teaching baptism, of not teaching obedience, is that you are really not teaching salvation.

Richard Quebedeaux: You've hit another thing, now, not only the sacraments and the church, but obedience...

Mark Branson: Well, that's where I think baptism is optional.

Richard Quebedeaux: I, too, have somehow made that optional. If you will ask an Evangelical after witnessing, etc., he or she would not say that; but in the pragmatic working out of the theology, that's been the problem...

Evangelical X: The struggle, though is in between, and it goes back to baptism. We're very afraid that you're going to have works without faith. We don't want to do that because we want to maintain vigorous faith, whereas a person who takes a leap of faith and just commits his life to Christ (and that really is salvation) is now in Christ. And we talk about obedience—do we do this, and not do that, be baptized, or not baptized?

Warren Lewis: We just don't want to add up our fasting and our keeping of the law, our merit. But, because God commands baptism for obedience to God's grace—that's where the essential nature of baptism comes in—if, in knowing the Scripture, you have not been baptized, you are not obeying God, you're not faithful.

Paul Eshleman: I think it harkens back to some of these other questions you want answered, one of them being at what point forgiveness occurs. In the Unification church, Frank mentioned, people might be in for a number of weeks or months, or whatever, during which time they would learn about Jesus and learn that He had forgiven their sins. Gradually, as they looked at all Unification teachings, one of their teachings would be simply that Jesus forgave all of their sins, and they would accept Christ too. I think that Evangelicals would say that, at the point when an individual exercises his faith and, in Warren's case, is baptized, at that moment he is forgiven for all sins, past, present, and future. Satan's bind on him has been broken, and now the sins that occur in his life are the sins that keep him from communion with God. So, there is a need for a continual repentance and confession, day by day and moment by moment, so that communion with God can be kept open.

Warren Lewis: What if you change your mind? What happens if you don't believe in Jesus, and repudiate your baptism, and return like pigs to wallowing in the mud?

Paul Eshleman: I leave that to the Lord.

Evangelical X: Well, it depends on whether you're a Calvinist or an Arminian. (laughter)

Don Deffner: Just in terms of phrases you used earlier, it is not really *our* struggle, but I like the way that Paul paraphrases I John 4:17, "So that our life lived in this world is actually His life lived in the world. Christ in us now, a new creation."

Warren Lewis: It doesn't have anything to do with being an Arminian. When the Israelites passed through the Red Sea, they were baptized, and they were forgiven all the Egyptian connections; and then they wildernessed for forty years, and later crossed the Jordan into Canaan. But, how many of them fell from grace during those forty years and didn't enter Canaan-land?

Paul Eshleman: I think the question Dan raised was how the blood of Jesus affects your life in the kingdom. You don't get into the kingdom outside of the blood of Jesus; without accepting His shed blood, you don't enter the kingdom.

Dan Davies: What I am wondering is what your relationship to Jesus will be when you're in the kingdom. You now have a way of reaching God through the blood of Jesus. But, when you're in the kingdom, will you still need the blood of Jesus for salvation? What happens to the blood?

Paul Eshleman: It washes away the sins. My purpose, once I'm in the kingdom, is to be conformed into the image of Christ.

Dan Davies: But that would take on a secondary importance, then, wouldn't it? Wouldn't you then be under salvation?

Paul Eshleman: Once we start talking about being conformed in the image of Christ, then we are into what you talk about in terms of restoration. We're talking about becoming all that God originally created us to be—that we might be energized by His spirit and we might demonstrate the qualities of His life. If our purpose, to get back to the Westminster Catechism, *is* to glorify God, so that if people looked at us they might see who God really is, and how great He is, then what keeps me from glorifying God is my ego-centered self-nature. What I need now is God's nature to come and live in me. I need to give Him total, unlimited access to live and walk around in my body. I still have the problem of my sinful nature. I don't deal with my sinful nature by trying to be physically married to another family. I deal with my sinful nature by means of the indwelling Holy Spirit, who I allow, then, to reflect His nature in me.

Johnny Sonneborn: How do you allow it? It seems that one moment you're having difficulty, and the next you are allowing the Spirit to indwell?

Paul Eshleman: When I realize that my life is not reflecting God's life, it usually means that I am going my way rather than His way, and that simply calls for a confession of that attitude, to say, "I now affirm again that I want You to direct my life, God." In repentance, it calls for growing up in that faith, and many things are involved, but it's not a grinding out of my own energy. It's totally centered on Him who works in me, to help me want to do what He wants me to do.

Johnny Sonneborn: Isn't confessing and repenting the same thing as cleaning up your life? Repentance is cleaning up, and then you give the Holy Spirit more room to act.

Evangelical Y: No, not really, if I could speak to that—it's known in good evangelical terminology as besetting sin. What do you do with some sinful habit pattern in your life that continually keeps cropping up? In my own experience, it's a matter of confession and turning from that mentally...

Don Deffner: Once we commit ourselves to the meaning of baptism and the holy communion, that inner commitment is what saves us, and the sacraments are the means by which we express outwardly that inward experience. And so, I'd like to explain my experience by putting on the board the formula for salvation: $S = F \rightarrow W$. Not F & W (faith plus works), but F with an arrow pointing to works. So, I like what Warren said: that baptism is the first step of obedience after faith, so it's not the baptism that saves...

Warren Lewis: That's not what Warren said.

Don Deffner: Isn't that what you said? Baptism is faith's work, faith's first work, or something like that?

Warren Lewis: Baptism is not a "work." Baptism is a part of faith. Just because it's a physical action, doesn't make it a "work." "Works" were the doing of the Law of Moses.

Evangelical X: I think it's a matter of semantics...

Warren Lewis: No, because you have posed the question to which the Quakers return the proper answer, "Well, if baptism accomplishes no more than what you say, then why bother? Go ahead and have the internal stuff and forget all this external show. It doesn't really accomplish anything."

Evangelical Y: No way. Faith without works is dead but a saving faith is a faith that works. You can't isolate the two...

Warren Lewis: Then what does it accomplish?

Evangelical X: I draw a circle around the faith with an arrow pointing to works...

Warren Lewis: But I'm not talking about "good works."

Evangelical X: ...and that is, it's all packaged. You can't separate the two. The faith and the works go together.

Warren Lewis: I perfectly agree, but I'm not talking about "works." I'm talking about baptism, which is faith—bodily, active faith.

Evangelical X: Yes, but the danger of suggesting that you're saved by going through a ritual...It's not mature.

Warren Lewis: It isn't a ritual.

Evangelical Y: But for some people it may very well be.

Warren Lewis: For some people *faith* is a ritual.

Evangelical X: Not in other people's minds.

Warren Lewis: And not in the sense that I'm defining baptism...

Evangelical Y: Well, you're talking about the inner reality, aren't you?

Warren Lewis: No. I'm talking about your physical body which is going to be resurrected someday; just as surely as your heart needs the invisible blood of Jesus, your physical, visible body needs the washing of the waters.

Evangelical X: What do you do about the soldier dying on the battlefield who has no opportunity to be baptized?

Warren Lewis: He is in the same situation that the unwashed Hindus are, and we can go through that if you like.

Evangelical Y: You mean he's not better off than they are? Even if he confesses Christ as his Saviour?

Warren Lewis: He's no worse off than they are. We don't change the biblical doctrine of baptism to cope with a special case. The New Testament teaches what it teaches about baptism, namely that it washes sins away—Acts 22:16. What are you going to do with that?

Evangelical X: It isn't the water, it's the blood that cleanses.

Richard Quebedeaux: Is that a doctrine throughout the whole Campbellite tradition, or just Churches of Christ? Is it also the Disciples?

Warren Lewis: The Disciples have given it up playing footsie with the Presbyterians.

John Scanzoni: I've just a few observations. I was discussing with a few Unification people at lunch today how, when the Evangelicals talk here, we constantly bicker with each other, and disagree violently, whereas when they present things, why it's very much a systematic and orderly whole.

Paul Eshleman: Well, we didn't invite Warren to be on our side! (laughter)

Warren Lewis: That's just the grace of God! (laughter)

John Scanzoni: The other observation was—I'm not sure if it's appropriate here—that we're talking about salvation on such a personal level. And I notice that before, when the Unification people were talking about salvation, they moved from the personal level to the group or societal level, and one of the problems we have is that we don't know how to do that. I mean, there are various ways, the Anabaptist way, the Calvinist way, but neither has worked very well. We don't have as neat a way as they do of going from personal salvation to group salvation. We just don't have that.

Dan Davies: I'd like to go back to the question that Paul brought up, namely, will the blood of Jesus and the sacraments still be necessary for salvation in the kingdom? In other words, how do you see life in the kingdom?

Paul Eshleman: You're talking about after the King comes back?

Dan Davies: Right. Will it be necessary to preach the salvation through the blood of Jesus when He returns?

Paul Eshleman: When Christ comes back again, it will be a different situation. There will be a separating of those who have expressed faith in Christ from those who have not expressed faith in Christ, and those who have expressed faith in Christ will be taken to heaven, and those who have not will be entirely separated in hell. We would say that only those people who have accepted Christ will be in the kingdom, when it is established here on earth, or in a new kingdom in heaven.

Jonathan Wells: Were you just espousing the doctrine of eternal damnation, then? Some people eternally will be in hell?

Paul Eshleman: Yes.

Jonathan Wells: And do you also say that God has foreknowledge of which people are going there?

Paul Eshleman: Yes.

Jonathan Wells: So God creates certain people knowing very well that they're going to be eternally damned?

Sharon Gallagher: But it's not His will. He doesn't will that any of us should perish.

Jonathan Wells: O.K. So people are saved because God's grace saves them. Is that correct?

Paul Eshleman: Because they respond to His offer of grace.

Jonathan Wells: Well, maybe I'm pushing the Calvinist position too far. Do believers respond because of God's grace?

Paul Eshleman: Nobody can come to God unless the Spirit draws him. He can't come on his own.

Jonathan Wells: So God is now in the position of creating two classes of people. One class He knows He will give His grace to, and thereby save. The other class He already knows He will not give His grace to, and, whether He wills it or not, He knows that they are going to hell forever.

Paul Eshleman: What you've done is equate creation with foreknowledge.

Jonathan Wells: As I understand it, you're maintaining both of those, right?

Paul Eshleman: You've said that God has created some men as a class of people who will go to hell. I'm saying that God creates mankind and His foreknowledge says that He knows who will reject and accept; that doesn't mean that He's created us to reject.

Jonathan Wells: No, but He has foreknowledge before He creates them. Is that correct?

Sharon Gallagher: You're speaking on a human time continuum, though, and I don't think that time exists that way in the mind of God. I think it's a mystery, but I wouldn't say that God is creating and damning at the same time. I think He's creating and you're choosing.

Jonathan Wells: Yes. I know that doctrine and, you see, what the doctrine is saying is that people are saved only by the grace of God, and that, when He creates those people, or even before He creates them, He knows which ones He's going to give His grace to, and thereby save. And He knows before He creates someone what that person will do, namely reject Him, and therefore go to eternal damnation. But the person only rejects Him because God withholds His grace, because he's only saved by the grace of God.

Evangelical X: No. The person rejects because he misused his free will, his...no, scratch that. (laughter) "The origin of sin is the wrong choice of a free moral agent," was the phrase I wanted, so that my misuse of my freedom to reject God is the origin of my lostness. God had the intuitive feeling, the fore-knowledge of those who would not have faith but God didn't damn me. God would have all men saved and come to the knowledge of truth.

Jonathan Wells: O.K. If God knows in advance that a certain individual will in his free will reject God, why did God create that person?

Paul Eshleman: That I'll leave in the mystery of God. I'm not God. I cannot know the mind of God, but I can declare a loving God who wants all persons to be saved.

Jonathan Wells: But who creates someone knowing very well the person will spend eternity in hell.

Evangelical X: Free will is a bonafide choice to accept or reject.

Jonathan Wells: Not to accept, because we accept only by the grace of God. We don't have the free will to turn to God.

Joseph Hopkins: What you're describing is fatalism.

Jonathan Wells: Some people would argue that, but what I'm arguing is the Augustinian viewpoint maintained by Calvin, namely that we come to God only by the grace of God and that, if we turn away from God by misusing free will or by rejecting the grace, God knows before He creates us what we're going to do and yet creates us anyway to spend eternity in hell.

Warren Lewis: And just to lend a little bit of support, because Jonathan is accurate in his historical theology at this point; what about the babies who inherit original sin who will burn forever in that same devil's hell?

Sharon Gallagher: What I'm hearing is that God picks and chooses who He gives His grace to. But He gives common grace to everybody. You see this in Romans I, which is the basis for which God can judge everybody and set down certain things. We're made in the image of God, and we can see God in creation. It's a common grace, so nobody is without excuse. So I'd say the point is not as though God would say, "Well, I'll give you some grace;" we all have some kind of grace and we accept or reject it. An infant does not reject God's grace and so is not accountable.

Jonathan Wells: O.K. Well, there are two different doctrines. One says the grace is irresistible. The other says it's not. You're saying it's not irresistible. But I'm saying that, according to Augustine and Calvin, God knows before He creates someone that that person will reject the grace and therefore spend eternity in hell. O.K., now what I'm saying is that God knows beforehand if someone is going to accept that grace and go to heaven. Right? Is that true? God knows beforehand what we're going to do with the grace that he offers. Now it's no restriction, presumably, on our free will for God to know that I'm going to accept His grace and go to heaven, according to that doctrine, right?

Rod Sawatsky: It's irresistible?

Johnny Sonneborn: It's not irresistible at a given time, but it *becomes* so irresistible that finally the last person who is left by himself—he's been with Satan, a hold-out—says, "Now I see."

Rod Sawatsky: So that Unification church is ultimately universalistic.

Johnny Sonneborn: Oh, yes, for sure.

Jonathan Wells: Wait. A person can stay in hell as long as he wants. Nobody is automatically saved. Somebody could conceivably choose to stay in hell for a very long time. God can't force him out or even, maybe, attract him out. But that's not the point I want to address. You mentioned foreknowledge. If you have an omnipotent, omniscient God (one who foreknows) and, at the same time, a benevolent God, then you have a contradiction if you have eternal damnation. It's like saying that God can make a square circle. You're no longer making sense. If God knows before He creates me that I will reject His grace and go to eternal damnation, then it does no good to say that we are talking about two different time concepts, because you've already called the consequences of my temporal sin eternal. O.K., so you've already transcended the time boundary, whatever it is. Foreknowledge is a problematic concept. What Unification theology would say on this point is that God gives man free will, and thereby voluntarily limits His own foreknowledge. I mean, He doesn't know what you are going to do with your free will, in an absolute sense.

Evangelical X: Where does it say that in the Bible?

Jonathan Wells: But that's the clear implication of it. Well, I'll explain. God didn't know that Adam and Eve would fall.

Johnny Sonneborn: He saw they were going to fall but He didn't intervene.

Jonathan Wells: Here we go. Here's a disagreement. He knew they *could* fall, Johnny; He didn't know when He created them that they *would* fall. If, from the beginning, He knew they *would* fall, that would be absolute foreknowledge. Now, it also says that, when Jesus came, God wanted people to accept Him. We come right back to the problem of the mission of Jesus. God knew there was a possibility that Jesus would be rejected, but God did not foresee 100% that Jesus would be crucified. Now, all these issues tie together and hang on this question of absolute foreknowledge. Given the fact of evil, it is contradictory to maintain absolute foreknowledge, free will and benevolence at the same time.

Richard Quebedeaux: And, in that context, you can have a suffering God, who suffers when a person chooses hell, and a God who dialogues.

Jonathan Wells: Right, in a real sense.

Dan Davies: One thing I would like to draw out of this argument when we're talking about justice: actually, there can't be justice without mercy, without love. Mercy is an aspect of justice; any good judge knows that. I think, in this respect, we have something to learn from the Buddhists. Because, in their concept of the Bodhisattva, the person who comes to the highest experience of God goes back to the world until every last person returns to God. I think this shows God's heart. God will not be happy until every person returns to Him.

Richard Quebedeaux: Could you explain heart? That's been mentioned a million times. How does that fit into your theology? What does it mean?

Johnny Sonneborn: God's heart is His impulse to give love, unceasingly. That is God's heart in relation to creation. God's heart in relation to the fall is His suffering heart. Then, there is God's heart in relation to restoration. This is the heart of compassion that desires our growth in faith and the learning and doing of his will.

Richard Quebedeaux: And the word "heartistic" which you have invented, what does that mean?

Patricia Zulkosky: I think it means pertaining to matters of the heart. So, if you say someone is a very heartistic person, we use that to mean that he is a person who radiates God's love and somehow emanates goodness and a good feeling.

Richard Quebedeaux: Can you identify people who have that quality?

Patricia Zulkosky: Yes. I think they are people who have grown and have developed a parental heart.

Nora Spurgin: We don't necessarily always put a value judgment on it. Sometimes we use it — heartistic — just as a description.

Tirza Shilgi: How about simply the German *Herz*. Isn't that the same thing, Franz?

Franz Feige: Yes, but I think heart is deeper. It does not just pertain to emotional feelings. It also pertains to intellect and will, having the right understanding, and right purpose. *Herz* is not enough.

Rod Sawatsky: Let's call it a night!

HERESY AND COOPERATION

Rod Sawatsky: I wonder if we can switch gears again, and introduce one more subject—the question of heresy. I think there's no doubt that the Evangelicals consider the Unification people heretics...

Jonathan Wells: And also some other Evangelicals! (laughter)

Rod Sawatsky: ...and I sense that most of the Unification people aren't too upset about being considered heretics; in fact, they own that category for themselves, in terms of the Christian orthodox tradition. But the question that I'd like to raise for the Evangelicals is this: "Is Unification Christian?"

Paul Eshleman: I think that whole area is one of the questions I had to wrestle with the most before even coming to the last dialogue here, and I think that before coming someone from the Unification church may not have understood the things going through the mind of an Evangelical. The Moonies say, "Why can't we simply have fellowship? Yes, we have disagreements, but why can't we simply get together?" There is a very strong allegiance by most Evangelicals to the scriptural passages which say "Whosoever preaches any other gospel outside of this one, let him be accursed.... Come out from among them and be separate. ...Have no fellowship with the unfruitful works of darkness." These kinds of Scriptures come to the mind of an Evangelical as he relates to a doctrine of heresy leading people not to trust *fully* in Jesus for their salvation. These verses cause a person to ask himself, "Am I doing something that really is against a direct commandment of Scripture by coming to have fellowship?" At the same time that those words go through the evangelical mind, there are also the commandments of Jesus to love one another. I just give that as a context for the discussion so that there's a realization on the Unification side that these are questions probably not totally sorted out in everyone's mind. And because Evangelicals rarely come in contact with outright heresy—usually it's doctrine-splitting items between denominations—these are issues that haven't been dealt with very often.

Frank Kaufmann: In light of that, when it really becomes a matter of how an Evangelical responds to a command in Scripture, then I'd like to consider more precisely what heresy is and the question: Is the Unification church, in the most strict and most serious sense of that word, heretical? Then the word heresy isn't just our usual joke, considering how the Evangelical has to respond to the Unification church. I personally don't consider Unification doctrine heretical.

Rod Sawatsky: What do Unification people say? Do you call your faith Christian heresy? Do you call yourself Christian? I wonder how many Unification people would not consider themselves Christians.

Paul Eshleman: There are some.

Rod Sawatsky: What I sense is that some don't.

Franz Feige: I think that when we Unificationists refer to ourselves as Christians, we mean something different perhaps than orthodox or evangelical Christians do when they refer to themselves as Christian.

Rod Sawatsky: Let's let Evangelical Y go first.

Evangelical Y: It seems to me that words, to have any function in language, have to have boundaries. And the question I would raise to Unification people would be this: Are Christian Scientists Christian? Are Jehovah's Witnesses Christian? Are Mormons Christian? If the answer is yes, then I'll go on and try Jews and Zoroastrians and Buddhists, until I find the answer "no." Then I'll begin to work my way back and ask how you sorted them out. And I would object to using the word "Christian" for Unification theology on the same ground that I object to using "democratic" for East Germany or some of the Eastern European countries. Because, it seems to me to mean something fundamentally different from what I mean by the word "democratic," and that isn't a very helpful thing to take a word that has a reasonably established meaning and toss it over to cover a whole bunch of other things that just weren't originally covered by that term.

Richard Quebedeaux: Yes, but if you don't like to refer to the Unification *movement* as Christian, in view of what people have said here, does that mean that Unification *people* are not Christian? Or if they are, is that by accident, or because they don't understand Unification theology thoroughly enough?

Evangelical Y: Well, now, we're making a distinction, aren't we, between the Unification movement as a movement and as an institution versus individuals in it.

Richard Quebedeaux: Right. But if individuals are in a movement which is not Christian, but *they* are Christian, is that an accident? Do you know what I mean?

Patrick Means: Not necessarily. You take the movement, for instance, of Witness Lee and the "Local Church." My experience has been that the majority of the members in that movement are born-again Christians, in that case, primarily because their whole proselytizing strategy is to go to new Christians and suck them into that movement. Their doctrine, however, is heretical in a couple of key areas, and we couldn't label the movement as a Christian movement or a Christian belief system despite the many Christians within it. The Christians are there because of the strategy of the parent organization. I'm not saying that's the strategy here.

Richard Quebedeaux: I'm not sure that I would agree with you that it's not a Christian movement. I would call Witness Lee's "Local Church" a heretical (or heterodox) Christian movement; I personally would call the Mormons a non-Christian movement. And heterodoxy isn't quite as bad as heresy. Or so orthodox Christians would say.

Jonathan Wells: We need a more precise definition of what *Christian* is.

Warren Lewis: That is exactly what I was going to say. It'll turn into a semantic wrangle if we're not careful, but we do need to get our definitions clear. Is a Christian a person who belongs to Christ? (Which, I take it, was the New Testament meaning.) Is a Christian a person who thinks he's a Christian and tells you so? Or, is a person a Christian who *you* think is a Christian? Can you be a heretic and still be a Christian? If you're heretical, if you're in error, if you're nonbiblical, in some of your doctrine, in the majority of your doctrine, can you still be a Christian? Is a Catholic a Christian if he still believes that the Blessed Virgin is the mediatrix of grace along with her Son?

Rod Sawatsky: We have several comments open. Do you have anything?

Evangelical X: The Christian is an impossible notion. Besides, it just doesn't work when we're talking about individuals. I think you have to hold to institutional theologies or positions, because if you get down to individuals it's impossible. Finally, anyway, it's God's business.

Warren Lewis: Is the Divine Principle, then, as a system of theology, a Christian one? What characteristics would it have to portray in order to be a Christian system of theology?

Johnny Sonneborn: I would hope that either your impression of this dialogue or the previous dialogue will give you a basis for understanding our position. This is how I would summarize the situation: the Unification position has agreed with important aspects of the evangelical position—except on the questions of the second coming and whether or not Jesus intended to die, but for me these are not crucial differences. What's crucial is what's left to be done! Of course the Evangelicals here have not agreed with the Divine Principle position on the second coming, but the Evangelicals themselves are not sure what is going to happen at the second coming. Therefore we are preaching, in my judgment, the same gospel. But we're also adding some understandings— everybody has to, to a certain extent, in order to live—and these can be debated as to whether or not they are dangerous under- standings. I hope you would not say that we are not Christians.

Paul Eshleman: That's the same gospel in India, though. I pick up a little thing that in India or other cultures it may not be so necessary to believe or trust in Christ as personal Saviour.

Johnny Sonneborn: I'd also like to say, suppose the Divine Principle is wrong and Jesus comes on the clouds, then what will happen to us? First of all, in that case we will see Him, and also He will gather to Him not those saying, "Lord," not those with a bright theology, but those who acted and cared for other people. And maybe also those who were not ashamed of Him. And also Jesus said anyone who was healing or exorcising in His name was not to be hindered. So maybe we would be those Christians.

Evangelical X: I would think the Apostles' Creed would be a good test of who is or is not a Christian.

Warren Lewis: What's your chapter and verse for use of the Apostles' Creed there, brother? That's good *second* century

Christianity.

Evangelical X: I mean, you have to start somewhere, and I say most of the evangelical churches would agree on the Apostles' Creed. If you want chapter and verse, of course, you can go through it and then go to the Scriptures.

Jonathan Wells: Is that true, Richard?

Richard Quebedeaux: That's a confessional credal position. I would say that more universal among Evangelicals is that we start with the Bible. The creed is a testimony to the truth rather than a requirement. I happen to feel that a lot of people who join your movement do become Christians in the process, but they may go *beyond* that belief-wise. I think it's the "beyond" that is wrong, yet much of the *practice* beyond that is right. That's why you're a judgment on us "orthodox" Evangelicals.

Sharon Gallagher: I really want to ask just one thing that will help clarify some of this discussion for me before we get into all Evangelicals saying what a Christian is. It relates to something Paul asked about for Hindus. "O.K.," he said, "some of the members in your group wouldn't consider themselves as Christians; some would." Do the people who consider themselves Christian in the Unification church do so because that was their second step? In other words, they were born into a Christian culture. If you went to Japan and someone was into Confucianism would you see that as the preparation for accepting the third advent? Would you preach Jesus Christ?

Johnny Sonneborn: Yes. Jesus Christ. And many people who weren't Christian before they came to the Unification church consider themselves Christians now because Rev. Moon has identified himself as a Christian, and he's urged us to. Yet you've all been given, by people who are critical of us, selections from *Master Speaks* and passages from it, and from training manuals, but once you read a large quantity of *Master Speaks* you'll find out that what he's teaching us about Jesus is that he's exalting Him, and teaching us to love Jesus and walk Jesus' way or come to His standard.

Anthony Guerra: It is interesting to note that recently a few missionaries to Islamic countries asked Rev. Moon if they could teach the Divine Principle with less Christian emphasis. He said, point blank, "no" to that request.

Nora Spurgin: I wanted to comment on that. Actually this has happened. We have our own little territories within our own movement that are trying to relate the Divine Principle to other cultures, especially our missionaries who are out there translating *Divine Principle* into these languages. The question has come up frequently, and always the answer is absolute. The Divine Principle stands as it is, going straight through the Christian concept of salvation through Jesus Christ. Therefore, the desire to translate the D.P. from a Koran point of view using Koran verses—which are very supporting many times—is absolutely forbidden; you can't do it. The same thing did happen in Japan, where some of our members tried to do it from a Buddhist point of view and Rev. Moon came through and said absolutely not. So our Japanese members many times become much more devout Christians than we are. They're reading the Bible. Why? Because they don't have that background and they have to gain it in order to understand the Divine Principle.

Mark Branson: I see a basic problem which permeates everything, so I really disagree with Richard. I see that you've got a different definition of sin, a different definition of what happened on the cross, a different definition of salvation, a different definition of glorification. I believe that once Jesus is not *the one* trusted for salvation, you do not have a Christian system. That's crucial. Now, I'm not saying that there aren't Christians in the movement. I have to say that, as a Christian, I understand the theology to be far wide of Christianity.

Richard Quebedeaux: Let me ask you, are they not trusting Jesus for salvation? Let's not talk definitions. Are they? Or aren't they?

Mark Branson: I'd say they teach "Jesus plus other ingredients."

Richard Quebedeaux: But that's different.

Warren Lewis: So do the Catholics.

Evangelical Y: The church ran up against a parallel situation in the second century when it had to deal with gnosticism. They used the same vocabulary that the church used but the church said, "You mean by this something very different," and it totally excluded gnosticism. I hear the same vocabulary being used, but I hear very different kinds of meanings being put into it, so I have to say it's a very, very parallel situation, and I don't see it as being Christian at all. It's the same vocabulary, but different kinds of concepts are being used.

Richard Quebedeaux: Gnosticism is a heresy. We're talking

about heresy. Pelagianism was a heresy. But there are degrees of heresy. Would you say that all Pelagians weren't Christians?

Evangelical Y: I'm not talking about who's Christian. I'm talking about...

Richard Quebedeaux: Yeah, O.K., but we *are* talking about systems of heresy. Now Mark said, "Trusting Jesus." I know that when Unification people speak they do use different definitions. I'm not so sure that it's *altogether* a different definition. I think there is a spectrum of meaning within the definitions. I don't think all Evangelicals agree on what salvation is. Jim Wallis of *Sojourners* does not agree with Bill Bright (of Campus Crusade) on what salvation is, and his new book, I think, is going to show that. Now that's what I'm talking about. This whole issue of heresy versus orthodoxy—that's the problem.

Patricia Zulkosky: I guess for me it's hard to really get into this whole topic. The way I deal with the whole question is very simple. I think the way of life that Jesus taught is the most essential. I went to the Jesus '78 rally last year, which I understand was charismatic and not evangelical, and Jim Bakker, from the *Praise the Lord* television show, told a story that made an impact on my life such that I can't accuse *anyone* of heresy.

Jim Bakker was getting criticized for having all of these heretics and other people on his television show who weren't fundamental. And so he really had to pray about it and ask God, "Well, what am I supposed to do?" and the message he received, and the message that's become the slogan for *my* life is, "You love them, and I'll judge them." I can't know what's going on inside the hearts of people, and if I make judgments such that I fail to love, then I'm definitely not Christian. Therefore, for me that one sentence has been the most powerful thing in my life, when it comes to loving people regardless of their system of belief. I think I can really say, "I'm Christian" and do really what Jesus said to do.

Jonathan Wells: Just two points. One, two years ago Herb Richardson asked a class of students here at the seminary from all different religious backgrounds to take one of two positions: that the Divine Principle, that is, the theological position of the church, is a new Christian interpretation of the Scripture; or that the Divine Principle is post-Christian, going beyond the Scriptures. And I was in the class, and it split right down the middle. I mean, not physically, but half and half. O.K.? So, the membership of the

Unification church does not have an unequivocal answer to this question that we're discussing. That's one point.

Now the other point is a more confessional point on my part, and I'm not going to try to answer the question, except from a confessional standpoint. Too many times in the past four or five years I've found myself defending Unification theology, and in the course of that defending, at some risk to myself, God's creatorship, original sin, and the perfection and sinlessness of Jesus Christ. I think Evangelicals, more than any other class of Christians, know that the way you come to love Jesus most is by putting yourself out for Him. I mean, a love relationship is not a passive thing. And I just want you to know that Moonies risk something to defend Jesus in a world that has pretty much turned away from Him. Now, you may disagree with some of the other things that we say, but you can't take that away from us.

Paul Eshleman: I think, Jonathan, there's really good evidence to the fact that there has been much interaction between individuals about Moon and Christ. However, when you say that Rev. Moon is somehow on a par with Christ, you're denying the plan of God that everything would be summed up in Jesus. I can't put that together. As soon as I think of Rev. Moon and people praying to Moon or thinking about him...

Jonathan Wells: We don't pray to Rev. Moon.

Paul Eshleman: Well, meditating about him, thinking about him in their thoughts, dreaming, looking at his picture, all these kinds of things in a meditative situation. "Sometimes I think of Jesus, sometimes I think of Moon—I can't think of them apart from each other"—that's what just throws me, and throws me toward the heresy side.

Johnny Sonneborn: A couple of things. We tend to dream and think of Rev. Moon because we love him. You do with people you love, and it's different from thinking of God. He's not God.

The Lord of the Second Advent is not God in our theology. We think that all things were summed up in Jesus and they're actualized by the Lord of the Second Advent. It's a broadening out. It's doing greater things which Jesus promised every Christian can do.

Paul Eshleman: If you would say that Jesus is higher than Moon I would feel a lot better. Jesus is higher than Moon.

Johnny Sonneborn: Sorry, I can't make you feel better on

that.

First of all, we're a movement, we've a theology, and we're individuals. As a movement there isn't a single Unification person who doesn't want the whole country, America, the whole country of Korea, to turn to Jesus Christ. Maybe we don't know the right way of doing it and you do, but we have a strong desire, I mean, we always hope that Campus Crusade is going to turn everyone to Christ. We want Christ to be Lord. Those are the conditions for whatever else may happen. And also, Rev. Moon has said, and I don't think you'll find it in print, when he was giving instructions to a group of people who were being prepared to be married very shortly, that what you really must do to be blessed is to love God more than anyone else, and the standard for this is to love God as Jesus loved God. So Jesus was the standard in this way. I think this is an example of how he exalts Jesus to us.

Warren Lewis: That's really the right question. Where the piety is at is where the theological rhetoric has had its greatest impact. Whatever's tucked away in a "Black Book" somewhere, we can debate; but where does the movement live? Theology aside, I would say that Moonie preoccupation with the person and work of Rev. Moon is no more pervasive than some Catholic preoccupation with the Blessed Virgin, yet, we've learned not to excommunicate the Catholics. Rev. Moon himself is the paradigm of his movement; you have to take his person seriously. It was after all Jesus—not Buddha, not Confucius, not Mohammed—who appeared to Rev. Moon on the Korean mountainside in 1936. Now what do we Protestants do with Lourdes? With Fatima? With La Salette? Did she or didn't she? And if she did, what does it mean—for the grace of God, for continuing revelation, for the fact that God didn't retire 2,000 years ago, and that He might really do a new thing, a genuinely revelatory new thing in this world? Of course, the Catholics believe that He did by allowing the apparition of the Blessed Virgin. Now, in complete parallel to that, it was even God Himself, Jesus Christ, Our Lord, who, Rev. Moon says, appeared to him, and said, "Finish my work." That's what the Unificationists are trying to do: finish Jesus' work for Him. Now, isn't that Christian?

Joseph Hopkins: We Evangelicals see this as just one such phenomenon among many. Joseph Smith claimed that the Lord appeared to him in visions, too. Many other religious leaders have made similar claims—all of them in total contradiction to one another. So somebody has to be wrong. And we assume, from an evangelical viewpoint, that they're *all* wrong. In other words, and I don't mean this unkindly, they are all false prophets.

Johnny Sonneborn: Rev. Moon implores you, for your sake, to be humble about your beliefs, because so many people have thought they understood something, but there was more. This happened in Jesus' time and to other Christians many different times. You can't be sure that what you understand is revealed gospel.

Evangelical X: What about all those warnings that false prophets would arise in the latter days and deceive many, and so on?

Warren Lewis: But what you're saying is, "no prophets." You're not just saying "reject the false ones," you're saying, "no more prophets at all."

Evangelical X: If what they come up with coincides or is in harmony with the Bible as we understand it, then it's O.K.

Warren Lewis: You're operating there with an exclusiveness paradigm. But the Moonies are suggesting, and Catholics would have to agree, as would Mormons, that a paradigm change is needed. God is a God of pluralism, not uniformity; but in your psychological insecurity, when you exclude everybody but those who agree with you, that's an old-style paradigm which simply cannot cope with the reality of the world as the creation of the God who loves dappled things. God does not contradict Himself, you see.

Evangelical X: We find in the new movements contradictions to what the Bible seems to teach clearly about the nature of Christ, the nature of man, the way of salvation, and so on.

Jonathan Wells: You see, your interpretation of the Bible is inherently self-contradictory, as we realized earlier.

Johnny Sonneborn: The point is that it *seems* to you to contradict what *seems* to you to be the right interpretation of the Bible. But they said the same, too, of Jesus—they judged Him as a law-breaker and all these things. *Divine Principle* goes to great lengths to explain this, for *our* caution, not for any other reason. That's also one of the reasons for talking about how Jesus failed to be accepted; it's a message to us Christians now.

Warren Lewis: During the wars of religion we Arminians and Calvinists and Catholics and Lutherans were drowning one another and burning one another at the stake because of the point of view you have just expressed. Haven't we learned after four hundred years that that kind of rationalist approach just doesn't embrace all the reality there is?

Sharon Gallagher: I really feel that I have to say that in reading, to prepare for this weekend, a lot of the writings of Rev. Moon I was overwhelmed by his sense of blasphemy. I see him perpetrating for himself the descriptions that we have for Jesus Christ in the New Testament.

Thomas Bower: My comment will follow somewhat on that. I think that as an Evangelical, I'm sensitive to anything that comes on the scene as being defensible biblically. I had hoped that I could be a bit more exposed to Unification thinking about messiahship, and I have in private conversations. We haven't done a lot with it in a group. I have a feeling that although the definition of messiahship is probably quite new to me, that it may be defensible biblically, or at least plausible, and for me that's the crux of the issue: whether or not this is heresy or not, when Moon says these things about himself. What is the content of messiahship that allows him to do that? There's a whole pile of things there that I don't know and I have to reserve a whole lot of judgment until I study that issue.

Franz Feige: You know, Jesus Himself said very clearly what a Christian is. He didn't give us any creed. Did He give us a creed? I think He said, "You will know them by their fruits." It's very general. And He said another thing, that there are only two commandments that He gives us. The one is, "You shall love the Lord your God with all your heart..." (that comes from both the Old and New Testaments) and the other one, "You shall love your neighbor as yourself." I believe somebody who lives by that spirit lives according to Christ and lives with Christ, whether he's a Hindu, a Baptist, a Catholic. an Evangelical, or a Moonie. Christ did not give us a rational explanation. He really left it very open. I think we should not impose our own judgment upon it. Let's leave it open by Christ's words. Let us know them by their fruits.

Dan Davies: I agree with you in this respect, Franz, that that's the great commandment. I think it's also true, frankly, that anyone who really lives by that way will come to know Jesus Christ. You're right on target. I think that should be our focus. We should live loving God and all mankind.

Charles Barfoot: I'd just like to throw out a couple of things.

In my studies in theology and sociology of religion, I found that the worst thing that happened to pentecostalism, number one, was that it was influenced early by fundamentalism, and that, secondly, it became evangelical. In pentecostalism there was a spirit, there was a finding of truth, not in dogma but in dance, and those were beautiful days. Now pentecostalism is blending with everything else. So for me to become a Presbyterian was really no big switch. But it's the genuine sense of community I miss. I still feel at home, I guess, theologically, in a Presbyterian church. But I think what you people have—that spirit of community, you're brothers and sisters—I'll be hard put to find in the mainline church, or in an evangelical church. I worked in the fourth largest Presbyterian church in the U.S.—a church which considered itself evangelical as well—and if I ever have to repent for a year wasted of my life, it was that year. I don't sense a lot of that hostility here; there's a uniqueness here, and I'm saying that more I guess out of being a sociologist of religion than anything else.

Patrick Means: Let me just say something which I'm sure that all of us Evangelicals feel. There's never an excuse for a lack of love on our part toward you, and for those instances where well-motivated individuals have mistreated you, and have not related in love to you the way Christ would have us, we ask your forgiveness. We want to relate in love toward you because Christ commands us to do that and He empowers us to do that. I don't think as long as we have an agreement and a covenant among ourselves, Evangelicals, to be doing that toward our friends here in the Unification church, that we're going to see a new holy war break out. But the issue of loving you is a different issue than agreeing with your doctrine as it stands.

Evangelical X: I can say Amen to that.

Warren Lewis: Your personal attitude is great; it's your grasp of the situation that's rotten.

Evangelical X: I hope I'm not coming through as one who hates the Moonies or puts them down or as one who is about to lead an inquisition against the Moonies or anything like that. It's just a matter of what you identify as heresy. And that is what we're talking about. My spirit is one of love and I want to communicate that.

Warren Lewis: It's important for me to say that I acknowledge that: I am not impugning your motive or your love. But if it weren't for the federal court system in the United States, there would already be a holy war going on because of the deprogramming activities that have been unconstitutionally perpetrated against Moonies and other new religionists, precisely by American, middle-class Evangelicals, linked up with religionless hucksters. Fortunately, because of the separation of Church and State, and constitutional protections, it isn't going to get anywhere. It's being stopped; American civil liberties have protected them. But let's not forget that by fixing these nasty stigmas "heretic" and "cult" with all of their historical meaning, the National Council of Churches and the media and you all in a fine spirit of the Dark Ages are saying, "Open season on Moonies!"

Rod Sawatsky: I think we're going to stop right here, if for no other reason than simple exhaustion. (laughter) Dinner is at 6:30. We've an hour to recover a little. See you all there.

(BREAK)

Rod Sawatsky: What we want to do is continue the question of how Evangelicals read Unification and Unification reads Evangelicals, but in this case we want to begin by talking about what, if anything, Unificationists and Evangelicals can do together. Is there any kind of enterprise, say in the area of concern for religious liberty or for social issues, that these two groups can do together? Can heretics and evangelical Christian people proceed together?

I'd like to ask the people here from, for example, Campus Crusade and Inter-Varsity if you would allow Unification people to work with you in building the kingdom of God.

Patrick Means: Why do you pick on us? (laughter)

Rod Sawatsky: I had to pick on somebody! (laughter)

Patrick Means: Could you work with them in the Mennonite church? (laughter)

Rod Sawatsky: My answer is no! (laughter)

Paul Eshleman: I think the question is an attempt to understand what the Scriptures, as we interpret and understand them in Campus Crusade, say about having fellowship with those who do not preach the gospel. I think that we spent the day trying to ask, does the Unification church approach the basics of the Christian faith in a way that would allow us that kind of working together situation? Because I can't hear that Jesus is greater than

Rev. Moon, I sense that He is not the only begotten Son of God, our Saviour, and that pushes me in a direction that the doctrine is heretical. Because of this and other obvious teachings that border on blasphemy, I would be disobedient to Scripture to enter into any united venture.

Could I ask it from the other way? Why would Moonies want to work with the Evangelicals?

Rod Sawatsky: O.K., let's ask that question.

Anthony Guerra: There's a large area of activity that our church is involved in right now, from social programs in Harlem to daily newspapers and, of course, several direct witnessing and teaching programs. For some of those programs we probably would gladly work with any organization or individuals who would be willing to help. In our view of restoration, we believe that we have to carry out activity on all levels. Our primary activity in the church, of course, is spiritual: witnessing and teaching. But at the same time we feel responsibility for social programs and we would want to work with anyone with the necessary preparation in carrying out the work of God. I know we certainly wouldn't require anyone to sign a confessional statement.

Paul Eshleman: You wouldn't want anybody around, though, that thought Rev. Moon was just another man.

Anthony Guerra: Well, I'm not sure about that. We certainly have worked with people who don't think of Rev. Moon one way or the other. I would certainly find it uncomfortable to work with anyone who had a very disparaging view of Rev. Moon, but I would be uncomfortable with anyone who had a very disparaging view of any human being.

Dan Davies: It may be good to draw a distinction between working with somebody and joining them. I think it's all right to have your own convictions and faith and to work with somebody else who has his own convictions and faith. Let me make that clear. But if we work on a common project, this is not saying you believe what I believe.

Mark Branson: The difference is between co-believers and co-belligerents. Inter-Varsity has published a book which disagrees with the Unification church and discourages deprogramming. Being identified as a common fellowship, with the appearance of agreeing on the same motivation, the same ultimate goals, would not be acceptable.

Warren Lewis: It's a characteristic of Rev. Moon's whole program that the people who follow him shall cooperate in every possible way with all the religions of the world; and that doesn't exclude evangelical Christians. Christianity is conceived of as the highest religion on earth. Whether the Unification church itself is Christian or not, it has a built-in, permanent respect for the spiritual pinnacle of Christianity. I head up a project here to convene a global congress of world religions, and I'm in daily contact with all kinds of religions all around the world which, I must say, are much more irenic and ecumenical than half you Evangelicals. Take the Anglicans, for example. I went over to England and talked to Archbishop George Appleton, who used to be Bishop of Jerusalem and ran the World Congress of Faiths, and has lived all over the world. I came in and sat down, and he said, "I'm not interested in what the newspapers say. Just tell me about the man." You know how I talk and what my characteristic comments are; I was my characteristic self in his presence. At the end of an hour of talk as fast and hard as we could go, his comment was, "Well, unless there's something more that I don't know about" (and I told him more than I've told you) "there's no reason why we can't cooperate with you people."

Charles Barfoot: I'm sitting here with a mental picture of Sproul Plaza in Berkeley 3,000 miles away: there are three tables that you pass by if you go through there; one's Campus Crusade, one's CARP, one's Inter-Varsity. I wonder how much dialogue goes on among those three tables. I have a suspicion that they're almost like competing gas stations. (laughter)

Warren Lewis: They don't honor one another's credit cards.

Tom Carter: Somebody here mentioned causes. I'd like to address that and put it in a very broad perspective. God's three problems, the three problems that God has with the world, as we see it, are the decline of Christianity, the rise of immorality, and specifically, the rise of communism, which we think is a problem for all religions. So, in that kind of a broad perspective, as Warren said, we would be willing to work with just about anybody on those kinds of issues.

Tirza Shilgi: I think that a good example is this very seminary. The seminarians will become the leaders of our church, and Rev. Moon himself hired the faculty, ten of whom are not members of our church. So, speaking about cooperation, he took people that are not of our faith to educate the leadership of our church. You can't go much further than that, and they don't have any guidelines about what to say, what to teach, or anything. Warren can tell you that better than I can, but I think that's a pretty good example. That's Rev. Moon's direction, and he's not involved in the curriculum here at all; he doesn't give anybody direction.

Evangelical X: I bet you come pretty well steeped in Unification theology before you get here, though.

Patricia Zulkosky: Not necessarily. It depends on our previous experience in the church; a number of people have come from fundraising teams which have been fundraising two, or three, or four years. This means the only studying they did was on their own and not through any formal, systematic training. Some people volunteer to go on fundraising teams after having formal education of maybe a 7-day or at most a 21-day workshop. So many students have a very fundamental understanding of the Principle when they get here, and we don't have any formal Principle classes at the seminary, with the exception of one called Unification Theology and Christian Thought, which is a comparison of Unification theology to traditional Christian thought. Any other study is completely the extra-curricular activity of the students.*

Thomas Bower: Rod, this comment may be just a bit tangential, but maybe not. I can think of two areas where the Unificationists can help me in my work. One is dialogue with Islam. I think the Evangelicals are getting into that now in a more realistic, comprehensive way than they have been ever. And the Unificationists may have some insights there, at least on a dialogical level.

The other thing is that when Virgil asked me if I'd be interested in coming out, I thought, "What do I really want to learn from those people?" I'm not sure I'm going to learn it now because we're just going to run out of time, but I work with young people at a university, and I said, "Virgil, I'd like to know what those people are doing with what I consider to be the two most profound problems of our society: number one, sexuality; number two, authority." Perhaps these are separate agenda items, Rod, that we don't want to introduce, but they are agenda items that I think we could usefully tackle sometime.

Rod Sawatsky: Well, Tom raised the question of being able

---

*Subsequent to this dialogue, formal Divine Principle classes have been added.

to do things against communism. I know many Evangelicals who are very concerned about communism, and I know a lot of Evangelicals who are very concerned about immorality, and those are two key concerns of Unification. These are two areas where the two groups seem to have a common task.

Dan Davies: There's one further area—the decline of Christianity, or in other words, a need for the revival of Christian values. I think that's also a major concern for the Evangelicals.

Richard Quebedeaux: I just want to raise some questions. I don't expect answers but I have to raise the question. For example, Campus Crusade put together two programs called "Here's Life, America," and the "I Found It" campaign. Apparently, Campus Crusade had a set of standards about what churches could participate in this. Right? In terms of the basic Christian tradition, I happen to know that there were churches with ministers who as "functional atheists" were in "Here's Life" because the congregation may have wanted them, and the ministers said O.K. Is that bad? Is it worth working with a liberal Protestant who is a functional atheist? I say that with charity. Is it more O.K. working with him or her than working with a Moonie who is not?

Patrick Means: For clarification, it was up to the individual organizing committees in each city, committees made up of pastors, not Crusade staff, to decide who they would cooperate with.

Richard Quebedeaux: An hypothesis: Let's suppose that another situation parallel to Nazi Germany arises where the Christians, the believers, become the minority, and must resist. Would the Evangelicals refuse to cooperate with the Moonies in resistance to this sort of situation? What if the Moonies and Inter-Varsity, or some other group, are working underground in a communist country, and the same sort of resistance problems come. Are you going to say, "I can't resist with you. We're just going to have to work alone." It's interesting that the ecumenical movement was born on the mission field because of the competition when people there said, "Well, should I go with the Baptists or should I go with the Presbyterians? The Baptists say I have to be baptized by immersion; the Presbyterians say I don't." So the missionaries found out they *had* to get together or people wouldn't believe. I mean, they wouldn't know *what* to believe. They'd be confused. I think we're so much in an American context where there's so much freedom, maybe we ought to start thinking about a situation where there's persecution. Then we'll say, "Can we work together?" O.K.? Then, a harder issue is that of Evangelical statements of faith. I have the feeling that a lot of Moonies could sign many of those statements of faith with integrity. Wouldn't that be interesting? (laughter)

On the issue of social action, let's say, very few evangelical organizations have social action as a *priority* because they have other things to do. Campus Crusade has evangelism established as a priority. But almost all evangelical organizations feel that they need, somehow, to get into social action. What if the Moonies, with other people, put together some inner-city organization or work where there's a concrete possibility of really helping raise the oppressed? Wouldn't it be better, easier, for an evangelical organization to plug into *that* organization by sending representatives, than having to do it alone? I think that's one of the problems—that we need to work cooperatively because we just don't have the time and the personnel to do it ourselves. If our goals are the same in raising the oppressed in the city, say, through whatever means, is it O.K.? Religious liberties are something I think we'll get into a little later, but I would hope there would be some possible cooperation there.

Christians are commanded biblically to love not only one another, but even our enemies, which is the ultimate love. Evangelicals have for too long *spiritualized* love. It's so easy to say, "I love you," and do nothing about it. Words are words. I don't like the idea expressed this way: "Well, we're not going to persecute you. We'll tolerate you, but we're certainly not going to have any kind of fellowship with you." That is not love, that certainly isn't *agape,* because *agape* is self-giving, unconditional love. What is unconditional love? How do you demonstrate to somebody that you really love them unconditionally? That is, I think, the fundamental issue. Furthermore, I think that is the fundamental issue of the New Testament message, and that's what I have to grapple with in this whole business of relationships— not just working relationships but fellowship. I don't have an answer to that, but if we as Evangelicals and you as Moonies begin to contemplate that, and pray about it and think about it, we're going to come up with some very interesting answers, because I don't think we have ever really thought about it. We've thought about how we relate to our own, to our own brothers and sisters. You know, we've had a hard enough time with *agape* there. But what about our enemies? Didn't Jesus say, "Love your enemies?" *Agape* with your enemies—how do you do it? And it's unconditional, so what does that mean? That's what I have to say.

Paul Eshleman: Could I pursue that?

Rod Sawatsky: Sure, please do.

Paul Eshleman: To any Moonie, how can I show you that I love you?

Dan Davies: I can give you an abstract answer. I would feel you really love me if you love God with all your heart and mind and your whole strength, and also all mankind. If you sacrifice your life for God and that world, then I would feel you really love me.

Paul Eshleman: It's not very concrete to you, though.

Dan Davies: It is, actually. You know, it's hard to imagine, though, how many examples of this love we see. It's easy for us to be nice and pleasant, but that is far from the highest expression of love.

Warren Lewis: I'm absolutely moved by what Dan just said, because I know his answer is straight from Rev. Moon. That's exactly what Rev. Moon would have wanted said. He would not have wanted Daniel to say, "Well, may I come work for Campus Crusade?" or "Will you come to teach a course at the seminary?" Next time I'm with him, I'll tell him that you're a good boy. (laughter) That's really great.

Tom Carter: Maybe this isn't what Rev. Moon would want me to say. (laughter) To me a love relationship is exactly that—a love relationship. Yet this weekend, having met some of you and so on, I'm afraid somehow, that this might be the end of that relationship, and I don't want that to happen. So how can I show you I love you? It also means how can you show me you love me? I think we have to find a way to continue our relationship centering on God. Exactly what that means, I don't know. I don't know your specific programs, I don't know what your goals are, exactly, specifically. I'm sure you don't know what ours are. But I'm sure there's a way, for the sake of God, we can continue our relationship, and put our energy and efforts into a common direction, into a something.

Richard Quebedeaux: ...because love implies *continuance.*

Anthony Guerra: I feel love from all of you, and I feel love for you. I think love is a vague word, but taking the time to be together in this kind of serious dialogue, and further, for many of us, taking risks for each other, is love. I know, for example, Dr. Hopkins, who wrote a fair article on our first evangelical dialogue and received persecution for it, is a man who knew very well what he was doing in writing the article and that he would probably receive that kind of response. I felt that was an act of love and something I appreciate very much. Many of you are coming from backgrounds and from friends and colleagues who probably dislike Unification. If they, for instance, are on the extreme left politically, I am sure you will have to bear some criticism because we are anti-communist. If you are in an academic setting, your professors might suspect you are in danger of losing your critical powers of thinking. I would certainly cast your attendance here under these circumstances as love. Our church has for years received persecution from quarters with which you would identify yourselves, and yet the fact we have opened our seminary and invited you here, and we welcome you in the deepest sense, this is our expression of love for you. For all of us, our commitments that we will continue to do this is a further test.

Thomas Bower: I think that Dan's statement is something we dare not take lightly. I've been in both the liberal and conservative wings of the Presbyterian church. I think both need what Dan said about a theology of love. I was hit by it. I had really never heard that before either in the liberal or the evangelical wing of my church, and in many ways I would claim that neither wing really knows how to love, either. They both claim they know how to love better than the other wing. I have some questions about it.

Jonathan Wells: I'm also moved by the reciprocal nature of this relationship. I think that when we're talking about love, part of it involves confidence in each other. You know we're not going to leave here and bad-mouth you. I think one of my supper comments makes it clear that your press is as bad as ours is (laughter) in some places, and a dialogue like this, especially when it continues, gives us a foundation to testify to you as much as you can testify to us, of our basic desire to do God's will. And I think that's important.

Warren Lewis: Straddling the fence as I do, and genuinely trying to see it from both sides, I'm asking myself the question, "What does each side of this conversation have to gain from the other side?" At the level of genuine religion and morality, is there a trade-off between Evangelicals and Unificationists? I will try to formulate theologically what I could see happening. On the one hand, the Unification movement was born in a charismatic context in Korea. I am researching the roots of the movement and writing a book to be published by Beacon Press next year. It's clear to me at this point that the Unification movement is a cooled-off pentecostal movement; the experience of the gifts is a kind of an unexploded hand grenade. It's all there ready to go off. If I could get my Moonies together with some real charismatics, the potential for genuine, biblical, Spirit-directed charismatic piety would be great. It would be yet another Pentecost. That's what they could get from that kind of evangelical Christianity. In exchange for that, what they've got to offer is a specific charisma which St. Paul puts in the list: revelation. The Apostle Paul lists the gifts—tongues, singing, preaching, and words of wisdom, discernment of spirits, and includes revelation as one of the charismas of the spirit. Without getting into the particulars of Rev. Moon's doctrine, as a church historian I want to say that Sun Myung Moon, whether he's the Lord of the Second Advent or not, is probably the greatest living religionist alive. He is of the caliber of a Thomas, or a Luther, or an Augustine. He is a great living saint and mystic, and we will write about him for a thousand years in church history books.

Now, what do these great people contribute to the great church? One thing they contribute is a new vortex for the human storm during their lives. They come on the scene full of foolishness and full of potential. I wish Don were still here: think of Luther! What a difficult character he was, and yet how important he is to us all! What a fool Calvin was! Talk about the "puppet master!" Calvin's influence in Geneva was horrendous, and yet we wouldn't be anywhere without Calvin today. Now, Moon is with us. To live in his proximity, to know him, to eat supper with him, to watch him and his wife, to watch a truly great man of that caliber reformulate the Christian faith from his perspective, as Thomas and issue something that is genuinely new, something we've never had before in the history of the Christian faith—namely oriental Christianity—is an experience of revelation. Thorough-going oriental Christianity didn't exist before Moon. We're in the presence of a creative, theological novelty. The Unificationists have that to contribute, with everything it means. As an historian of Christian thought, I could literally go on for hours about what it means; and that's why I'm writing a book which I hope you will all buy and read. (laughter) I want to keep it in the charismatic context: Moon is a charisma that God has given the church, a special gift of heavenly grace.

My other point is this: the Unificationist understanding of Christianity and Jesus is that it is the highest religion. But half of these folk are, at best, half-pagan. Most of my Unificationist friends don't have much of a background in Christianity, haven't lived with it all their lives, like a lot of us Evangelicals have. Now, I know a lot of you guys are probably converts, too; but many Christians forget that most of the Moonies are half pagans; they're still learning and they admit it. They're still learning to catch up with us spiritually, because Rev. Moon has defined that Jesus Christ is the highest spirit in the universe. They're trying to internalize that teaching and they're trying to experience it. So, if they could rub shoulders with you Jesus-freak Evangelicals, then, the spirit of Jesus, whom they are taught to love and revere and worship and pray to and try to internalize, would rub off on them. And that would be good for them.

Patrick Means: I'm available for shoulder-rubbing. (laughter)

Warren Lewis: In return for that, in return for that close spiritual proximity (this is really off the wall, but I've got to say it) they could give you morality. I don't know an evangelical or pentecostal enclave where about half the people aren't messing around with the other half of the people. I often go to evangelical and pentecostal groups where the preacher is having an affair with the deacon's wife and the pianist is having an affair with the youth minister. Why is that?

Sharon Gallagher: That's a generalization you're making, Warren.

Warren Lewis: Well, that's my personal experience. If your place is doing better than my generalization indicates, then I congratulate you from the bottom of my heart. But I've tried to think theologically about this as well as emotionally, and I ask myself, why is this generally the case? Why is it that America is a moral wasteland? Why is it that the Christians are as susceptible to that as the pagans are? Why is there not a clear fix on sexual morality. As I was growing up, what could they tell me that would keep me out of bed with my girlfriend? "Jesus doesn't want me to?...The Bible says I shouldn't?...It's against the Ten Commandments?" All of that remained external, and unless I could be scared sufficiently of eternal hellfire, none of that stuff ever washed for me. It didn't wash for any of my friends, either, and I've never heard anybody yet from a standard Christian theological base make a cogent argument why you "shouldn't." I shouldn't quote stories from Harvard (we all know they're liberal), but usually the best reason there was, "It's not good for your person." And that made more sense. Now, what Unificationists have got is a rational program that is directly rooted in their theological world view which says it isn't just a "do" or a "don't" for Christian boys and girls. It relates directly to the innermost, essential nature of God. Every time one of God's children commits fornication or adultery, it absolutely rends the Father's heart because it tears Him in two. And there's a lot more to it than that, but the effect is that you've got people who are living for genuine holiness in an unholy world. And that's great stuff.

John Scanzoni: But Warren, that notion has been present certainly in pietistic Christianity, that rending of the Father's heart, that you're really obeying Christ because of an intimate personal relationship with Him. I don't think that's been absent, but it is certainly not part of the standard fare that is preached on Sunday morning because of the reasons that we were hearing this morning. But certainly it's been there. And that's been the motivation where it's worked to keep Evangelicals in a traditional obedience to the Ten Commandments.

Richard Quebedeaux: Yes, but I have to agree in terms of my experience. I agree exactly with you, Warren. I don't have to tell you, but everything he said is true in my experience, and I know that there are others here who would say the same. There are others whose experience is different.

John Scanzoni: But that's not the point. The point is we had that in our tradition.

Warren Lewis: You have to be patient with me 30 seconds more. That doesn't get it yet for the Unificationists. Because God for them is both male and female, God distilled His very essence in the first incarnation of His Logos and wisdom, which are His external attributes, in Adam and Eve. But, because of their sexual abuse of love, the original sin distorted all of human society in a pervasive, Freudian way. Unificationists thus have a theological grounding for morality, and for an indemnification of sexual immorality, which we do not have in traditional Christianity.

It isn't just that feeling of, "Oh, dear, it will hurt our Father in Heaven's feelings if we do it," but that the very Tao of the universe will be disrupted.

Evangelical X: But the problem there is that it exalts sexual sin. It gives it a proportion that is simply not in the Bible, at least from a traditional orthodox point of view. And it overlooks so many other sins, which are far more catastrophic in terms of their consequences.

Warren Lewis: That's easy to say when your great teacher was a celibate Jesus, a celibate Paul, and a widower named Peter. But we don't get good clear teaching from Scripture on sexuality and family life precisely because we're dealing with perpetual virgins. And that was capitalized upon by 1500 years of Roman Catholicism, which left us simply without decent teaching about sexual morality. We've had to do patchwork there. The Moonies, now, are saying: God has revealed Himself as a family.

Sharon Gallagher: I would like to say that I'm very grateful that I don't run in the same circles as Warren and Richard, and I'm glad what has been described here is not in my experience at all. I'd like to say that in my church and community, people are excommunicated for sexual immorality that we know about. In the Christian evangelical school I went to it was the same thing, and I think if anything, sexual sin is overly stressed. I don't think that it should be ignored, but it has been stressed to the exclusion of almost any other sin.

Evangelical X: That's exactly right.

Warren Lewis: Oh, I perfectly agree with that. The question is, are you as good at putting sinners back together again as you are at excommunicating? I know precious few who are.

Evangelical X: Well, Sharon's point may not be the same kind of answer that you're arguing it is.

Charles Barfoot: I'd have to say that at least in classical pentecostalism, ministers are defrocked for immorality for at least a year, and that stigma usually stays with them unfortunately.

Jonathan Wells: The point that interests me about this particular approach is that I find that Unification theology gives me an internal strength that I did not find in traditional Christianity for prevention of this problem. As I listen to this, personally, I'm less concerned with how we punish somebody after the fact, than how we build in people the internal fortitude to overcome it altogether. And you can say that other sins are more damaging, but I would say, consistent with Unification theology, that they all can be traced back to a form of selfishness which is best overcome on the personal level by this kind of internal strength that we're talking about.

Dan Davies: One thing I can see, in terms of what Warren is saying, is that in looking at Christianity in terms of a process, right now evangelical Christianity is a bastion of morality for the Christian world. But isn't it true that evangelical Christianity is beginning to liberalize now, and that as it begins to liberalize and take a different view of the Bible, then Evangelicals' morals may begin to deteriorate? That's a real great danger. Frankly, I don't want to see that happen. I mean, I'd like to see narrow attitudes toward the Bible change, but I don't want to see morality deteriorate.

Evangelical Y: There's no official policy, Quebedeaux excluded here, for Evangelicals. They're not liberalizing; they're not becoming worldly—you know, Richard claims they are—and they may be going through a transition, but there's no attempt to liberalize sexual morality.

Dan Davies: No. It just happens. I can see it in the dorm at Perkins. People who are liberal tend to think much less about sexuality.

Evangelical Y: There's no policy. People may be behaving that way, but no one's sitting down and saying, "Well, now we're becoming more sophisticated."

Dan Davies: No, but it's happening.

Evangelical Y: Well, it may be happening. We don't really know.

Dan Davies: I know.

Evangelical Y: Well, you don't actually know in terms of actual numbers and statistics. We still know, for example, that people who are religious, who are devout, are much less likely to engage in pre-marital sex than people who aren't. It's still a very powerful indicator. It's not quite the barrage of sexual looseness that some people think it is.

Richard Quebedeaux: You're right. It's not like the rest of the world, so to speak. I can say that if you just check it out, you'll find out that it's true that there is a liberalizing trend. And I must say, I am impressed with what Warren said about the Moonies because there is something there that is true. There is something foundational about sexual morality that turns me on to it. I have to agree with you that there's nothing from my evangelical background that has ever turned me on to sexual morality. There's a lot of hypocrisy. There have been rules; there's been the threat of hell, you know, but there is something about you Moonies, that even if people accuse you of really being sexually immoral, I can say they're basically crazy.

Letha Scanzoni: I don't think you've read my book! I've for years been talking about an evangelical view of sexuality in a very positive way, and it's called the *Joy of Sexuality.* Sexuality is something positive, but there are abuses of sexuality, and if we want God's best for us, we will be watching...

Richard Quebedeaux: O.K.! I think you're right. I think inherently in Christianity that's the way it ought to be, but I find there is very little *power* there to really do that and to really feel that. Most people I know in seminaries—Catholic, Anglican, "liberal"—when you talk about being celibate, who's celibate? Celibacy is a joke! You know, where and with whom are you doing it? The fact is that people just don't believe it's possible. But I feel that it *is* possible. I feel it is a gift, a vocation, and there's something about the Unification people that makes me really believe it's possible. Sex is creative, and ought to be reserved for marriage; it is joyous, and there's something very holistic about it. I'm not saying that all Evangelicals are out screwing around all the time—that's a great exaggeration—but in my experience, there is a great deal of truth in Warren's point.

Patricia Zulkosky: Somehow we dragged this in from the question of how we can work together, and I find that to be unfortunate. I think morality is something that touches each one of us, because sexuality is one of the most precious things to ourselves, and we hate to see and to hear that these problems are going on, and often we hate to face the things that we've done in our own lives. So I can appreciate this kind of struggle, but I would hope that somehow we could swing back around to the question of how we can work together.

Evangelical X: Pat, I disagree. I think that that is a very relevant topic. Warren's premise was that he felt this is what Unificationists could give us Evangelicals, and then Richard followed up by saying in his judgment it was empirical fact that we needed that, and we've been disputing that. (laughter)

Thomas Bower: I have to agree with Richard on that. I've worked with young people; I have worked in an evangelical school, and I'm now *not* in an evangelical school. I don't see very much difference, to be honest with you, between the evangelical school and the secular school. I think that adds to the pile of empirical facts, which we needn't go into, but I believe we're on to something very important.

Patricia Zulkosky: So long as it continues in a direction of Divine Principle.

Jonathan Wells: I'd like to make it clear, just so we know we're working together, that Unificationists aren't accusing Evangelicals of immorality.

Patrick Means: Oh, no. It was Richard! (laughter)

Warren Lewis: Why doesn't Richard write a new book: *The Sexy Evangelicals*? (laughter)

Evangelical X: I think Jon has a very good point. It's like the old saying "the squeaky wheel is the one you always pay attention to." I don't believe that we don't have problems. We have weekends where we work with 100-150 college-age kids and we deal with the business of sexuality, because it's an important relationship.

Warren Lewis: And there's a real problem.

Evangelical X: Yes, sociologists and men and women of that caliber, sit there and listen to that stuff and say, "I wonder how much research he's ever really done. Listen to him. They probably know two people who've gotten into trouble, so they start telling everybody, but they haven't done any research." So whenever we talk about these things I think we ought to be very careful to do research. I think another thing we've got to realize, which was said today, is that there are many phases of evangelicism.

Paul Eshleman: We're doing a number of things in Campus Crusade in that regard. After the Congress on the Family several years ago, we initiated a number of different things within our movement. We first of all started setting up conferences for people who were engaged, just to be sure there was a commitment there ahead of time, and to understand what marriage is. One of our key speakers who travels continually, Josh McDowell, speaks on a Christian view of sex. We're speaking in classrooms in many, many universities on a Christian perspective on love, sex, and marriage. Within our movement we don't tolerate sexual immorality, because you can't have that close intimate relationship with the Father if you're in willful rebellion against Him in that area of your life. When you get close to the Lord, the overwhelming desire is, "I want to be a clean vessel of the Lord."

Dan Davies: I think that Evangelicals and Unificationists share a common concern about morality, but I see a problem in the future of the possibility of morality declining even further. As Jonathan has asked, how do we at this time unite to solve the horrendous problems of immorality in our society? In California I believe the divorce rate is higher than the marriage rate. What's going to happen if our morality gets any worse? Things aren't getting better morally; frankly, they're getting worse. What are we going to do about that?

Richard Quebedeaux: And there's another kind of immorality besides sexual immorality. There are things like racism, sexual discrimination, and poverty. God does not will poverty on anybody; poverty is not good for anybody, and I think you people are concerned about those things too.

Franz Feige: What has hurt me the most deeply in the history of Christianity is that there were people, groups and churches believing very fervently in God, and yet splitting up and persecuting one another, instead of working together for the same goal—to change the heart of man. I believe that if we want to work together we have to get the answer from God. I believe that the degree of unity that can come about depends upon our unity with God, our seriousness in trying to serve God. I think the beginning of anything should be praying together, asking God how we can work together. On that basis we can try to find goals that we both agree on, trying to help to change the people's hearts, because both the Evangelicals and the Moonies are interested in changing people's hearts. So, if we focus on that, based on prayer, then God will inspire us; because God is the one most interested in changing the world, more than we are.

Rod Sawatsky: Any comments?

Joseph Hopkins: Here's something to think about with regard to cooperation on an official level. I don't identify with Paul's anger in putting down the Judaizers. At the same time, I can't imagine Paul, even if he *hadn't* been angry, cooperating with the Judaizers. He felt they were guilty of a heresy which occasioned an emphatic warning to the Christian community with regard to a legalistic requirement for salvation added to faith. We Evangelicals look at Unification theology in somewhat the same way. We see it as "another gospel," where something is being added to simple faith in Jesus Christ as the basis for salvation. If we really are committed to that position, then we must be careful lest friendly cooperation be construed as endorsement. If Campus Crusade and Inter-Varsity were to work side by side with CARP on a college campus, that would be a way of telling the community, "Let's be tolerant: these people aren't so far off base," and so on—instead of warning them, "Now here is a heresy which is subverting the Christian message." It would create a kind of an acceptance that most of us, as Evangelicals, would not want to encourage. I have to be frank and say that, though I say it in love. I don't love the Moonies any less, but I feel that I couldn't work in an official relationship of cooperation, at least on the local level.

Franz Feige: What would be the concrete problem?

Joseph Hopkins: Well, the danger, I think, would be the same as that we read about in the book of Galatians, that the "other gospel" the Judaizers were fostering militated against the gospel which Paul was preaching, the gospel of salvation by faith alone—making a faith response to the atoning sacrifice of Christ as the means of reconciling us sinners to our Heavenly Father.

Franz Feige: Are you talking about losing converts?

Joseph Hopkins: No, I'm not worried about that. *That* isn't the threat. The threat is to those who might be drawn into the movement through my cooperation with it. It's a matter of encouraging a philosophy or religion that I feel undermines the Christian gospel. In other words, if I am committed to steering young people in a direction of faith in Christ alone as the basis of their salvation, I should be steering them *away* from what I believe to be *false* beliefs—the sexual basis of the fall, the unique role of Rev. Moon as prophet—messiah in fact—the whole structure of Unification theology.

Warren Lewis: Do you cooperate ecumenically with Catholics and Jews? Do you ever do any ecumenical things with Catholics or Jews?

Joseph Hopkins: Yes, I've spoken in a Jewish synagogue.

Warren Lewis: Why is it O.K. to believe in Mary but not Rev. Moon?

Richard Quebedeaux: Catholic charismatics are getting back into the rosary. What you're talking about is, if Evangelicals do *anything* with Moonies it tends to legitimize them and cause some rethinking. Well, as I said before, dialogue always involves the risk of conversion.

Joseph Hopkins: I'm in favor of dialogue. In the Jewish

synagogue I dealt with the points of agreement, and then points of disagreement. It was in a friendly context, and I wasn't pushy about my belief in Jesus Christ. But dialogue is different than entering into an official relationship of cooperation on a college campus or in a local community.

Dan Davies: I would like to bring out something Dr. Hopkins said. Frankly, I think none of us are *really* preaching the Christian message. Not Unificationists, not Evangelicals, no one. Why? Because our example is our strongest sermon. Until every church in this country is a living example of what we preach, we can't really say we're preaching. What we are doing is reducing our faith to doctrines. Let's take a look at this from the point of view of those people we're attempting to influence, the secular world. What do people want? Do they want to hear about doctrine? They couldn't care less about our theology and our philosophy. They ask, "What do you have to offer me? What do you have to offer the world?" And because we haven't really offered much to the world, communism has been able to step in where we have failed. That's why it's affecting young people. That's why drugs come in. That's why we're finding ourselves confronted with a very serious ideological problem. And unless we get together and start living what we're preaching and make that our criterion, I think we're going to find ourselves in serious trouble.

Nora Spurgin: I just want to talk a little bit about goals. Even if we may not all have the same personal philosophy of life, we should be able to unite around a goal. If that goal is to make Evangelicals out of people, then of course the two of us cannot work side by side. Nor can we work together if the goal is to make Unification church members out of people. But if the goal is some other issue, around which we can both unite, it seems to me we could work together. Rev. Moon often says that our goal is to build the kingdom of heaven on earth, and anything we do that promotes or works toward that goal is of God; that's God's will. But basically, if you put it in light of the guidelines we've been given, what we're working toward, to build the kingdom of heaven, is God's will. If we're working against that then we're pleasing Satan, and therefore not doing God's will. So if we're working jointly with anyone to raise the moral consciousness or to make a better world, we feel we're doing God's will no matter who it is we're working with. But, if whatever we're doing side by side with even somebody who is a very wonderful Christian but who's working against God or feeding into Satan's world, then we would consider that not good. So I'd just like to put the emphasis on the ultimate goal.

Evangelical Y: Let me ask Nora or someone else perhaps from the Unificationists if you all would work side by side with a Marxist inner-city development project where the goal had nothing to do with philosophy, but it was simply helping people socially. Would you work side by side with communists?

Tom Carter: I think there are situations where we would work together, if the goal isn't to turn young people into Marxists. I've been wondering, could we rub shoulders if nobody said anything about their beliefs, to dig the foundation for a new youth home for somebody else? That's a very practical or very simplistic example. I think we could picket with Marxists at pornography theaters. And we could work with pornographers against the encouragement of communism in our society and feel no contradiction, or compromising of our faith, because both of those goals work toward accomplishing our goal of establishing the kingdom of God on the earth.

Warren Lewis: That's an honest answer. In terms of the plans for the Global Congress, the question came up almost immediately: Do Marxists get to come to the Global Congress of World Religions?—Marxism is a world religion! That was a hard one, but the word has come down from higher up: "Yes. If they want to be there, and really want to deal with the other religious people in the world in a responsible way, then they have a right to be there, too."

Tom Carter: Also, Marxists come to our science conferences.

Rod Sawatsky: I've been wondering if maybe one of the things that could be done together is a conference on the family. Moonies love conferences on many things (laughter)—science, world religions, and so on. Maybe the two groups could get together and do something on the family sometime, and maybe if Moonies like that idea they could even speak to the Scanzoni's and see if they would like to do something with them on an international conference on the family. Let's move on—is this a quickie?

Jonathan Wells: Yes. There's another level entirely that I think is open as a possibility, and that's prayer. For example, I pray that Evangelicals succeed in teaching people in Russia about Jesus Christ. I've prayed that many times. When the Campus

Crusade Fellowship has Bible classes, I pray that they'll get a big crowd. And it's a sincere prayer. Now, I'm not going to tell you what to pray, but I think it's possible we can pray for each other on a level of heart, not just "I hope all those Moonies will join Campus Crusade." (laughter) I know you could pray that, too, I mean, I could pray that all you people join *our* church, too. But prayer on the level of heart, that's my suggestion. It's food for thought...

CONCLUSION

Rod Sawatsky: I think that we should spend half an hour talking to each other about this kind of dialogue experience. We don't want to discuss the theological issues as such, but rather what this kind of experience means to us. Richard is going to start us off, and then maybe some of you can chime in, as you will.

Richard Quebedeaux: Some of you may not realize that I am a very passionate person. (laughter) I'm a Calvinist, but I've got to read you something from John Wesley, because I really like this. It's from a little thing he wrote called, "What Are the Distinguishing Marks of a Methodist?" What really is a Methodist anyway? It reads:

> The distinguishing marks of a Methodist are not his opinions of any sort. His assenting to this or that scheme of religion, his embracing any particular set of notions, his espousing the judgment of one man or of another, are all quite wide of the point...
>
> Nor, lastly, is he distinguished by laying the whole stress of religion on any single part of it.... By salvation he means holiness of heart and life. And this he affirms to spring from true faith alone. Can even a nominal Christian deny it?...
>
> ...A Methodist is one who has "the love of God shed abroad in his heart by the Holy Ghost given unto him;"...
>
> And while he thus always exercises his love to God, by praying without ceasing, rejoicing evermore, and in every thing giving thanks, this commandment is written in his heart, "That he who loveth God, love his brother also." And he accordingly loves his neighbor as himself; he loves every man as his own soul. His heart is full of love to all mankind, to every child of "the Father of the

spirits of all flesh." That a man is not personally known to him, is no bar to his love; no, nor that he is known to be such as he approves not, that he repays hatred for his good will. For he "loves his enemies;" yea, and the enemies of God, "the evil and the unthankful.". . .

The love of God has purified his heart from all revengeful passions, from envy, malice, and wrath, from every unkind temper or malign affection. It hath cleansed him from pride and haughtiness of spirit, whereof alone cometh contention. And he hath now "put on bowels of mercies, kindness, humbleness of mind, meekness, long suffering:" so that he "forebears and forgives, if he had a quarrel against any; even as God in Christ hath forgiven him.". . .

By consequence, whatsoever he doeth, it is all to the glory of God. In all his employments of every kind, he not only aims at this (which is implied in having a single eye), but actually attains it. . .

. . .He thinks, speaks, and lives, according to the method laid down in the revelation of Jesus Christ. His soul is renewed after the image of God, in righteousness and in all true holiness. . .

. . .And I beseech you, brethren, by the mercies of God, that we be in no wise divided among ourselves. Is thy heart right, as my heart is with thine? I ask no farther question. If it be, give me thy hand. For opinions, or terms, let us not destroy the work of God. Dost thou love and serve God? It is enough. I give thee the right hand of fellowship. . .*

I think that's the most powerful ecumenical statement I've ever seen.

There is one other thing that I hope for all Evangelicals; I've been thinking about this for years. We Evangelicals must recognize that no matter how convinced we are that we have the truth, biblically speaking, *no one* is promised *all* of the truth in this life. We see through a glass darkly. Others: Catholics, liberal Protestants, and maybe I should say Moonies, too, may have as much to teach the Evangelicals as we them. God is the ultimate judge of all our theologies, and Jesus has commanded us to love everyone whether Liberal, Evangelical, Moonie, atheist—even our enemies. As an Evangelical—now I speak only for myself—I really have lacked in love. Let me tell you what you Unification people have taught me and how you have affected me. Eight months ago, I wanted to pretend that you didn't exist. I got sick and tired of walking across the Cal Berkeley campus and Telegraph Avenue

*John Wesley, *Selections from the Writings of the Rev. John Wesley,* compiled by Herbert Welch, Nashville, Tenn.: Abingdon Press, 1942, pp. 292-302.

and having people walk up to me with those "glaring eyes,"
wanting to walk with me all the way across campus. It was a very
un-Christian attitude on my part. I really wanted to treat you as
non-persons; not that I hated you, but I just wished you weren't
there. Then I met one of you—which is always the key—who was
a very persuasive person and very "non-Moonie" in my stereo-
type. He was auditing a class I was teaching in the G.T.U. and he
knew I had a new book in press, so he said, "Why don't you go
back to Barrytown and lecture on your new book?" I said,
"That's interesting," and he said, "O.K., I'll arrange it." So he
arranged it, yet I really didn't want to go because I thought, "Oh,
God, how boring." (laughter) But I had to go meet Bill Bright in
Washington, D.C., and it was nice to get my way paid. (laughter)
So I thought, I'd go and spend a few boring days in Barrytown,
and then I'd have my way paid to the East Coast. Besides, it
wouldn't be all that much work. So I came here expecting to be
terribly bored. I never really cared about your theology because
it's hard to get me interested in anything. I get bored rather
easily.

So I came here and wasn't bored at all—not one minute—
and to think that Stillson Judah, who's been working on me for a
year, was right! You people *are* very interesting. The truth of what
he'd been trying to say to me about you people started to become
clear to me. I do have a passion against injustice. I left here
feeling very, very bad about what I consider the media's unjust
treatment of you. But it was really more than that, because I
found something here that I've never found anywhere, and I've
had a lot of experience with Christian groups and other religious
groups. There was a phrase, I think, in Sontag's book that said he
thought that you were the nicest people he'd ever met. Now, I
looked at that and said: big deal! We all have people that we can
say that about. But it's true. More importantly, I have never seen
a place where *agape* is worked out so well. That is quite an
admission since I've had a lot of experience, and I'm very critical
and very skeptical. What I mean by *agape* is the kind of genuine
hospitality and concern that really comes across here.

Secondly, I'm really impressed because, as an Evangelical,
I've spoken a lot about trying to *do* something about justice in
our society but I personally haven't done much. Like a lot of
other people, I talk a lot. But I have always been concerned that
we Evangelical believers *do* something about our beliefs: that we

put our faith into action in terms of the suffering world. I see that you're trying to do that. Theologically and intellectually, I think you're wrong. I cannot accept your doctrines intellectually, but emotionally I feel you're right, which is kind of a paradox. I'm very glad I'm not in the position to judge, because I do think that when we meet our Maker, we're going to be surprised by who else is there! (laughter)

Seriously, I am extremely impressed by your openness. I have always felt that one of the marks of a mature Christian is the ability to be self-critical, and even beyond that, the ability to laugh at oneself. Your seminary here must be unique in the world. I've never seen another seminary that would allow, much less recruit faculty on the basis of who's the best they can get, without worrying that a given faculty person might perhaps destroy the faith of a student. You're not afraid to be opposed, to have dialogue, even with people you strongly disagree with. According to my information, there are few conservatives in liberal seminaries and in conservative seminaries, there are no liberals. But you're not afraid to have people of different kinds of faith, and that really impresses me. In conclusion, I could say that I have always been a person who has appreciated the Christian command to love everybody, but I've not been able to do it, by a long shot. I love my friends, but I don't love most other people, and I know that's not right; but you challenge me. I really do love you, not because I feel I have to, but because I think you deserve all of our love. And even though you may be heretics— let God make that decision—I am really glad you're around, and I think that the world's going to be a better place because of your presence here.

Jonathan Wells: I doubt if I can match that, but I will say a few things from the Unification side. A few years ago, when many of us here joined the Unification church, we came from all kinds of strange backgrounds—Christian, atheist, agnostic, neo-Buddhist, Hindu, etc. When I joined the church and went out on the street and witnessed to people about the Divine Principle, I was totally unprepared for the Evangelical onslaught that I got. Quite frankly, I think it's a common experience for Unification church members to develop a very deep resentment toward Evangelicals and Fundamentalists. I can remember an afternoon in Burlington, Vermont, when I had a little portable blackboard set up on a street corner, and I was lecturing on the Divine

Principle. A crowd of young people gathered and some of them were Evangelicals and some of them were communists. The Evangelicals had their objections to what I was saying, and the communists had their objections. And by the time they finished mocking and persecuting me, the Evangelicals and the communists were embracing each other in their mutual hatred of me. And I was just trying to teach people about God. This is why our members quite commonly distrust Evangelicals. Of course, not all Evangelicals do this, but I just want you to know that this does occur. So when Richard set up this conference, my first reaction was gladness that I wasn't going to be in on this one. But I began to get interested in the idea when I read Richard's book, *The Worldly Evangelicals.* As I read the book, I realized that actually I had a lot of respect for the people Richard was writing about; in fact, I admired and loved them. I ended up asking to be part of this conference. I looked forward to it. For me it has been a real eye-opener, and I feel like I've grown a lot in Christian love.

When I look at America today, I see a lot of dying churches and a lot of people dying spiritually, and a lot of militant activists who hate God; except maybe for the Unification church, the only group that seems to be doing a whole lot about it is the Evangelicals, and I think it's great. I think that's what it's going to take to save this world. I think *your* theology is wrong. I think you'd do better to read the *Divine Principle* and realize that Christ is coming in the flesh again. But I know you're not going to walk out of here with that opinion. At least—and this will have to suffice—I feel a real bond of common purpose, of working to bring people to God. And, as Richard said, I think when we finally do meet God, all of us are going to be surprised. I expect to be. God's always surprising me. So I'm really glad you came, and I want to thank you on behalf of everybody here.

Warren Lewis: I'm a little bit surprised at what I am about to say. This isn't what I rehearsed at all. I doubt I can get through it and keep my dignity. Surely you have noticed that an awful lot of what I've had to say was motivated by a very deep bitterness. One of the reasons for that bitterness is that I'm a church historian. I know the history of the church so well that I hate, with Christ's passion, what you Evangelicals stand for. I hate what you've done to one another through history and what a lot of your people would be willing to do to these Moonies right now. Evangelicals have done it to me in my personal history, as they sat there in their smugness with their scriptural proof-texts and lowered their axes, and said, "I love you personally, brother Lewis, but I don't agree with your doctrine; so get the hell out of my church." Frankly, I just don't trust you to walk out of this room and treat these people honorably. Members of the Unification church have been interviewed by all three major networks, French TV, *Time* and *Newsweek*; they are met with smiling faces and then are stabbed in the back as the editors fix it to suit themselves. I am deeply bitter. I'm not bitter because I am a Moonie, which I am not, and never will become one, but because I just see it all happening again. I could provide you more historical examples than you want to hear. Consider this patchwork unity that you talked about. Have you forgotten, Brother Baptist, that these Presbyterians and Lutherans conspired to drown you and your wife in the 16th century? And that was after they got through burning one another at the stake. As Evangelist Spurgeon said, "The only reason we Baptists have never persecuted anybody is because we've never been bigger than anybody." So now the Moonies take their turn to be the new kid on the block, and everybody gangs up against them. Persecution doesn't prove their theology, right or wrong; it's just that old human thing over and over again. Philosophically, I suppose I shouldn't be so bitter. It's just that it is in the name of the Prince of Peace that we keep doing it. It's the greatest argument against the existence of God I know. So, what I'm doing is asking you, because I'm a Christian, to pray for me, and forgive me for how much I hate you, for what you've done to one another, and for what I have done to other people in the name of the Bible, and in Jesus' name. The only way I know to exorcise this is to confess it. [long silence]

Rod Sawatsky: Would anybody like to make any comments?

Johnny Sonneborn: Jesus taught us to pray for our faults, to be forgiven as we forgive other people. Once we know that, and do it, then we will be forgiven.

Nora Spurgin: I'll just say one last thing regarding this conference. At some point during the conference, I felt that what I believed and felt was too precious to share with you. I wasn't trying to evade your questions. When I walked home, the biblical phrase "throwing pearls before swine"—pardon the expression—it kept running through my mind. I often felt my faith wouldn't or couldn't be appreciated by someone who did not have the same convictions. But then I realized that you must feel the same way. We are intellectualizing about Jesus and His work, and you must feel as though you, too, are throwing your pearls before swine. I hope that we can come to the end of the conference with at least an appreciation of each other, not necessarily believing what each other believes, but with a real appreciation for each other's beliefs. I hope we will feel that we are sharing some deeply meaningful parts of one another's hearts. Each of us has a faith that's very, very deep and precious. So I want you to know that I appreciate your convictions and what you're doing. I also apologize for those many times when we didn't do justice to what you were feeling.

Paul Eshleman: I was sharing briefly with someone else this afternoon about what my reaction is going to be after leaving here. I think it speaks to the things that Warren has raised. I will go back, and since three thousand Campus Crusade staff know that I've been here, the issue will be, "My goodness, you went to Barrytown, and you got out?" Who knows what they'll say? I want you to know what my conclusions will be and what I'll say to them. First of all, I would say I believe that there are some Unification church members who know and love Jesus Christ and are Christians. I would also say that there are numbers who aren't. I believe beyond that, that Unification doctrine is all screwed up. But I can't be any more condemning of Moonies whose doctrine I think is all screwed up than I am of the Presbyterians in my church who don't believe in the virgin birth.

So, therefore, I come to you to say, and not flippantly, Warren, that I do love you, and I want you to know that. At the same time, I think it's become very clear to me why in the Evangelical world there have been so many bitter attacks on the Unification church. It's simply because nobody has ever taught an Evangelical how to deal with a person who seems to be cutting the heart out of everything that we Evangelicals believe. An Evangelical can feel much more compassion for a prostitute who is having trouble with faith, or a drug addict, or a drunk, than for somebody who says something that would indicate that Christ is less than God, that He didn't quite do everything that He should have done. It's like saying that everything your whole life stands for isn't good enough and it's not really true and it's not enough. If that's what you're giving your whole life for and working twenty-four hours a day for and you have left everything to

follow Christ, and somebody tells you that; and if you've poured
your life into a number of people, and someone comes and tries
to lead them away, you're heartbroken and you don't respond
with God's love in those situations. I think one of the great
lessons that all Evangelicals need to learn is simply that God has
commanded us to love in every situation, no matter what. I think
there's another role that I must play as a leader in Campus
Crusade for Christ. I have a responsibility for those God has
placed under my leadership. And so I must say I don't believe
that what the Unification church teaches is biblical. In my role as
a leader, I warn, as the apostles warned those with whom they
were, not to pay attention to certain teachings. But, you see, I
think that's something different from backstabbing. That's what I
go away from this conference with, the prayer that I can communicate.

Lloyd Howell: I hope that people in Campus Crusade can
listen to or talk with us. That has been a problem. Their faith is
solid and so is ours. Part of the problem has been an unwilling-
ness on both sides to talk. We just built walls which excluded
each other and God. You could recommend that people in
Campus Crusade talk to us and not just see us as zombies.

Paul Eshleman: That's going to be a challenge on the street
level. Maybe I should say that I've seen your camp—come see
mine.

Lloyd Howell: We have a lot to change, too, and repent
about. We have to love in every situation also. I can say that I
haven't and I repent for that.

Joseph Hopkins: Well, Warren has asked that we pray for
him. I would like to ask that we pray for each other and pray
together before we part.

Rod Sawatsky: That's a very good suggestion. I was going to
suggest that myself unless somebody else has something they'd
like to add.

Virgil Cruz: I have appreciated very much the summing up
that we've all done. In addition to drawing those kinds of conclusions from the conference, I think I also operate on a person-to-
person basis. I've talked with a number of you while I've been
here. I guess I've talked mostly with Dan and Pat and Jonathan
and others and that's meant an awful lot to me. *People* are the
thing. It's been really great to know you. When I put a face on
something, I put names with that face, and it changes the whole

thing for me. I don't accept your doctrine—I hope I've made that clear (laughter)—but I want you to know that I accept *you*, and I can also say that I love you.

Dan Davies: I'd like to say one thing. I won't be happy until every one in the Unification movement has the experience of Christian love you have. I've been working for that.

Roy Carlisle: As an editor, I usually get the last word. I don't know if I will tonight, but I do have to tell you that when I first shared my testimony, I said that I came because the only thing I'd ever seen was hundreds of pages of anti-Moonie material. Hence, I felt led to be here to observe and to increase my own sense of understanding in order to maintain my integrity as an editor. I know I'm going to be challenged in the months to come. I want you to know that I have come away from this event with a new awareness of your human and spiritual vitality and integrity. My prayer is that as a person and in my role as an editor I will be faithful to God. I hope that I can maintain that sense of responsibility and fairness in my job. It's a responsibility that I live with twenty-four hours a day, because a book, frankly, can change lives in a way that almost nothing else can. So that's a weight and responsibility—and I'm grateful for what you've meant to me. I thank you for it.

Rod Sawatsky: When we went around introducing ourselves, I said I was neither liberal, nor Evangelical, nor Moonie. I guess I'm probably still there; Warren and I share that in common. I still also believe that in terms of the future of the church—despite all that Warren has said, and also as a student of the church—I put a great deal of faith in the evangelical movement. This confidence has been reconfirmed here because of the new dynamics and new life which are obviously emanating from some leaders in the evangelical movement. At the same time, I also see some new light and new life, coming from the Unification movement. I hope the Evangelicals can take that seriously, and, as well, that Unificationists can take seriously the strengths of the Evangelicals. I think the Evangelicals have much to teach Unification, and since Unification thought is in process, there may be some coming together down the road.

Earlier I wrote a little article for *Theology Today* on the conversations which were held last year, and I concluded in a way which, I think, still holds true for these conversations:

Indeed, we found that communication, dialogue if you wish, is something Unification members anticipate with great enthusiasm. Isn't this the better way to respond to a new religion, rather than bringing out all the old techniques out of the Inquisition, under modern guises like deprogramming? Or is the more orthodox Christian church too insecure to listen before reacting in hostility? The process of conversation may well reintroduce the category of heresy as functional in contemporary Christian theology, and it may well force greater clarity on critical issues in modern Christian thought. Conversation with Unification will possibly reconfirm traditional Christianity in its understandings of human nature and human destiny, and reinvigorate the church in its proclamation of the gospel. If so, Rev. Moon may indeed be a providential personage. Maybe not exactly as he foresaw it, but at any rate, as God would have it!*

If there are no other comments, I think that we might pray together. If two or three would like to offer some words, I'll conclude.

Paul Eshleman: Lord, Jesus, You've said that wherever two or three are gathered together in Your name, that You're in their midst, and so we thank You for being present with us this evening. We ask that we might have learned in these last days together how very, very important it is that we love one another, and that truly, all men would know that we are Your disciples, because we do have love for one another. You cause us moment by moment to walk in Your love as we reach out to so many people in this world that have never met you yet, and don't know the living God.

Joseph Hopkins: Father, we thank You for these days together. Thank You for the bonds of love which have been developed among us and between us. We pray that we may learn to be more loving and more tolerant of those who believe differently than we do. Help us to have a genuine love for every person in this room, and to carry that love with us wherever we go. We do pray for Warren, as he requested. You know the hurts he has suffered, and You know the truth of that which he described to us. We confess our sins of intolerance and bigotry, our lack of compassion and understanding for one another. We pray that we may grow in the Christ-like spirit and in the knowledge of Your

---

*Rodney Sawatsky, "Dialogue with the Moonies," *Theology Today,* April, 1978, v. 35, no. 1, p. 91.

truth. We thank You for the promise that if we seek after You sincerely, You will reward our search for You and for truth. So bless us all and help us to devote ourselves to loving and serving You and one another, as we seek to grow in the likeness of Christ, and to achieve our common goal of building a better world. This we pray in His name.

Nora Spurgin: My beloved Heavenly Father, Your presence in this room is so beautiful. The love which flows among us, Father, is beautiful. Father, I pray now that this love can flow, can be fluid enough, that You can teach each one of us Your will for our lives, and what You want us to do in terms of leading other people's lives. Thank You.

Jonathan Wells: Dear Heavenly Father, we confess our sinfulness and ignorance before You. We're so sorry that we've been unable to love each other as You've wanted us to. Heavenly Father, every person in this room wants most of all to see Your sovereignty established on this earth, and everyone in this room wants to see Your Son, Jesus Christ, receive the full measure of glory which He was denied 2,000 years ago. He sacrificed His life for us, and we rejected Him. Heavenly Father, please forgive us.

Rod Sawatsky: Our God, we are not sure how to pray together. We're not sure how to pray together because our understandings of Your revelation to us differ. They differ rather widely and the chasms are fairly deep. Yet we know that You are a God of love, and that we share that love and are called to share that love. We do not ask for bridges over chasms that are artificial or false, but we do ask for light where there is relative darkness; we do ask for truth; we do ask for the infilling of Your Holy Spirit to guide us; and we do thank You for what we have together, and we know that ultimately the end is Yours. May we be Your servants to Your honor and glory in the way, the best way we can at present know Your will in our own and different ways. Thank You for bringing us together, dismiss us with Thy blessings, send travel mercies to those who go a distance. Be with the students as they write their exams and guide them in their summer activities. We pray these things together in the name of our common Father, our God, Yahweh, Amen.

SERMON

Sermon given by Dr. Donald L. Deffner, on October 29, 1978, at Sunday morning worship service during the Evangelical-Unification Dialogue at the Unification Theological Seminary, Barrytown, New York.

Have you ever felt like running? Running to get away from it all. Running to escape some of the pressures and tensions in your life. Running to try to find some meaning and purpose in life.

Well, the Scriptures are filled with examples of people who tried to run away—from God. Take the first case of a runaway in the Old Testament: "And Adam and his wife hid themselves from the presence of the Lord God among the trees of the garden."

This is a vivid and true picture of what mankind has been trying to do from the beginning of time. We have tried to make our selves, our will, our interests, our desires first and foremost and final.

And that's what the "original sin" really is: the deification of self, with, as its inevitable consequence, a tragic separation from God. And the trend is as "old as the hills." Take the case of Jonah: "Now the word of the Lord came unto Jonah the son of Amittai, saying, 'Arise, go to Nineveh, that great city, and cry against it; for their wickedness has come up before Me.' But Jonah rose to flee to Tarshish from the presence of the Lord."

It was the Genesis story all over again. Jonah made his own interests first and final.

Or take the case of Augustine, the famous church father. As

told in his *Confessions,* his is a most moving story—the story of a man running away from God, using every trick in the book to put distance between himself and God. He turned to passion, then to rhetoric, then to philosophy, then back to passion again. And finally, with every escape route cut off, Augustine surrendered to what he had so long feared, and out of his experience came that unforgettable saying: "Thou has made us for Thyself, and our hearts are restless till they find their rest in Thee."

Or take the case of Francis Thompson, the famous poet. Few people realize that his poem "The Hound of Heaven" was a transcript of his own religious experience. For years he tried to escape God. He turned to nature, to his friends, to love, but all in vain. "I fled Him," he wrote, "down the nights and down the days; I fled Him, down the arches of the years; I fled Him down the labyrinthine ways of my own mind; and in the mist of tears I hid from Him, and under running laughter...From these strong feet, that followed, followed after..."

I was a campus pastor at the University of California in Berkeley for twelve years; I was there in the fifties. And one day a cherry-blonde graduate student in chemistry walked into our University Lutheran Chapel on College Avenue and said to one of the students: "I'm an atheist. Argue with me." To which the student replied: "We don't argue with anyone around here. Come on in." She did. And she stayed for three years. Even sang in the chapel choir—but she never became a Christian. And yet, before she left, she told me: "You know, Pastor Don, the Hound of Heaven may get me yet!" She could not accept Christ as her personal Lord and Saviour, and yet she had to admit that she could feel the warm, loving breath of the Almighty on the back of her neck—brooding over her, wooing her, chasing her, saying in effect: "Angry young woman, I love you!"

And it was in that same spirit the Psalmist said the words of Scripture: "Whither shall I go from Thy Spirit? Or whither shall I flee from thy presence?...If I make my bed in sheol, behold thou art there! If I take the wings of the morning and dwell in the uttermost parts of the sea, even there shall thy hand lead me, and thy right hand shall hold me." (Psalm 139:7-10; KJV)

But we have been talking about other people so far this morning. How about you? Have you been running away from God?

The story I have been telling is really the story of "Everyman"

—as they used to say in the old British morality plays. And may I suggest that "Everyman" and "Everywoman" is right here today.

What are the ways in which you—even while being in a church for many years—can run away from God?

Well, one of the most common ways is to "fall in love with the things of this world." Now don't turn me off yet...I know the feeling... How many times I have sat in a pew and gotten sick and tired of a preacher storming away at "the material things of this world" with the implication that we are not to enjoy, in a balanced way, the blessings which God has given us here on the earth. I am quite aware that the church has "come of age" in baptizing the secular, in seeing this as God's good world, a world which we are to properly enjoy in our life "under the sun."

And yet is there no danger at all in falling in love with this "island colony" called the earth, and forgetting who we are, and whose we are, and forgetting about the home palace above "...from which also we look for [the return of] the Saviour, the Lord Jesus Christ"? (Philippians 3:20 KJV)

Even for the Christ-man and the Christ-woman there is always the temptation to feel—whether it's a mighty new bridge, a towering skyscraper, or another satellite: "These things will last forever!" "What hath man wrought!"

> But the angels from their thrones on high
> Look down on us with wond'ring eye
> That though we are but passing guests
> We build such strong and sturdy nests.

And in our daily lives we can "run away from God" by putting our trust and our zest into the wrong things... There is the worker who lives to get, rather than to give. There is the teacher who really likes his or her job—but frankly, hasn't liked students for a long time. There is the Midas in each of us in a thousand different ways, by which we place self first, others second, and God third.

True, it is God's world, and we are to enjoy it. But has our blessed Lord's parable no application today? And the man said to himself: "Soul, thou hast much goods laid up for many years; take thine ease, eat, drink, and be merry! But God said unto him, 'Thou fool, this night thy soul shall be required of thee; then whose shall those things be, which thou hast provided?' So is he

that layeth up treasure for himself, and is not rich toward God."
(Luke 12:19-21 KJV)

Yes, the Christ-man and the Christ-woman can still "run
away from God" by an inordinate love for "the things of this
world." John's words still speak to you and to me: "Love not the
world, neither the things that are in the world... For all that is in
the world," (and now note the qualification) "the lust of the flesh,
and the lust of the eyes, and the pride of life, is not of the Father,
but is of the world. And the world passeth away, and the lust of it;
but he that doeth the will of God abideth forever." (I John 2:15-17
KJV)

There's another way to "run away from God" however. And
that's in doubts and disenchantments about our God and His
relationship with us. Oh, I don't mean those old chestnuts they
used to talk about on college campuses: "Who was Cain's wife?
...How many angels can dance on the head of a pin?...Can God
create something so big He can't lift it?" etc. No, I'm speaking of
those ongoing, nagging doubts that can come into the heart of
the most faithful Christian...about whether God really loves us,
whether He really cares...or if He does care, then why doesn't
He show and reveal Himself more to us in our lives?

It's like the instance of the teacher in Sunday School who
had just very carefully explained that God never "tempts" us in
our lives (that word has two different meanings in the New Testament). We are "tempted" by our own sinful nature. But God does
"tempt"—that is, test us—to make us realize our need for Him,
our dependence on Him. "Any questions?" asked the teacher.
"Yes," said an eighth-grade boy. "I know God only tests us to
strengthen our faith, but you know, I still think that sometimes
He overdoes it!"

And so we can "run away from God" in doubt and despair
and disenchantment with our Heavenly Father. But God does
care, and He does reveal Himself to us in Word and Sacrament if
we but let Him come to us through His Means of Grace, and use
them with an open mind and a penitent heart.

May I suggest that this often is right where the greatest
difficulty in our Christian lives rests? The problem is not that
God does not care, or will not reveal Himself to us, or help us in
our time of need. The problem is that *we don't really believe the
mighty promises of God*! As James put it: "Ye have not, because
ye ask not." (James 4:2 KJV) For this is the God who has

promised: "As thy days, so shall thy strength be." (Deuteronomy 33:25 KJV) This is the God who says: "Be not dismayed; for I am thy God. I will strengthen thee; yea, I will help thee; yea, I will uphold thee with the right hand of my righteousness." (Isaiah 41:10 KJV)

A coed walked into a campus pastor's office and said: "I'm an atheist." To which the pastor replied: "Well, tell me what *kind* of a God you don't believe in." And for an hour she told him. And when the hour was over, the pastor said: "Well, that's very interesting. But you know, I must be an atheist, too, because I don't believe in *that* God, either." And then he proceeded to share with her the kind of a God we have: a loving God, a forgiving God, a contemporary God, who does reveal Himself to us when we but use the Means of Grace—His Word and the Sacraments. And even then, after we have used the Means of Grace, and may still not be hearing God's response, and we are saying: "Why, God?" "Where are you, God?" there will be times we will have to say with the Apostle Paul: "Oh the depth of the riches both of the wisdom and knowledge of God! How unsearchable are His judgments, and His ways past finding out! For who hath known the mind of the Lord? Or who hath been his counselor? Or who hath first given to him, and it shall be recompensed unto him again? For of him, and through him, and to him, are all things: to whom be glory for ever. Amen." (Romans 11:33-36 KJV)

There is a third way in which we can "run away from God" and that's in religion itself. "The greatest peril of the church is always from within," said Presbyterian theologian James Smart.

One of my favorite stories has always been about the man who was going to a masquerade party just at this time of the year—October. And he decided to dress up in a devil's costume. It was a rainy, stormy night, and he was driving on a lonely country road when his car went off the road into a ditch. He couldn't get the car started again, so he got out of the car, and walked across a corn field until he came to a small country church.

Some people were in that church having their evening prayer meeting—singing hymns and praying. And just as this man got to the door of the country church, and opened the door—dressed in this devil's costume, mind you—well, there was a bolt of lightning and a clap of thunder. And all the people turned around and saw this man in the devil's costume standing there. And they went out of the doors and windows right and left. Except for one little old lady, standing in the center aisle, scared stiff. And she said: "Mr. Devil, I don't know what you want here, but I've got only one thing to say. I've been a member of this church for forty years, but I've really been on *your* side *all the time!*"

Some time ago there was a graduate student at the University of Michigan who flunked his exams. He was embarrassed to go back home overseas and face his family, so he hid in the bell-tower of the local Methodist church. Well, there were some strange goings-on in that church for a while. The spaghetti disappeared from the refrigerator after the Ladies Aid dinner. There were some strange creakings and groaning sounds in the building at times, and no one could figure out what was happening until it was discovered that there had been a man hiding in the church.

Are you the man—the woman—"hiding in the church"? You know, there's a big difference between saying a creed, and doing a Christian deed. There's a big difference between "going to church" and being in the church.

And there's a big difference between being a part of a loving, sincere group of religious people...and being a true disciple of Jesus Christ.

A businessman was speaking to 1200 other businessmen, and he said: "Give me all your criticisms of Christianity." And for an hour they did...and he wrote them down. When it was all over, the man said: "All of your criticisms have been against the church as an organization. And I admit that the church has its faults. But none of you has said anything against Jesus Christ. Now let me tell you about Him."

And let me tell you about Him....

You may not have heard much about Him in a church you grew up in. Or, you may have seen a contradiction in the lives of those who called themselves Christians but did not live it out.

But that does not make Christ and His claim on you any less real. For He says: "I am the way, and the truth, and the life; no one comes to the Father, but by me" (John 14:6) "I am the vine, you are the branches. He who abides in me, and I in him, he it is that bears much fruit, for apart from me you can do nothing." (John 15:5) "...if you confess with your lips that Jesus is Lord and believe in your heart that God raised him from the dead, you will be saved." (Romans 10:9) "And this is the testimony, that God gave us eternal life, and this life is in his Son. He who has the Son has life; he who has not the Son has not life." (I John 5:11-12)

And this Christ cannot be added to by another Gospel or another Lord, or one loses the true God Himself. As Paul wrote: "There is...one Lord, one faith, one baptism, one God and Father of us all, who is above all and through all and in all." (Ephesians 4:4-6)

And in this God-man Jesus Christ and in Him alone is there forgiveness before Our Heavenly Father. He alone is the Son of man who has power on earth to forgive sins. (See Matthew 9:6)

And so I call you to faith in and forgiveness from the God who is only revealed in Jesus Christ.

No matter how great a guilt you may have felt from anything in the past, let me tell you of a God of forgiveness! "Herein is love, not that we loved God, but that He loved us, and sent His Son to be the propitiation for our sins." (I John 4:10 KJV)

Corrie ten Boom tells of how the Dutch feel very close to the sea. And when she speaks of God's forgiveness she says it is as if God takes all of our sins, when He has forgiven them, and He casts them into the deepest part of the ocean, and then He puts up a sign: "NO FISHING ALLOWED." We are not to go back again and again in remorse over sins which He has already forgiven. As He says in Isaiah: "I, even I, am He who blotteth out thy transgressions for mine own sake, and will not remember thy sins." (Isaiah 43:25 KJV)

As former President O.P. Kretzmann of Valparaiso University put it: "We need to learn how to pray the prayer: 'O God, forgive me the sin of coming back to you and asking forgiveness for a sin that you forgave—and forgot—a long time ago!'"

What a God! What forgiveness! What a Friend!

Your parents may fail you. Your friends may fail you. A religious group in which you invested your whole life and commitment may fail you. But Jesus Christ will never fail you. I will never leave you nor forsake you, says the Lord.

Is your faith in this Jesus Christ? Is He the heart and center of your commitment, exclusive of all else...and of all others who would displace Him?

You and I may be sincere members of a religious group (regardless of what it calls itself) but Christ's words may still apply to us: "This people draweth near unto me with their mouth, and honoreth me with their lips, but their heart is far from me." (Matthew 15:8 KJV)

And so, many and devious are the ways people try to "run away from God." But none of them is of any avail. You need stout defenses against the devil; you need stouter against God. You may crowd your walls with sentries but there is one invasion you are powerless to withstand. That is the universal experience. God is inescapable. Sooner or later, in life or in death, we must come face to face with Him. As the Psalmist said: "Whither shall I go from Thy Spirit? Or whither shall I flee from Thy presence? ...if I make my bed in sheol, behold, Thou art there. If I take the wings of the morning, and dwell in the uttermost parts of the sea, even there shall Thy hand lead me, and Thy right hand shall hold me." (Psalm 139:7-10 KJV)

And the beauty, the wonder of it all is, that once you stop running away from God and really let Him declare Himself to you, you find that He isn't the kind of God you thought He was at all!

Once you confess, "Lord, be merciful to me, a sinner," once you confess the selfishness of wanting to run your own self-centered life and stop long enough to look at that cross and see that it was your sins that nailed Him to the tree...and it was your sins for which He died... Then you can see that the God from whom you in your folly tried to run away is not your vindictive judge, but your loving, forgiving Heavenly Father.

And that the reason He follows you down the nights and down the days, and down the arches of the years, down the labyrinthine ways of your mind, and in the mist of tears and under running laughter, the reason why He will not give you up, will not let you go, is that He longs to rescue you from yourself, from your waywardness and your wandering, and wants to bring you home.

And so, if you have been running away from God—like Adam and Eve, like Jonah, like Augustine, like Francis Thompson, like the cherry-blonde graduate student in chemistry...if you have been running away from God in an unbalanced love for the things of this world, in dishonest doubts, or in just going through the motions of church membership, then listen to the loving and concerned call of your Saviour as He says: "Behold, I stand at the door, and knock; if any man hear my voice, and open the door, I will come in to him, and will sup with him, and he with me." (Revelation 3:20 KJV)

In closing I would like to tell you the story of a young woman from Japan who came to the University Lutheran Chapel in Berkeley which I served some years ago. She was engaged to a young doctor, also from Japan, who had recently become a Christian. When she arrived in Berkeley, I baptized her, after instruction, and married the couple in our chapel. Both of them were rejected by their families for becoming the hated "Christians." Gradually they felt compelled to return to their native land, also to share their new faith with their people. Their life was difficult, and his work at the medical center in the old conservative city of Kyoto was particularly strenuous. Then one day our students and I received a cablegram from the young wife, whose name was Toko. She said her husband had died in her arms of an acute heart attack at 12:30 a.m. "Please pray for me," she concluded. And some time later a letter came from her:

> Oh, Pastor, I am so weak these days in spiritual life. It is sometimes unbearable to wait *our* first Christmas in Japan *alone*. The same old questions come up in my heart so repeatedly. 'Oh, Lord, why, why did You not take my soul with my dearest one? And why didn't You allow me to have our first Christmas together? And why did You not allow me, us, to have a small family?' Oh, Pastor, I am such an undisciplined girl, such a spoiled girl! I am singing Christmas songs, remembering you and your students, your home with Christmas trees, doughnuts, hot chocolate, ice cream, and singing voices! I am singing alone songs, songs he played with his flute.
>
> But, Pastor, I am not complaining what God has done. I am learning everyday, through this small cross of sorrow and loneliness loaded upon my shoulder, little by little how to trust and how to obey God of love. Beyond sorrow, I find a joy and hope, even though the joy to live may wane so soon. God does not leave me long in despair, He never, never leave me down...
>
> I thank God giving me such beautiful memories of Christmases received with my dearest _____ and many, many good friends from all over the sea. I'll never stop singing songs to praise my Christ Child whom he trusted and loved, even in tears and smiles... Pastor, Lord makes me brave. I take Bible everywhere and do not hesitate to sing and pray among non-Christian friends. I cannot die, because He insists me to live and work for His glory. I am His slave. Please remember me and encourage me to live. Yours in Christ, _____*

What better prayer can I have for you than that, no matter what burden or loss in life may oppress you, you like this young woman, though you lose family and friends for the sake of your faith or lose your loved one, may still be able to say:

> "Christ never, never leave me down. My eyes are full of tears with happiness, remembering these *small* treasures. I'll never stop singing songs to praise my Christ Child. I take Bible everywhere and do not hesitate to sing and pray among non-Christian friends. I cannot die, because He insists me to live and work for His glory. I am His slave."*

God give you that faith—through Jesus Christ!

---

*Devil's costume story adapted from "The Devil and the Masquerade Ball," and Japanese woman's letter quoted from "A True Story of Christian Faith," pp. 83 & 93-94 in *The Possible Years: Thoughts After Thirty on Christian Adulthood,* by Donald L. Deffner, St. Louis: Concordia Publishing House, 1973.